The True Story of the Wooden Horse

For Tom Wilson, who was there …

The True Story of the Wooden Horse

Robert J. Laplander

Pen & Sword
MILITARY

First published in Great Britain in 2014 by
Pen & Sword Military
an imprint of
Pen & Sword Books Ltd
47 Church Street
Barnsley
South Yorkshire
S70 2AS

ISBN 978 1 78383 101 2

A CIP catalogue record for this book is available from the British Library

Typeset in Ehrhardt by
Mac Style Ltd, Bridlington, East Yorkshire
Printed and bound in the UK by CPI Group (UK) Ltd,
Croydon, CRO 4YY

Pen & Sword Books Ltd incorporates the imprints of Pen & Sword Archaeology, Atlas, Aviation, Battleground, Discovery, Family History, History, Maritime, Military, Naval, Politics, Railways, Select, Transport, True Crime, and Fiction, Frontline Books, Leo Cooper, Praetorian Press, Seaforth Publishing and Wharncliffe.

For a complete list of Pen & Sword titles please contact
PEN & SWORD BOOKS LIMITED
47 Church Street, Barnsley, South Yorkshire, S70 2AS, England
E-mail: enquiries@pen-and-sword.co.uk
Website: www.pen-and-sword.co.uk

Contents

Foreword		vii
Author's Notes and Acknowledgements		ix
Prologue: Confessions of a latent escaper		xiii
Part I: Capture		1
Chapter 1	The Demise of O for 'Orange'	2
Chapter 2	Sagan	15
Chapter 3	'One of Our Aircraft Failed to Return …'	32
Chapter 4	Under the North African Stars	43
Chapter 5	'A Rum Sort of Place …'	52
Part II: Captivity		61
Chapter 6	Back in the Sandpit	62
Chapter 7	Inspiration	74
Chapter 8	First Steps	88
Chapter 9	'It *Cannot* Last, Old Boy …'	100
Chapter 10	Exhaustion and Ingenuity	116
Chapter 11	From Here to There	126
Chapter 12	'You're not thinking of *leaving us*, by any chance, are you?'	138
Part III: Escape		155
Chapter 13	Through the Looking Glass	156
Chapter 14	Exhilaration	167

Chapter 15 Meanwhile, back at Sagan … 176

Chapter 16 'Jon Jorgenson' Takes a Trip 188

Chapter 17 The Varied Adventures of Marcel Lavasuer and Michel Conde 210

Chapter 18 Complete and Free 228

Postscript: 'Margaret' 244
Notes 252
Glossary 262
Index 269

Foreword

When I was first asked to pen a few words to introduce this fine work, I was filled with a mixture of honour, pleasure and not a little trepidation, for the part of the world which is central to the story is known only too well to me. I have travelled to Sagan many many times and, more than most in this late, day know the significance of this bleak setting in what has been called the 'Upper Silesian Dustbowl'.

However, after but a momentary pause for thought I realized what a fine opportunity it would be to become involved in what I consider to be the definitive account of not only the 'Wooden Horse' escape, but of the East Compound at Stalag Luft III as well. It would be fair to say that this early compound, its characters and history, often become overshadowed by the neighbour who joined it later, the North Compound. History recalls the North Compound to have been the location of one of the most inspirational acts of World War Two. There, one snowy night in March 1944, seventy-six RAF officers made a daring bid for freedom during what has become known as 'The Great Escape'. While three men made a successful 'Home Run' to freedom, the remaining seventy-three were recaptured and, in one of the most flagrant breaches of the Geneva Convention governing the treatment of Prisoners of War (PoW), fifty of those were selected at random and murdered by units of the Nazi regime.

Though the story of 'The Great Escape' is vitally important to our understanding of the many aspects of PoW life – not the least of which is how hundreds of men were able to work together in secret for so many months – it does sometimes overshadow literally hundreds of other escape attempts made at Stalag Luft III and other PoW camps.

There have been many fine accounts by former prisoners of war regarding their own personal experiences in the war which make reference to either first hand eye-witness accounts, or refer to stories that were passed on to them. While absorbing pieces in themselves, they do often remain just that; solitary accounts of personal experiences. Until now there has been a general void in accounting for the early history of Stalag Luft III, as seen through the 'eyes' of the inmates of East Compound. However that void exists no longer. In this book, Robert Laplander has painstakingly and meticulously researched the history of this dramatic piece of land that measured only a few hundred yards by a few hundred yards.

I would urge all that can do so to make the pilgrimage to Sagan; once in Germany but now renamed Zagan and, due to the post-World War Two border changes, now in Poland. Primarily due to its isolated location it has, in many ways, remained unchanged after all these years. Here one can stand where these fine men stood and close ones eyes and be transported back in time. The camp was created when trees were cut and cleared from the dense forest, and in places 'Mother Nature' has sought to reclaim it to her fold. The tall trees surrounding the camp still make for a foreboding sense of isolation which is only reduced when one remembers that one can leave the scene at the end of the day and return to the comfort of a hotel in the town beyond the woods and train station just a few kilometres distant. Such comfort could only have been the subject of dreams by the men held there during the war.

Yet this book, while containing a definitive account of the East Compound at Stalag Luft III, goes still further and frames the camp and compound history around what I personally feel to be one of the most ingenious escapes of the war: 'The Wooden Horse'. Here Robert successfully balances the components of all great stories – characters and plot – to recreate one of the most endearing of escape tales; one which saw all the participants succeed in their objectives of obtaining freedom. Along the way we meet and greet the characters involved and we participate in their detailed experiences which gradually see their paths intertwined before they collaborate on the escape.

To tell the story in a way that educates and entertains is no mean feat, and it takes excellent primary research, patience, and passion for the subject matter. Robert has blended all these ingredients and has created a literal feast for the reader to taste and enjoy. I highly recommend this meal to you.

Gavin J.F. Worrell
Sunbury-on-Thames

Author's Notes and Acknowledgements

The story you are about to read is true. It happened in my grandparent's time and I have striven to retell it as authentically as possible. It has always been my favourite escape story, although I was made aware very early on that there was more to the story than had been told in Eric Williams' classic book. Thus I have diligently searched out whatever sources I could find in order to tell as complete a rendition of the tale as possible. Some may feel initially that this book is redundant and unnecessary; that the story has already been popularly told, at least twice. However, it is only now – some seventy years after the events described – that all the pieces necessary could come together and the *full* story can be finally told.

Eric Williams' book, *The Wooden Horse*, was the public's introduction to the story. However, even by his own admission it was not exactly the book he wanted to write. If it all were not based in fact and written by one of the principal participants, today it could very well be conceived as historical fiction. Only those pertinent facts keep it from being regarded as such. Outside of the three main characters, all others are composites of several real individuals that worked on the escape, and many of the incidents related in that book are composites of events, all of which is set along a compressed time-line. Because of that, initially sorting out who was who and what was what in order to maintain accuracy for this book turned out to be quite a chore! There was also the 1950 film *The Wooden Horse*, based mostly on Williams' book, and on which he was technical advisor, which also helped muddy the waters. Oliver Philpot's book *Stolen Journey* (the second popular telling of the tale) was a big help in regard to straightening things out, but even his work held tantalizing omissions; not the least of which was his maddening habit of providing no last names and his prolific use of nicknames. Then too, printing space considerations of the time, the British Government's Official Secrets Act, and a public that was not nearly so detail demanding, meant that general retellings of this most exciting tale were considered quite good enough.

Such is not the case anymore, and thus my retelling of the story is in far greater detail. I have gone to great lengths to provide accuracy and element for this account. For this, I have searched archives and other information sources in four countries; also sought out those individuals that I could find who were still alive and who had actually participated in the event (few though they are today). In one unfortunate case, I received contact information just two weeks too late. I have also consulted dozens of previously written accounts, both published and unpublished, and spoken with many individuals who are as 'PoW driven' as I am. Of course, Williams' and Philpot's books provided the basis from which to begin. However, in comparing the books with the official escape reports written and filed after the event, I found glaring inconsistencies between them. When that was the case, I tended to rely more upon the escape reports for accuracy, if for no other reasons than that they were written much closer to the event than the books, as well as without the novelistic 'fluff' which both lean toward; Williams' far more so than Philpot's. A lengthy interview Oliver Philpot gave to the Imperial War Museum in 1987 also expands the story well and has been worth its weight in gold for detail.

As no period photographs of the actual wooden horse are known to exist, despite extensive efforts to locate any that may, I constructed one especially for research and illustration for this book, using as many descriptions of the original as I could locate and checked against the memories of ex-prisoners. The reproduction was authentic in every detail save one: it was built with one removable side in order that the interior might be visible. Ex-prisoners who vaulted over the real horse were very pleased by its authenticity. I also constructed a full scale, authentically-built tunnel, as it appears that the Germans did not photograph the original in the chaos that reigned in East Compound following the breakout. Photographs of both these efforts, as well as period photographs I have gathered concerning the men and the escape (some quite rare), appear in this book. Photographs are credited to the source most closely associated with that image, as near as could be determined. If no source is given the image comes from my own collection. Should anyone have questions concerning any of these sources, or any other question concerning the facts in this book, I encourage the reader to contact me.

In relating the story, I have also woven in background information that I felt was relevant to the account, although it may seem to some who are familiar with PoW and escape stories as superfluous. The list of consulted sources for my work is in the back of the book. Endnotes meant to flesh out a particular point are also included. As British prisoners of war had their own slang words that grew out of their experiences, and members of the RAF had their own slang on top of that, a Glossary of Terms is included at the end of the book.

I would like to take this opportunity to thank the many persons who were of assistance in my journey through time to bring this book to fruition. A noted author once told me, 'No one writes a book on their own; the author just takes the credit.' So it is here. Inevitably, I will forget one of the many who assisted me and to those who are missed here please accept both my thanks and deepest apologies. If you are missing here it is entirely my own fault, and may I be 'sent to coventry' for my incredible mistake.

First and foremost, my deepest appreciation goes especially to Mr Tom Wilson, and his dedicated wife Gabrielle, both of whom have taken much time out of their lives to correspond with a nosey 'Yank' from across 'The Pond'. My respect and admiration for Tom knows no bounds, although in saying so I risk his modesty and humility. I do so anyway. I would also like to thank Don 'Pappy' Elliot, Dallas Laskey, and Ewen McDonald for spending the time they did with me back in the place they looked forward to getting away from for so long. I hope in relating your memories and experiences you were able to reconnect with only the positives of that era in your lives. To Michael Codner, I am deeply indebted for opening up the family archives concerning his uncle and namesake. His uncle's role in the escape has always been drastically underplayed, in my opinion, and hopefully together we have corrected that terrible omission. My deep appreciation also goes to Mr Martin Rowley Calnan, for taking time to discuss his father, Thomas Calnan, with me. 'Tommy' Calnan has always been one of my personal escape heroes, and it was a thrill to learn about him from someone who knew more of the man himself, rather than just the airman. Still further, my eternal gratitude is extended to Gavin J.F. Worrell, not only for his excellent ground research at the former site of Stalag Luft III, but also for his unending belief in this project, his sound advice, and his inspirational, abiding devotion to the reality of enemy incarceration and escape, rather than just the myths that have grown up around the subject. (Nor does it hurt that he is unfailingly British.) Also, my gratitude to Mr Nick Jackson for much the same support.

And to the extended legion of many who have contributed assistance in other ways, my sincere and unending thanks go to: Peter Wilson (without who I would never have been in contact with his father and mother,); Marc Stevens, for information on his father, Peter Stevens; Jonathan Vance, expert on all things PoW; Brendan Foley and 'Tex' Ash; Cathy Pugh, at the Second World War Education Centre in London; Frank Drauschke and Tanja Katharina Thomaschky, MA, for searching the German Records at Freiburg, Germany; Sebastian Laudan, for special advice on all things German; Alex Bateman, for his work at the Imperial War Museum on my behalf; Dr Stuart C. Blank, at Military Archive Research, for finding whatever I needed; Michal Juran and Filip Procházka, my Czechoslovak ground source men; Josephine Garnier, at the Imperial War Museum, London; Bruce Zigler, for all things RAF related; Scott Bellis for much the same; Dr Janet Bobby, for her deft editing skills and unending faith in my writing; Lewis Wood and Mike Shackel for the same; Tony Lynham; Tyler Butterworth; Marilyn Walton; Dave Windle and Allan Hunter (whose father made Philpot's forged papers), for reading the manuscript and giving me an honest, objective opinion; the much talented Katie and Lynn at The Ink Spot, in Waterford, Wisconsin, USA; Tim Carroll and Steve Martin, for answering the Stalag Luft III questions I could not find answers to; Rob Davis, expert on all things 'Great Escape'; Jim Liesenfelder, who never laughs at my stupid ideas; Kathy Strasser; Sue Lea, expert acquisitionist at the Waterford

Public Library, Wisconsin, USA, who regularly works miracles at laying hands on some extremely rare works for me; David and Jenny King; Mike and Jenny Jetzer; Tamara Truitt, for her deft location of the unfindable; Major Howard Aprill, US Army Reserve; the members of my former command, Headquarters Company/339th Battalion, Wisconsin Military Cadet Corps, especially 1st Sergeant Greg Dams, Sargeant Jim Babcock, Corporal Andy Falkner, Private Patrick Blasing and Major Mark Menting; Ray Pirus, David Zajicek, Mike Ahl, Brad Pearson and Kristen Mastricola for their unending interest; Andre Hubbeling for his research into Eric Williams' capture; Ms Laura Hirst at Pen & Sword for extending the hand across the ocean; Jasper Spencer-Smith, whose enthusiasm and clean editing on behalf of Pen & Sword made a keen Yank's writing fit British form far better than it originally had and thus worthy of the story; and to my late mother, Rose, for handing down to me the passion to read, explore, and ask questions.

Finally, and most importantly, a big thanks to my 'long-suffering' wife Trinie. It is primarily because of her that I am able to escape myself and really live my adventures – which she allows me to do, with never a word, no matter how strange or bizarre those adventures may seem. She is my chief editor and critic; main support and motivator; and unfailing companion on the journey, no matter where it leads. Thanks for putting up with me doll – I really love you.

And finally to Eric Williams, Michael Codner, and Oliver Philpot, for their ingenuity and courage, and for whom there is no further need to escape.

Well done chaps!

Per Ardua Ad Astra!

Robert J. Laplander
Lake Tichigan, Wisconsin
USA

Prologue: Confessions of a latent escaper

The reality of exactly what Prisoners of War were came to me when I was 7 years old. The US involvement in the Vietnam War had recently ended and I distinctly remember watching television (TV) as the first of our downed flyers were returned from Hanoi. Amid a huge throng of people at an airport somewhere, thin, emaciated men were slowly treading down the stairway from a large jetliner, stopping briefly at the bottom and saluting the welcoming officer. I recall thinking how generally grim and ill they looked – their huge smiles not withstanding – and asking my mother who they were. She looked at the flickering black and white screen briefly and told me they had been taken prisoner by the enemy after their aircraft had crashed. They were called Prisoners of War, she said, and now that the war was over they could come home. How long had they been gone, I asked? She paused, waiting for a fresh camera angle on the small screen before pointing out a tall, skinny man who looked very old. (It was Commander James Stockdale.) 'He's been gone for nearly seven years, if I remember correctly,' she said and turned away.

Seven years! My young mind was staggered by the number. At that age, I could barely stand to be away from my mother (my only parent) for much more than a day or two. And here was a man that had been away from his family for 7 years! Away from his friends, from his family and the comforts of home and locked up in a prison for all that time. The thought terrified me. No wonder the man on TV looked so sad. Little did I know.

Like most American boys, my fascination with the experience of the World War Two escaper, however, goes back to the 1963 John Sturgis film, *The Great Escape*. My friends and I waited all year for it to be shown on TV, which it usually was sometime around Thanksgiving. It was like getting an early Christmas present! Sitting with a bowl of popcorn and a glass of 'Kool-Aid' amid an array of pillows on the floor; being allowed to stay up late and watch it with all the lights dimmed ... It was one of those rare times (in those days at least) when a 10 year old actually saw the clock reach 11.00pm. The film – even with all its flaws and inaccuracies, of which there are many – is terrific high adventure of the best kind, suitable for even a younger viewer and the one that has remained my all time favourite to this day.

I was in middle school when I really caught the escaping bug. We moved a lot when I was a child and my school that year was a new one. Being an avid reader, I checked out the library situation immediately and it was there that I first came face-to-face with Paul Brickhill's classic on which my favourite film was based; tucked at the back of the bookrack was a 'dog-eared', paperback copy of *The Great Escape*. It took me barely two days to read it and I remember very clearly that I was in science class, with the little paperback stuck cleverly into my textbook, when I came to the parts where the fifty officers were murdered. I knew it had happened of course, but all the hair went up on the back of my neck nonetheless. They had really done it. They had really killed all those men in cold blood and it had been far more chilling than the film had led me to believe.

Yet despite the horrifying outcome of the whole 'Great Escape' drama there was still a fascinating adventure about it all, and I soon learned that Brickhill's work was not alone. There were others who had written about escaping – lots of others – and each story was just as exciting and daring. That is when I first came across Eric William's classics *The Wooden Horse* and *The Tunnel*. Later, I was to find P.R. Reid's *The Colditz Story*; Thomas Calnan's *Free as a Running Fox;* and Sydney Smith's *Wings Day*; as well as Robert Kee's *A Crowd Is Not Company* and Paul Brickhill's wonderful work on the incredible Douglas Bader, *Reach For The Sky.*

I had discovered an exciting new world, and I was there alongside these men as they carved their way through the wire in broad daylight, or tried to bluff their way through the front gate. I was there with them modifying an RAF uniform jacket to look like a civilian suit; digging tunnels and shoring them up with wooden bed slats; and hand-forging documents copied from originals brought in by bribed guards. My rations were short and I brooded around the 'circuit' just inside the 'warning wire' for hours while wracking my brain for another way out, something that had not yet been tried, and analyzing why others had failed. Because, of course, my all-encompassing goal in prison camp life was always centred on escape; getting beyond the wire, across Germany, and safely back to England.

And, as I began to spend more and more time in the 'Stalags' and 'Oflags' in the Poland and Germany of my grandfather's time, I began to experiment with some of the things I was learning. I haunted 'flea markets' for an old World War Two army uniform, which I took home and attempted (poorly) to modify into my 'escape suit'. Working from pictures in my books, and using my mother's typewriter and a set of coloured pencils, I tried to make the 'documents' I would need (which proved early on that I am definitely no artist). But the crowning achievement was the 'escape tunnel'.

My grandparents lived on 15 acres in northern Wisconsin right on the edge of the Nicolet National Forest, and it was there that I spent all my summers. There was a sandy, flat patch of clear ground a short distance to one side of the gravel road near their house, extending toward the forest for about 25yd and some 50yd long. It also happened that in that summer of 1979 someone had cut up a large number of pallets and given the wood to my grandfather to burn in his fireplace. The boards, as it turned out, were about 6in wide and cut to just under 2ft long – perfect tunnel material! You can probably guess what happened next.

It took about three days to build and cover the tunnel, which was assembled in a 30ft ditch I had dug in the sand. Construction gave way to one further concession toward reality: the tunnel was only 6in below ground, since I had read enough to know that I did not want to be buried under a large amount of sand if things went wrong. When complete, the trap door was level with the ground, but the other end – the 'escape' end – I had not built open, instead leaving about 2ft of sand in place in order to make my 'break out' as real as possible. Although I had no railway or margarine-fuelled lamps flickering along its length, the tunnel looked to me just like the images in my copy of *The Great Escape,* and I was very pleased with my effort.

On the night of my 'escape', I slowly crawled down the tunnel in the weak light of my Ever-Ready flashlight and, using a small coffee can fashioned into a shovel, I hacked the last feet of sand away. I remember how I sweated, despite the damp coolness of the sandy tunnel. Then, all at once, I was through and looking up at the stars framed through the broken ground, with fresh air caressing my face. What a moment! Breaking out the width of the exit, I pulled myself up and out and then nipped off into the woods. Squatting behind a small pile of brush, I paused and looked back toward the tunnel exit, now bathed in moonlight. It had been quite an experience and one that I have never forgotten.

All of that came back to me several years ago, when my wife and I bought our first home. While moving in, a book fell out of an old cardboard box marked 'My Stuff'. It took only a moment to recognize it –*The Wooden Horse*, by Eric Williams. I had purchased it from the library of my middle school when it had closed years ago, and it was a well-worn, much loved copy. In putting it back, I looked in the box and there they were – all my favourite escape books, almost as if saved in a time capsule. Excited, a few days later I sat down with Tommy Calnan's *Free as a Running Fox* for the first time in years, and once again was back in the old familiar world of tunnels and barbed wire and finding that none of it had lost its thrilling adventure.

However, the subject has changed some from what it was in my youth. I see escaping in quite a different light now. There is earnestness and a stark reality about the activity that I had not understood before and the intensive research that has been done on the subject in recent years has since brought a very heavy sense of pragmatism to those events. It is now easy to see that, in a way, the Germans were right when they informed the PoWs that escaping was not a sport. There was far too much at stake from their point of view for it to be so flippant a thing and they had every intention of going to drastic measures to prevent escape. Nazi Germany, a nation with 6.5 million foreign workers, lived in dread that they could be organized into a serious resistance effort that would attack the interior of the Reich. And the German High Command recognized the possibility that escaping airmen – highly trained and motivated individuals – might be capable of organizing that resistance.

Although there is no proof that any such clandestine efforts were in the offing, in a similar sense it is broadly true that escape was truly recognized as a serious subject by Escape Committees in the camps, despite what the Germans might have thought. Even if they had no means to hit back at the enemy in a conventional manner, the prisoners honestly believed they could still cause trouble behind the lines by drawing the attention of as many troops into guarding or searching for them as possible; troops who might be better deployed elsewhere in the Reich. Often then, committee members saw their activities as a way of continuing the fight on a 'different front'. This is especially true of the erstwhile Roger Bushell; mastermind behind the 'Great Escape'. By and large, however, it appears that the majority of the *general* escapers did not commonly see escape in that light – or in the light of seriousness that the Germans tried to impress upon them. At least not until after March 1944 that is, when the fifty were murdered following the 'Great Escape'. After that, it all changed.

So too, then, have some of my own views on the subject changed with the clearer understanding of life, death, and risk that only time and maturity can bring. That said, in my youth I was convinced that had I been a PoW alongside those men in World War Two I would have been one of the 'escaping class'. Now, some 30 years later, after having read through the stories again, and this time understanding what was at stake far better than ever before, I can honestly say that I still believe I am a latent escaper at heart.

It is in that frame of mind that I here present to you the story of one of the most wonderful escapes of all time.

During the years 1939–1945, Royal Air Force and Dominion forces losses in the air war over Germany totalled some 70,253.

Of that number, 13,115 were taken prisoner of war.

Out of that total number taken prisoner, only 34 who managed to escape from Nazi PoW camps ever made it back to England.

This put the chances at roughly 1 in 385.

The likelihood of success was, therefore, decidedly against the odds …

Part I

Capture

Chapter 1

The Demise of O for 'Orange'

December 1941–April 1942

The round, yellow rescue dinghy drifted sluggishly on the icy, open expanse of the North Sea. Waves lapped at the sides, occasionally sluicing up and over, sloshing water into the interior and sending a fine spray through the air. Above, the sky was a leaden grey and all was quiet except for the heavy, hollow sound of the water as it beat against the inflated dinghy, and the chilling rush of a 32mph December wind. In the yellow dinghy, slowly freezing to death as the hours dragged interminably by, were four shivering figures in RAF aircrew flying kit. Taking turns, they occasionally bent forward to bail the icy water out of the dinghy's interior with a leather binocular case whenever the level in the bottom reached the point where it was lapping into their trouser pockets. Otherwise, they simply held on and rode the waves of the rolling sea, ducking ever deeper into their fleece-lined Irvin flying jackets against the bitter North Sea wind, and waited for something to happen.

Only hours before they had been the crew of a Bristol Beaufort torpedo bomber, call sign O for 'Orange' with the serial number AW 243 of No.42 Squadron, assigned to Coastal Command and flying out of RAF Leuchars, Scotland. That morning, they had been detailed to fly an anti-shipping patrol off the Norwegian coast. They took off just before 10.00am that morning, and at 12.25pm were photographing a German radar station just inland from the coast when they spotted a German convoy of some eighteen or twenty ships, steaming in two long columns for the safer waters of the Fatherland. In the centre was a 10,000-ton freighter, a valuable and tempting target. Immediately swinging west off the coast, they went in for a mast-height, high-speed attack and were just starting their run in against the freighter when the Beaufort was hit by anti-aircraft fire from one of the escorting Flak ships, destroying the starboard engine and damaging the flight controls. Having no height with which to play, and unable to properly control the badly stricken aircraft the pilot, Flying Officer Oliver Philpot, called over the intercom for the crew to prepare for a rough ditching. Coming in much too fast, the Beaufort snapped in two when it struck the waves, and from there on it was all rushing water and adrenaline as the crew of three officers and one Flight Sergeant scrambled out and into the dinghy. Safe, if severely shaken, they then watched the two pieces of O for 'Orange' silently slip beneath the waves. It was 11 December 1941, and they were no longer the crew of a Bristol Beaufort. Now, they were simply a group of men floating along silently under a leaden sky who needed a small miracle in the vast open expanse of the North Sea.

Cold and wind and water ... water and wind and cold; nothing to the north, south, east or west, except bleak openness. At least no one had been seriously injured. The air gunner, Flight Sergeant 'Freddie' Smith, had cracked his head against a bulkhead in the aircraft when they had hit the sea, but other than that everyone had escaped unscathed. Yet that was certain to change as they faced the December North Sea in only their flying gear. Worst off was Flying Officer 'Ollie' Philpot. He had taken off that day in just his service shoes, leaving his fur-lined flying boots behind and now, even after just a couple of hours, he was already feeling the effects on his feet of the icy water that entered their dinghy. Flight Sergeant Smith was feeling much the same effect in his hands, since he had lost his heavy gloves sometime between hitting the aircraft, hitting the sea and being pulled into the dinghy, unconscious, by the Wireless Operator, Pilot Officer Roy Hester.

All in all, the prospects of their situation were not good. Never mind the immense areas that needed to be covered by Air/Sea Rescue in order to locate and then pick them up. The basic facts were that it was unlikely that any of the crews that had flown the mission alongside them and after witnessing the amount of Flak that the Beaufort had absorbed would assume them to be dead, and would likely report them as such upon return to Leuchars. More to the point, it was a well-known fact that few who survived a ditching that far north in the North Sea (particularly at that time of year) stood much chance of surviving the extreme weather conditions for long. Their only real hope was to be picked up by either a friendly Norwegian trawler, which looked highly unlikely, or by an enemy ship, in which case they would find themselves in the unenviable position of becoming Prisoners of War. But at least they would be alive.

All this ran through pilot 'Ollie' Philpot's mind over and over as he sat in command of the small group in the dinghy and felt his feet slowly freezing. The next 48 hours or so would be the most telling of their young lives, in which their fate would be decided. Around him, each of the other three sat buried in their own thoughts, huddled deep in their Irvin flight jackets. Personally, Philpot's main regret was that his wife, Nathalie, would have to wait before knowing his ultimate fate – and, in fact, may never really know at all. She was the mother of his twin girls – Nathalie Anne and Barbara Alison – born only a little over a month before, on 1 November 1941, and he worried what the shock of his loss might do to his new family.

Oliver Laurence Spurling Philpot was born in Vancouver, British Columbia, on 6 March 1913, the son of a London electrical engineer who had come to Canada to work for the British Columbia Electric Company. He attended two public schools in Canada before his parents returned with him to England in September 1925. There he received his secondary education before attending Radley College near Abingdon between 1927 and 1932. While at Radley, he served in the Officers' Training Corps (OTC), later remarking, 'It was one of these very English things – voluntary but compulsory.' Following that, he took his undergraduate studies in Philosophy of Politics and Economics at Worcester College, Oxford University until 1934.

In 1928, before Worcester, Philpot had had his first brush with what was to be very much the centre of his youth – the air services of the British Empire. While visiting with cousins in Derbyshire, an RAF biplane made an emergency landing in a field nearby, pitching over onto its back in the process. They all went up to see the wreckage, taking photographs and marvelling at the modern design of the aircraft, and it brought to mind for Philpot dimly remembered stories from an uncle in Canada who had won a Military Cross (MC) while flying in World War One. Shortly after, while in the OTC at Radley, he was given a flight in an RAF Vickers Vimy, a great, lumbering World War One-era bomber and, standing in the forward gunner's cockpit with the wind in his face high above the Oxfordshire countryside, his fate was sealed. He wanted to fly.

Having seen photographss of the trenches in France from the last war, Philpot determined that in the event of another war he wanted no part of an existence in the mud. And, having already decided to go to Worcester College at Oxford University following Radley, he therefore applied for admission into the Oxford University Air Squadron (OUAS), into which he was accepted in 1931. In vogue at the time, university air squadrons were to form the basis of an expanded national air force in the event of war, and were a place for eager young men to show their metal – or lack thereof. Far from a natural airman (it took him the then-unheard of total of 27 hours dual flying before going solo), he nevertheless eventually settled down and gained his wings. In fact, one of his instructors was Flight Lieutenant F.J.W. Mellersh who, in 1918, had been involved in the shooting down of the most famous fighter ace of World War One, Manfred von Richthofen – the legendary 'Red Baron'. In due course, under Mellersh's instruction, Philpot represented OUAS in the 1934 college aerial competition, where he earned high marks for his flying skill.

After graduating from Worcester in 1934, he joined the Unilever Corporation as a management trainee and in 1936 was appointed assistant commercial secretary in Unilever's Home Margarine Executive. This proved to be a most interesting post, which required him to travel to Berlin, Germany, and work at Unilever's Margarine Sales Union. There he learned to speak German and lodged with a German family who were ardent supporters of the Nazi regime. Over the next several months his work had him carefully studying the German rationing system and travelling extensively around Hitler's early Reich visiting clients. During this time he observed in detail Nazi Germany and much of the control and overtly militaristic nature of the country that he saw both shocked and appalled him. He returned to England in the autumn of 1936, sadly convinced that Germany was again a threat to Great Britain. He would not realize for another seven years, however, just how useful the whole experience would turn out to be for him.

By September 1938, Philpot was married to Margaret Nathalie Owen and the couple had settled in Chelsea, a prosperous, residential part of West London. That next year was a good one for the new couple. He was a well-bred, employed and upwardly mobile young man with a beautiful young wife and a bright future. The roses were truly blooming in that last summer of peace.

Then, in September 1939, war was declared on Germany and Great Britain began to mobilize once again. His service in the Oxford University Air Squadron automatically made Philpot a useful member of the British war effort. However, due to his married status, the government held him back initially and it was not until January 1940 that he entered the Royal Air Force Volunteer Reserve (RAFVR). Official RAF instruction followed – during which he found that he had much yet to learn about the Royal Air Force (RAF), which his instuctors gleefully drilled into him. Turned down for fighters (he was considered too old at 27), he volunteered instead for torpedo bombers, and received his operational training in No.269 Squadron; a No.18 Group (Coastal Command) unit based at RAF Wick in north-east Scotland. There, during October and November 1940, he served as a Pilot Officer on probation. He was immediately assigned to No.42 Squadron (also from No.18 Group) then operating the Vickers Vildebeest a single-engined, biplane torpedo bomber from RAF Leuchars (also in Scotland). Just before his arrival, however, the squadron had re-equipped with the redoubtable Bristol Beaufort and immediately began taking part in anti-submarine patrols off the British coast and the campaign against enemy shipping off the Norwegian coast. He was gazetted as a Pilot Officer on 15 January 1941.

His first difficult hour came during the night of 9-10 May 1941. During a night bombing raid against the Luftwaffe airfield at Kristiansand, Norway, his Beaufort took heavy anti-aircraft fire while on the bombing run, killing the navigator instantly and severely wounding the wireless operator. Still managing to drop his bombs on the target, Philpot then swung the badly damaged aircraft around, debating whether to land his dead and dying crew in neutral Sweden and take their chances with internment for the duration, or attempt to make it back to England. Damaged or not, the aircraft's controls still answered to his touch, so in the end England was chosen and he pointed the smashed nose of the aircraft out over the North Sea. Four hours later he landed in the pink light of dawn at RAF Northcotes in Lincolnshire and, without any hydraulic power, made a spectacular, wheels-up landing. The award of the DFC for his efforts was announced in the London Gazette on 1 July 1941. Promotion to Flying Officer soon followed.

Now fully aware of what war was, he realized his chances of not returning from a sortie grew with every flight, and in his own way he had begun to try and prepare Nathalie for that possibility. He himself had grasped it the moment he had turned his head in the cockpit over Norway and saw his navigator crumpled forward over his instruments, dead. But for her, what could he say? The question became even more troubling when his twin daughters were born. How could she have been expected to prepare for his loss while welcoming two new lives?

In any case, as the cold water now lapped around Philpot's slowly freezing feet, it was clear that no amount of preparation would have been likely to make the blow any easier for Nathalie to take, children or not. For some time to come their aircraft would simply be listed as one of those that had 'Failed to Return'. This would create a false hope inside her that he might yet be alive and well somewhere. He had seen it with other wives of men who had 'Failed to Return', and it was a most depressing prospect. But then, after an appropriate time had passed, the status of the crew of O for 'Orange' would be changed to 'Missing: Believed Killed in Action', after which she would have no recourse with which to fool herself any longer. She would be a war widow with two babies to care for and an uncertain future ahead.

Yet there was still the possibility of capture; a possibility that brought some chance of survival and even the possibility of escape and return. And although being captured by a sometimes brutal and cruel enemy was, at best, an unknown fate, perhaps imprisonment would prove the better of the two possible futures facing them. An intriguing thought, which was interrupted by one of the crew asking him whether he thought they had any real possibility of evading capture. He did not have to think about it very long, but did so for a few seconds anyway to give the impression of weighing the odds. Eventually, 'No; I'm afraid not.' was all he could say.

But at least they would be alive.

The coast of what they took to be Norway came into sight, through the dank, dull mist of the afternoon, some kilometres off giving rise to hope of landing and finding friendly folk to help them evade capture. They took it in turns to paddle in its direction with the tiny oars provided with the dinghy, but after several painful, exhausting hours, during which they made no progress whatsoever, they were forced to give up and each fell back, utterly exhausted. With the coming of night, the wind and sea became calmer and the tantalizing view of land, however dim and distant, slipped away into the darkness, seemingly taking their hopes with it as it disappeared. Completely exhausted and thoroughly disillusioned, they settled down to a fitful sleep, only to be repeatedly woken up at intervals throughout the night, shivering in the bitter cold.

The next morning they found that the view of land had totally disappeared; they were obviously drifting farther out to sea. The effects of exposure to the December weather was taking a firm hold on everyone. They spent the day each grabbing the arms of the man across from him and heaving them back and forth, in an attempt to generate some circulation and warmth, but the effort did little good. In the afternoon, two German Heinkel He115 seaplanes passed within three quarters of a mile of them, but with fingers frozen no one was able to grab the only flare pistol fast enough to fire it.

Philpot had insisted, when this second crew had originally been formed, that they regularly practice ditching drill in the hanger where their aircraft was kept. Many of the other crews had laughed at them, but they had kept training until they were reasonably proficient at the task, 'Just in case, old boy.' After all he had experienced in the RAF thus far, he was determined to take no chances. Let them laugh. His crew would be prepared. Now, as darkness of their second night fell upon them, with hope rapidly becoming a thing of the past and the miserable cold keeping them from sleeping at all, he began to wonder if it had really been worth the ridicule.

Their third day in the dinghy found the dawn revealing that they had again drifted within sight of land; in fact to what appeared to be within only 3 or 4 miles! However, peering through the binoculars revealed no beach but instead sheer cliffs, leaving nowhere to land the dinghy. At the same time, in the distance they spotted two columns of smoke from ships steaming across their route, both of which came round a cove and into sight a short time later. Now suffering from severe exposure and frostbite, there was little dissension when Philpot eventually managed to hook his frozen fingers onto the flare pistol and fired it in the direction of the lead ship. A few minutes later they received an answering flare and saw the ship swing around toward them. Shortly after, they were being hauled aboard a German *Flugzeugabwehrkanone* (Flak) ship by members of the *Kriegsmarine* (German Navy) dressed in heavy foul-weather gear. The time was 9.30am on 13 December 1941 and Flying Officer O. L. S. Philpot, RAF: Service No. 77131, along with his crew entered their term of captivity.

His feet were in truly bad condition when he was finally pulled over the side of the German ship, and kindly crew members carried him below decks. There they made him as comfortable as possible while they tried to thaw him out, along with the other members of his crew. Since Philpot was the only member of the crew who could speak German he translated for them, and they grew more despondent with the continuing bad news the crew passed to them of events in the Pacific. There, the Japanese had escalated hostilities just six days earlier with the attack on Pearl Harbor and continued to win oustanding victories. Further, though a medical attendant on the ship worked on Philpot's badly frostbitten feet with dexterous care, they were all nevertheless worried that he might yet lose one or both. Additionally, the Flight Sergeant's hands were nearly as bad. However, they comforted themselves by reminding each other that at least they were alive.

The ship took them to Kristiansand, where they were taken off and since they were aircrew, officially handed into the custody of the Luftwaffe, who immediately took them to a local hospital for further treatment. Late the next night, they were taken out, travelling through the remainder of that night and all the next day to another hospital, this time in Oslo. There Philpot and Flight Sergeant Smith began to receive real care for their injuries, while the two unwounded crewmen were separated from them and sent away. After a day or two of being warm and dry and well-cared for in a comfortable room at the Oslo hospital, the two airmen were beginning to feel much better and were visited by an officer from a Luftwaffe Flak (anti-aircraft) unit, who spoke excellent English and claimed to have shot them down. With a breezy, friendly manner that smacked smartly of the military intelligence services, he sandwiched into the conversation nearly every forbidden question in the book and truly seemed to expect answers. With Flight Sergeant Smith barely acknowledging him, and Philpot making it clear that the German was not going to get any of the information he sought, the officer departed indignantly and the two RAF men were quickly moved to less comfortable accommodation. However, from the window of their new room they could see the Luftwaffe airfield, and for the first time 'Ollie' Philpot felt his first desire to escape surge through his veins. Yet his feet were not in good enough condition for even the short snowy walk necessary to take him over to the airfield, and anyway the Germans had taken their clothes, leaving them with short, cotton hospital robes and no shoes. That night, he dreamed of flying off over the snow-covered landscape to neutral Sweden in a stolen German aircraft and the next morning sat for hours silently planning an escape that could never be achieved. Damn his feet! Time passed very slowly.

On 15 January 1942, the hospital staff informed them that they were to begin the move to Germany the next morning. The thought of going to 'The Fatherland', to a proper prison camp, was as depressing a thought as either of them had ever had. Philpot's feet were better now – at least it was now plain that he was going to keep them – as were Smith's hands. With their clothes returned to them only on the morning of their intended departure from Oslo, they made a desperate, unsuccessful attempt at unscrewing the window in their room using a table knife when their guard was not around. Success would have meant that his feet would probably have frozen (again) in the sub-zero temperatures, but it shows that the flame of escape was already burning bright. Nevertheless, before they could get the window loose enough, two Luftwaffe guards arrived in the afternoon and shuffled the two prisoners out of the room, and the first, fumbling escape attempt came to an end.

From Oslo they boarded a ship that took them to Aalborg, Denmark. From the ship's rail, flanked by their two guards, Philpot and Smith could clearly see the coast of Sweden in the distance, wistful and tantalizing in all its neutrality. If only there was a way! But there was not, and at Aalborg they were escorted to a train that carried them south, first to Vaarhus, then to Flensburg, then on to Germany where they passed through Hamburg, then Hanover, and on to Brunswick, until finally they arrived at Frankfurt-am-Main. During the entire trip the two guards never left their sides, except when they went to the lavatory. Therefore, he reasoned, that was the place to make his bid. During one of his visits in the darkening evening, just as the train was slowing down he forced open the window and leaned out. Looking left he saw the dim shapes of the rattling carriages ahead. Looking down he watched as the sleepers slowed from a blur into individual ties. So far so good! But when he looked to his right he saw one of the guards looking straight at him through their adjacent coach compartment window, puffing cigar smoke furiously past a scowl on his face. Wisely, he withdrew and retreated to their compartment with a sheepish grin at the still scowling guard. After that one of the guards always accompanied them to the lavatory and made them keep the door open.

At Frankfurt, they stayed the night in a German troop hostel and long before dawn the next morning boarded an open-air tram that would take them to their new camp. They were standing right next to German citizens on their way to work who largely paid them little notice. Getting off the tram, they walked off into the cold, snowy, January morning down forested country lanes until the pools of light from arc lamps around a long perimeter fence came into view through the trees. After they halted in front of a pair of log framed, barbed-wire gates they were bathed in the intense glare of a searchlight that swung around onto them from a watchtower off to the side. Inside the barbed-wire enclosure they could make out several low-slung huts through the dim, grey morning light as their guards and the gate guards fumbled their way through some paperwork. Soon they were being led into the camp, past a man walking a large Alsatian dog, and into a pleasant continental-style house converted to a prison. Here they were separated, and though Philpot would not see Smith again for some days, he could hear him in the cell next door and they kept up a loud conversation until a German guard yelled for them to be silent. His clothes were taken from him again and he was left sitting in the cold, cramped cell in just vest and underpants.

'*Fur sie ist der Krieg vorbei*,' (For you the war is over) the guard had told him flatly with a slight, icy smile full of bad teeth as he left to take his uniform 'to be X-rayed'.

He had arrived at Dulag-Luft.

Durchgangslager der Luftwaffe, or Dulag Luft as it was commonly referred to, was the Luftwaffe's intelligence and interrogation camp for newly captured aircrew. It was located at Oberursel, a suburb some 7km northwest of Frankfurt-am-Main and had been opened at the end of 1939 on the site of a former agricultural school. The first residents had been a small contingent of RAF officers that had been captured early in the war and first held at Spangenburg Castle (Oflag IX A/H). In the spring of 1940, a purpose-built camp was constructed adjacent to the permanent buildings of the school and the prisoners were moved in. The camp then officially became the Luftwaffe's transit camp for RAF PoWs and therefore a new prisoner's first experience of the German prison camp system. A new prisoner could expect to be kept in one of the 6ft by 9ft intake cells from a week to 10 days, during which time he would be subjected to various interrogation techniques by the Germans. Following that, he would be released to languish for up to two months in the main compound before being transferred (or 'purged') to a permanent camp; his time at Dulag dictated by the current rate at which aircraft were being shot down. The original RAF prisoners to Dulag, however, were kept on as a permanent British staff, ostensibly to help soften the transition period of the new prisoners from what had been life to something totally different. For the permanent staff, life at Dulag was relatively pleasant, mostly because the International Red Cross (IRC) had had plenty of time to set up a supply line to the camp. Therefore, the all important Red Cross parcels had begun arriving early in the war and were plentiful. New prisoners benefited from this as well.

There were also other benefits to life in Dulag; no overcrowding, a general relaxation of many of the more petty rules by the Germans, and occasional parole walks outside the wire. However, all of these benefits bestowed by the Germans had a purpose, which was to present a better picture of prison life to the newly captured, and therefore sap their resistance to go against the system and attempt escape. And, it must be remembered, that interrogation (seeking information from men still in shock from what, in many cases, had been the terrifying experience of being shot down) was the main purpose of the camp. Later, the permanent RAF staff frequently came under attack from many new prisoners for 'helping' the Germans, when in reality they were only trying to ease a new prisoner's shock of capture which, as stated, could be considerable. They also used the benefits provided by the Germans to their own good, dispelling many of the allegations against them when, in the spring of 1941, a number broke-out from the camp through the first successful RAF-dug tunnel in Germany

Time in the holding cells at Dulag Luft usually passed with a painful slowness, so it was a blessing that Philpot was not there long. He got his uniform back within a few hours of it having been taken to be 'X-rayed' and almost immediately afterwards was taken to be fingerprinted and photographed. The next day, a short man in an immaculate Luftwaffe officer's uniform paid him a visit with a false Red Cross form that asked all kinds of forbidden questions. Knowing that the IRC would hardly need to know what kind of aircraft he had been flying or what their mission had been, he refused to fill in any of the blanks on the form save for name, rank and number. The officer immediately became incensed and stormed out of the cell yelling that Philpot would never be allowed to write to his wife.

'She will never know what has happened to you!' he said, pausing in the doorway to see what effect his words had on the prisoner. Seeing no response, the little officer left in a huff, slamming the door violently. Philpot turned toward the small barred window for the hundredth time, and for the hundredth time renewed a vow to himself to get out and away from such churlish people.

The next visitor was a well-presented officer who announced himself to be the assistant camp Kommandant, a tall, older man with a duelling scar on his cheek, who asked more leading questions to which Philpot again gave no answers. After a short time of getting nowhere with his prisoner, he also left in an insistent huff. Soon after Philpot was hustled out of the holding cell and taken over to the main camp where, much to his delight, he found the rest of his crew waiting for him.

The next three weeks at Dulag Luft passed mostly in a flurry of 'There I was …' stories swapped with his fellow new prisoners, and in learning the ropes of being a 'Kriegie'. The nickname was a self-imposed one by the prisoners; a bastardisation of the German word *Kriegsgefangenen* (Prisoner of War). At Dulag he learned what it really meant. 'We were the left-overs,' Philpot would later recall. 'Death had made a mistake – we should all have been blotted out, together with our companions, and appeared on the 'Killed in Action' lists. But some fantastic twist of fortune had favoured each one of us.' Now they were stuck in some dim, twilight world; trained for war, but not able to perpetrate it while the world continued the struggle without them. The years ahead looked long, if one cared to look in that direction.

However, with his feet again in some semblance of reasonable shape, and with the prospect of spring just around the corner, he began to make inquiries of the older prisoners about the chances of escape from the little compound. The small flicker that had sparked within him back in Norway was now becoming a raging fire as he learned more and more of the life that lay yet ahead for him; the more he learned, the less he liked of what he heard. In England, he had never met a single escaped prisoner that had made it back (or an evader, for that matter) and instruction in what to expect if he were shot down and captured had been rudimentary at best. The older prisoners were largely not enthusiastic about the escape subject however, and usually tried to steer the conversation toward what were the latest shows playing in London, and whether the price of a pint of beer had gone up yet at 'The Lion' pub.

But not all the prisoners were as blasé on the subject as they seemed, and he was able to learn about an escape that had taken place the spring before. A tunnel had been driven out from under a bed in one of the huts, and twenty or so men had slipped clean away, including the Senior British Officer, Wing Commander Harry Day. The Germans had become understandably agitated and went to great lengths to recapture the absconders; not one of the escapees had made the coveted 'home run' back to England. Within 2 weeks, all had been recaptured and sent off to other camps as punishment. Philpot was enthralled by the story, as was a new prisoner he had recently met who had just been released from hospital and into Dulag; Squadron Leader Thomas 'Tommy' D. Calnan. Both immediately began plotting and planning, but before either man could bring any escape plan anywhere near to fruition, they found themselves among a purge of new prisoners being loaded on a train heading for Oflag IX A/H, the officer's prison camp at Spangenburg Castle, near Kassel.[1]

Oflag IX A/H was actually a camp divided in two, holding mostly army prisoners that had been captured at Dunkirk and in the fall of France. The first section was a barbed-wire ringed camp located actually within the town of Spangenburg. Dubbed 'Lower Camp' by prisoners, this was 'A Lager' and it held mainly non-commissioned men. The second part of the prison was Spangenburg Castle, built high on a hill overlooking the town. This was the Upper Camp, or 'H Lager' (short for *Hauptlager* – Main camp) which held officers. While it was all very scenic – the blond German frauleins could readily be seen going about daily life in the village from almost everywhere in the Lower Camp – the officer contingent from Dulag Luft was only in Lower Camp for some two weeks before being moved up the hill to the castle. And a real castle it was, complete with battlements, 3ft thick walls, and a drawbridge over a 30ft deep dry moat running along three sides. Along the fourth side was a drop of indeterminate depth, but generally considered to be 'a whole lot of down' by the inmates. The Senior British Officer (SBO) of the castle, Major General Victor Fortune, had been taken prisoner at St Valery with the 51st Highland Division and talked to the new contingent about escape first thing upon their arrival. Besides being the duty of each officer, he reminded them, it had generally become the camp's main focus, though too little good thus far. But they must keep it up; must keep trying, no matter what. New men meant new ideas. The general's talk, not so much a lecture as a hearty greeting to a new club of achievers, was inspiring.

However, escape from the castle was very difficult, and it seemed at first to the new boys that most of the ideas to get out had already been tried. Nevertheless, Philpot and some of the other RAF contingent quickly got busy on several schemes (in no small measure under army advice), which were duly registered with the camp Escape Committee. He had agreed to join in a plan put forward by Squadron Leader Woodruff, an Australian Spitfire pilot, to ride a small trolley down some electrical wires that ran from the castle over the moat to a post, though no one seemed to be able to convince Woodruff that the likely resultant sag of the wires caused by the additional weight placed upon them would probably leave the escapers stranded halfway across with no way to traverse the last uphill stretch. Tommy Calnan had found a grappling hook hidden in a huge, old table and was in the process of procuring a rope in order to scale the moat face with two other men. Diversions would keep the attention of the guards. Another team was making some replica German uniforms to attempt (yet another) walk out of the front gate by some new prisoners posing as two of the guards. Maps began to appear from secret hiding places ready to be traced, as were the few German documents that had been collected by army prisoners, while men with a skill for tailoring suddenly found themselves very popular. Within a few short weeks then, the 'Arab Quarter' (the nickname given by the army to that portion of the castle occupied by the RAF) was alive with illicit activities and furtive men talking in low tones in dark corners.

But, once again, it was not to be. Rumours had been circulating almost from their arrival that the RAF contingent was only at Spangenburg temporarily while the Germans put the finishing touches to their huge new, escape proof, air force-only prison camp. While no one doubted the move was an absolute certainty, the timing was under considerable question, and so escape activities moved forward relentlessly. Yet despite the weeks of careful preparation, before any of the various plans could materialise, one cold morning at the end of April 1942, the RAF personnel were roused early by the shouts and tramping boots of their German guards echoing off the cobblestones outside the 'Arab Quarter' and told to pack quickly. As they did so, their quarters and belongings were thoroughly searched, during which much of the escape equipment they had so painstakingly gathered in the last few weeks was found and confiscated. They were then marched out of the castle and down to the railway station in the town, where they were again thoroughly searched, during which any remaining items of their escape equipment was found and confiscated. Crammed into cattle trucks and third-class carriages, their destination, the English speaking German guards among them explained in surly tones, was indeed the Luftwaffe's newest camp, near the town of Sagan in Upper Silesia.

The train ride was typically long and uncomfortable; more so for Philpot and the main group, accommodated in cattle trucks, than for those few still lame with wounds or other sickness, who occupied third-class compartments with wooden seats. In Philpot's truck a small group got together and started to cut a hole through the floor with a saw blade filed out of a German issue table knife that had somehow made it through both rigorous searches. Meanwhile, Philpot and a companion decided that a true opportunity for their own escape had definitely presented itself in the form of a small window at one end of their truck. On the afternoon of their second day, just as the train slowed as it began to climb a long, winding hill, he asked a group of men to gather around a fellow inmate playing a violin to form a screen between him and their two guards. Just as the train seemed at its slowest, he jerked the barbed wire covering loose from across the small window at their end of the truck and began to wriggle out. Getting one arm and a portion of his torso out the window, he turned toward the head of the train to get a better purchase for the final wriggle out and as he did saw a German railway worker leaning far out of a truck ahead, looking straight at him. Quickly he pulled himself back in, replaced the wire he had torn away and he and his companion dispersed themselves into the crowd. Immediately there was a shrill whistle and the train stopped. Within minutes the Germans were yanking the door open and searching the truck. It was another chance gone, but at least it was another attempt made.[2]

The train pulled into the station at Sagan, later that night and the prisoners were off-loaded away from the platforms. They were then herded into the yard of the local granary to be counted again in the glare of floodlights before being handed over to the Luftwaffe. (Spangenburg had been run by the German army and was indeed an army camp.) All around them were tall pine trees whose trunks blocked the view from every direction. Then their new guards – younger than those at Spangenburg, more alert and with rifles at the ready – formed them up and began marching them away from the station and through the thick pine forest along a narrow road. At first all was quiet and somewhat serene. Then, after about a kilometre, Philpot spotted through the trees the familiar site that he had first seen several months ago, in the early morning hours outside of Oberursel; the thick fence of barbed wire, the stark shape of a 'Goon box' (guard tower) with the guard swinging a searchlight all around, and a lonely looking sentry slowly pacing a beat outside the wire. The barrenness of the scene behind the wire as they drew closer to the large double gates was somewhat foreboding in a desolate way, even in the gloom of night. Here was a proper prison camp, well thought out and designed for one purpose and one purpose only – to house air force prisoners within its confines, and to keep them there. They had arrived at the now infamous Stalag Luft III.[3]

Chapter 2

Sagan

April–September 1942

S*tammlager der Luftwaffe* No.3 was located deep within the pine forests of German Upper Silesia, just a short distance from the border with occupied Poland, immediately adjacent to the ancient town of Sagan. A 'Stalag' was commonly the term used in reference to an 'other ranks' or non-commissioned officer's (NCO) camp (*Stammlager*), while an 'Oflag' was generally a camp for commissioned officers (*Offizierlager*). The Luftwaffe did things their own way however, and Stalag Luft III, which would hold both officers and other ranks, received a 'Stalag' designation.

The camp lay along the ancient route between Berlin (209km distant) and Warsaw some 402km distant. The location had been carefully selected by the Luftwaffe's high command for three very important reasons: First, it was a long way from any friendly, or even moderately friendly, border. Switzerland was over 644km away and the French coast was some 1,207km distant. This meant that any sucessful escaper had a long distance to travel through 'hostile' country.

The second reason was the location that the camp actually occupied. The site had been carved out of the middle of a vast pine and birch forest, and left no view of anything but tall trees in all directions. This unchanging landscape gave a strong feeling of total isolation that, over time, had a detrimental effect on many of the prisoners. This effect was further increased by the area of ground occupied by the camp, which was either a hot, dry and dusty barrenness in fair weather, or else a dirty, muddy barrenness in bad weather. Either way, the very austerity of the location, combined with the isolating panorama, gave way to a certain hopelessness that sometimes took on the effects of an actual sickness, tempting many of the imprisoners to just wrap themselves in a blanket of hopelessness and wait for the war to end, which is precisely what the Germans hoped for.

The third reason that the Germans had chosen the location of Stalag Luft III so carefully had to do with some of the men to be housed in the new camp. Philpot and many of his companions, who were among the second contingent of prisoners to arrive at the camp, were comparative newcomers ('new boys') to the escape business; willing and eager and champing at the bit to make their attempts, but wholly lacking in practical knowledge. Not so among the group in the first contingent to arrive at the camp however, who had been transported from Stalag Luft I, the first air force camp the Luftwaffe had established which was located near the town of Barth, on the Baltic coast. The RAF men in that first contingent were the prisoners of long experience; the 'old lags' and the naughty boys, many of them dedicated escapers who had become exceptionally ingenious at tunnelling, cutting wire and even bluffing their way through the gate. They were forever giving their captors problems and it was hoped by the Germans that the isolated location of their new camp, combined with all that they had learned about security from trying to keep them 'caged' for 3 years already, would blunt these escapist tendencies. In fact, the entire staff of Luft I had moved to Luft III along with the prisoners for just that reason. It was largely a vain hope however, for in the end all the Germans succeeded in doing by throwing the two groups together was to increase the size of what would become a group of dedicated escapers.

Yet there was further method to the German scheme as well; method at first not readily recognizable. If the general 'scenery' of the camp make up did not act as deterrent enough, then the make-up of the 'soul' of Stalag Luft III probably would; that being the very earth on which it stood. The dark grey topsoil of the camp was the typical loose forest flooring made up mainly of pine needle mould and other natural forest debris that spoke of a good soil makeup underneath. That was a fallacy however, as the Barth escapers that first dug the earth for a tunnel out of their new camp (by far the escaper's preferred method of egress) would quickly find out. Once past the first 6 to 16in of grey topsoil, came soft, unstable and unpredictable sand; a dim yellow-gold in colour when wet, but drying to an unusual whiteness in the sun.

This was something new to the tunnellers from Barth. There the soil had been good, firm earth, with the main deterrent facing the diggers the fact that, through being so close to the sea, the water table had been very high (an average of just 7ft below the surface) necessitating shallow tunnels that the Germans had been able to often collapse by simply driving a heavy wagon around the compound. A further consideration was that the water table typically rose and fell through the year, sometimes flooding tunnels before they could be used. Therefore, tunnels at Barth had had to be driven out fast, both before the elements might turn against their completion and before the Germans had got it in their heads that one might exist; by far the most important factor in a camp where the German security system had been highly developed through experience.

At Sagan, the diggers were faced with a whole new set of problems. There, the sandy subsoil made tunnelling an extraordinarily dangerous prospect. The sand collapsed easily, necessitating that the roof of any tunnel had to be firmly supported by wooden props for every inch it went forward. A roof fall in a tunnel was therefore incredibly dangerous, when sand could give way quickly and bury an unfortunate digger in seconds, with more coming down at any time while efforts were made to rescue the digger. Sourcing all the wood needed for a tunnel without the Germans knowing what was going on also proved to be a problem; the bed boards used crosswise in the double-tier bunks provided for the prisoners proved just the ticket, at approximately 30in long, but there were only a finite number which could be taken. Soon prisoners were ripping the double flooring off from under the huts and pulling bracing rafters out as well, until it seemed a miracle that some of the huts remained standing.

However there were a few positives discovered at Sagan by the ever optimistic escapers. First, much to the delight of the Barth crowd, the water table at Sagan was deep; an average of 78ft down, far deeper than any escape tunnel would ever likely be dug. Further, it was eventually also discovered that at a depth between 4 and 6ft, there was a layer of sand that had clay within its composition, and over that layer, just below the loose, grey topsoil, were the pine roots from the tree cover that had once filled the space the camp now occupied. This pine-root layer was itself some 2ft thick and, when combined with the sand/clay layer below it, provided a fairly solid soil base of some 6ft in depth before the softer sub-strata sand was reached. These discoveries, over time, would eventually prove to be extremely beneficial for escape.

Yet even with the seeming benefits, the experienced RAF tunnellers that arrived at Sagan in that spring of 1942 soon found that they almost preferred

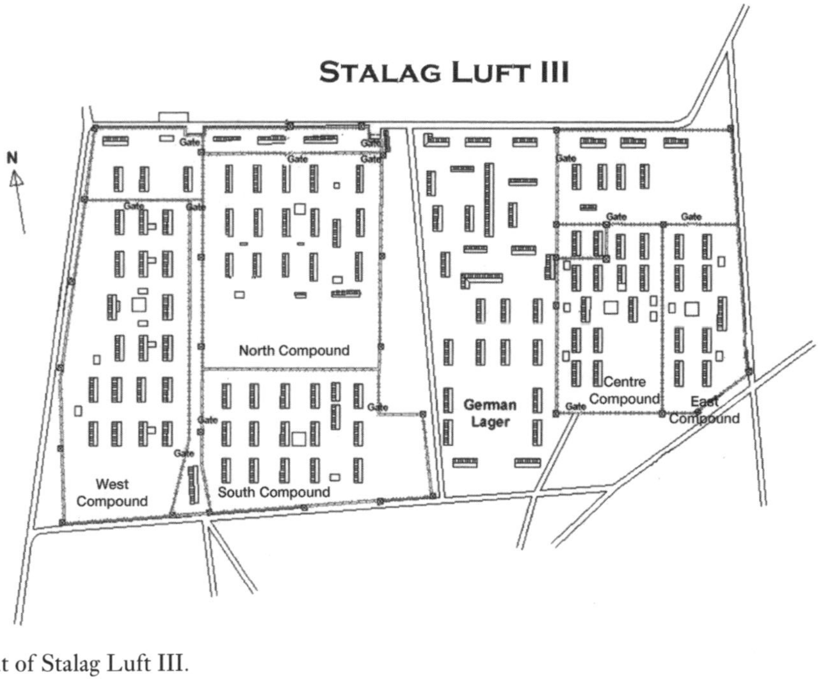

Layout of Stalag Luft III.

the digging at Barth. They quickly discovered that the Germans had planted sound detectors in the ground outside the perimeter wire, and this meant that any tunnels driven out of Stalag Luft III would have to pass deep through that lower, shifting sand layer in order to avoid the sounds of the digging being picked up. And, as with any tunnel, there would be copious amounts of spoil to be dealt with; a particular headache at Sagan where the golden-yellow sand contrasted brightly against the top soil of the compound, meaning that it had somehow to be hidden in the open grey drabness.

No matter how you looked at it, tunnelling from Stalag Luft III would not be easy.

When the camp first opened at the end of March 1942, there were only two compounds, later to be known as East (officers) and Centre (other ranks). By end of the war however, the camp had expanded to five compounds, containing some 10,500 captured aircrew, mostly RAF and United States Army Air Force (USAAF) personnel. East Compound was the first exclusive air officer's compound in the camp. Its dimensions were approximately 350yd by 150yd of drab, dreary solitude surrounded by a double fence, 12ft high made up of some twenty strands of tightly strung barbed wire for each. The fences were set 5ft apart and in the intervening space were piled more coils of barbed wire, so thick in some places that it was hard to see through. Sunk into the ground just outside the fence were the seismograph microphones, connected to a main listening post in the *Kommandantur* (main German administrative area, just west of Centre Compound that would eventually handled all Luftwaffe PoW camp affairs in Germany). Further augmenting the defences of the fence line was 'Goon boxes' positioned every 100 to 125yds apart along the perimeter and standing some 20ft high. In each was a guard connected by telephone to the main guard house and armed with a rifle, a searchlight, a machine gun and orders to shoot, without warning, any prisoner caught near the wire without authorization. (In prisoner jargon, a German was never known or referred to as anything but a 'Goon'.)

Running the entire perimeter of the camp a set distance inside the main fence was the single 'warning wire', set on posts some 2ft above the ground, although in the original East and Centre Compounds before too long this was changed to a wooden 'rail' for most of the perimeter instead of a wire. The space in between this barrier and the main fence was the 'danger strip'. Strictly off limits to the prisoners, anyone who entered this area without permission from the camp staff could reasonably expect to be shot at by the nearest sentry. Just inside the warning rail was the walking 'circuit', a path some 5yd wide that ran around the camp perimeter where the prisoners walked endlessly (always counter-clockwise), brooding; talking of home, women, or liquor; planning 'nefarious activities'; or just looking for that ever elusive commodity within a tightly packed community – privacy. 'Bashing the circuit', 992 paces, was one of the main activities of the camp population.[1]

Within the East Compound there were eight, untreated wooden huts 160ft long and 40ft wide, each divided into living rooms some 16ft square, as well as a small washroom, night latrine and kitchen, which contained a small stove that was barely capable of boiling water. Each room had a compliment of double-tier bunks, a trestle table with benches, a few stools, also a wall locker for each occupant, and a shuttered window. Additionally, each room had a small stove for heating, but there was usually not enough coal issued to keep the room anywhere near warm. As the wood used for the barracks had never been allowed to dry properly, and thus had shrunk after the barracks had been built, there were gaps that let the wind in. Therefore it was not unusual after the first winter the camp was open to see the cardboard from Red Cross food parcel boxes tacked on the walls. In the beginning, there were usually no more than six men to a room sleeping on double-tier bunks, however, by the end of the war, rooms were holding up to fifteen officers, and bunks had been converted to triple tier. Each hut was set on piers, about 30in above the ground. This served a dual purpose; first, it provided an air current under the huts that kept the moisture down under the floor. Second, it gave the camp security staff the ability to, as author of *The Great Escape* and former PoW there Paul Brickhill wrote, 'check to see if anyone was tampering with the soil of the Fatherland.'

Each room had a single electric-light bulb of 30 Watt (or less) for lighting at night, and lights out was at 11.00pm. German time was one hour behind ordinary British time and the camp ran on German time, though the prisoners preferred to use a more 'sensible' British time. Lock down of the huts was at 10.00pm, with the doors locked until 6.00am the next morning. In the winter months, the window in each room was kept closed with blackout shutters locked from the outside, while in the summer months the shutters could sometimes be left open, allowing the prisoners to open the windows and gain fresh air provided they showed no light, which would draw immediate fire from the nearest sentry to notice. The same went for anyone who crawled out a window and was caught in the compound after hours; he could either expect to be shot, or face the *Hundeführer* (Dog handler) and his Alsatian. Neither was a promising prospect. Additional repercussions from the 'Goons' could mean the blackout shutters would be locked permanently, no matter how hot it became, which would make the person(s) responsible very unpopular with his fellow inmates. For emergencies at night, when the doors and windows were locked, there was a single red bulb on the roof of each hut that could be switched on from inside in order to summon a guard. Often the light did not work, or failed to draw any attention from the guards.

North of the two compounds was the *Vorlager* (Fore-camp). This was the administrative area for the compounds, large and airy and lightly guarded, as few prisoners were allowed in except for special reasons. The main gates for each compound opened into it, from which there was one main entrance/exit to the area. Inside it were eight buildings; the solitary confinement cell block (the 'Cooler'); a Red Cross parcel distribution building; a bath house; a coal storage building with a huge pile of coal next to it (painted with wide diagonal stripes to prevent theft); and buildings that held the book censor's office; the camp Sick Quarters and dentist rooms; clothing storage area; facilities (such as they were) for a small contingent of Russian prisoners, (kept on site for manual labour); a barracks for the night guards and kennels for the dogs. In the south-east corner of the area, next to the coal pile, was the dump for tin cans collected by the Germans from the prisoners' Red Cross parcels, and below that along the east fence line, was a tomato garden planted by the Russians and fertilized by effluent from the camp latrine. To the west of Centre Compound was the *Kommandantur*; the administrative base for all Luftwaffe controlled prison camps in the Reich and was almost the same size as the East and Centre Compounds together. A good example of the work done in the *Kommandantur*; by the end of the war almost all air force prisoners' mail from all of the other Luftwaffe camps around Germany was being routed through there for censorship; a monumental task largely accomplished by a staff of hired female civilians.

From an administrative side, the basic camp was a fairly complex, though under-staffed, organization. In the first year of the camp, the Kommandant, Oberst (Colonel) Wilhelm von Lindeiner-Wildau, only had around thirty staff officers under him at any given time, and a guard company totaling some 250 men, controlling some 2,500 prisoners. However, by the time the camp was evacuated in January 1945, the number of guards had risen to nearly 800 for over 10,500 prisoners. In order to ease some of the burden of operating the camp the Kommandant had, from the outset, allowed the prisoners to set up an internal structure charged with assisting in the running of daily activities and administration directly related to the prisoners, such as mail, Red Cross parcel and clothing distribution, as well as organization of hot showers and other matters. Not only did it help bring calm to the general chaos, but it gave some of the prisoners with administration skills something to do.

German administration of the camp was divided into several main departments, each of which handled a different task in the actual operation of the camp. Almost the whole of the original staff had come to Sagan from Barth and were therefore wary to the ways of the prisoners. This included the camp internal security organization. This administrative branch (Department No.3) was commonly known as the *Abwehr*, the Intelligence and Clandestine Warfare Service of the German High Command. The *Abwehr*, while considered to be a part of the Kommandant's staff, with whom they worked and reported, were actually a separate entity and also reported to their superiors at the High Command. The primary function of the *Abwehr* in camp was to prevent escape and they had learned as much at Barth in the previous year about preventing it as the prisoners had learned about perpetrating it. To this end, each compound at Sagan was assigned an *Abwehr* staff of one officer and six NCOs, along with a host of lesser ranks, whose duties ranged from searching incoming and outgoing prisoners, searches of the huts and other compound buildings, and generally being on constant guard for suspicious activity. The *Abwehr* staff did this by making themselves an almost constant presence in the compounds; they crawled under the huts looking for evidence that the soil had been disturbed or the level had risen, barged into rooms unannounced to catch someone involved in 'inappropriate business', climbed up into the rafters of rooms with an ear to the ceiling listening to conversations in hopes of hearing about *verboten* (forbidden) activities, and generally making a complete nuisance of themselves. They obtained the nickname of 'Ferret' from the prisoners, and were easy to spot. Dressed in dark blue overalls and a forage cap, they carried a thin, 4ft-long steel rod, which they used to probe the sand or poke into any crack that looked suspicious. They were usually everywhere a prisoner did not want them to be, and it was a difficult task to hide illicit activities from their keen sight. Most were highly trained, although in times of need regular camp staff was sometimes pressed into service for compound duty. Most 'Ferrets' spoke at least some English, though none were likely to ever admit it. They were the biggest threat the prisoners faced when it came to escape activities, and a very dangerous one. Little went unnoticed by them.

The prisoner's version of the *Abwehr* department was the Escape Committee, commonly referred to as the 'X Organization'. The designation was solely for secrecy, not drama, and the leader of the organization was known as 'Big X'. Each compound of the camp had a 'Big X' and under him a staff of 'department heads' that dealt with individual jobs to facilitate escape – security ('Big S'), tailoring (for making escape clothing), engineering (who made everything from bracing for tunnels to wire-cutters for those brave enough to tackle the fence), forging (who hand-made copies of all the paperwork needed for an escaper to move in Hitler's Reich), mapmakers, compass makers, and 'Scroungers' whose job it was to bribe or blackmail the camp guards in order to obtain needed items. This last was not really all that hard in a country where rationing became more restrictive with each year of the war, while the prisoners' Red Cross parcels fairly bulged with items of temptation like real cigarettes, chocolate and soap. There was also a 'Little X' assigned to each hut in the compound whose job it was to assist in arranging escape for those who had an idea, by first bringing the idea to the general escape committee and, if the idea was approved, helping then in any way to bring the plan off. A 'Little S' in each block helped to arrange security and look-out duties ('Stooges') for the various clandestine activities, as well as creating diversions to draw German attention away from anything the prisoners had going that they felt would be better kept secret. While escape committees were common in virtually all PoW camps, the 'X Organization' at Sagan, headed by Lieutenant Commander James 'Jimmy' Buckley, RN, was a well organized and developed unit. It had its real beginnings at Barth the previous year and by the time nearly all the RAF prisoners in Germany had been gathered in Sagan, the organization had true direction, purpose, and – most importantly – had been officially sanctioned as the prime institution by the senior Allied officers in charge of the prisoners at Sagan. Escape then became the official focus of PoW life at Sagan and that first summer of 1942 the 'X Organization' really came into its own.

The problem of escape from a square wire compound can be broken down into three basic methods of escape; over, under, or through. Over – climbing the wire – was a difficult prospect at best, and was more likely than not destined to end with the escaper being shot in the back. There were exceptions, of course. Several prisoners had managed to scramble over the wire in various camps during blinding snowstorms. However, escaping in the winter, with hundreds of kilometres to travel on foot to the nearest friendly border, usually only led to frostbitten feet and ultimate defeat.

Yet, August of 1942 would see the most spectacular 'over job' of the war, from Oflag VI B, the officers camp near the town of Warburg. Called 'Operation Olympia', prisoners had secretly made special scaling ladders from wood and disguised them as shelving. One fine night, when all had been prepared, the camp's electrical circuits had been fused by a prisoner who had been an electrician in civilian life, plunging the fence line into darkness. Like Olympic sprinters, forty-one men dashed forward, slammed the ladders up against the fence, and twenty-eight of them managed to scramble over before the guards became alerted to what was happening and opened fire. Eventually three men got safely home following the brave escape, while only one man had been slightly wounded by gun fire on the other side of the fence. After that episode, it became common practice at prison camps all over Germany to always have some type of emergency lighting system in place.

A through escape involved either cutting the fence wire, or bluffing the guards to get through the gate. Escaping this way had been achieved successfully several times at various camps, as prisoners impersonated either members of the camp staff or visiting officials. However, impersonation involved plenty of groundwork, from preparing camp-made German uniforms ('Goon skins') or civilian clothes good enough to fool the gate guards, as well as obtaining and properly copying the correct gate passes to allow exit; an extremely difficult prospect, as passes were generally changed weekly. Each also depended on at least one person in the escape group being a fluent German speaker. And even with all that in place, chances of success were slim as a hundred details needed to go right and just one uncontrollable element could destroy months of preparation. One man, who bore a passing resemblance to one of the camp staff in the compound he was in, managed to successfully bluff his way through the gate as that very staff member – only to come face-to-face on the other side with the very man he was impersonating!

Cutting through the wire was even more difficult. Every inch of the wire at Sagan was under the observation of a number of guards positioned in at least three 'Goon boxes' along the fence line in various directions, as well as sentries patrolling the perimeter. And even if their attention could be distracted, there were also the mounds of coiled wire between the fences to contend with; meaning that time would run out long before anyone got through, and anyone caught in the danger area would be shot on sight, without warning. It seemed, therefore, that cutting the wire was a practical impossibility. In fact, Philpot himself later frequently referred to it as 'a suicide game'.

The possibility of cutting the wire was proven that first summer at Sagan, however, by the incredibly daring escape of Flight Lieutenant William 'Red' Nichols, an American of No.71 RAF 'Eagle' Squadron, and Pilot Officer Ken Toft, formerly of No.82 Squadron. Nichols and another 'Eagle', Pilot Officer Morris Fessler, insisted to the Escape Committee that the distance between the guard towers on the long eastern fence of the East Compound, coupled with the masses of wire and the multitude of poles supporting the fence along that distance, would provide a vision 'blind spot' of around 8 to 10ft directly in the middle of the fence line between any two of the three 'Goon boxes' along the fence. To prove the theory, they built a scale model of the wire and the towers which allowed the committee a view along the model fence line from the guards' perspective in the tower. The theory seeming to be viable, the two were given the go ahead, however Fessler was sent to another camp before the attempt could be made. Undaunted, Nichols went in search of another partner, finding the only one with the daring to give the plan a go with him was Toft. One afternoon in mid-September the atmosphere in the camp became tense as diversions distracted the attention of the 'Goons' in guard towers for the few moments necessary. Calmly Nichols and Toft, dressed in their escape clothes and each carrying a small bag of escape gear, stepped over the warning rail, crossed the danger strip to the correct place halfway between the middle tower and the south tower along the east fence, then lay down next to the wire and began to cut. Once through the first fence, they then used notched wooden sticks they had brought with them to prop up the wire coils in between the fences, crawled under, and went to work on the second fence. Diversions continued to distract the guards as a precaution. Once through the outer fence, they pulled out the props, crawled through the grass over to the road adjacent to the fence line, got up, dusted each other off, and simply walked away. The whole operation had taken just four terror-packed minutes.

Though they were only out for a few days it was enough to get them some 113km from the camp before they were picked up and brought back to Sagan for two weeks' punishment of solitary confinement in the 'Cooler' (which was the usual sentence). It was an inglorious end to one of the most nerve wracking and daring escapes of the war. Nevertheless, on their return the Kommandant had both men brought to his office, where he congratulated them for their daring and presented them with a bottle of whisky in admiration for their nerve.

Within a week of the escape, extensions had been built on the front of all the 'Goon boxes' in the two compounds so that there were no longer any blind spots along the wire from their view, and extra foot guards were placed to patrol the entire fence line of the camp. But the escape also did more than the 'X Organization' ever realized. Word also was sent around through the *Abwehr* detailing the method of escape to all other camps, where each then added extra fence patrols. The result was that by the end of the war approximately an entire division of German home-front class soldiers were patrolling the wire around PoW camps instead of providing other service to the Reich – all because of one single escape.

However, wire and gate attempts aside, tunnelling was the chief escape activity of 'X', and the organization became very busy that first summer at Sagan. Drawing in part on what they remembered from the books most of them had read in their youth about British exploits in German prison camps in World War One, and working out the rest from trial and error, the organization set to work with some purpose. Within a brief period of time the escaping 'stars' emerged from within the prisoner's ranks. A Canadian Spitfire pilot named 'Wally' Floody, who had actually been a mining engineer before the war, proved to be the master of tunnel design and digging, along with another Canadian miner, John 'Scruffy' Weir; under their guidance the tunnels became deeper, longer, and more sophisticated than they had ever been at Barth. But the 'Ferrets' had also been learning, setting seismograph microphones in the sand outside the wire all around the camp, and were listening virtually around the clock. Time-after-time the 'Ferrets' pounced once a tunnel had reached beyond the 'Circuit'. (Previously, the prisoners constant tramping around the 'Circuit' had made the sound detectors ineffective.) The only answer to the problem seemed to be to dig down even deeper. Tunnels then began reaching the unheard of depths of 20 and 30ft – but still to no avail.[2]

The trapdoors to the tunnels became the next problem. Where to start a tunnel that the Germans could not find the entrance? As all the huts had been built on piers some 30in above the ground, this left the majority of the space under the huts open to inspection, and it was routine for the 'Ferrets' to carefully scrutinize the ground under a hut during a search, which in practice happened to each hut about once every ten days or so. If a hut was suspected for some reason though, inspections came more frequently. The only place not available to their prying eyes was within the solid foundations around the chimney in each room under the stove, and under the washroom.[3]

Of course it was possible to start a tunnel through these foundations, and there was also a brick and concrete floor in the camp communal 'wash house' also on the side of each *Abort* (pit latrine). However, it was very difficult to camouflage work that had been done in these areas, and once the Germans had found a tunnel entrance and studied it, they then usually had a keener eye to noticing anything out of place in a similar environment.

That summer of 1942, was the true 'golden age' of escape in East Compound, Stalag Luft III. Escape morale was extremely high and besides the various wire and gate attempts they foiled, the German staff also located an estimated forty tunnels in that first summer. As autumn approached that year, it was beginning to look more and more as though tunnelling might just be a waste of time and that the German boast that escape was impossible from Sagan could possibly have a ring of truth.

However it was the digging of three particular tunnels and the quick failure of another during that golden summer of 1942 that would have a great influence on events still to come in the future for 'Ollie' Philpot – as well as on others yet to join him in captivity.

Lieutenant Colonel Albert P. 'Bub' Clark, a young West Point graduate in the USAAF, had been blasted out of the sky on 26 July 1942, making him the first US fighter pilot to arrive at Stalag Luft III. Coming in early that August (where he would occupy the bed vacated by Douglas Bader [the legendary legless RAF ace] only the day before), as he walked through the gates he was immediately shocked and appalled at the wholly unsanitary conditions of the compound's two latrine buildings – and to the German, as well as British, indifference to the unhealthy situation. Thick, black, clouds of flies swarmed everywhere, along with swarms of hornets and wasps; all of which bred quickly in the unsanitary, open buildings. Also a problem, were large brown and orange slugs that trailed throughout the buildings. And if that were not enough, the cesspit underneath the latrines, besides smelling abominably, was only emptied infrequently by the Germans and was prone to overflowing on a fairly regular basis. With nowhere else to drain, the sludge oozed out into the compound, exacerbating an already dangerous unhealthy situation. Clearly something had to be done, before a major disease erupted and spread like wildfire through the densely occupied compound. However the British did not see it as their job to correct the situation, and the Germans simply did not care.

Clark's father, however, had been a surgeon with President Roosevelt's Civilian Conservation Corps in the 1930s, and taught him much about health and sanitation in a crowded environment. Therefore, the first thing 'Bub' Clark toward the middle of that long, hot, August of 1942 did was request permission and supplies to sanitize and properly seal the latrines. Granted the request by both British and German authorities in the camp, and with plenty of Dominion volunteers assisting, Clark and company cleaned and effectively sealed each building. They then set to digging drainage sumps to deal with the run-off problem. In this endeavour, Clark was assisted by Flying Officer Leslie 'Bill' Goldfinch, a member of the pre-war Royal Engineers who arrived at Sagan via the 'second dickie' seat of a Shorts Sunderland from No.288 Squadron. From the back of each hut they dug three 18in wide drainage ditches sloping away from the buildings, which terminated in a 20ft square by 10ft deep pit, some 20yd from the warning rail along the eastern fence. The ditches and pits were then filled with gravel to assist the drainage.[4]

However, before the filling could occur, one of the most ingenious tunnels of all time was dug from the drainage pit of the North *Abort*. While assisting on the drainage project, Goldfinch and his pilot when shot down, Flying Officer Henry 'Piglet' Lamond, a short New Zealander, saw their chance to enact a plan that Goldfinch and he had thought up and registered with the Escape Committee at Barth, but which had been prevented from implementation by the move to Sagan. The idea was a 'blitz' project and simplicity in itself. They proposed to dig a short tunnel from inside the pit, only some 30ft long and running just 3ft below the ground. Here at Sagan this would make use of the pine root layer in the soil above them as 'bracing' for the roof of the tunnel, while the entrance shaft would pass through the firm sand/clay layer, negating any need for shoring. Once this short section of tunnel was ready they, along with a third man, would then crawl in with all their escape kit and the tunnel would then be completely sealed. Inside, the front man would dig forward and push the excavated sand back past his hips to the second man, who would then pass it back to the third, who would then tightly pack it into the tunnel behind him, thus effectively filling in the tunnel as they proceeded forward. In this way, encased in a constantly moving section of tunnel, the men could proceed rapidly and unhampered by the traditional tunnelling problems of shoring the sides and dispersal of the excavated soil. For air, they carried along a hinged wooden rod with which they would pierce the tunnel roof at intervals. Dubbed 'The Mole' system, it had the advantages of being both rapid and simple and therefore stood a better than average chance of success.

Lamond and Goldfinch were given the green light by an enthusiastic Escape Committee, and they in turn coerced Pilot Officer John 'Jack' Best, a pilot from No.69 Squadron, into the scheme as the third member. Taking it in turns, while two of the would-be escapers dug the soak-away pit, the third would be busy digging the starter tunnel. Then, with their escape kit packed in bags hidden in the pile of gravel for filling the pit, on the last evening of the *Abort* project they enlisted the help of Pilot Officer Phillip Searcey (an Australian, formerly of No.99 Squadron), who sealed them and their gear into the tunnel at around 7.30pm. Then the remainder of the working team filled the pit with the gravel, gathered up their tools and walked away.

But tunnelling is a physically demanding business, and the three diggers had underestimated the project; despite the relatively short distance to freedom. The next morning, walkers out on the 'Circuit' scanning the ground outside the fence found no sign of exit, but instead noticed some thin wisps of steam rising from a short line of air holes in the ground on the opposite side of the warning rail, indicating both the direction of the tunnel and the fact that the three would be escapers were still alive, but had yet to emerge. They had only made it to the outer fence, still a few feet short of the goal. Meanwhile underground, the three had noticed daylight streaming in through the air holes and had then settled in for a sweaty day of waiting. Their watches had stopped because of the sand and it was only through careful judging of the light through the holes that they could estimate the time. That second night they then dug the final short distance and in the darkness beyond the fence were seen by 'stooges' watching from nearby hut windows to emerge from the tunnel, completely covered in sand. Helping each other out, they then dashed off into the dark forest. It had been a nearly perfect get away.

Nearly perfect for two reasons: Firstly, because all three were brought back within the week; the luck they had had in getting away from the camp having failed them. And secondly, because of the repercussions the discovery of their method of escape had brought. The next day, the Germans went into frenzy when the hole was discovered, and once they had brought in a few Russian prisoners to excavate the track of the tunnel and figured out how it was dug, they immediately took preventative measures. Their first order of search was to walk the perimeter of both compounds just inside the fence line, driving long, thin steel rods down into the ground every 12in or so to try and hit upon a tunnel, then moving on and trying again. The effect of this was almost immediate; in Centre Compound, Sergeants John Fancy, William Street, and Alf Miner had started a tunnel from a garden alongside their hut – which the Germans now found. The three men had camouflaged the entry hole under a wooden tray in which the plants for the garden had been growing. The edges of the tray had then been carefully covered over after each digging session in order that it would blend in with the rest of the garden. This tunnel, another that made use of both the pine root and the sand/clay layers, had been dug in the space of just a few days and was only hours away from completion, which caused nearly as much excitement among the 'Goons' as the 'mole' had in East Compound.

To prevent these sorts of quick and easy tunnels, the Senior *Abwehr* Security Officer for East and Centre Compounds at the time, Major Peschel, decided to dig 6ft deep 'anti-tunnel trenches' around the perimeter of each compound inside the danger strip just beyond the warning rail. The project had barely begun, however, before Squadron Leader Tommy Calnan and Flight Lieutenant Tony Barber, along with a third man, hid in the trench one afternoon, determined to 'mole' out from the trench itself! They nearly succeeded, but ran into problems underground when the third member became claustrophobic. This caused them to fall short of their goal, forcing them to 'lie up' for the day as Goldfinch and his team had done. However, in this instance the dogs found the air holes the next morning and the attempt was quickly over. Calnan and Barber were sent to the 'Cooler', while the third man was taken to the infirmary. The Germans quickly filled in the anti-escape trenches.

Oliver Philpot surveyed all this from the excellent vantage point as something of an interested outsider within the camp; not actually involved in any of the escapes, but certainly connected. That busy summer of 1942, found him initially involved in the workings of the 'X Organization' at Sagan. By now considered an older prisoner, wise in the ways of 'Kriegiedom' among a growing number of the newly captured (and having tried at least twice to escape) he found himself a minor figure among the escaping elite that had come from Barth, at least in the eyes of the new boys. In truth, his initial contact with the 'X Organization' was less than thrilling, his jobs usually revolving around the most boring tasks, such as map-making, 'stooging' and sand dispersal duties. It was work that, though with a purpose, was nevertheless among the most endless and mind numbing within a setting where each day was an exercise in trying to escape inescapable boredom.

Then came the much waited for chance to actually work in a tunnel; an experience he found both exciting and frightening all at once. But tunnels rarely had a lifespan of more than a few weeks at Sagan (the Germans had improved internal security in the camp) and he found himself involved in first one scheme and then another before they were discovered by the 'Ferrets'. Always late in coming into a plan, and thus comparatively low down on the selection list for escape, he so far had failed to come up with any real useful ideas of his own, and thus he remained at the mercy of the escaping 'Gods' – the 'Barth Elite' – whose days were filled with nothing but planning escape. However, they largely preferred to surround themselves with those they knew and thought as they did, namely more 'Barth Elite'. After those first few initial impatient months of getting nowhere on several schemes, as the summer drew on toward autumn Philpot's patience grew thin and he began to view escape efforts within the camp with some scepticism.

Further, the effects of being a prisoner had a surreptitious way of slowly taking a greater hold on all who suffered incarceration as time went on. As Philpot later described, '[After a time] we were well on our way to adopting a Kriegie attitude of mind; "Everybody has forgotten me. I've landed in a half-world between the lively world I knew, and Eternity. We're not properly alive, and we're not dead. Nobody gives a damn."' It was an attitude that had to constantly be fought against, or else it could literally overwhelm a person, often with disastrous consequences. For most, activity was the answer, which ranged from escape activities to any one of the various classes that were constantly being taught within the compound. If the mind was active, then the corrosive effects of prison lethargy could not make progress.

For his part, mildly disgusted by a seeming inability to become more deeply enmeshed in viable escape activities, Philpot began shifting more of his daily efforts into taking a greater interest in making his life within camp a better one. To that end, he found himself devoting more time to camp theatre, also to maintaining a cleaner personal appearance, and taking charge first of administration of his room and then, eventually, his hut. This also involved helping the new prisoners settle in to the strange and alien environment of camp life; sometimes a trying exercise in patience. Escape still filled his thoughts, but it had now tempered by a realization that many of his fellow prisoners within the escape group largely belonged to two main factions.

The first were mostly from the actual escaping elite, no matter where they had come from. These were the thinkers, the plotters and the planners. There is an old military saying that 'amateurs think tactics – professionals think logistics', and it was into the professional category that the hard-core elite escapers fell. Often it was not they who actually thought up original ideas for escape, but it was them who ran the 'X Organization' and thus they had the means to bring a plan to fruition, be it a success or failure. Yes, there was always definitely a certain element of luck involved as well, but overall without the professionals of the escape organization few of the truly original ideas that had been thought up would have ever seen a start. They organized and made things happen, sorting out the crackpot schemes from the truly insightful and brilliantly original, as well as keeping people out of each others' way when attempts were to be made. Time in the 'bag' usually had nothing to do with belonging to this element, only brains, talent and insight.

Also, these were also the men that had a better than average chance of evading capture once outside the wire. They were the ones fluent in German or French, and had the capacity for remaining cool in any situation. They planned ahead, and knew what to do and where they were going. They lived on their nerves and determination drove them farther than most. The head of the 'X Organization' at the time, Lieutenant Commander Jimmy Buckley, and his second in command, Squadron Leader Roger Bushell, were these types of men. So was Wing Commander Harry Day, one of the first RAF prisoners who had been captured in October 1939 and therefore usually the Senior British Officer (SBO) in any camp in which he was interned.

The second group was made up of those who wanted to get out, at almost any cost, but who often lacked an original idea to get them beyond the wire. These were the tireless workers that kept the escape system functioning. Many in this group committed themselves to several ideas at once in their great efforts to get out, but this was a double-edged sword as they were then unable to commit themselves fully to any one single idea. And if they did commit to one, it was rarely an idea that worked, as their judgment was often clouded by the overwhelming desire to get beyond the wire in the quickest way possible, and the quickest way was frequently not the idea that worked.

These were also the people who usually failed to have a cohesive plan in place to carry them across the second and most difficult part of their journey – crossing of occupied Europe to a neutral country. Their imaginative powers carried them only outside the wire. Once there, they remained largely ignorant of what was truly required to complete the journey. Tommy Calnan later recalled of this class, 'So many – too many – were suffering from wire psychosis. They had a compelling impulse to get outside the fence. At that point however, their thinking stopped. From then on it was a matter of luck and providence. They had no plans … [but] every tunnel depended on prisoners with this attitude. They were the hardest workers, the most fanatic, [and] the indefatigable. But once outside the wire, they were lost.'

Philpot did not fall into either category. Instead, after almost a year 'in the bag' he lay somewhere in the middle; anxious to escape, but aware that the possibilities were very remote. Though occasionally involved in different escape activities, from providing security ('stooging'), to dispersing spoil dug from tunnels, to actually joining in with the digging of several, thus far he had yet to come up with what was truly required of any serious attempt: an original idea. He considered 'wire jobs' as suicide, and 'gate jobs' had been over attempted, as far as he was concerned. And the 'Goons' were finding around two tunnels a week by that time; many of which had a life of no more than a few days. Therefore, as the busy Sagan summer faded and autumn approached, signalling an end of the prime escape season, Philpot became even more convinced that it would take a *very* exceptional idea to get beyond the wire at Sagan and that those were few and far between. The latest failed attempt he had been involved in was a fair example of that.

One afternoon, his hut 'Little X' had collected him, along with some twenty-four other men and ushered them all out into the compound near Hut 63 and not far from the 'Circuit'. There they had all stood around in a tight circle in their greatcoats in the early autumn weather while one man stood in the middle playing his accordion. Then they had all been ordered to sing. Philpot quickly noticed activity in the middle of the group and, edging his way forward, he noticed a man down on his knees, shielded from outside view by the legs of the singers, digging a hole and passing the dirt and sand to those around him, who were either stuffing it into their pockets or kicking it into the grey topsoil. Philpot duly did so as well, bellowing out the song *Roll out the Barrel* along with the others. By the time the party broke up, after an hour of heartily singing every song everyone could remember (and with everyone waddling along under the weight of sand stuffed pockets), the man had managed a hole of fair dimensions and depth, which he covered over with some bedboards then with sand and soil.

But that night one of the 'Ferrets', ostensibly suspicious of the spontaneous sing-song, had been seen wandering around the general area that they had been working in that afternoon and he had the misfortune of cracking through the cover over the hole, nearly breaking his leg in the process. It was another idea gone by the way and after it, Philpot was more firmly convinced than ever that it would take an idea of a minor genius to crack the defences of Stalag Luft III.

The autumn brought a splash of colour as the leaves of Silver Birch trees 'flamed' among the Fir trees surrounding the camp. It also brought an ever increasing flood of new prisoners, among them the first Americans shot down as the USAAF daylight bombing campaign got underway. Sagan was filling up fast and running out of room. Therefore, in September the Germans started clearing an enormous space to the west of the *Kommandantur* for a new compound, which would eventually be dubbed the North Compound. At the same time they made the decision to round up a good many of the trouble makers from East Compound (ostensibly to prevent them from instilling the new prisoners with escape knowledge, as well as making some much needed room until the new compound could be opened up) and transport them to another camp. The announcement was made of those who would definitely be going, and then a call was also sent out for volunteers who would like to go. To his surprise, Philpot found his name on the former list and immediately packed his things – such as they were – for the move, and on 14 September 1942, found himself again in a third-class German railway carriage speeding across Germany for the Polish border and yet another camp.

Chapter 3

'One of Our Aircraft Failed to Return ...'

December 1942–January 1943

The night of 17 December 1942, started out as many had in the war for the men of No.75 (New Zealand) Squadron. Orders had come through during the day for them to take part in a heavy raid on the Volkswagen plant at Fallersleben, in the Ruhr Valley of Germany (sarcastically known to RAF aircrew as 'Happy Valley'), and the afternoon was spent in preparation for the little-appreciated trip to the hated place. And as they prepared for the coming operation, little did the seven-man crew of Short Stirling number BK 620 realize (and much the better for it) that it would also be their last trip with the squadron. Just after 11.00pm that evening their aircraft would be falling in flames through the sky over Germany.

Leaving their base at Newmarket behind them, soon after the English coast, they climbed into the ever-darkening sky; on time and in formation. It was not long after that however, that things began to go wrong. First, the oil pressure for one of the starboard engines began to fluctuate; not serious enough to turn back, but enough for the pilot, Flight Sergeant Kenneth J. Dunmall, to be concerned. Then, while trying to steer around the heavy anti-aircraft (AA) fire over Hanover, they inadvertently flew over the blacked-out city. The better of the two starboard engines was hit by AA fire and stopped, causing severe problems with the trim characteristics of the heavy bomber. It now became obvious that they would never reach the target. Holes from AA fire were appearing, as if by magic, in the fuselage and wings of the Stirling when Flight Lieutenant Eric Williams – the bomb aimer, as well as the only officer of the seven-man crew – jettisoned the bombs. That done, Dunmall, now turning back and losing altitude far too rapidly for safety in enemy territory first called for a direct course to base from the navigator, and next for Williams to come up from the nose and assist with the piloting the aircraft. Williams abandoned his gun which he had been firing in an attempt to shoot out the searchlights illuminating them and crawled up to the cockpit. Dunmall, following the new course, trimmed the damaged aircraft as best as he could to steer them towards the bacon and eggs breakfast that would be awaiting them in the squadron mess. They were flying at an altitude of just over 1,000ft with full power set on the remaining engines, and in less than 15 minutes they would be over Holland. Shortly after that, the crew would be holding their breath during the North Sea crossing (always dangerous in a damaged aircraft, especially in winter), and looking forward to again seeing the friendly smile of the WAAF driver who drove the dispersal truck that would take them to debriefing and breakfast.

Ever after there would be controversy among the crew as to whether they made the Dutch border or not, though Dunmall would later insist that they had. Just minutes after they had settled down for the uncomfortable ride home the rear gunner, Sergeant James Voice, chillingly called to the pilot on the intercom that a Junkers Ju-88 nightfighter was coming in fast on their tail – he could clearly see the glow of the enemy aircraft's exhausts – and everyone began to sweat a little more, despite the cold December night. Almost with the first rattle of the nightfighter's guns the crippled bomber was caught in the beams of at least two searchlights. After that, events happened confusingly fast. Dunmall and Williams did everything they could with the damaged aircraft to shake off the fighter, but the Stirling was just not responding. Inside the damaged aircraft, the eerie glare from the searchlights shining through the gaping holes in the fuselage played across the darkness, while the airframe shook violently with every impact of the night-fighter's cannon shells. Sergeant Voice's machine guns rattled almost continuously and a burst from the nightfighter raked the fuselage from nose to tail, shattering the perspex of the cockpit and setting the aircraft on fire. Inside the damaged cockpit the air was thick with smoke. With airspeed dropping alarmingly fast the situation was hopeless; Williams shouted to Dunmall, 'We've had it – give the order!' and the pilot in turn called out in a firm voice over the intercom: 'We've had it chaps. Abandon aircraft – Go now!'

They were only flying at around 800ft by then, making time of the essence. One-by-one the crew called their leaving into the intercom, unplugged, clipped on their parachute pack and stepped through their assigned escape hatch into the full glare of the enemy searchlights. With the flames outside the shattered cockpit lighting up Dunmall's silhouette, Williams took the sweating pilot's parachute from its rack and set it on the seat next to him before he turned to exit the aircraft. Dunmall, struggling to keep the aircraft straight and level in order to give them all a chance, even as the tail section slowly burned off, raised a hand in acknowledgment without ever looking away from his instruments. His chance of escape was just about impossible at that point and he knew it. So did Williams as the slipstream grabbed his legs and yanked him out the hatch and away from the blazing aircraft.

Though Williams later never remembered pulling his ripcord, the canopy opened above him with a sharp crack and a stunning tug between his legs. Then there was nothing; nothing but a startling silence after the recent cacophony of sound, and then his slow descent into Nazi occupied territory, lit up brilliantly from below by the searchlights. Turning in the harness he watched as the Stirling, burning fierce and with the pilot still at the controls fell like a comet through the darkness beyond the glow of the searchlights.[1]

The violent sway of the parachute was just settling down to a gentle swing when, barely discernible through the solid darkness, the shadowy shape of a forest rapidly began to rise up. He saw he was heading for a small grassy clearing, and before he had time to prepare for landing there came a sharp 'thump' as he hit to ground, stunning in its unexpectedness followed by a short roll across the floor of the forest. Then, there was just the cold, clear, starry December night above, silvery clouds of his heavy breath in the moonlight, the pounding of his heart in his ears, and the resinous smell of the pine forest around him.

Flight Lieutenant E. E. Williams, RAF No.117660, had just flown his twenty-fifth, and last, operational sortie.

Eric Ernest Williams was born 13 July 1911 in London, the son of Ernest and Mary Elizabeth (Beardmore) Williams. He was the eldest of five children who, early on, learned how to entertain his siblings with a seemingly natural flair for storytelling that flowed freely from an active imagination. 'Bill', as he was universally known to close friends (a derivative of his last name), grew up with the burning ambition to become a novelist and painter. He sought all throughout his young adulthood the inspiration he felt he needed to accomplish these goals, while attending Christ's College in London and working at one time as a painter, architect, and refurbishing old houses with his father. He also joined a local yeomanry unit of the Territorial Army, which he thoroughly enjoyed. However, bowing to a need to support him following college, Williams set his sentimental artistic ambitions aside. Displaying a maturity that would stand him well later in life by using his artistic gift to best advantage in the circumstances, he accepted a permanent position with the well-known retail company Lewis's of Liverpool in 1932 as an interior architect, working first at their new store in Birmingham. He was a dedicated and hard-working young man and promotion came quickly. However, with promotion came more responsibility and therefore, with the daily routine of work leaving little room for free time, he resigned from his beloved yeomanry unit in 1935.

Then war was declared on Nazi Germany.

Williams' first stop after the 3 September 1939 declaration was at the yeomanry barracks, then in the process of assembling for war, where he was told that in order to get in he would have to join the regular army first. Not wishing to do that, for fear of being immediately sent to the infantry due to his age, he instead reassessed his options. His romanticism stirred by declaration fervour, and hoping against hope to be accepted as one of the dashing pilots of the youngest of Britain's services, he applied and was accepted for a commission in the Royal Air Force. In the spring of 1940, he left Lewis's with the best wishes of all his seniors and employees and reported for training.

Williams, however, was a highly unlikely RAF pilot candidate. At 28 years old he was much older than what was then considered the norm for pilot material in a new recruit. Worse still, he developed a pronounced stammer when excited. Those two points, in combination with the high marks he had scored in mathematics in his entrance aptitude tests, had found him instead assigned to navigational training. For this he went to Ontario, Canada, which he enjoyed enormously. There, among men 8 to 10 years his junior, he was known as the 'old man' of the class by his fellow trainee navigators, but was also the one who studied hard and actually *knew* what he was doing when he took his examinations, instead of relying on 'cribbed' notes. His maturity brought the realization that if he failed at his job, his whole crew would suffer – not just him.

That same year, before he had left for Canada, he married Joan Mary Roberts, with whom he had lived before the war in a small flat in London. They were deeply in love, but it was during the operational training phase of his service on squadron, once again in an embattled England, that she was killed in Hitler's 'Blitz' on their London neighbourhood while working as a nurse. Earlier in the war one of his two brothers had been killed – while flying with the RAF – and now his wife. But he would not let himself fall apart. Instead he buried his pain and shock as best he could (as did so many others at the time), throwing himself deeper into his training; gaining even more maturity and strength of resolve.

By the middle of 1942, Williams was in No.75 (NZ) Squadron ('The New Zealand Squadron'), flying operations out of RAF Feltwell. The squadron was originally formed with New Zealand airmen sent to England, in May/June 1939, to train on the Vickers Wellington Mk IC at RAF Marham, but most of the original members had long since been rotated out of operations, or killed in action. Williams found himself as the only officer in the crew, who were inclined to be a little aloof until they discovered that he held few ideas of class distinction. Then, once out of earshot of other crews or in the air, he was just 'Bill'. By November 1942, the squadron had moved to RAF Newmarket and converted from the Wellington to the Short Stirling heavy-bomber aircraft, a sturdy workhorse, and he had been promoted to Flight Lieutenant, on which occasion his crew had thrown him the mother of all parties.

Now Williams lay, slightly dazed after his drop through the December night, in a German pine forest listening to the rumble of aircraft engines fading into the distance. It had been a good thing he had landed in a clearing, otherwise he might have been left dangling helpless from a tree, waiting for the enemy to come and cut him down. It was that thought of the enemy which finally spurred him into action. The searchlights had followed the parachutes all the way down, and no doubt the woods would soon be filled with the shouts and calls of German troops searching for them. Stiffly he got up, gathered together his parachute, harness, and 'Mae West' and buried them under a nearby bush, covering them with moss and forest debris. Then, sweating freely despite the cold of the December night, he set out to avoid capture. The last 'fix' the navigator had given was still fresh in his slightly shaken mind. They had been just outside of Osnabruck and now, guided by the Pole Star (Polaris – North Star) above, he set his course for the Dutch border, which he estimated to be no more than 80km away. Suffering from some bruising but otherwise unhurt, he felt he stood a better than average chance of making it across the border. There he could reasonably expect to obtain help and, with any luck at all, would be back in the squadron mess in a few days; perhaps a week at most.

Setting off through the forest the second wave of bombers for the operation (Short Stirlings of No.218 Squadron) droned overhead, and he felt a shudder of lonely fear run through him. His one remaining brother was in one of those aircraft. They were all going home, while he was here on foot in enemy territory with every man against him; left behind, forgotten … He must get to Holland; he must find help. One way or the other, he promised himself as his flying boots crunched across the forest floor in the darkness, he was going to get back to England.

He started off through the seemingly endless expanse of the dark forest, stopping often to hear if there was yet anyone in pursuit. Alert, he soon detected a small noise beyond the undergrowth in the darkness ahead and froze in his tracks. There were more rustlings amongst the pine needles. Finally he could stand it no longer and, his voice quivering, called out softly, 'Who's there?'

'It's me, sir,' an equally nervous answered, and Sergeant Voice stepped out of the darkness.

'Good God; is it you Jim?' he exclaimed and the two men eagerly shook hands before setting off hurriedly through the trees, each happy to have a companion for the unfolding adventure.

Using the small rubber bladder and purification tablets Williams found in the 'escape kit' most aircrew carried, they stopped at a stream to get water. Also they chewed some of the Horlicks tablets he found in the kit. Though their travels eventually took them onto the road network, Williams insisted they still trudge the fields in order to avoid any villages and hamlets they might encounter, though the task of moving through the rough country tired them out considerably. Williams soon discovered that his flying boots, never designed for long walks of any kind, began to chafe his heels and blister the sides of his feet badly, and at a barbed-wire fence he tore his trousers. Once during the night they encountered two German soldiers out with their sweethearts on bicycles, but were able to dive into a nearby ditch and escape notice. Soon after that, the two were hailed by a guard at a railway crossing as they stepped under the gate, but managed to scamper off into the darkness without further notice. Other than those two times though, they travelled undisturbed in this part of Nazi Germany, 'enjoying' the solitude. Williams thought they were keeping a fairly good walking pace.

Toward daylight, exhausted but satisfied with their progress, they decided to lie up for the day hidden in the dense undergrowth of a wooded area just off a narrow lane they had been following. Here they shared a piece of birthday cake Voice had in his pocket (his celebration had been to be shot down – not a birthday he would ever forget), before settling down to some much-needed sleep. Within a few hours, however, they were awakened by the deep, penetrating cold of a December morning. Williams got up and stamped his aching, blistered feet to restore his circulation and found that his right leg and arm were sore from his parachute landing. Then he lay down and attempted sleep again. The day was passed in such a manner, alternating catnaps with stamping around to keep warm. Once, they was very nearly discovered by some children, but were able to burrow deeper into the undergrowth just in the nick of time. In the afternoon, Williams tore his flying brevet and rank tapes from his uniform but kept them in his pocket to later prove his identity, if necessary.

That evening, as darkness came they set out again. Williams was stiff and sore and it took a few kilometres before he once again found his stride. This night's travelling found the country becoming increasingly waterlogged, making detours around the inhabited areas progressively more exhausting and difficult in the dark. They often found themselves suddenly up to their knees, and sometimes hips, floundering in the mud and water of ditches and dykes that bordered the fields. As the night wore on facing these obstacles began to prove too much, and more often than not they began skipping the detours and chancing the villages. Hunger had also grown, so much so that Williams contemplated robbing a farmhouse they came to, but was scared off by the furious barking of a dog. With the morning looming, they came across a lonely-looking barn at a farm far from anything and climbed quietly up into the hayloft, which was well stocked. Crawling gratefully into it, they burrowed down deep and were soon warm and fast asleep.

Rising that afternoon, Williams found some raw swedes in a corner of the barn which he tried. However, they turned out to be largely unpalatable, causing him great thirst, and they had forgotten to fill the water bag before hiding. At the same time a careful search of the barn revealed no civilian clothing they might wear over their uniforms. During the day several people visited the barn, but none came up to the loft and so they were able to sleep on and off all day, grateful for the warmth.

With evening the pair set off again, but much more slowly. Though the sleep had done them good, hunger was now becoming a severe problem. Williams' chafed and badly blistered feet were really giving him problems now, but still he hobbled along, determined to escape from Germany any way he could. Later, after dunking his head in a fast moving stream and soaking his feet, he felt a little better. This night, however, the two just did not have the energy to bypass any of the villages they came upon, nor could they manage to avoid those people whom they met, instead answering their curious stares with a simple, if tired sounding, '*Gute nacht*. (Good night)' Williams' stomach was a knot and he was sick several times during the night. Getting more and more lightheaded as the night wore on, they waited too long before looking for a hiding place and the grey light of dawn forced them to hide in a small, exposed stand of fir trees. Flopping to the ground as a weak sun streaked the clouded horizon they waited for exhaustion to bring sleep.

But the cold was far too intense for sleep and a steady, freezing, drizzle began to fall. Before long both were up again and trying to generate warmth. Peering out of the meagre hiding place, some distance across a wide field Williams saw what looked to be a better one in thicker woods and decided they should go there instead. Cutting across the field the two did their best to ignore the hard stares of several peasants working there, which Williams had failed to see before, and tried to walk with purpose, but it was painfully obvious from their mud-covered uniforms and 4 day's growth of beard who and what they were. Once deep in the wood, now worried about the farm hands, they hurried on despite their exhaustion and soon came to a marshy plain backed by a wide river. They followed the line of the bank for a time rather than attempt to swim across in the December cold. Before long they came to a town and spotted a bridge ahead. Pushing quietly around and onto the edge of a road, they cautiously crept forward to see if it was guarded.

There was indeed a guard at an improvised barrier and he seemed to be checking the papers of anyone wanting to cross. There was little doubt as to who he was looking for. Then the thought slowly drifted into Williams' tired mind – they must be near the border, and this must be the River Ems. Safety lay only a short distance on the other side; the journey was nearly over! Quietly pushing into the bushes on the side of the road and studying the bridge, he felt he could manage the climb under it and cross under the cover of darkness. He had no doubt that Sergeant Voice could as well, if only they could get a little sleep. There flagging spirits revived, the two determined to rest up as much as possible. The workers in the field now temporarily forgotten, they moved deeper into the undergrowth and were soon fast asleep.

It was almost dark when the shouts woke them with a start. Peering through the bushes in the direction of the noise, Williams saw a line of men in green uniforms carrying shotguns, slowly approaching in his direction. Obviously, it was them they were searching for; the field workers earlier had no doubt reported their presence. Williams' thoughts ran furiously. To get caught now, after all he had endured and so close to their goal, would be stupid. He must get away! He was between the line of men and the river – he did not know where Voice was at that moment – and the searchers would soon overtake him, unless he could quietly slip into the water and swim across now. Carefully getting up, he backed away slowly, crouching down so as not to be seen. Then, turning to make his stealthy getaway came face-to-face instead with an old man in a dark green uniform pointing a huge, old-fashioned looking revolver directly at his stomach. Expressionless and heavily moustached, the old man merely muttered *'Hände hoch'* (Hands up) and gestured with his gun. Feeling empty inside, Williams slowly raised his hands above his head and stood upright.

The march into the nearby village of Steinbild was almost circus-like. The policeman that had captured them led the way, followed by the rest of the search party and a crowd of children and villagers. In the middle of the crowd were the two bedraggled and dejected flyers, limping along, and hands at ear height. A German officer in riding breeches mounted on a bicycle met them at the edge of the village and directed the men leading the procession to a hotel near the local railway station, where they were allowed to wash and given a meal in a back room. Here an English speaking Kreigsmarine officer (local to the village and home on leave) paid a visit. He was very sympathetic and told Williams that guards from the Luftwaffe camp at Frankfurt were on their way to collect them in the morning. He also told him that they had nearly made it; the border, he said, was just a few kilometres away, which Williams took with quiet resentment.

Later they were led into the hotel bar, run by an old woman of resigned features, where they had their boots taken away and placed behind the counter. For a while a parade of villagers trooped into the building to have a look at them, which Williams detested intensely. Before long though the parade had ceased and Williams – an officer, and thus a true prize – was allowed close to the warm stove and made welcome among the men who had captured him, while Voice – a mere sergeant – was locked in a side room. There was a girl behind the bar, young and pretty, who gave Williams a blanket and took his uniform away to dry. When she returned it a short time later he saw that she had brushed most of the mud off and even sewn up the tears for him.

With much singing and frivolity the night, along with many rounds of drinks then slowly passed until, by 4.00am, everyone had drifted home, save for the policeman that had taken him (who was exceedingly drunk by then) and two foresters. Williams, keeping alert for any exit which might become possible, had already noticed that just outside the front door there was another shotgun-armed guard, and no other form of exit presented itself. Escape seemed out of the question.

Then the policeman passed out, suddenly and without warning and, laughing, Williams saw his chance; motioning the policeman's partners to throw water in the man's face, the foresters, laughing as well and struggling against their own load of alchohol, manhandled the old fellow from the room and into the lavatory. As the door closed behind them, Williams was quickly up, grabbing his boots and Irvin jacket from behind the bar and quietly running up the staircase to the upper floor of the building. After a quick reconnaissance, he slipped through a window in what was the old lady's room and onto the roof of a small outbuilding. Dropping to the ground he was again off into the early morning at a dead run, blisters notwithstanding.

Crossing the bridge, he noted sardonically that it was no longer guarded and pressed on, determined to get as far into Holland as he could before the search was in full swing. The rest and food had done him good and he did not stop until dawn was clearly streaking the sky. Then, just off the road he had been dangerously following, he noticed a small farm and ducked behind a stand of trees to watch for any signs of German occupation. He saw no Germans but instead a mother and a small girl, perhaps 8 or 9 years old. Deciding to take the chance, he stumbled up to the door of the farmhouse, keeping a sharp look out in all directions, and knocked. The little girl opened the door and, with a terrified look, quickly retreated into the large kitchen. Williams stepped in behind her and found the woman he had seen earlier, looking equally terrified. Knowing no Dutch, the conversation was all sign language and muddled German between them, but Williams nevertheless managed to tell her his name, the fact that he was a British flyer, and that he wanted food, a shave, and help. The woman grudgingly helped after speaking briefly to the girl, who ran out the door and down a path away from the house.

As he ate, he wondered absently if she might be fetching the police. However, aware there was really nothing he could do about it he sat down comfortably in front of the fireplace afterwards and was soon fast asleep in the warm glow.

The bed in his cell at Dulag Luft three days later was not nearly as comfortable as had been the chair in that farmhouse. The police (Dutch SS) had indeed come, mounted on bicycles, to snatch away his freedom and had taken him to the nearby town of Kluse, where he was locked in the cellar of the town hall. There had been no drinks by the fire the second time he was captured; only four blank walls until the Luftwaffe had come to collect him the next morning. It had been a cold, uncomfortable rail journey through the German countryside to Oberursel, though the guards were friendly enough and one spoke reasonable English. During a visit to the lavatory, he had forced a window and stuck his head out as the train was moving slowly along a soft grass embankment. However, turning to one side he found the head and shoulders of one of the guards leaning out another window, grinning and waving a pistol at him. Back in the corridor he merely gave a weak smile at the German and then sat down in their compartment. But he was never left alone for the rest of the trip.

Now he sat in silent misery, lamenting his bad luck and wondering what the future held in store for him. Over the next several days spent in solitary confinement in his 6ft by 9ft cell at Dulag Luft, he was visited alternately by a young German officer who claimed to have been the pilot of the nightfighter that shot his Stirling down; a phony Red Cross man with the usual fake Red Cross form asking far too many questions that the Red Cross need not know;

and a German Feldwebel (Sergeant) who urged him to 'fill in the forms necessary and answer the simple questions asked of him' in order to speed his transfer to a permanent camp. Otherwise, he said, the prisoner might never find himself out of the cell again. All of them, despite their air of good intentions, were hustling him for information and tried hard to unnerve him, but none succeeded. Although his clothing had been taken from him and searched, as he had been (embarrassingly so), he had nevertheless managed to secrete away the compass and map he had kept from the escape kit. Through the night, his cell was alternately heated and cooled, and he was usually kept from visits to the latrine until the last possible minute. As a matter of principle, he refused to use the chamber pot provided. With little to occupy his time or thoughts at first he slept a great deal, glad to be indoors, dry and reasonably warm again. Only as the days dragged by did his mind begin to wonder if the Feldwebel had been telling the truth.

Then, despite the predictions of the Feldwebel, he was let out on the tenth day and was led down the road through the trees alongside a number of other men into the main camp; a barren quarter mile square enclosure containing four equally barren-looking huts. Strolling along, he thought that they looked more like a line of refugees than airmen of the RAF; all types of uniform (or lack thereof) seemed to be represented. Walking next to him, Williams noticed a young, brooding figure dressed in a filthy khaki battledress of a Royal Artillery regiment with a fringe of downy beard gracing his thin face. He seemed ill at ease and aloof from the others in the group, and Williams wondered what a 'brown job' was doing here among these airmen.

Once through the gate and into the black mush of the camp compound, the group was given over to a British officer, who introduced himself as the compound adjutant. He was accompanied by the compound doctor and padre. These men then led them all into a dreary looking greeny/grey hut, warm and dry inside, where they were given a mug of strong, hot tea and a long lecture on camp life and how the progression of things would be from then on. Following this, they were taken into another room and issued with shaving and washing gear, toothbrush and toothpaste, two blankets, a set of long woolen underwear, a pullover, and a fresh RAF uniform (all sent out by the Red Cross). Lastly, was a greatcoat picked from a large, musty pile provided by the Germans; captured from one of the various armies defeated by the Nazi war machine. Most often these were of Polish origin.

It was 2 January 1943, and Williams struggled to remember which day had been Christmas Day, but quickly realized he could not discern one day from the next during his time in solitary. Thoroughly dejected, he trudged with the group again through the black mush outside, but carefully examined the surrounding barbed wire with one all-consuming thought engulfing him – 'I must get out; I must escape!' He resolved, somehow, some way, to escape.

Led into another hut and assigned to one of the rooms, immediately most of the new intake of prisoners, piled under the hot showers in the compound bathhouse. Shot down on 17 December, it had been nearly 15 days since Williams had been able to properly wash, shave and change his clothes and he lingered long over the process, revelling in it, taking as much time as possible, and for a few minutes almost forgot his situation. Once back sitting on his bunk in the warm room assigned to him, feeling at ease in clean underwear and a fresh uniform, Williams found himself in conversation with the now equally clean and shaven young army artillery officer he had noticed earlier, who had drawn the bunk across on the other side of the room.

Chapter 4

Under the North African Stars

December 1942–January 1943

The small gaggle of British prisoners shuffled forlornly through the Tunisian dust under the burning North African afternoon sun, looking more like a khaki-clad band of migrant itinerants rather than British soldiers. Only the shoulder patches on the tunics – the yellow axe of the 78th Infantry 'Battleaxe' Division – identified their unit. The heat, the dust, and their situation had stifled any early-morning spirit they might have had by that time of the day and there was little conversation among the ranks. At rest breaks the line, almost as a single man, flopped to the sandy banks along the side of the road and sat or lay down as the waves of desert heat continued to waft over them. Their guards, standing along the sides of the column, also seemed swallowed up in the overwhelming blanket of heat from which there was no escape. Their sweat ran in thick rivulets down their dusty arms and along dusty rifle stocks, to drip on to the dusty desert floor and evaporate almost immediately. The dust of the desert lay thick along the band just above the back of their open tunic collars, mixing with their sweat to form a thin, dirty, dun-coloured paste around their necks. There was no animosity between guards and guarded; it was too hot for anger or reproach, and whether one was among those doing the guarding or one of those being guarded, the situation was certainly the same. It was hot, it was dirty, it was miserable and there was no relief in sight for either side until the sun finally dipped down below the horizon. When it did, they could go back to the normal insanity of war, where there were two sides determined to destroy each other. Until then however, they were all just miserable beings sharing a similar hell.

These British were the ones with the luck – if that was the right word – to have been spared death and, in most cases, wounds and now allowed to shuffle forlornly along that dry, barren Tunisian highway into captivity. For them the war was supposed to be over. They had now ceased to be a factor in the war effort; years of tedious imprisonment lay ahead. Once, the small band was briefly engulfed by a cloud of dust kicked-up by a passing open staff car, carrying the distinctive palm-tree emblem of Rommel's famous *Afrika Korps* emblazoned on the door. In the back seat, a young, scowling British officer prisoner was sitting next to a German officer in immaculate uniform.

The march into captivity was a miserable and demeaning experience which was not improved by riding in a car; the collection cage much better. At least there had been the welcome and camaraderie of the 'rankers' to ease the situation, providing that special brand of cheer unique to the British soldier. However, the young officer spent little time in the overcrowded enclosure before being separated from the 'rankers' and locked in a stifling and spectacularly dirty cell in a nearby building. There was no table, no chair, nor bed in the cell, just a filthy, bug-ridden blanket foldded up in one dirty corner. No food was offered but there was water out of a tin can, which tasted strongly of petrol. Eventually sleep came as the sun went down and the heat dropped. Then the blanket – bugs or no – came into its own, though the insects prevented any real sleep.

How long he was there before they came and collected him he could not remember, for time had ceased to be a factor by then. But eventually they did take him up to a different part of the building; still dirty, but less stunningly so. There he was interrogated, fingerprinted and had his particulars taken by a Feldwebel who was somewhat less than enthusiastic about his work. Initially, he was left standing in front of the desk for what seemed an eternity, the young officer's own attitude toward the situation, already destroyed during the depressing journey and further deteriorated during his stay in the dirty cell, hit rock-bottom. His demeanour was surly and obstinate by the time the Feldwebel at last looked up at him from behind the untidy, small desk to begin the interview.

'Your name?' the German asked laconically, in accented English.

'Codner … Lieutenant, Royal Artillery … 200507 …' he replied.

Richard Michael Clinton Codner was born on a rubber plantation near Kajang, Malaya on 29 September 1920. He was the second son of John Edward Seppings Codner and his wife, Frances Eva formerly Hollway. J.E.S. Codner came from Somerset, England, where his father was a well-respected local doctor. He had gone to work for the Connemara Rubber Estate at Kajang (at that time a British protectorate) in 1912 at the age of nineteen, and by the time of World War One had risen to the position of manager. When the war in Europe broke out, he had travelled back to England and joined the Royal Field Artillery, and saw action in France. Returning to Connemara and his beloved Malaya immediately after demobilization, he would stay there until his retirement in 1948.

By the time R.M.C. Codner (always known as Mike) and his older brother Christopher John Codner (born the year before and known as John) were of school age, their parents had made the decision to send the boys back to preparatory school in England in order to ensure they had the best education possible. Arrangements were made for the brothers to be under the care of their paternal grandparents at the family home of 'Redferns', in Burnham-on-Sea, Somerset. Here they stayed for their holidays from school where their grandmother, Mabel Clara, was very much the centre of their family life.

At the age of 13, Michael was sent to Bedford, a public school in Bedfordshire, while John was sent to Haileybury School, near Hoddesdon, Hertfordshire. For the first time the two boys were separated. From there, John's educational path led him from Haileybury to the Royal Artillery Academy, Woolwich, south-east London, and a career as a professional soldier, no doubt spurred on by the exploits of his father in France some 15 years earlier. Mike entered Exeter College, Oxford to study Colonial Administration. He was tall, had a lean stature, dark hair and was somewhat wild-eyed; but quiet and yet full of youthful impetuosity, but nevertheless a deep thinker who favoured the classics. He was later remembered as a good student by his tutors. A university existence obviously suited him. Life was good.

But the war quickly interrupted that, as it would the lives of many in the world, and Codner soon left Oxford, volunteering for the army on 17 October 1940. He was commissioned on 2 August 1941 and, following in both his fathers' and brother's footsteps, joined the Royal Artillery. Every inch the epitome of a British officer, in putting on his uniform the new Lieutenant Codner had unknowingly taken the first steps toward his own fate of adventure and immortality.

Army life sat well with the young Lieutenant Codner, as had college life and his batman seemed dedicated to ensuring that he was looked after as an officer and gentleman. Before long, a weekly bulletin on the young officer's activities and health was being sent to Malaya and to his home 'Redferns' on his progress under King's Regulations. Reports noted, 'Madam, you will be pleased to hear that we have received further promotion …' were balanced out by, 'Madam, our shirts are becoming a little worn …', while the youthful lieutenant received liberal doses of unrequired laxatives and was ensured of a fresh change of socks and underwear regularly. A series of assignments eventually deposited him as a member of the 78th Infantry Division.

The division had been assembled in June 1942 from troops of 11 Brigade, 36 Brigade, and the 1st (Guards) Brigade. They immediately began training as part of what was first known as Amphibious Force 110 but which later became British First Army. In August of that year, they held their one and only divisional exercise, 'Operation Dryshod', before embarking for action in North Africa that October. Then, under US command, the division began its active campaigning of the war on 8 November 1942, when Commonwealth and US forces made the series of landings in Algeria and Morocco as 'Operation Torch', with the 78th Infantry Division's landing force supporting the advancing US troops.

Following the successful landings, on 14 November the division was ordered to send a mobile force of infantry with supporting armour, artillery, and combat engineers to move rapidly along the coastal highway from Bône to the port of Tabarka. This overland march would be supported by two British airborne drops the next day. The three operations together would therefore place Allied forces within Tunisia at two strategic northern points, each of them covering a major route from Algeria, as well as along the Algerian-Tunisian border on the southern flank. The mobile force assembled for the mission was known as 'Blade Force', a provisional formation that drew chiefly from the 78th Division, but also from the 6th Armoured Division.

The Germans responded almost immediately to the threat posed by 'Blade Force' and the supporting airborne elements by sending a force of their own from Sicily to northern Tunisia. This force halted the Allied advance eastwards in early December. Some 60km to the west of Tunis, Medjez-el-Bab would prove to be a key position in the battle. Known as the 'Gateway to Tunis', once captured by the Allied force (as it would be in late November), the town needed to be held at all costs. With German forces advancing in the hills surrounding the town, 'Blade Force' commanders ordered the defending infantry outside the city to dig in and prepare for the coming assault, while positioning artillery support to the rear. The battle that followed during the first half of December was fierce and costly to both sides as the fighting 'see-sawed' back and forth in the desert heat. The wounded made their way back to the dressing stations as best they could, doing all they could to keep the dirt, sand, and sweat out of their wounds; the more lightly injured even going so far as to looking forward to a day or two of rest.

Lieutenant R.M.C. Codner found himself in the middle of the action, acting as an artillery spotter with the 457th Light Battery, Royal Artillery, equipped with the British-built Ordnance QF 25-pounder field gun/howitzer, and part of the main artillery compliment. On 13 December, he received orders directly from the Commander of Artillery, 78th Division, to carry out an important reconnaissance of a series of hill tracks on the high ground northwest of the main Medjez-el-Bab to Terbourba road. He was to attach himself to the 5th Battalion, Northamptonshire Regiment, which had responsibility for the area, and carry out his reconnaissance in conjunction with one of their patrols. That afternoon, he set out on horseback accompanied by one of their captains and followed the battalion's Bren gun carriers. The tracks on the ridge were easily located and the patrol may well have been routine, had their location not been frequently given away by Arabs in the area working for the Germans, who repeatedly sent up smoke signals indicating the progress of the patrol. The fire they drew was not severe however, and by nightfall they had returned to their position north of Medjez-el-Bab, where Lieutenant Codner phoned in his initial report, then settled down to stay for the night. He would return to his unit in the morning; it was safer than travelling at night in unfamiliar territory.

The next morning, 14 December, before returning to file his report with Divisional Artillery Headquarters, the Battalion Commander requested that

Lieutenant Codner pass the information he had gathered to an isolated forward company. The route up to the company had been one of those they had used the previous day, and so was thought to be safe. Codner set out on a BSA motorcycle as the hot morning sun warmed the terrain, little realizing that overnight the Arabs that had caused them so much trouble the day before had led the Germans into positions which gave them a commanding view of the very road the young officer was now riding along.

Motoring along (there is some speculation that he may have been lost, but this is unsubstantiated), Lieutenant Codner suddenly began to take fire from the left and front. Surprised, he swung the BSA around to make a getaway but it was already too late; several bullets had hit causing the engine to sieze and the motorcycle slid out from underneath him. He got up and sprinted for a nearby shallow ditch alongside the road almost before his machine had stopped skidding across the sand. Two Germans armed with machine pistols some 20yd ahead had him covered from the left and right front with enfilading fire and were aiming rounds in his direction at an alarming rate. Fortunately, their aim was none too good. Using his Webley Service Revolver, he fired a few rounds back at the Germans in an effort to buy time to think, but in the end found his situation to be impossible. All around him was mostly open desert; no escape. He would be cut down in seconds, poor aim or not. Calling out, he hesitatingly raised his hands. When the firing stopped and the enemy called back to him, he stood up hesitantly. The next thing he knew, he found himself uncomfortably surrounded by German troops with rifles. Calmly, and with some resignation, he handed his pistol to an officer who had stepped forward. It was perhaps the most humiliating thing he had ever done, and the instant he did it he wished that he could have the pistol and just one cartridge back for just a moment.

His initial interrogation was nothing more than a formality, as the Germans were actively engaged with 'Blade Force' by that time. But he *was* an officer, captured alone and who obviously had been on some sort of 'special' mission. That alone might make him a valuable commodity. The harassed infantry officer who had captured him, decided to put Codner in the back seat of a staff car accompanied by a staff officer and send him to area command HQ. Later that day, Codner arrived at a place known as 'Ferryville' (Manzil Bū Ruqaybah), where the Germans had set up a PoW collection and processing compound on the southwestern shore of Lake Bizerte (16km from the Mediterranean Sea). There he was perfunctorily searched, stripped of his steel helmet, gas mask and dispatch case and had his basic particulars taken. His initial interrogation at 'Ferryville', was thorough and to the point. He was then transferred to the nearby airfield at Sidi Ahmed, and immediately flown to Trapani, Sicily; the main Luftwaffe Wing HQ for the area. It was the first time he had ever flown and the interesting experience was tempered by the thought that it seemed the Germans were going to an awful lot of trouble over a lone artillery officer. At

Trapani he was again detained in a cell (though far cleaner than his previous accommodation) while further interrogations – none of which were anything more than pointed and probing – were carried out. As these progressed however, and he wondered more and more why the Germans had such an interest in him, the picture rapidly began to come into focus; The Germans had somehow garnered the notion that he was part of one of the 'Blade Force' airborne units. When he was eventually presented with this allegation, Codner argued *ad naseam* that they had made a mistake, insisting that he was just an ordinary artillery officer, and a junior one at that, but it made no difference. The longer the interrogations went on and he denied the assertion, the more his captors became obstinately convinced otherwise.[1]

On 26 December, he was flown to Naples and immediately bundled onto a train for the Dulag at Cinecitta, near Rome. Though there was an escape chain working from within the Vatican by then, Codner was wholly unaware of it, and in any case had no contact with the outside world had he been in possession of such knowledge. For three days he 'vegetated' in a cell while further visitors came through to interrogate him concerning his unit. As a supposed 'paratrooper' he was considered a *wichtigen Gefangenen* (important prisoner) by the Germans; highly-trained, highly-skilled and highly observant. Therefore he was deserving of extraordinary measures to insure he did not escape, having now spent time behind the German lines. Further, as a 'soldier of the air' it was policy of the Germans that he be detained by the Luftwaffe for his imprisonment. To that end, on 29 December he was sent by train to Rome and then on to Dulag Luft in Frankfurt-am-Main, Germany.[2]

At Dulag Luft he was given his first embarrassingly thorough search before being locked in one of the solitary-confinement cells. He received what was by then the standard treatment: no reading or writing materials were provided and he was not allowed to smoke. The cell window remained firmly closed and locked causing the cell to become overheated. When he asked to speak to an officer he was initially told that all the officers were on leave. Within the first 48 hours however, the usual fake Red Cross form was presented to him. Recognizing the form as a fake, he filled out as much as he was allowed by rules of war, but was not pressed for more detail by the supposed Red Cross man who read what he had written. On the contrary; the Red Cross man seemed puzzled as he left with the form. Later, when an officer who spoke excellent English finally did arrive to interrogate him, around his third day in the cells, the German was seriously nonplussed to find that Codner was obviously in earnest when he said he was neither RAF nor a member of any airborne organization. The interrogation degenerated from there into a string of complaints on the German's part against the organization in Italy that had sent an ordinary British army officer to a Luftwaffe interrogation centre.

On 2 January 1943, the day after the officer's visit, Codner was led out of his cell and taken across the road toward the main prison compound. There he found a ragged crowd of mainly RAF personnel, milling around in the black mud in front of the main gate to the camp. In his dirty army battledress, Codner stuck out among the men in RAF blue, dressed in khaki he was a curiosity, a point of interest, when he wanted more than anything just to become anonymous. Later he noticed a Major of the Royal Army Medical Corps (RAMC) among the group whose uniform had the badge of an airborne regiment and after that felt somehow less ill at ease.[3]

In the main camp, they were ushered into a hut where an RAF man wearing a cloak, who had met the group at the gate, introduced himself as the compound adjutant and addressed them all about what they could expect from prison life. Almost immediately Codner asked about the chances of escape. He was told rather abruptly there was virtually no hope from the transit camp, especially in winter, and that his chances would be better if he would wait to get settled into a permanent camp. The adjutant then hastily changed the subject and asked where he had been captured.

'Tunis,' answered Codner.

'What were you flying?'

A faint smile glowed from within the fringe of beard now growing on Codner's young face, 'A BSA!'

The adjutant had no answer.

After an initial pep talk, they were issued with bedding, toiletries and other sundries necessary for basic life – including a new RAF uniform battledress – before being directed to a series of rooms in one of the huts. In the one Codner was assigned to there were six double-decker bunks, each with a narrow, wooden double locker beside it, and a cast-iron stove which heated the room reasonably sufficiently. Initially, he found he was sharing the room with a Canadian, a New Zealander, the RAMC major and another Englishman. He briefly introduced himself before dumping his kit and heading for the luxury of his first shower and shave in weeks. When he returned to the room, the Canadian and New Zealander had already swapped the light, khaki RAF desert uniform they had been captured in, for new, warm, blue serge. He soon found himself in conversation with the other Englishman, who had taken the bed across the room from his. Slightly paunchy, but with a patient face and easy smile, he introduced himself as Eric Williams ('Call me Bill; everyone does.'), who Codner recognized as the fellow that had walked beside him when they first entered the camp, though now clean shaven and far more at ease.

When Williams excused himself to go and track down the rest of his crew, Codner went in search of the RAMC paratrooper doctor, who he found out walking the camp. They discussed escape; Codner was keen to try a tunnel from their room, but realized they needed more hands. At lunch, Williams came and sat next to him, thinking the young army lad looked lonely, and Codner broached the subject with Williams, who said that he would be interested.

Later the doctor told them both that the Germans had agreed to transfer him to the large PoW hospital at Obermassfeld, and that during the journey he intended to try and escape from the train if he was presented with an opportunity. He left the camp a few days later, and it was after several days later when they heard that the doctor had indeed made his escape but had been killed in his attempt.

Over their weeks in Dulag Luft, Williams and Codner quickly became firm friends. Williams, older than Codner, was methodical in his thinking, taking things slowly and working them out in detail before he expressed an opinion. Codner was his alter ego; bubbling with optimism and ideas and eager to express them – to Williams. Perhaps it was the shock or shame of the circumstances surrounding his capture (which few in the camp shared); perhaps it had to do with Williams being an older and more understanding figure than the average prisoner; or perhaps it was nothing more than Codner's own personality, but Williams appears to have been his only really close friend while in captivity. Though many remember him, most only remember him as shy and reserved; a quiet fellow in khaki within a sea of air force blue, truly an odd man out. But some remember a little more. One former prisoner recalled him as 'a classical fellow; always reading Latin and he could spout it by the yard.' But none claim him as a friend; only as an acquaintance.[4]

Perhaps Marcus 'Rackets' Marsh, a famous race-horse trainer (he had led 'Windsor Lad' into the winner's enclosure before the war) who as a Flying Officer from No.214 Squadron became a PoW on 8 May 1941, recognized Codner's austerity more realistically than anyone other than Williams. 'Codner, as one of the few army officers [with us]', he later recalled, 'felt his position keenly. We had been shot down – he and his men had surrendered. To him, and to nobody else, it was a mark of shame that could be washed away only by escape. That was his Eldorado; the moment of which he dreamed by day and night.'

That dream would eventually become reality, it was still 9 months as a 'guest' of the Luftwaffe away in the future. But early on, as fate would have it, he was lucky enough to find a kindred spirit in Williams, who was equally determined in that regard. Williams also shared a similar shame of capture which he himself wrestled with on his own terms, though it did not involve the voluntary transfer of arms, as had Codner's surrender. That shame had quickly hardened into a cold resolve to eventually make good his own escape, and in Codner he had found a quiet reserve of strength that had gained his respect. 'I was lucky,' he would later remark concerning their eventual escape, 'because I found [a] staunch companion, and with him made that dreamed-of journey.' It may be believed that Codner held much similar feelings, though if he did he never recorded them. And although Williams would be better remembered later on by his fellow prisoners, he himself could count only Codner as his one true, close friend behind the barbed wire. And that is how they would be most often remembered; as 'Williams and Codner' – a team – rarely separate as individuals.

Every week a list of prisoners to be transferred to permanent camps was pinned up on a notice board outside the German administrative building in the compound. Some two weeks following their arrival, Williams and Codner noted their names on the list and found they would be leaving the next morning for Oflag XXI-B near a town called Schubin, in occupied Poland. By then the two had resolved to escape together, if possible, and despite the outcome of the paratrooper doctor's attempt, the train journey to the new camp offered a very real possibility. Together they began to make what meagre preparations they could; collecting the little food they managed to save and stow it safely away in their clothing, tracing the few maps the censors had failed to delete from the books in the Dulag library, which they then sewed into the waistbands of their trousers, along with the silk escape map that Williams had managed to get past the searches. In the late January sunshine of the next day, the group destined for Schubin assembled in front of the gate and, looking for all to see like a band of miscreant refugees, began the slow walk to the railway station.

It was a long way from Medjez-el-Bab; also London.

Chapter 5

'A Rum Sort of Place …'

September 1942–April 1943

Oliver Philpot and his fellow captives stretched in the September sun of Poland as they descended from the train that had carried them from Sagan. It had been a miserable, tiring three day journey. Cramped into stifling third-class railway carriages on seats as hard as any rock, not once had they been allowed off the train; indeed, the only time they were allowed out of their six-man compartment was to use the evil smelling lavatory at the end of the corridor. Even then, guards armed with bayonet-mounted rifles either stood in the compartment with them, or roamed the corridor outside, peering in on them frequently. They had been forbidden to open the windows as well, and the atmosphere inside the compartments soon became stale and heavy with cigarette smoke, body odour, and bad breath. Along the way there had been long, unexplained stops when the train had been shunted into a siding; there to sit and wait for hours as the late summer sun slowly roasted them in the oven-like carriages. Conversation came to a standstill as each said what they had to and then tried not to get on each other's nerves, or let anyone get on theirs.

The only break in the monotonous routine had been when Major Johnny Dodge – a veteran of World War One and old enough to be the father of almost everyone on the train – made a break for it through the lavatory window while the train was travelling at nearly 30mph. He sprinted off over the fields with bullets whizzing all around him, only to be rounded up within an hour and brought back to the waiting train, smiling and enormously pleased with himself. It was a brief morale booster for everyone on board. The Germans then confiscated his boots for the rest of the journey.

Once off the train, the march to their new camp took them through the ancient Polish town of Schubin. First settled in the year 1434, the town was dirty and uninteresting; just another of the many such towns in Poland under Nazi occupation. The few inhabitants that came out to watch stood silently along the street, occasionally smiling and giving the 'V for Victory' when the guards were not looking. The road they followed out of town ran alongside fields as flat, dull and uninteresting as any the prisoners had ever seen, merely adding to the sense of desolation initiated by the train journey; although they did take notice of the Polish girls out working those fields.

What they found on arrival at the new camp however, perked up the flagging morale of many enormously. Located some 3km outside the town, the camp proved to be an almost unbelievable site to the eyes of those would be escapers, as few locations in the extended Reich could have been less suited as a site for a prisoner of war camp.

Oflag XXI-B had started life as a boy's school, and the white-washed main buildings of the camp reflected that original purpose. There was a large, secure looking main building known as (of course) the 'White House', two stables, a sanatorium, cookhouse, chapel, several other smaller outbuildings, and a large greenhouse and potting shed. The grounds, laid out across a hill behind the house, were very pleasant looking, with trees, shrubs and footpaths, alongside gardens of vegetables and flowers and a small beechnut grove. In 1939, when war appeared imminent, the Polish government had closed the school and four cheap brick and mortar barn-like barrack buildings were rapidly built, converting the school to accomodation for a cavalry unit. After the Germans overran Poland and the country surrendered, they incarcerated a large number of Polish prisoners there, who built four more barrack buildings and surrounded the new camp with barbed wire and sentry boxes before being sent elsewhere to labour further for the Reich. Following that, the camp then held Polish officer prisoners until the fall of France in May 1940. The Poles were then evacuated to make room for French officer prisoners. These had only recently been moved out to another Oflag in order that the Germans could gather together all the RAF prisoners from the various other camps in the Nazi system, as well as those serial escapers and others from Sagan, to relieve the overcrowding there until the new North Compound could be built.

The camp was run by the Wehrmacht, not the Luftwaffe, and it was largely because of this fact that it became an RAF escaper's paradise. The Luftwaffe had already gained an understanding of the RAF mentality toward escape, which was to embrace it with a will. The Wehrmacht however, having become used to holding men at Schubin from countries which were already under occupation, and would thus have far less incentive to escape, did not have security uppermost in their mind when they laid it out as a camp. Consequently, to the 'professional' eyes of RAF escapers it was like being handed an 'escaping gift'. In spots there was tree cover nearly up to the double fence line; far less rolled 'concertina' wire between the fences than at Sagan; the barracks were ridiculously close to the wire; and 'blind spots' existed all over the camp where a man could be completely hidden from any German view. Nor was there any real *Abwehr* department to speak of; just one lazy officer (a former German university professor of English) originally commanding two very bored Gefreiters (privates), who wandered the camp with little idea as to what they were supposed to be looking for. Only later did a Wehrmacht form of 'Ferret' dressed in green army overalls appear in the camp, but by then it was largely too late; RAF escape activity had already far outstripped the German's meagre efforts at control.[1]

Additionally, as the camp Senior British Officer, the redoubtable Wing Commander Harry Day, was to quickly discover, the rest of the German staff were little more than 'a bunch of bastards'; totally unhelpful to him and his staff. Having become used to dealing with Luftwaffe officers that, by and large, conducted themselves with dignity, offering and thus expecting respect, Day instead found himself being treated with extreme disrespect right from the outset. The *Kommandant* was a World War One veteran of extremely dislikeble character and attitude. The Czech-born *Lageroffizier* (officer in charge of the compound) was a Nazi zealot, given to violent fits of temper, while his assistant – known to the British as 'The Butcher Boy' – was a mindless product of the Hitler Youth with an intractably vicious disposition.

Because of the attitude of the German staff, conditions in the camp were grim. 'It was a rum sort of place,' one prisoner remembered. 'Surely not the sort of place you'd take your old mother!' The overcrowded barn-like barracks had no ceilings, just open rafters, and there was never enough fuel for the stoves to keep them anything like warm in winter. The double-tier bunks in the cavernous buildings had been shifted around to form individual semi-private 'messes' of eight men, with a corridor running down the middle of the building. A washroom occupied one end of the building, usually inches deep in dirty waste water from blocked up drains. For night use, a foul smelling, bucket-type latrine was located the other end of the building. At night, the buildings were noisy with conversation and the atmosphere quickly grew worse than stale; a condition exacerbated by a German order that all windows were to remain closed and shuttered at night, summer and winter, with no exceptions. Red Cross parcels were regularly held up from distribution as punishment for minor infractions of the rules, as well as the electricity being switched off at the most inopportune times. And, as a further measure to prevent forebidden activities, every month all the prisoners had to pack all their belongings and move to another barrack hut.

Yet, despite all these factors morale among the prisoners ran exceptionally high; perhaps higher than in any other RAF prison camp in the Reich. Hardship shared, after all, is hardship endured.

Escape quickly became the main focus of the camp inmates, and an Escape Committee had formed almost at once by the first RAF personel who arrived in early September. These came from Oflag VI-B, a camp near the small German town of Warburg, supposed to be exclusively for captured British army officers. At Warburg, those members of the RAF that the Germans interned there had studied escape under the brilliant minds of a very active Escape Committee. Conditions at Warburg had also been almost equally as grim as they were at Schubin, so the RAF men felt 'at home' in their new surroundings, though some quickly began to suffer a mild neurosis from trying to pick the best escape route out of the camp before anyone else did! The second intake to the camp arrived from Sagan later that month and contained the majority of the troublemakers from East Compound, which included a good number of the 'Barth Crowd' who quickly fell into collusion with the 'Warburg Gang'. What the Germans had unwittingly done when they made the transfer of troublemakers and volunteers from Sagan in that autumn of 1942 and thrown them together with the 'Warburg Gang', was effectively gather together a mass of escape talent into a rather old and non-purpose built location. This provided the stage and cast for a series of spectacular escape attempts and the cohesion of a serious and dedicated, 'X Organization'.[2]

Almost immediately tunnelling began. A hole was started under one of the boilers in the cookhouse, another from under the altar in the church, and the redoubtable Tommy Calnan attempted a 'mole-type' escape from the middle of an asparagus bed not far from the north fence. But troubles began almost immediately; the tunnel in the cookhouse ran into seepage from heavy autumn rains and had to be closed down; the one from the church was hampered as it was only possible to disperse soil during services and then into the pockets of those involved; Calnan's effort collapsed, almost suffocating him. Three more tunnels took the place of these, but all were found in rapid succession through pure bad luck.

More bad luck dogged a number of 'X Organization' efforts as autumn faded into winter. A new USAAF prisoner, still wearing his flying boots, was found entangled in the barbed wire one night, his own poorly planned attempt in defiance of orders. A young RAF officer, drawing maps for the escape committee, leaned too far out from a top-floor window of the 'White House' in his efforts to see something in the distance and accidentally fell to his death. Ironically, the details he was trying to record were actually collected by his burial party. One tunnel was near completion when a guard noticed a man dumping a load of soil onto one of the muddy paths, to be trodden in by the prisoners' boots. Stupid as the majority of the Wehrmacht guards at Schubin were, even they could not help but notice that something was happening in light of such activity on the part of a prisoner, and the tunnel was quickly found.

Success finally came, however, early that December when Sergeant P.T. Wareing, one of fifteen NCOs sent from Sagan ostensibly to look after officer's needs, escaped from a working party sent to Schubin railway station to collect bread. Word eventually filtered back to the camp that Wareing had made the coveted 'home run' back to England in time for Christmas. Buoyed by Sergeant Wareing's success, two other officers tried to swap places with two NCOs in order to get onto a working party being sent to town to collect coal, but were caught at the gate. Another officer, hiding in a garbage truck, was winkled out at the gate by guards using a sharp metal rod. One prisoner climbed up onto the canvas tilt of a German military truck leaving the camp and actually did get through the gate, only to be picked up the next evening trying to steal an aircraft from a nearby Luftwaffe airfield. Another succeeded in concealing himself in a laundry van, only to be picked up a few days later sneaking around the same airfield.

Slowly it was beginning to become obvious to the Wehrmacht guards as to what they were up against. By Christmas 1942, they made the prisoners move from barrack to barrack almost on a weekly basis to try and foil any escape plans then in progress.

Nevertheless, efforts continued as the initial escape fever of that balmy autumn swept on into a positively freezing winter, which merely dampened, but did not extinguish, the escape flame. In November, just before the hardest freeze in decades began, a serious, long-term effort was commenced. The brainchild of Pilot Officer Eddie Asselin, a Canadian Spitfire pilot, and Pilot Officer 'Tex' Ash, a US-born Spitfire pilot in the RAF, a tunnel was begun through the side of the brick wall inside the large pit under the *Abort* along the western fence line. The hole was an evil, dank affair, dipping down to a depth of 17ft to avoid the sound detectors, and occasionally seeping with effluent when the elderly Polish farmer, who came to pump out the pit was a day or two late. However, the diggers had three things in their favour. Firstly, the soil was solid earth and clay, which collapsed rarely compared to the sandy soil at Sagan. Secondly, they had a ready dispersal point for the earth they dug in the great latrine pit itself, although the old Pole who drove the sewerage cart did grumble to the prisoners once or twice about the amount of soil in the bottom of his tank when he emptied the cart onto his fields. And thirdly, the trap door – the most vulnerable aspect of any tunnel – was below the floor of the *Abort*, making it very unlikely to be discovered by any snooping German, unless he was willing to stick his head down through one of the toilet seats; a dubious prospect, at best. Slowly then, the tunnel progressed toward the wire as the New Year came and went.

A fine sleet was falling through the late January darkness when a group of dishevelled, tired 'kriegies' arrived in front of the gate to the camp from Dulag Luft. There were nearly as many guards as prisoners in the group and all were bathed in the bright dazzle of the arc lamps above the double fence stretching out on each side of the gate. It was freezing, and silver clouds of breath floated dreamily above the scene, mingling with the sheen of the sleet in the glare. Remarkably, for the Germans, there was very little shouting; just the squelch of boots through the almost frozen slush and the creak and rattle of the gate closing behind them. After being counted several times, the tired and miserable prisoners were finally led single file to a room in a large white-painted building where they were searched before being taken to a large mess hall. There they were fed by British camp staff. Afterwards, the SBO addressed them at length on the general operation of the camp, stressing escape and co-operation with the escape organization, before they were divided into small groups and assigned bunks in the various messes around the camp.

Much to their pleasure, Williams and Codner found themselves assigned to the same mess. Led out again into the night they found that it had stopped sleeting and the camp, under the soft beam of the searchlights sweeping the white surface took on an almost iredescent glow. Any congenial feelings they may have had quickly disappeared however, when they were ushered through the door of their assigned barracks by a guard and were greeted with the realities of their new home and way of life. The walls of the building were grimy and damp, while there was a layer of fug hanging low from the roof; half tobacco smoke, half dampness from lines of washing stretching down the corridor. The smell of the building was almost overpowering; a mixture of stale tobacco smoke, warm body odour, wet soot, and human excrement. They were greeted by a mass of dishevelled, haggard-looking men, among them was the 'Little X' for the hut, who took them to their mess and introduced their fellow inmates. Like it or not, they were 'home'.

For the next few days, the new prisoners were pestered by their messmates and pumped for the latest news of the war and of life at home. There were also invitations from other messes for much the same reason and occasionally become re-acquainted with old friends. They found there was a dramatic society in which to become involved, as well as sports. In between all this activity was the routine of getting settled and learning the repetitive monotony of daily life in a permanent camp. Gradually the newness wore off of them slowly – almost imperceptibly – the dreary January gave way to an equally dreary February and they became 'woven' into the fabric of life as a PoW.

'When I was a boy,' Williams wrote in 1953, 'I read and re-read all the well known escape books of the First World War … I entered into [the prisoner's] strange world of improvisation, derisive laughter and unity against the common enemy. I forged passports and made civilian clothes, toiled for hours underground or, heart in mouth, scaled the walls of formidable ancient castles. Finally, alone or with a staunch companion, I crawled exhausted across the border into neutral Holland or stowed away in a ship for Sweden. In those days my hero – for a boy must have a hero – was not a famous cowboy, nor yet a musketeer; he was not even Tarzan of the Apes. He was a dirty, bedraggled British officer stalking the border on hands and knees, or hanging furtively around the barrier to a Baltic port.'

It is small wonder then that, fairly brimming with enthusiasm and thrown into the escape atmosphere that prevailed at Schubin, he and Codner would be among the first of their intake that January to volunteer their services to the escape committee in the hopes of getting on 'a scheme'. But enthusiasm was not enough to be welcomed into the world of the escape elite – much as Philpot had found out in the previous year – and they wracked their brains for an original idea, but failed time and again. Each idea had been tried, each location for a tunnel already used. They learned a mess-mate was on the *Abort* scheme and envied him, dreaming of the day they would have a scheme of their own to progress. Finally, their services were called on to 'stooge' for the *Abort* scheme, as well as a new tunnel being started from the main washroom next to the cookhouse. Never turning down any task for 'X', no matter how menial, they soon were identified as keen types by the escape elite. When the decision was made during the February freeze to re-open the derelict tunnel under the cookhouse boiler (closed due to autumn weather making it dangerous), Williams and Codner were quizzed on their interest in the scheme. A short time later, much to their delight, they found themselves below ground tunnelling through the earth of a frozen Poland.[3]

The night of 5 March 1943 virtually ended the cookhouse scheme however, for on that night the tunnel from the *Abort* was opened in the potato field outside the western fence, and thirty-four men made their escape. It had been the perfect escape. The next day, all hell broke loose within the camp once the Germans realized at morning *Appell* (counting parade) what had happened. The prisoners were immediately locked in their huts and within a short time several car loads of Gestapo arrived. A Russian PoW was ordered to go down the exit hole with a rope around his waist and in a short time he emerged from the *Abort*. With the method of escape discovered, it only remained to find out who had escaped. An individual identity parade was initiated, with each prisoner being checked against the photograph on his identity card held by the camp staff. The count was further confused by four men who went into hiding within the camp, so as to seemingly increase the number of escapees in German minds. Within 24 hours 'Wanted' posters and descriptions of the escapees had been put up across the Reich, and eventually some 300,000 people were called out to carry out a manhunt in the countryside. Meanwhile, the Gestapo searched the camp (for precisely what nobody was quite sure) while some inmates sold them glasses of weak beer from a barrel they had left over from the New Year. The barrel had a false bottom, where much of the forgery department's stock of original German documents was hidden.[4]

Gestapo control over the camp lasted almost the entire month. In the end, the *Kommandant* was removed from command and court-martialled, while many of the camp staff awaited (with much trepidation) sentencing for dereliction of duty in allowing the escape to occur. Within two weeks of the break, however, all but two of the escapees had been recaptured and they could be seen peering out of the windows in the 'Cooler' block. The last two – Jimmy Buckley (head of the 'X Organization') and his travelling companion Jorgen Thalbitzer, a Danish-born member of the RAF – were drowned while attempting to cross to neutral Sweden from Copenhagen when their boat was presumably run down by a larger vessel. The loss of Buckley, the mastermind of escape at Sagan the previous summer, was a serious blow to the 'X Organization'.

Filling in his spare time by performing with the dramatic society, Philpot had also joined a tunnel scheme which showed every promise of being a success. Starting from the night latrine in a barrack hut on the hill above the *Sportzplatz* (Sportsground), it was being dug at the same time as the *Abort* project, heading in the same direction and had just reached beyond the wire when the latter had broken, destroying any chance of success. Much to the bitter disappointment of the tunnellers, it was quickly discovered in the search following the *Abort* break. A group of Russian prisoners were brought in to fill in the tunnel, but not before two RAF men managed to avoid the sentry guarding the entrance and enter the night before, intending to break out before the tunnel was destroyed. The work by the Russians was to take two days. Early on the first day, watchers saw a Russian stop work and smile broadly; he had discovered the two would be escapers, but the Russian carried on digging as they crawled toward the end of the tunnel. That night the two men did break out, but were almost immediately recaptured by a cordon of guards that nobody was aware that the Wehrmacht had positioned outside the wire. It seems they were finally beginning to understand the RAF escaping mentality.

The following week, the men who had gone into hiding following the *Abort* escape were accidentally found living in the attic of the 'White House' by a Polish chimney sweep, who reported their presence. Their sudden reappearance caused considerable controversy with the camp staff, already awaiting sentencing, as well as among the Gestapo men who had ostensibly searched the entire camp for nearly a month – and not found them.

At the beginning of April, word came through from Sagan that the new North Compound at the camp was finished and occupied, leaving plenty of room in the East Compound for the 'Schubin Gang'. The Wehrmacht could at last say goodbye to their troublesome charges as they marched off into the distance. The prisoners were moved by rail in batches of 200 at a time and transported in cramped third-class carriages, but this time without their shoes. The irrascible RAF men began to move back to what they sarcastically called 'Göring's Luxury Camp'.

'It was doubtful as to which side desired most for us to move from the camp; ourselves, or the German Army,' Oliver Philpot later laconically recalled.

Part II

Captivity

Chapter 6

Back in the Sandpit

May 1943

The medieval town of Sagan lies along a centuries old major travel corridor linking Eastern and Western Europe. Logically, this corridor has also seen considerable service as a primary military marching route over the years. In deference to the age old political rivalries that existed in the region, at the advent of the industrial age much of the geographical area had been starved of railways to impede military progress, making those major routes that did exist and the towns along them key points of military interest. Sagan was just such a point; the railway marshalling yard quickly grew to be an area of substantial capacity.

During the years of World War Two, the heavily-laden railway traffic that rolled through the town on its way to the Nazi disaster of the Eastern Front was considerable. So too were the trainloads of wounded returning. And usually strung together on those trains were more than a few cattle trucks full of Russian prisoners, some of whom would be bound for Stalag VIII-C and Stalag VIII-E, both part of a large complex of prison compounds located in the area very near Stalag Luft III. This situation was nothing new to the district. As far back as 1813, Sagan had been a collection point for prisoners of war. The graves of those who died while being held in the area from the Napoleonic period on up through the World War One can still be found there today. During the years 1939-1945, Russians and Poles died in great numbers (an estimated 120,000) within the prison complex around Sagan, of starvation, neglect, and selective extermination. These are remembered in mass graves located in the neighbourhood. And, for a time, located there also would be the remains of fifty Royal Air Force and Dominion officers murdered on the order of Hitler in March and April 1944 for doing their duty.

The trip back from Schubin was every bit as difficult and uncomfortable as the trip to Schubin had been seven months previous. However, no one had escaped this time, or even tried to, and when they finally pulled into Sagan the stiff, fed up prisoners tumbled numbly out of the carriages into the cold trackside dust of the baggage docks, stretching, grumbling and very relieved that the journey was over. Many remembered their arrival the last time, and pointed out the road they would follow to the camp to the 'Warburgers' and other new boys. Immediately the German guards did a head count and again herded them the short distance down the road and into the yard of the tall granary building that dominated the sky line above the surrounding forest, there to wait while the guards telephoned the camp to tell them they were coming.

For Ollie Philpot, it was depressing déjà vu of almost exactly a year before as he and the other returnees stared morosely at the all too familiar forms of the gaunt pines they had tried to block out all the previous summer. Shortly after, as they trudged down the road carrying all they owned, the rabble once again reminded him of 'a mob of down at the heel gypsies' rather than a group of the British Empire's best and brightest. And all too soon the familiar site of rusting barbed wire and 'Goon boxes' came into view through the trees and the guards halted them in the dust in front of the familiar gate to the *Vorlager* for East and Centre compounds.

But there had been changes at Stalag Luft III while Philpot and his comrades had been digging in the Polish earth at Schubin that winter. The new compound – North Compound – had been built to the west of the *Kommandantur* and most of the prisoners that had remained in East Compound when the move had been made to Schubin the previous September and October had been moved over there on 1 April. East Compound, now a year old, looked bare and empty, shabbier and more used. It was all too familiar; all too dirty; all too depressing.

The new SBO of East Compound was Group Captain Richard 'Dickie' Kellett, who had been shot down while in North Africa in 1942. His assistant was Flight Lieutenant Aiden Crawley, one of the Schubin escapers who had travelled the farthest during his attempt (Innsbruck). 'Stafford', as he was generally known, also did duty as chief information/intelligence officer for the compound 'X Organization', was official compound interpreter, and worked in liaison with the 'Kitchen Goon' concerning the German rations (such as they were) prepared in the compound cookhouse. Compound Adjutant was Group Captain Donald MacDonnell.[1]

The 'X Organization' was organized very quickly in the familiar environment, with virtually no changes made to the set up assembled at Schubin. The notable exception, of course, was the substitution of Wing Commander Joe Kayll in place of Jimmy Buckley as 'Big X'. 'Big S' was Flight Lieutenant Dudley 'Dud' Craig. As such, he was also liaison officer to all new PoWs. Both he and Kayll would share one of the end rooms in Hut 66. Clothing Officer for 'X' was Squadron Leader Ralph Bagshaw Ward, while his assistant and officer in charge of colour dying cloth, was Flight Lieutenant John Paget. Their department was code named 'Puller's of Perth'. The forgery department, formally known as 'Thomas Cook's Tours' at Schubin but since changed to 'Dean & Dawson', was generally under the charge of Squadron Leader Ian Brownlie and Pilot Officer E.H.L. 'Bushy' Shore. Map making was the responsibility of Flight Lieutenant John Clayton, and meteorology was under Flight Lieutenant Phillip E. Bressey.[2]

That first day in camp was an important one, for each mess set itself up and it was an opportunity to settle in with new people, should that be desired. Philpot's mess at Schubin had decided before they left Poland that they had been together long enough and would not continue as one at Sagan. A few others had followed suit, so it was with an easy drift that he had fallen in with some new faces. He and the others had wandered into a room in Hut 67 and were making themselves at home when a broad, slightly paunchy fellow strode through the door inquiring if there were any spare bunks available – two actually. He was a newer prisoner, certainly not an old lag as he was unknown to any of them; just the type to perhaps lend some fresh colour to the drab monotony of a prison mess. The man set his kit down on an empty bunk, and introduced himself all around as Bill Williams. The other bed, he said, would be for his pal, Mike Codner, if that was OK; 'That army type with all the hair? Yes, let's have him. Good type.' Soon Codner, a slim, dark figure, quietly engaged and somewhat aloof walked in, set down a parcel on the last empty bunk and wandered out again.

It was an incredibly inauspicious meeting between the two and Philpot, but was one which would soon grow to be the single most favourable association in East Compound history.

Within a day the experienced members of the mess had moved the facility into a free room in Hut 62 which had two stoves for cooking instead of one, thus making meals somewhat less of a challenge for the weekly room 'stooge'. The only drawback to the arrangement was that Hut 62 was the 'flagship' hut of the compound, where the SBO and his adjutant lived. But as most in the mess were either older individuals or seasoned prisoners, and thus far less given to much youthful exuberance, that did not appear to be much of a problem. This was demonstrated when, soon after, word came through that Philpot had received his promotion to Flight Lieutenant, and the new faction quietly celebrated with nothing more than a cake.

Since this was his second spell at Sagan he was well used to the idea of keeping busy behind the wire, Philpot quickly began to fill his time with camp tasks. He took on the job of Coal Officer, supervising the distribution of coal to each room in the compound; Shower Officer, arranging groups for the weekly hot showers (a difficult task to encourage in the summer, but for which there was a waiting list in the winter) in the *Vorlager*; and Cook Officer, supervising the delivery of the German rations to the block each day, making him familiar with the cookhouse and the 'Kitchen Goon'. He also joined the theatre company along with Williams, where the two got to know each other a little better. Later he let himself be cajoled into the thankless job as 'Little X' for Hut 62 as well. His only consolation in this was that the block 'Little S' at the time was the irrepressible Tommy Calnan. The weekly meetings with the 'X Organization' through the job put him into direct contact with all compound escape activities

– few though they were. In fact, East Compound looked to be as secure and impregnable as ever it had in the summer of 1942; if not more so.

Further, when his new mess mates Williams and Codner found out that Philpot had accepted the job as 'Little X' for the hut, they bombarded him with questions concerning escape activities during the previous summer. Over and over Philpot found himself forced to explain the Lamont/Best/Goldfinch effort, the almost suicidal Toft and Nichols effort, and any others he could remember in detail. To describe the two as enthusiastic about escape would be an understatement, and Philpot's attitude toward their naked ambition on the subject swung from mere tolerance to genuine incredulity. Their relationship with Philpot naturally also brought them into contact with Calnan, whose efforts they also questioned at length. Yet in the end, despite their exuberance on the subject and fresher outlook on the camp, neither had Williams nor Codner any original ideas to get them beyond the wire.

However, beyond the moves to Schubin and after the major shift to North Compound, there had remained in East Compound a small group of prisoners charged with taking an inventory of what was missing, such as bedboards, bunks, towels, blankets and generally anything else that had previously proved useful for escape, and restocking the blocks in preparation for the returning prisoners. In addition to enjoying the relative peace and quiet of a virtually empty compound, these men had taken further advantage of the unique situation and had been able to deceive the Camp authorities into providing more than was actually required. One of them was Pilot Officer William G. 'Bill' White who, in late February, had started a major tunnel project from the washhouse side of the northern *Abort*. It was a worthy scheme that stood every chance of success since the *Aborts* were positioned nearer the wire than any of the huts and also were rarely searched. The tunnel shaft went down for 18ft, to where there was a roomy working and dispersal chamber. This was used for storing tunnel spoil until it could be disposed and contained a portable winding device for lifting water jugs full of sand up from the tunnel below. The entrance trap had been cut irregularly along the edges of the bricks and had been fitted into a frame. The cracks between the trap and floor being filled with a special mixture of cement dust and soap, making it virtually undetectable. From the washhouse the tunnellers only had approximately 140ft of digging to clear the east fence then under the road and freedom. However, the project was hampered first by dispersal problems, and then by lack of manpower when the big move to North Compound had occurred. Once the East Compound began to refill with the returning prisoners from Schubin, White found plenty of willing helpers. Prominent among these was Pilot Officer Daniel A. Webster, who had been one of the escapees from Eddie Asselin's attempt at Schubin. He, in turn, recruited Philpot into the scheme, at first to help with dispersal and then, as the tunnel progressed, for a few shifts underground.

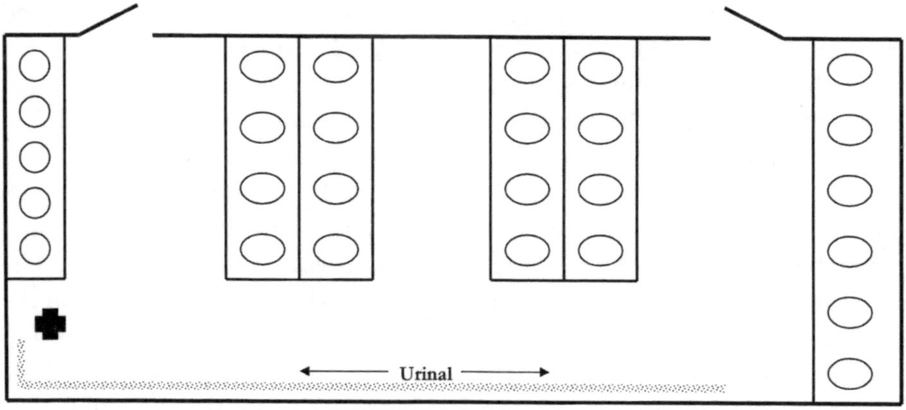

The *Abort/Waschhaus*.
Both north and south buildings were the same in construction and layout. On the left note the five wash basins, equaling a total of ten in the compound – for over 800 prisoners to wash their bodies and clothing. One of these would usually be converted to a makeshift shower in the summer, using a piece of hose and an empty food tin with holes punched in the bottom. The seats were nothing more than holes cut into enclosed benches above the pit with cardboard covers (part of Colonel Clark's 'Crap in Comfort Campaign') and thin plywood dividers between each. The urinal was simply a tarred section of the wall above a sloping half pipe in the floor which emptied into the pit at one end. The black cross marks the approximate spot of Bill White tunnel entrance. There was a constant problem with urine leaking into it.

When he had left Sagan for Schubin the previous autumn, Philpot had been determined never to return to the hated place. Yet here he was – back again, in much the exact position as he had been then … shut off from the world by the tall, bare fir trees standing silent sentry to his enforced incarceration. But not for lack of trying! Dickey Edge's tunnel at Schubin had been a mere 36 hours or so from success. And now he was on White's effort, which stood a good chance in the long run, without any unforeseeable bad luck. Also he had moved a few more rungs up the ladder to escape by actually joining the Escape Committee. Hard work for committee members had paid off for four of them at Schubin when they had been included on the Asselin attempt as a reward for all they had done in helping others to escape.

But suppose success had come at Schubin? What if it came this time? Once outside of the wire, what intentions had he; what actual preparations had he made? Or was he, like so many others, simply willing to let the committee guide him with what they felt was best for any potential escape? All good questions! And, as methodical as ever, he began to examine the problem of escape along a line he had not thought of before.

What Philpot quickly realized was that he had not been prepared for an escape while at Spangenburg, nor at Schubin, nor during his first stay at Sagan. Though he had thought about it, he really had not given it the intense thought necessary. True, it was a challenge to break free of the wired compound (or ancient castle) but the large majority of challenges that faced an escaper began *after* he had escaped. What if, just for a change of direction in order to clear the mind, he started to prepare for a 'sudden departure' from the camp? Let the 'how' of escape from the compound go for a moment and concentrate on his subsequent journey. Prepare for escape – believe it will come – and succeed in the end. With that thought in mind, Philpot slowly began assembling a second persona for himself that he would fully assume in the event of his escape. He eventually decided to become 'Jon Jorgenson'.

Philpot placed a great deal of effort into this guise, since it was important that any escapee be both plausible and as unobtrusive as possible. It must also make use of what actual attributes the escapee could bring to the role, as well as those to be assumed. 'Jon Jorgenson', Philpot had decided after much debate, would be a Norwegian. Not because he held any natural Norwegian attributes, but largely because he deemed it very unlikely he would ever run into a real Norwegian among the general German populace who would challenge his authenticity. As 'Jon', he would also be a devoted follower of the infamous Norwegian collaborator Vidkun Quisling, something which would also likely set him above suspicion to most Germans, should he be stopped and questioned.

Most importantly, however, 'Jon' had to have a real occupation which gave him reason to travel across Germany. 'Stick to what you know,' had been the advice given him by Aidan Crawley. Philpot, drawing on his own experiences with Unilever before the war as an exchange worker in Germany with the Margarine Sales Union, 'Jon Jorgenson' would work for much the same type of corporation, in almost the same role. After some research, he decided that his employer would be De-No-Fa, an edible fat company at Frederikstad, and he would be on a six month exchange programme with a German union worker; each gaining useful insight into each others' companies and countries. This exchange status would therefore enable him to travel to any of the union's network of companies throughout the Reich, giving him reason to be travelling. A further plus was that he actually had been to several of those locations before the war and knew something of De-No-Fa, and could easily describe them if questioned.

And in order to make the persona as completely accurate and detailed as possible, with little room for question or misgiving – since he had virtually no knowledge of Norwegian customs or the language – Philpot sought the help of a Norwegian prisoner who had escaped to England when Norway fell to fly with the RAF; Lieutenant Haldor Espelid. Through hours of conversation and coaching with Espelid, 'Jon Jorgenson' began to take on a real personality. In the end, he had a full personal, as well as professional background. His demeanor and attitude would support this – he was an 'authentic' Norwegian.[3]

Next, he went in search of the forged papers he would need. Initially, he sought out a representative of Dean & Dawson, explaining that he wanted a complete set of undated papers prepared and waiting for him should he get out of the camp, no matter what the scheme or when. But paperwork for a complete identity was a big job and the agency was still a small organization, totalling some five forgers, who were already preparing papers for washhouse tunnellers. This meant that little effort could be given to such a request.

Undaunted, and realizing the best way to make things happen was by being proactive, Philpot went in search of more personalized help, which he found in the form of Coastal Command navigator (No.217 Squadron) Pilot Officer William 'Red' Hunter, who had been shot down at the end of July 1941. During an earlier attempted escape, Hunter had emerged from a tunnel at Warburg to find a German guard pointing a rifle directly at his face. At that moment, Hunter decided that his part in escape should be more directly associated with 'camp based' activities. He was an accomplished artist with an eye for detail, so centred his activities on forgery. Philpot found him in his room in Hut 64 and introduced 'Jon Jorgenson' to him, asking primarily for a *Kennkarte* (Identity card) and personal visiting cards. An enthusiastic Hunter began work with a will.

Philpot's next stop was to see Flight Lieutenant Peter Stevens in Hut 69, perhaps Dean & Dawson's most knowledgeable forger and the recognized expert of East Compound on all things German. Entering Stevens' room the next afternoon, Philpot explained his idea in great detail, what he already had Hunter working on, and asked Stevens what other travel documents would likely be necessary to make 'Jon Jorgenson' official in Nazi eyes during his trip. Stevens remained thoughtful for just a few moments before disappearing down the hallway of the block. A few minutes later he came striding back through the doorway to the room, a little sandy and with an equally sand-covered book under his arm entitled, *Auslander Arbeiter im Deutshland* (The Foreign Worker in Germany) an official government publication which carefully detailed what documents were required by which foreign workers and in what capacity. Here was an invaluable bit of 'gold' smuggled in by a bribed guard, in which the official persona of 'Jon Jorgenson' lay. Together, Stevens and Philpot put together a list and sketches of the required items, not forgetting to include the text of a personal letter of reference from 'his' employer. Philpot, in turn, took all this back for Hunter to work on. The 'status' of 'Jon Jorgenson' was being created.[4]

The forger's task was made infinitely easier that summer by the ever resourceful team of Tommy Calnan and 'Rackets' Marsh. Calnan – of all people – had managed to get himself appointed as the British Book Censor for East Compound, though not through any love of books but instead to facilitate an escape idea he was working on starting from the *Vorlager*. Having become friendly with Marsh (Parcels Officer) while the two were at Spangenburg, together they had corrupted Corporal Eberhard 'Nikki' Hesse one of their

German supervisors in the *Vorlager* the previous summer. Just behind the Parcels Office was a small office occupied by a German clerk who had a typewriter, which he guarded very carefully. However, Marsh would request 'Nikki' to distract the clerk, during which time Calnan would wander over to the Parcels Office, slip into the clerk's office and work undisturbed on the typewriter. Soon forged blanks for the most difficult of documents produced by Dean & Dawson were being smuggled into the *Vorlager*. The task of reproducing typescript by hand (very difficult and time consuming) had been somewhat negated.

Calnan had also collected the cockpit layouts and starting drill for some of the most common German aircraft that may be found on any given German airfield. In fact, sewn into the lining of his greatcoat as he leaped from the train coming from Spangenburg to Sagan that first time, in early 1942, had been these same items, and Calnan had actually been caught just outside of a German airfield while giving it a good 'recce' in anticipation for stealing an aircraft. While no escaper had ever managed to actually steal one and fly it home, the idea naturally appealed greatly to any RAF pilot on the run, and few felt that they could ignore such an opportunity if it were at all possible. Calnan had managed to keep the documents hidden during numerous searches already and was more than willing to share the information with Philpot, and though it might have seemed a far-fetched scheme, as a back-up plan both he and Calnan felt it was not all that bad.

Meanwhile, in the new North Compound, the 'X Organization' had been quickly set up and was making headway towards escape with a will. The 'Big X' over there was a tall, brooding Squadron Leader shot down in a Spitfire of No.92 Squadron during Dunkirk named Roger Bushell. An extremely intelligent barrister in civilian life, he was a brilliant, determined escaper with a 'target' on his back put there by the Gestapo for his efforts, and he had been sent to Sagan following his most recent attempt while everyone was still at Schubin. The parting warning from his Gestapo captors had been eminently clear: to escape again and be caught meant his death. Bushell, however, had no intentions of being caught again. He had been Jimmy Buckley's second in command within the 'X Organization' ever since their days at Dulag Loft and with the blessing of the overall SBO for Stalag Luft III, Group Captain Herbert Massey, he assumed the mantle of leadership in Buckley's absence at Schubin. Then, learning of the impending move to the new compound, Bushell had devised a plan for a mass escape the likes of which the Germans had never seen, nor the British ever tried.[5]

Gathering together his most dependable and experienced people as department heads, and even before the move was carried out, Bushell's plan had already begun to take shape. Occasionally today the media refer to it as 'Operation 200', but it is best remembered as 'The Great Escape' and would turn out to be the largest combined escape effort of the war. Three tunnels would be dug simultaneously; code named 'Tom', 'Dick', and 'Harry'; the theory being that at least one should be successful. In any event, plans were for at least 200 officers to escape into the 'Third and Last', scatter into the countryside causing inevitable and considerable consternation to Nazi leadership. Each escaper was to be provided with maps, rations, all the forged papers needed for a new identity and a plausible travel plan. The 'X Organization' would engineer the whole process, and North Compound in its entirety would work toward the escape. Some PoW working parties had even been allowed to go over to the new compound early, with the Kommandant's blessing; ostensibly to help with the building of the place, though in reality to conceal supplies they had stolen from the workmen and to survey the situation in order to pre-plan for escape activities. From the German point of view, the new compound was being built to incorporate everything they had learned about interning RAF prisoners. However from the prisoner's point of view, their sole purpose in the new compound was to escape.

Word had also been passed around the entire camp that there were to be no escape attempts which had not been approved by Bushell and his organization in North Compound. That did not mean that all escape attempts were to cease except for the activities in North Compound, it just meant that nothing was to jeopardize Bushell's plan. That was how good security was on the scheme.

Before long, the end of May had arrived, and with it the Silesian summer. Another Sagan day had only just started, and across East Compound the morning routine was playing out in its usual way. With the bars on the doors removed at 6.00am, the loudspeaker sprang into life over Hut 64, blasting German martial music and announcements across the compound. Wing Commander Roger Maw lived in the room directly under the speaker, and inevitably the morning would be pierced by the Wing Commander's shouted cursing against the aural assault. Many of the prisoners were already up by then however, either it was too hot and uncomfortable to sleep, or they were just fed up with being locked in all night. The room 'stooges', quickly going about their business of getting breakfast ready, headed to the kitchen block for hot water to brew tea, or carefully cutting the sour, German black bread into equal portions, adding a small smear of margarine or jam. Conversation, hesitant at first, for fear of robbing away the last peace of the day, would begin; low and calm initially, and then slowly it would grow. Before long there would be an argument somewhere, short and growling, and then growing louder, perhaps to be followed by a slammed door … and so would life come to another day in 'Göring's Rest Camp For Tired Aviators'.[6]

The sound of guard's jackboots clumping through the corridors at 8.30am accompanied by the familiar shout of '*Raus!* (Out!), announced *Appell*. The standard prisoner shout of 'Goon in the block!' went up in reply. Dress for the morning event came in an array of clothing supplied to the prisoners and took little time. In the winter it was easy; one paraded wearing everything one possessed. The warmer weather, however, made for more options. Many never left on their now ragged and faded pyjamas the Red Cross had sent while others insisted on parading in full uniform. The vast majority of individuals, however, fell somewhere in the middle. There were also those who waited until the last minute to get out of bed, to attend the parade wearing 'whatever', and since the summer had arrived one or two were even seen to appear clothed in nothing more than a home-made jock strap.[7]

The prisoners stood in ranks of five by hut number in a very loose formation best described as 'indifferent' to the activity. One 'Goon' – usually the brutish Hungarian-born Feldwebel Stuhlmeyer, the German NCO in charge of the guard in East Compound – counted from the front of the ranks, while a second guard counted from the rear. At the end they compared totals. If all was well they moved on. If not they scanned that hut carefully and counted again. Another guard went into each hut to count those who remained *'krank im zimmer'* (sick in bed). Once all the huts had been counted and the totals agreed, the count was taken to the *Ost Lageroffizier* (East Compound Officer in Charge), Hauptmann (Captain) Hellfachs who stood, with his assistant, facing the British compound adjutant and his assistant. If all was well, the *Lageroffizier* permitted the parade to be dismissed. If all was not well, the parade could continue for some time as a recount commenced; not a bad thing in the summer, but in the winter it could make for a long, cold morning.[8]

With *Appell* over, the daily tedium of passing time began, which could be a difficult prospect. East Compound had become something of a backwater, even by PoW camp standards. The compound seemed stifling and old, most especially to those there for a second time. The tall fir trees that blocked any view; the wire and the wooden fence separating East from Centre Compound; the dirty *Vorlager*; all did their part to create just the impression that the Germans intended: that of isolation. There was plenty of activity; almost 800 prisoners were now in the compound. But the mood of the previous summer had changed and much of the character of the compound had been dissipated. No longer was escape activity as maniacal as it once had been. Many of the leading escape leaders of summer 1942 had managed to be transferred to North Compound to work on Roger Bushell's scheme. Additionally, the majority of new prisoners were being placed in North Compound, and the few that arrived in East Compound soon seemed to become affected by the general 'malaise' existing in the compound.

Nevertheless the prisoners sought ways and means of keeping boredom to a minimum and sanity within tolerable levels. Schools had been set up, and classes enthusiastically attended. Many 'Kriegies' were taking postal courses, using qualified persons in the camp to gain credits toward university degrees. Others, intent on making the RAF their post-war career, if possible, studied toward specific service related jobs. The Red Cross provided musical instruments and bands were formed. Quite a nice theatre had been built in Hut 64, and shows were always much anticipated and popular. Among the leading actors some would later become quite famous; they included Lieutenant Commander Peter Butterworth, RN; Flight Lieutenant Talbot Rothwell, and Sub Lieutenant Rupert Davies, RN. Even Philpot and Bill Williams became involved, painting and shifting scenery and generally lending a hand.

There were also languages to be learned. Virtually every common European nationality could be found in the camp, and many of those men were more than willing to teach their native tongue; some even going so far as to teach languages they themselves had learned as a second. A reading room/library had been set up in the end room of the cookhouse, shared by the 'Food Acco' (food bartering system) in the mornings, making it a popular place to spend time during inclement weather, but usually only used by Dean & Dawson in the fine weather. Discussion groups abounded, and lectures on almost any subject could be heard.

And there were sports on a large scale, during which the 'fitness wallahs' exercised control over the compound. Physical fitness classes met mornings and evenings; groups regularly jogged around the circuit; a set of parallel bars was supplied; rugby football was *very* popular, as was five-a-side ice hockey on the flooded and frozen football pitch in the winter. There was a basketball court of sorts, and a baseball diamond had been laid out by the Americans and Canadians. When Group Captain Kellett received a golf club in a personal parcel, he made a ball which he was soon pitching into tree stump holes. Soon after, the Stalag Luft III 'Pro Club' was founded and a nine-hole golf course would eventually be laid out around the camp, with smooth, sandy 'browns' in place of finely mown greens. All in all, the compound could be a busy place.

Still, for many, the wire could not be ignored, no matter what classes were offered, no matter what sport there was enjoy. It was always there as a reminder that they were not free; that the war and the world was moving on without them. It encircled more than just their lives; it encircled their spirits, and it would not let go. For these, escape was their only remedy.

Bill White's tunnel from the washhouse in the north *Abort* was discovered on the 26th, after some twelve weeks of intense digging. Feldwebel Stuhlmeyer had been seen one day to come and stand in the doorway of the hut during the morning cleaning and had apparently stared hard at the clean, concrete and brick floor for some time; fists jammed on his hips and a brooding frown on his face. The next morning the 'Ferrets' had descended, thrown everyone out of the hut, brought in the fire engine and sprayed a hose over the floor. Stuhlmeyer, watching carefully, quickly noticed that the jet of water had dissolved the sand

and soap filling hiding the crack around the edge of the trap door and the entrance to the tunnel was discovered.

At first, no one had been able to figure out why Stuhlmeyer had suspected the washhouse in the first place, as tunnel security had been very good. Had it been the sound detectors that had given the effort away, or had it been something else? Then, through the 'tame' guards, word filtered in: There were eighteen RAF and British Army NCOs that came into the compound on orderly duties to look after some of the officer's general needs, and one of their tasks was to keep clean the meager communal wash areas in the *Aborts*. They naturally knew about the tunnel and made every effort to ensure that there was no tunnel sand left on the floor around the trap. However they had apparently kept the floor *too* clean, which had attracted the attention of the ever suspicious Stuhlmeyer.

Few had believed the tunnel had stood much of a chance anyway as the distance to be dug was nearly 150ft; from the washhouse across that portion of the compound toward the wire, then under the circuit, the warning wire then the warning strip to the main wire. Then, under both fences the sentry path and the road that ran along that side of the compound, and into the trees beyond. Though he had chosen a building as close to the wire as any, for White's attempt it was the same old story; digging a tunnel that far would take too long, allowing the Germans ample time to discover the scheme. The longer it took, the more the odds turned against the success of any tunnel.

Oliver Philpot surveyed the loss of this latest bid for freedom with little more than a morose familiarity. True, it was another effort foiled; another disappointment to endure. He had been a prisoner for nearly a year and a half and despite his efforts to extricate himself from the situation he had been far from successful.

However, over the several weeks of effort in the 'sandpit of Sagan', his own attitude toward escape had markedly improved, thanks in large part to 'Jon Jorgenson'. Now, no longer did he view escape as an abstract idea that *may* work. Instead, since his return to the dreaded place he had somehow become inexplicably convinced that he *would* indeed get out of the compound, and went to bed each night repeating to himself, 'I am *going* to escape from this camp; I am *going* to escape from this camp; I am *going* to escape from this camp …' Now, with 'Jon Jorgenson' as his 'travelling partner', at night he dreampt not of the stifling hold the camp had on him, but of making his bid for freedom. And for the first time as a prisoner he now felt that he had a better than average chance of even achieving a 'home run'.

Now all he needed was an original idea to make his escape.

Chapter 7

Inspiration

June 1943

Sagan lies on the Silesian plain, which has a climate strongly influenced by the area of lowland topography in that part of Europe; namely a long corridor that stretches from France to the Ukraine. Air masses from the Atlantic or North Sea, unchecked by any natural barriers, move quickly into the area creating a mainly moderate climate with both maritime and continental elements. This is due to humid Atlantic air colliding over the plain with dry air from the Eurasian interior. Generally, in the warmer months this causes lower level winds to blow in from the west, mainly emanating from the area stretching between Scandinavia and what is now the Czech Republic. These winds are typically weak to moderate in strength. However, with such a diversified regional topography. In Silesia it is also not unknown for local winds, some of which can be strong, to develop. It was just such a local weather phenomena that helped trigger a brief moment of inspiration for one prisoner on a hot summer day in 1943.

A pleasant May gave way to a positively searing June, and the talk of East Compound that month was of an escape attempt made from the North Compound. On 10 June, the Escape Committee had faked an infestation of lice, necessitating the movement of groups of prisoners over to the 'delousing' shed in the East Compound *Vorlager*. The first group arrived at the gate, just after a change of guards, led by two prisoners dressed in fake Luftwaffe uniforms and carrying forged gate passes. Everyone held their breath for a few moments until – sure enough – they were allowed through and began walking down the road toward the 'delousing' shed. Once out of sight of the German guards however, they all dispersed into the forest and were off and running. Unfortunately, the alarm was raised within the hour, and though nobody was successful in getting home (all were either back at Sagan or sent away to other camps within a week), it had been a tremendous morale booster for the whole of the camp.

Once the fervour of that escape had died down however, everything quickly reverted to normal camp activity. The advent of warmer weather had brought the prisoners out of their huts in force, and outdoor activity of all kinds was flourishing. New gardens were started, while older ones were expanded. Sun bathing became the fashion, with plenty of pale, white skin quickly turning red, while education classes were moved out into the sunshine. By far however the greatest expansion in activity in the fresh warmth was for exercise, and certainly the leading light in all that physical activity was Flight Lieutenant John Stevens, who led a morning exercise class, every day, rain or shine.[1]

Over the compound the early summer heat was draping itself like a heavy blanket, a portent of another scorching Silesian summer day. Following *Appell*, Codner and Williams were out on the circuit walking, as was their usual morning routine. They wore 'Kriegie' summer attire: Codner a pair of ragged, blue-stripped pyjama bottoms cut-off at the knees, a pair of socks, and desert boots. His book of Latin verse was under his arm, which he had been reading at *Appell*. Williams wore shorts cut down from a pair of airman's old trousers and nothing else, his paunch far less noticeable now. They had both been prisoners for six months – three at Schubin and three at Sagan – and they both had agreed that that was quite long enough. As was usual, escape was their main topic of conversation.

Bill White's tunnel had been discovered just weeks before; neither had held much hope for his effort. They both had long since come to the conclusion that any successful tunnel needed to be short, dug by a small work force, started somewhere close to the wire where the distance to dig was the least it could be, and with a fool-proof entry trap. Nearly everyone else in the camp that had an interest in escape had long ago also come to the same conclusion.

But where was a good starting place for any tunnel? White had logically chosen the hut nearest the wire and had cut as good an entry trap as any previous attempt. What other options were there? They had discussed the escape subject with Philpot at length, since he was an 'established' prisoner and had been in East Compound during that golden summer of 1942. They had listened at length as he told them all about those efforts he cared to remember. But none of the old ideas had held any interest for them except two: the failed 'accordion attempt' Philpot had been involved with, where the crowd had gathered around the accordion player while a prisoner tried to dig a hole in the middle of the group; and the ingenious and successful Lamond/Best/Goldfinch attempt (although it was frightening). Now *there* were two original ideas! However, the accordion attempt could not possibly be tried again, as the Germans would surely immediately realize what was happening. As they had agreed several times before, the 'mole' idea was ingenious and might certainly be tried again, but from where? What they needed was some sort of new and fresh location from where to dig the initial stretch of tunnel.

They let their imaginations wander as they continued walking around the circuit … 992 paces … then another 992. A person could walk the circuit until he was numb and never get anywhere, in thought or in deed.

A location inside the compound was required, nearer the wire than even the Lamond/Best/Goldfinch attempt. That would be just the ticket! The distance to dig would be less than half of that from a hut. However, the compound was flat and open; a dusty expanse, unbroken by any object or obstruction. They walked on morosely. They were getting exactly where they had every other time they discussed the topic – nowhere.

Passing by the football pitch on the *Sportzplatz*, the exercise class was getting into full swing, and the two watched the 'physical jerks wallahs' as they slowly trudged through the rising heat of the day. The class was all lining up to play leapfrog, and all looked happy and content to be doing something.

Overhead the sky was clear, but in the distance clouds could be seen rolling toward the camp, bringing the rain that would quickly turn the dark-grey dust of the compound into a sea of sticky, thick mud that clung to everything. Because of it, the floor in their room would be dusty for days after the mud dried and was brushed out; the fine, hated Sagan dust that got into everything.

A gust of breeze picked up, gently cooling the camp and in the distance, to the south of the compound, the tops of the tall Silesian pines of the surrounding forest began to bend under the pressure of a strong wind. Anyone who had previously spent a summer at Sagan knew this was a sign of worse weather soon to come; there was a 'good blow' on the way.

Williams and Codner both noticed it at the same time, even as the fine dust began to whip the air around them. The flag over in the *Vorlager* flew, fully displaying the Nazi emblem and suddenly people were tumbling out of huts and snatching at laundry hanging on improvised lines outside, while sunbathers gathered up their meagre personal items and ran for their rooms. Others were slamming windows shut as the camp came positively alive with activity. Williams suddenly realized that he had left a pile of his drawings loose on the table in their room with the window open and rushed to the hut. The exercise class was quickly dispersing and Codner retreated behind a hut, shielding his eyes from the dust and sand whipping all around and stinging his bare legs. The wind was moaning through the wire and the guards in the boxes stepped further back into them, or slid the windows on the windward side shut. The temptation to rush the wire while the guards had momentarily dropped their attention was strong, but fleeting.

It was quickly over. Soon there was just a residue of fine dust hanging in the sunshine as the camp slowly settled back down to its normal midday routine. Stepping out from behind the hut where he had taken shelter, Codner noticed a stray piece of German newspaper flitting about on the gentle breezes still blowing across the compound. The light breeze snatched at it and it began to spiral upwards and finally over the fence and away toward the gaunt pines to the east. His thoughts wandered with it, even as he had to squint to watch as the paper finally disappeared over the tops of the pines. How grand it would be to float away from the wretched camp like that piece of paper! To be able to float up and away; just like Pegasus in the classic story he was reading in his book.

He imagined Pegasus winging his way down into the camp and prisoners lining up for a lift over the wire and away. Yes, that is what they needed: a true 'flight of fancy' to solve their problem of escape. And it was then that inspiration struck.[2]

That would certainly be ideal, would it not? Line up the prisoners to be lifted over the wire, just like the line queued up for the game of leapfrog played by Steven's hearty followers. A glance in that direction showed that the area of the *Sportzplatz* where they had done their leaping exercise was now bare.

Games, just like those at school; cricket, rugby, and when they would spring over the vaulting horse in gymastics class. That had certainly been great fun! He saw the vaulting horse they had used in his mind's eye; heard again the hollow 'thump' made when a foot knocked against the side, and the resounding 'crash' when someone had a hard landing.

An empty vaulting horse – not unlike the 'Trojan Horse' in the classic tale. Now *there* was a cracking story! The Greeks certainly outwitted the Trojans, did they not? A brilliant idea; hiding within a hollow wooden horse.

A vaulting horse! That was it!

Then suddenly he was off running across the compound in the direction of their room. He finally had it: the new idea he and Williams had been seeking.

The midday was calm and still and a quiet tranquility – the rarest of all things in a prison camp – lay over the sweltering room. Within that warm stillness, the lone figure of Oliver Philpot lay dozing in his shaded bunk. Through the open window, an occasional hot breeze wafted at a copy of the *Volkischer Beobachter*, still spread out on the table at which he had been reading it earlier, and a few flies buzzed lethargically around. Otherwise, all else was quiet and peaceful.

The sound of pounding feet in the corridor first threatened that peace, followed by the door to the room banging violently open, which shattered it altogether.

'Come on, Ollie! Wake up! We've an idea to tell you about!' Williams stood next to the bunk, positively beaming, Codner behind him.

'Oh go away, Bill. It's far too hot.' Philpot tried to doze off again.

'Come off that bunk Ollie! We're going to get out of here!'

'Oh, I've heard that before!'

'Come on Ollie; you're Little X for our hut! It's your *duty*. Come on for a turn round the circuit!'

'Oh, alright, damn you. I'll come round the circuit with you,' Philpot said and, relenting, lurched off the bed.

On the circuit in the sunshine, and out of earshot of any listening 'Goons', Philpot demanded to know what the fuss was all about.

'We're going to get out of here, and we want the committee's help,' Codner began. 'Tell us about that 'mole' effort from 1942 again.'

Philpot sketched out the bare details of the scheme and asked again what the fuss was all about. Williams was almost dancing by then and Codner could not conceal a huge, apparently permanent grin.

'Now, Ollie, how did the ancients move men around surreptitiously?' asked with all the authority of a university professor.

'What? the ancients? What *are* you two on about?' Philpot replied.

'Yes, the ancients. The Greeks, how did they move men about?' Williams beamed.

Philpot ventured that he supposed they were referring to the wooden horse of Troy. But what could some thing as big as a hut have to do with escape? The Greeks had used the beast to get *into* a place – not *out*.

'Do not worry about the direction; it's the principle of the thing, old man! It's the principle! Concentrate on that!' Codner said, barely containing his obvious excitement while still assuming an academic manner.

'What Mike is going on about,' Williams said, 'is this …' and Philpot listened, silently and slightly bemused, as the two excitedly sketched out the initial bare details of their idea.

They would build a vaulting horse, like those they had back at school, made of wood and with covered sides extending down to the ground. Then they should carry it each day to a set spot out on the *Sportzplatz*, close to the wire – with one of them inside. He would dig a tunnel from underneath the horse while the other chap held vaulting classes outside to complete the charade. In the end, the trap door to the tunnel would be solidly boarded over and covered with sand. The spoil would be carried back inside with the digger to wherever the vaulting horse would be stored, and be disposed of later. Once they had dug a certain distance, they could 'mole' out the rest of the way.

Philpot listened pessimistically and silently until they were finished. Pessimism was not just part of his attitude toward escape after a year and a half as a prisoner, but a part of his duty as 'Little X'; it was his job to separate the truly original schemes from the crackpot ideas. Concerning the project proposed by the two grinning officers before him, there were several sides and he had to admit that it had a lot going for it at first glance. It would be a relatively simple plan and a quick one to achieve, with such a greatly shortened distance to dig compared to a conventional tunnel. It was also bold, and boldness often played a big part in success, especially where escape was concerned.

On the other hand, audacious though it was, it could not work; it simply *could not*. The Germans were bound to stumble onto the idea before long. One could not expect that they could be fooled by a mere box for any reasonable length of time, especially when some of the best escape minds in camp had had produced some of the very best in trap doors in the past and been discovered. Now here were two relatively new boys – both of whom had almost driven the

Schubin escapers crazy with questions – with such a simple proposal. No, it did not really stand a hope.

Nor did Philpot realize that, unbeknown to any of them that day, the idea was not exactly an original one, or that it had already failed in the past. The year before, in the summer of 1942 at Warburg, the idea had already been thought up and attempted by an Australian army officer, Lieutenant Jack Millett, who had been captured during the fall of Crete. Millett, along with two others, had built a vaulting horse of their own, much the same as Williams and Codner were now proposing. This they had carried out to an open area in the camp that was used as a ice-hockey rink in the winter, and the other two dug under it while Millett conducted exercise classes. However, Millett was a known escaper to the Germans and had, in fact, not long before been among those working on a tunnel from his own hut which the Germans had discovered through sound detectors they had buried around the wire; something the prisoners had not been aware of until that time. When the guards had seen Millett involved in something out of the ordinary, they immediately suspected trouble, pounced, and the trio were caught red handed – and sentenced to an appropriate time in the 'Cooler'.

However, that effort had been at a Wehrmacht camp, where there had been few RAF officers. And what few RAF men that had been there that year were now mostly in North Compound when Codner had his brainstorm. Therefore the scheme had not been heard of and recorded by the Escape Committee in East Compound, even if those RAF officers that had been at Warburg had even been aware of Millett's effort. Nor did Wehrmacht camp officials often share information with the Luftwaffe, with the result that the *Abwehr* staff at Stalag Luft III also had never heard the story. Thus the idea would of course seem a fresh one, and had a lot going for it in the originality department when original ideas were at a premium in East Compound.

But, as stated, all of this was unknown to the three men as Codner and Williams at last fell silent. Then, after a short pause, Philpot looked into their expectant, excited faces … and laughed. The scheme had not a chance in hell; not a chance and, grinning, he recalled to them how something similar had been tried the previous summer when someone had built a wide deck chair with an attached table out of wood from a Red Cross packing crate and had tried to start a tunnel from under that; an effort that had ended almost as quickly as it had begun. Then there had also been the accordion stunt, which Codner and Williams now assured him had been part of the initial inspiration for their current idea. They again insisted it was foolproof and only needed a slight push from the committee.

Philpot wanted next to know what they would do for a vaulting horse; something the Germans were unlikely to provide. Codner interjected that they had already given it some thought and were reasonably sure that they could knock one together with little trouble. There were plenty of amateur carpenters in the camp, and Williams was on the scenery committee for the theatre, which might give them access to materials.

Philpot thought more, trying to come up with all the questions the Escape Committee might ask. They were not likely to approve the idea in any case – it was too far-fetched to actually amount to anything – but better to have all the facts together (such as they were) well ahead of time.

What time frame were they expecting the project to take, he asked? Codner reckoned somewhere in the neighborhood of three weeks, if all went well. Philpot snorted. More like three months! Williams interjected the possibility of doing a 'mole' as an option, which would put the time frame closer to 36 hours, and the three then got into a discussion about the effort and danger of doing a 'mole', as well as the hundred other details that would need attending to along the way. Impatiently the two urged Philpot to take the idea to the committee straight away, before it was lost to some other imaginative soul, but he kept up the tough questions a while longer. Nevertheless, in the end he agreed to present the idea, but warned the two not to get their hopes up. 'Actually, I thought they were crackers,' he later admitted, and told them that, if approved, he gave it no more than a couple days. However, he would let them know the committee's decision as soon as he could, and with that the meeting broke up as Philpot headed over to visit the compound 'Big X'.

In the oppressive heat he ambled into Hut 66, where he found Joe Kayll and 'Dud' Craig lying uncomfortably on their respective bunks in the fly infested oven of a room, talking. Neither showed much inclination to get up when he entered, though both did roll over onto one elbow as he presented the basic idea.

There was a short pause and then Kayll broke the silence saying tiredly, 'You're joking.' Philpot assured him he was not, and Kayll and Craig traded looks as they let the idea sink in a little. Though it seemed to Philpot otherwise, Kayll would later state that initially he actually thought the idea was a good one, but was sorry it had been thought up by two men such as Williams and Codner. It was not anything personal against the two, but Kayll was a 'Warburger' and a well-experienced escaper. To him the two were just young bucks; not part of the popular escape class and therefore amounting to less in his venerated 'Kriegie' eyes.

Further, it was Escape Committee policy to allow the initiators of an idea to have the lead on the project, and Williams and Codner – being such new boys – had now come up with the sort of scheme one would expect from an experienced escaper, without having had to pay any real dues as prisoners first. Six months in the camp was nothing to a man who had been a prisoner for over two years, and spent much of that time involved with escape. In short, it was because he and the other serious escapers in the camp held themselves in a class above the new boys that produced a certain amount of concern at the idea necessarily being left in the hands of Williams and Codner; totally inexperienced men, who in committee eyes would probably take a decent idea and make a complete mess of it, when such ideas did not come around all too often anymore.

But rules were rules, and as such the scheme belonged to Williams and Codner, no matter how much the Escape Committee might wish it otherwise. And as it did stand a chance, Kayll was willing to listen.

'But it'll never come off.' 'Dud' Craig interjected. 'The 'Goons' are not mad; the 'Ferrets' weren't born yesterday, you know!'

But Kayll persisted. 'Well, what goes on now?' he said, and Craig gave him the details.

'Well there's Tommy Calnan, who's got something going in the *Vorlager*, but we haven't heard too much about that. And someone registered to try going out on top of the laundry van, trying that one again, but they never seem to be going.'

'Well then, there's not too much going then, is there?' Kayll mused. 'And there's got to be something going … Tell these two jokers we'll back them to the hilt – provided they supply the vaulting horse.'[3]

The rest of the meeting was short. Once the horse was ready, the committee would meet with the two would-be escapers and listen to the finalized plan in order to find out what they might need. And since it fell under Philpot's authority as 'Little X' in their hut, he would be the committee representative on the scheme, lending an official hand in whatever way needed – which was likely to be a big job, what with two inexperienced men leading the project. He was also given permission to tell Williams and Codner the bare essentials of the operations over in North Compound, but to also strongly warn them to keep the information exceptionally quiet. In the meantime, word of the scheme would be passed to the Escape Committee over there.

Philpot found the two would-be vaulting enthusiasts in conversation about the scheme and told them they had the initial permission from the committee. Excited, they set to work to put their plan in motion. Where to get the materials – that was the first question. Williams and Codner walked the circuit that afternoon examining options. The first, and most important, element was strong timber for the framework and nails. Oddly, it was the Germans that provided a direct answer to the question. About midway along the line of the western fence, the Germans intended to build a bath house, with shower facilities and wash basins, to augment the inadequate amenities of the two existing *Aborts*. However intentions and actions were two different things to the Germans where the prisoners were concerned, and while the work had been started and much of the building materials were stacked and waiting, it was far from finished. To prevent enterprising prisoners from looting the site, rather than complete the project, they had instead ringed it with barbed wire. Within were the solutions to their every requirement. Seeing this as they walked the circuit, they immediately decided to rob the works site.

They arranged with the irrepressible Tommy Calnan to occupy the two guard dogs that the *Hundeführer* allowed out to roam the compound at night (which cost them both their share of the meat ration from the Red Cross food supplies for a week), the two would-be burglars slipped out through a trap door in the floor of their hut long after dark the next night and carefully made their way to the site. Slipping under the wire, they moved fast and quietly found all they needed and more, including a fine, small brick layers trowel for digging. Their pockets filled with nails, and dragging several 5ft long sections of 2in by 3in roofing rafter along with them, they slipped back under their hut, where they buried the wood until they could begin construction.

The next day, Williams went in search of help with building the horse, and headed over to see Pilot Officer Kenneth 'Digger' McIntosh, the carpenter for the theatre. McIntosh listened to their scheme but could not let Williams use his tools to build the horse however, as they had been supplied by the Germans for theatre use only and the agreement needed to be honoured on an officer's word. But he did suggest that Williams go see Wing Commander Maw in Hut 64, who had his own collection of illicit tools.[4, 5]

Williams immediately went to Hut 64, where he found the Wing Commander in one of the larger end rooms. Maw was hut commander, as well as 'Little X'. He was also an avid amateur engineer and was always building, creating, or 'bashing' something. To that end, his room was a litter of old tins, Red Cross boxes (some full of 'stuff' and some empty), bits of wire and string, broken bed boards, and a hundred and one other items. When Williams knocked on the door, on which was pinned a cartoon of a prisoner digging a hole in his cell, and entered he found Maw working on installing a hand operated air-conditioning system he had designed.

Williams introduced himself to Maw, a small, older man with a huge 'Bomber Command'-style moustache, and explained how he had been referred to him by McIntosh and what it was that he wanted. He detailed the whole scheme to the Wing Commander, as far as he and Codner had worked out at that point, and Maw, immediately interested, listened keenly before pinning a clean piece of drawing paper to a home-built drawing table under the light of the room window. It would need to be large enough to carry a man, but not so large that it could not be easily carried. Also the framework would need to be extremely sturdy in order to carry both the weight of the man and the spoil from the tunnel. Now, *here* was a problem worthy of his attention and, smiling like a conspirator, Maw leaned over the paper and got to work.

Meanwhile, Codner approached John Stevens, the South African bomber pilot that led the morning exercise classes, about organizing a 'vaulting class' for them. Out on the circuit, Codner filled him in on the whole scheme and found

Stevens, a dedicated escaper himself, intrigued by the idea and enthusiastic and agreeable from the start. Later that day, the two men went round the compound and pinned enrolment forms to several bulletin boards advertising the new vaulting class. The immediate response was not exactly overwhelming, so over the next few days Stevens, Codner and Williams, began making the rounds of every room in camp until, by the time the horse was finished a few days later, they had firm commitments from some sixteen or so fellow inmates.

One of the first to sign up was Pilot Officer Thomas Wilson, a navigator fom a Vickers Wellington who had been shot down near The Hague. Wilson came to Sagan at the end of May, kicking himself for not having evaded capture while in Holland, and determined to do something about that, looking almost immediately for a way into the escaping class. He did not have long to wait. 'Within a week Bill Williams came round asking for volunteers to vault over his wooden horse, under which a tunnel was to be dug ... Bill made it clear that only two were booked to make the escape. There was no hope that any of us vaulters would get out. That did not make any difference to me; I only needed to show future plotters that I was available and reliable.'[6]

Wilson had no idea the important part he would play in the scheme.

Dedication and focus did not come easy in prison camp. Men quickly latched on to an idea or scheme, only to abandon it just as quickly. Education classes that were offered and taught by other prisoners in various subjects were attacked with fervour for a few weeks before interest began to wane and then completely disappeared. With little directional guidance or real sense of purpose, life had a tendency to pass slowly by in the camp and time became unnoticed, spent frivolously on first one undertaking and then another as an individual's impulses rose and fell.

Therefore it was with no small measure of surprise to those who were initially aware of the scheme (Philpot included) when, the day after stealing the supplies from the washhouse site, Williams and Codner began working on the vaulting horse in earnest. They set up a 'workshop' in the cookhouse canteen following *Appell* that morning and, with Wing Commander Maw assisted by Squadron Leader 'Jimmie' Sargeaunt and Flight Lieutenant Douglas Cooper, before afternoon *Appell* that day they had much of the framework completed. They had worked out a security system ahead of time to cover the noise of their work, as they were using Maw's saw and hammer (among the very few proper tools available in East Compound) being extremely careful to only work when they were informed that any Germans were out of earshot.

The canteen where they were now working was not really a canteen at all, but just a large room in the hut that housed the compound kitchen and an office for the 'Kitchen Goon' on the north end, and a room on the south end used as a reading room, library, and 'Foodacco'. In the centre, there was a large kitchen storage room along the north end of the east side, where the potato and

German bread issue for the compound was kept. A barber shop was set up in a room along a section of the south-east side. The large room along the west side was the canteen which was almost empty, except for a battered old upright piano. The room was used mostly for lectures and classroom instruction, as well as by the East Compound band as a practice area. It was entered at one end through a single door in the west side of the hut, and from the other end through a short corridor next to the barber's shop which led to a pair of double doors in the east side of the hut. The room not only made a perfect workshop, giving plenty of room to Maw and his team to construct the horse, but also a perfect place to store it once completed, out of the way in the corridor near the double doors.[7]

For the sides of the horse, they used three-ply wooden sheets from Canadian Red Cross parcel containers. These they had been supplied by 'Rackets' Marsh, who had made sure that the timber would conveniently be available to be 'stolen' from the parcels area by Wing Commander Maw one afternoon. The next day they carefully cut and fitted all the plywood covering and made the long carrying poles. Most of the nails used for the covering had been pulled from the walls of the huts.

All had gone well and they had worked happy and undisturbed, save for the occasional prisoner, curious at all the noise. Then, on the last afternoon of construction, as they were sewing the Turkish Cotton cloth cover over the straw padding for the top (taken from the bales that the Turkish Red Cross shipped cigarettes in, and again obtained clandestinely through 'Rackets' Marsh), 'Charlie' the chief 'Ferret' wandered in to check on their progress.

His real name was Karl Piltz, but he was known to the prisoners as 'Charlie', and was the most dangerous German in East Compound. He was a tall, lean man from Hanover, who wore a seemingly permanent sombre expression on his sallow face. Piltz was an Unteroffizier (Corporal) in the *Abwehr* department of camp and one of the most aware that the Germans had at Sagan. He had once been a Social Democrat in the early days of the Reich, but nine months spent being 're-educated' in a Nazi prison had quickly changed his mind. Now he was a devoted Nazi follower and decidedly anti-British. Everyone in camp knew 'Charlie' by sight, and, whenever he was around, he posed a great danger to all escape activity.

He had been one of the first of the new *Abwehr* force that the Germans had put together in the days when Stalag Luft I at Barth was the only air force camp in Germany and the RAF prisoners there were giving their Luftwaffe guards so much trouble. While at Barth, Pilot Officer Vincent 'Bush' Parker, an Australian Spitfire pilot who bore a passing resemblance to 'Charlie', once escaped by impersonating him, only to come face-to-face with the real 'Charlie' just outside the gate. It was perhaps his time at Barth, which made him so very, very good at his job. He spent most of his duty time, as well as much of his off-duty time, in and around the compound, taking in everything and letting nothing new or unusual go unnoticed. He had a habit in off-duty hours of playing with the puppies brought in to be trained as guard dogs and would walk them around the perimeter of the camp outside the wire, his watchful eye noting everything from different view points along the way.

Yet he was a very human enemy too, despite his almost manic anti-British attitude. He had the ability that not many guards had of being able to overlook some of the small infractions of the rules in an effort to keep a greater peace with the prisoners, no doubt to help keep them as quiet as possible. He took great pride in his uncanny ability to sniff out even the best camouflaged of tunnels and was a great admirer of the prisoner's ingenuity. He kept a small escape museum of photographs of tunnels he had found, as well as escape items made by the prisoners that fell into his hands. A good tunnel received his great admiration, but a poor or amateurish one brought his scornful condemnation. His personal adversary in camp was Tommy Calnan, for whose escaping intellect he had the greatest respect. Calnan described him as, 'the cleverest … of the German *Abwehr* staff. He could smell a tunnel from a hundred yards away and had a nasty criminal mind which worked on exactly the same wave-length as any escaper's. Charlie was a menace.'

'Charlie' had, of course, been keeping note on the progress of the construction of the vaulting horse; nothing in the compound escaped his attention, especially something as unusual as a vaulting horse. It was not uncommon for the prisoners to build items and, in fact, one of the more popular made with wood from Red Cross parcels, to which 'Charlie' and the other 'Goons' frequently turned a blind eye, was a comfortable type of deck chair. Nor was it unusual for the prisoners to take part in physical sports; in fact, it was encouraged by the Germans. Now, watching Williams and Codner at work, 'Charlie' was even openhanded enough to sidestep the question of where the wood and nails for the framework had come from, although it must have been blatantly obvious. After all, busy 'Kriegies' – be they building a vaulting horse or using it – made for happy 'Kriegies', and happy 'Kriegies' did not try to escape. He walked around the horse, eyeing it professionally, and then patted the top with a smile. *'Ja, das ist ein gutes Pferd zum springen, nicht wahr?'* (Yes, this is a good horse to jump, indeed?)

Williams and Codner agreed, if somewhat warily; it was indeed a good horse for jumping over. 'Charlie' must come and join them some time, they said. But the wily 'Ferret' gave no indication of planning on participating, although both of the would-be escapers knew all too well that he would definitely be a part of the programme.

When they had finished, they had a sturdy piece of exercise equipment that was 4ft 6in high and covered an area of 5ft long by 3ft wide. The sides tapered towards the top, where the width was reduced to around 18in. The padded top had been sewn together and then tacked into place. The plywood panels on the sides covered an individual area of just under 2sq ft each, and the beading, surreptitiously removed from the walls of one of the huts, was used as bracing. Four slots had been cut in the sides, one at each corner, that were 4in long by 3in wide through which the carrying poles were slid. These were some 6ft long had been made from the same rafter material as the framework of the horse. When slid into place, from one side through to the other, four men carried the horse with ease 'in the manner of a sedan chair', as Williams himself later stated. They left the horse unpainted, since there was no paint available, leaving it unmarked except for the Red Cross shipping symbols stencilled on the wood. It was decided that the policy would be to never leave the horse outside when not in use but to bring it back into the corridor of the canteen after each vaulting session ostensibly to protect it from the weather.[8]

When the horse had been nearly completed, the SBO sent Philpot to bring Williams and Codner before the Escape Committee to explain their idea in full. At the meeting with the committee that day, Codner laid out the plan in as much detail as he and Williams could. They would carry the horse out to an open spot near the northern goal post on the football pitch along the eastern side of the compound, just west of the circuit. A man would be carried out inside the horse and a shaft would be sunk, with the trapdoor some 18 to 24in below ground. From there the tunnel would go out under the eastern wire, eventually to surface several feet beyond the sentry's path in a shallow ditch that ran next to the road, which was shadowed at night from the perimeter arc lamps. The distance to dig was only some 100ft or so and they were considering the possibilities of 'moling' part, if not all, of the distance. In any case, they would dig the tunnel only 2 to 3ft below the surface and use the pine root layer as shoring for the roof, just as in the Lamond/Best/Goldfinch attempt. They would use wooden shoring the first few feet however, to prevent damage to the tunnel from the vibrations of the vaulter's tread and the circuit walkers. At the end of each session, a strong trap door made from bedboards would be replaced and buried carefully over, so as to leave no trace of activity under the horse. The spoil from the tunnel would then be carried back in with the man inside the horse at the end of each session. With luck and hard work, they had figured they would be out in around three weeks, perhaps four, if they tunnelled the entire way. Far less if they dug using the 'mole' method. They had volunteers who had agreed to do the vaulting. What they needed now was the approval of the committee.

The meeting was short after Williams and Codner finished their explanation. It was clear that no one believed they would get away with it, and most committee members expressed that view. There just did not seem to be any way to keep it hidden from 'Charlie'. The odds were decidedly against them but, as when first presented to Kayll, since there were no current schemes in progress, and seeing as they had actually constructed a vaulting horse, official permission was given and with the full backing of the escape committee. Philpot would be their liaison, with orders to assist in every way possible. Most went away from the meeting feeling at the very least the effort might offer some light relief until discovered. Williams and Codner were elated; convinced they were as good as out. Philpot went away feeling as if he had been saddled with a cumbersome burden likely to produce – nothing.

For some weeks the compound had been preparing for a 'gymkhana', scheduled for Wednesday, 30 June. The morning was to be filled with rugby football and other events while the culmination, in the afternoon, was to be a series in the 100yd and 220yd sprints, pitting an RAF (New Zealand) Pilot Officer against a Maori army Private who worked in the camp as an orderly. Both were favourites. It proved to be a grand event and nearly the entire compound was on hand to see the exciting finish with the Maori who (unknown to all had raced for his country in the Olympics), went on to win the final sprint.

Codner and Williams were no exception, standing a little way off the finish line, which was very near the northern goal post, encouraging everyone there to scuff up the sand as much as possible in a certain area. People obliged and by the time the racing was over, the section of ground just outside the canteen doors that had interested them was completely churned up.

Chapter 8

First Steps

July 1943

The day after the 'gymkhana', at just before 2.00pm on July 1, a group of men from the exercise class, along with a few other recruits, wandered over with Williams and Codner to the canteen. A short while later the double doors on the east side of the building burst open to reveal four men carrying the wooden horse out, followed by the rest of the men of the new vaulting group. They carried the horse toward the east side of the compound, just north of the football pitch; the four carriers staggered around a little under the 'weight', giving the appearance that they were struggling. Setting the horse down in the centre of the area churned up the previous day, Stevens then held a brief meeting with all the gathered 'gymnasts'.

General activity in the camp stopped and all eyes turned toward the unusual spectacle, including the Germans. In moments the 'Goons' in the three guard towers overlooking the football pitch had their field glasses watching the procession, with the nearest immediately on the telephone to the *Abwehr* department in the *Kommandantur*; the 'mad' English were up to something unusual. Within minutes 'Charlie' and his No.2 man, 'Lofty', as well as two other 'Ferrets' on duty that day, came rushing in. Pilot Officer Don Elliot, a Canadian shot down over Cologne that April, remembered, 'Of course when it was brought out [the 'Goons'] were very suspicious, and they had a 'Ferret' over there looking at it immediately.'

A few hardy souls, under the direction of Stevens, gave a demonstration of vaulting before the class moved back a short distance ready for their attempt. Shirts were removed, and belts tightened around homemade shorts. Virtually no one had gymn shoes and those wearing only issue boots took them off and stood in bare feet. There was much stretching and good natured banter, and Stevens walked over and took a place at one end of the horse; the master of the class. Then, under a hundred pairs of watchful eyes, the vaulting started.

In the July heat, the horse being as high as it was and with no springboard, the vaulting quickly proved a difficult endeavour, even though Stevens was not pushing anyone yet, just calling for easy jumps. Many of the men had not (some never) been near a vaulting horse for some time. Among them had been a few who had been wounded when shot down and were still suffering from their injuries (as was Stevens, some would argue) which did not help matters.

It also proved to be a rather long session – nearly 2½ hours – as Williams and Codner strove to prove the validity of their 'animal'. Tom Wilson later recalled his impressions of that first vaulting session: '['Charlie'] and all the 'Ferrets' on duty stood watching our first session vaulting … We held 'dummy runs' with it for the first week and a half [sic] … He must have realized that 2½ hour vaulting sessions were an enormous demand on our strength, and totally unrealistic as physical exercise.'

But he apparently did not, and the prisoners kept it up as a crowd watched. Those who cleared the horse were greeted with cheers and further encouragement. Those who failed usually had bruised shins to show for it at the least, and were greeted with a chorus of catcalls and criticism. Williams and Codner took part in the vaulting, increasing the number of athletes, though Williams spent a portion of his time standing with Stevens, surreptitiously observing everything and anything. Though some of the crowd had faded away after the first 15 or 20 minutes, the 'Goons' in the towers were still keeping an eye on what was happening, even while they made sure to watch the stretch of wire they were responsible for guarding. They were all very aware that interesting activities in the compound were a favourite diversion of a sentry's attention while illicit activities were being perpetrated. Nor did 'Charlie' or 'Lofty' drift off.

It was quickly apparent who had an aptitude for the vaulting and who did not, and one man in particular seemed especially inept. Don Elliot was a gifted athlete, who should have had no trouble with vaulting. However, as Don recalled, 'For the first week or so … people who were a little bit clumsy, like me, arranged occasionally to knock it over. This was so the 'Ferrets' could see that there was not anything happening inside it.' Now, prepared to charge the horse again and with a grim look of determination on his face, Don set off like a rocket and hooked his foot on the side of the horse, crashing down in a sweaty heap in the sand. The horse was flipped over on its side in full view of at least a half a dozen Germans, most importantly 'Charlie', who practically leapt forward to look at the inside. The bare, interior of the horse was now wide open to all and quite clearly empty.

Amid a chorus of laughter and calls of false sympathy, Elliott was helped to his feet and dusted off while several pairs of hands righted the horse. 'Charlie', himself laughing, came over to where Williams and Stevens were standing and remarked in German that what they needed now was a good springboard. Stevens, who spoke good German, agreed heartily and 'Charlie' wandered off followed by the rest of the 'Ferrets'.[1]

Toward the end of the session, there was a meeting around the horse again before the carrying poles were slipped into their slots and the horse was carried back to the canteen. There it was set down in the corner of the passageway, along with the two carrying poles, and the team dispursed. Once the horse was inside, Williams closed the door and tied a length of black cotton thread across from the upper door jamb, and another from the baseboard of the wall nearest the horse to its lower edge. The two then went to clean up ready for tea, satisfied with good start to the project. Everyone in camp was told to refrain from using those doors for the rest of the day.

The vaulting had gone well, 'Charlie' had accepted the horse as genuine, at least for now, and the rest of the camp seemed to be interested enough to lend the activity the much needed realism the project required. Further, they had demonstrated to the 'Goons' that the horse was empty by tipping it over a number of times. Another week or so and the horse would become a camp institution, at which time they could begin digging.

The next morning when they went to check on the horse following first *Appell*, they found the black threads broken. Obviously 'Charlie' was taking no chances and the horse had been examined overnight – just as they had anticipated (and hoped) it would. It was just one more step toward having the vaulting horse accepted as part of normal camp activity.

After that first day, it all quickly became a matter of routine over the next week. Flying Officer David Codd, from No.35 Squadron who had been shot down that June and was now a resident in the neighbouring Centre Compound, remembered, 'An unusual activity had been taking place in the adjacent East Compound, the main part of which was visible from the Centre Compound over the boundary fence. One day there appeared a wooden vaulting horse which looked as though it had been constructed by the prisoners from Red Cross boxes. Vaulting took place every day for several weeks and it was noticeable that it was always put on the same spot in the compound. After a few days it was obvious to us in Centre Compound that something was afoot. No self-respecting 'Kriegie' would waste his precious energy day after day on such a futile activity.'

On 8 July, the two prospective escapees began the digging operation. That session would largely set the pace for those to follow. Codner went out in the horse just after lunch that day at the now routine schedule of 2.00pm. He had a Red Cross cardboard box containing a kit bag, the stolen brick-layers trowel, three large sacks made from old battledress trouser legs, a large needle and thread, four small pieces of black cloth, and a candle. He also had one sheet of three-ply wood from a Red Cross packing case and four cut down bed boards. At the all-clear from a 'stooge' at the window, the horse was tipped up and he crawled under. Set back down, the carrying poles were slid into place and he pressed his buttocks together while bracing his feet on the bottom framework. Then, steadying himself with one hand while the other held the equipment, he gave the word that he was ready, the horse was lifted up, walked out the door, down the steps, and into the sunshine.

In the compound, Philpot had control of security. After taking a quick walk around the camp to insure the location of all 'Goons' in the compound, he took the 'duty pilot' seat at the window in the north-east corner room of Hut 63, where he could keep an eye on the *Vorlager* for any approaching 'policemen'; the project parlance they had decided upon for the 'Ferrets'. Soon the last 'Ferret' in camp – a lazy character called 'Rudy' by the prisoners – had made his usual unhurried rounds and wandered out the gate. The horse would now be operating in a 'Ferret' free compound and he sent word around to the vaulters.[2]

Acting as instructor (for soon after the formation of the team Stevens had managed a transfer to North Compound in order to work on Roger Bushell's scheme), Williams ran the vaulting just as it had been on any other day, except that it was a landmark as the start of the tunnel, giving the impression of normality.

It was important that the 'Goons' did not notice that the horse seemed heavier than usual due to the extra weight of the digger. They knew it to be actually very light. To that end only the strongest of the vaulters would be allowed to carry it from then on, and then only with one hand. It was difficult getting the carrying poles through the double doors of the canteen with an empty horse, let alone the full one, and this was made more so by the attempt to make it look effortless. From there it was a careful trip down the three wooden steps into the compound, keeping the horse low so no one might accidentally catch a glimpse under it, and then over to the vaulting spot. The horse had been carefully and repeatedly positioned in the same place over the first few days of vaulting so there was little problem getting it right anymore; north and east of the northern football goal post, lined up directly with one of the poles of the fence line and in the corner of two soft patches of loose ground that had been turned over, ostensibly to soften landing for the vaulters, some 30ft in from the circuit. Once the horse was on the ground, the digger immediately got off the framework and the poles were withdrawn and placed to one side, out of the way. The instructor then stood off to the side of the horse near one end to assist the vaulters and make sure the horse was 'stabled down' securely – the team leader was always stationed at the end the horse for emergency purposes – and as the session started he slapped the side of the horse and quietly signalled to the digger that he could begin.

From the start the vaulting sessions had been demanding. Now, with the effort for real, Williams did not let up. From its beginning the Germans had been fascinated, and pleased, at the enthusiasm the British displayed for physical exercise in camp. The inmates were forever playing various games (rugby especially fascinated the Germans, as it does all who do not know the game), running, exercising, and generally keeping fit in any way possible. Therefore, the activities involving the horse quickly became accepted by them as just part of a British mania for exercise. In any case, 2½ hours of sweat and exertion was the eventual outcome of the sessions, and was readily accepted by the 'Goons'. But for the prisoners, stretched to make it all believable on short rations, it was a heavy strain. Tom Wilson later recalled, 'After the war, I became Headmaster of a Secondary School and my PE staff would have been horrified to hear of the demands made on us by the wooden horse escape.'[3]

Work inside the horse was no easier. Once it was placed on the correct spot, then with the vaulters hard at it the signal that all was OK would be knocked on the side and Codner began to work. Kneeling at one end, he carefully covered over the four carrying slots in the sides of the horse with the the small pieces of black cloth he carried, before lighting a small candle. In the dim, flickering light, he scooped up the top soil from an area something less than 2ft square and put it in the Red Cross box. Placing that off to the side, he then filled the three sacks made from battledress trouser legs with some of the bright under sand from the deepening hole and quickly sewed them shut. Placing these off to the side as well, he opened the kit bag and began filling it with sand from a slot he dug into the ground to one side of the hole. Once it was deep enough, he then slid the plywood down into it, making sure that it was about 18in below the surface, and then packed sand tightly around it. After that, he laid the four bed boards flat in the hole side by side, put the three bags of sand he had made on top of them, and tipped some of the loose sand from the kit bag onto these to level out the hole to about 6in from the surface of the compound. He then emptied the contents of the Red Cross box into the hole. Feet on the framework again, the kit bag of sand suspended from the top boards of the horse by a special hook, and the box of supplies positioned to one side, Codner then smoothed the dirty sand to look as much like what the compound surface usually looked like before he started, and then gave Williams the word that he was finished.

Since the digger had no watch with which to tell time (the sand would have ruined it), when the session approached the 4.00pm mark the instructor would begin calling to the digger in a low voice under the guise of coaching from close to the horse. Once he received acknowledgement from the digger, the two would co-ordinate the length of the rest of the session. Evening *Appell* was at 5.00pm, so it was imperative that the session be finished and the horse taken back into the canteen no later than 4.30pm. It took some 15 minutes to close the trap, so they could not afford any sort of emergencies.

In the first four days of digging, Codner sank four pieces of packing crate in the ground, making the sides of the entrance shaft, and in the next two days dug out the interior of the box he had created. When completed, the vertical shaft was approximately 20in square, the plywood secured together by four corner posts of 2in by 2in pine rails taken from a bunk. By the end of the first 10 days the shaft had been dug to a depth of 5ft, with the trap some 12in below the ground level of the compound. Beyond that first 12in, the plywood box extended down the next 2ft, where each corner post sat on a 2ft pile of ordinary construction bricks stolen from the new washhouse site in a clandestine visit. On the west side of the vertical shaft (the compound side) a small alcove had been cut at the bottom for a man to push his feet into, in order to get down low enough for him to pass his head under the framework on the east side of the shaft – the side heading out toward the wire – in order to get into the actual tunnel.

It was hot, cramped and airless inside the horse. They took it in turns but Codner, the younger and more enthusiastic of the two, did most of the digging while Williams was in charge of construction and vaulting. The diggers worked mostly by feel, as the light of the candle was feeble at best, and soon got used to the 'crash' as the vaulters threw themselves over the horse. Occasionally a stray football would slam into the horse, or someone in boots would impulsively 'have a bash' at it, which was followed by angry shouts from the vaulting team. But outside of being startled by these occurrences the digger remained focused on working fast yet carefully. Most importantly, he had to be cautious so as not to collapse the loose sand around the entrance into the hole; not at all an easy task, especially when digging out the shaft. Later, when they had dug down enough to where a man could actually get into the entrance shaft to work, it was then a minor athletic feat getting out of the hole and into the limited space of the horse without pushing in the lip of the entrance or disturbing the horse. This problem was solved by making a box frame assembly from bedboards. This was positioned on the storing of the entrance hole, then stored in the tunnel when the vaulting session ended

The digger also had to be very mindful of space and always on guard against spilling any sand on the top soil. This was eased somewhat as the work progressed when later on they spread a blanket over the ground under the horse to help ensure that no bright sand got on the surface soil. By then, the dirty surface sand covering the trap went into a bag made from a pair of striped pyjamas, while the dug sand was placed in two smaller kit bags. These, along with the trap boards and trap sand bags, were all placed carefully on the blanket out of the way at one end of the horse. Three steel rods had been added along the length of the top of the horse, and after he had covered the trap the digger then hoisted the kit bags of spoil up and hooked them to these for the return journey. During this, the digger then struggled to keep the heavy bags from swinging and rocking the horse as he hung on, balanced on the framework of the horse, while carrying the bag containing the digging equipment; not at all easy for a tired man at the end of a session.

The first major crisis on the project – and there were to be many, many, over the next 14 weeks or so – came some 10 days after digging had been started. By that time, the vaulters had been hard at it every day for nearly a month and the physical strain was really beginning to tell. The quality of vaulting that had been first set by John Stevens had quickly risen to a high standard. Though many of the men benefitted from this in mind and body, as Pilot Officer Bertram 'Jimmy' James later put it, 'The Red Cross parcels, with the German rations, were just sufficient to sustain normal life, but allowed for little extra effort.' Unfortunately effort, and plenty of it, was just what vaulting exercise demanded. Steadily, the number of vaulters began to dwindle.

Williams and Codner took to canvassing the compound once again on recruiting missions; cajoling as many men as they possibly could into agreeing to take part, and then trying to hold them to their word. Often they would have to physically go and find some people just prior to a session, which occasionally led to a late start – and thus less work done on the tunnel. It could be very frustrating and Williams particularly would occasionally lose his temper.

One of those that did answer the call however was Pilot Officer Martin Smith, a Coastal Command pilot who had been captured off Norway early in June. 'At first I did not connect [a] tunnel with this sudden enthusiasm for vaulting, and wondered out loud at the sense of some of those novice athletes as they hurled themselves at the horse. Word soon went round that more people were needed for the gym class and, realizing the reason, I willingly volunteered. I soon learnt that I would never make a career out of gymnastics!'

However, with no way round it, the two continued to kindly badger people to come to vaulting classes, but it was always a struggle. Most days they might gather enough to make perhaps two Lancaster crews' worth of men; hardly a crowd.

Despite the toll that vaulting took on the prisoners, digging was by far the toughest. The tunnel was a crude affair; cruder than any of the experienced tunnellers in the compound that lambasted the idea ever imagined. There was just enough room for a man to work in the entrance shaft, but only just. The horizontal shaft was even smaller. The smaller the tunnel, the less sand that needed to be carried away. The less sand carted out, the faster the project would be completed. To that end, the tunnel went out toward the wire at a bare 18in square, which was just big enough for a man to crawl through. The first 7ft of the tunnel was fully and firmly shored with solid box framing constructed using bed boards gathered by the Escape Committee from the double-tier bunks. The box frames fitted together with dovetailed ends that Williams cut at night in their room using a sharp knife and a red-hot poker. That first 7ft of shoring kept the tunnel together against the daily pounding of the vaulters some 3ft above. After that first 7ft however, the tunnel was dug without any shoring whatsoever, rising up gently about 1ft over the next 5ft, becoming little more than an 18in cylindrical tunnel bored through the sand 2ft down. The pine root layer of the earlier forest provided the support for the roof, while relying on the clay in the sand, that formed the soil in the camp, to hold the sides together.

There was no light and no ventilation in the tunnel; only what came in through the vertical shaft. In such a small area with only one man doing the digging, an air pump was obviously out of the question, and they did not put up air holes to the surface for fear they would be sniffed out by one of guard dogs at night. More light meant either an electric torch – a very rare item in the compound, as were batteries – or a camp-made 'fat lamp'. The prisoners made these lamps from a small cheese tin filled with boiled vegetable margarine (to extract the water) with a wick made from either pyjama cord or a strip of flannel. While they were a tried and true method for lighting underground, giving off just enough light to work, they also consumed oxygen which, in such a small tunnel, was already at a premium.

It was just as well that they could not see anyway, as working in the tunnel might be construed as a perfect nightmare. In order to enter the horizontal shaft, one needed to crouch down in the vertical shaft as much as possible; not at all easy due to the small size. Then, thrusting the feet into the small alcove at the back, one curled down tightly at the waist in order to clear the head under the lintel of the tunnel opening. In the shored section the digger could stretch out fully but only had just enough room to draw one arm above his head, while his body blocked out what feeble light came in from the entrance. There the first shiver of claustrophobia might tickle its way up his spine. Once past the shored section of the tunnel, it was worse. From there it was only possible to slide into the sandy shaft with one arm outstretched ahead and the other trailing alongside the body as the 18in diameter offered no room to do anything else. To crawl along it, the digger used his fingers and toes; there was no room to draw his knees up to use for leverage, or to bring the elbows into play. Once at the face, the digger hacked away enough sand with the small trowel to fill his outstretched, crooked arm. Then he slid his way back toward the vertical shaft side scraping the sand along with him. There he would scoop the spoil into the kit bag and then make another trip up to the face and do it again. Once the kit bag was filled, the digger hoisted it up into the horse and placed it at one end on the blanket. Each kit bag held some 50lb of sand, and every 7ft of digging of the 18in tunnel yielded about 1ton of spoil; all scraped labouriously back down the tunnel one arm load at a time.

Williams and Codner worked completely naked, as clothing scraped small amounts of sand from the walls of the tunnel adding to the spoil which had to be laboriously removed for disposal. Before long their knees and elbows became scuffed, but this was easily explained to any questioning 'Ferret' as being caused by vaulting and many hard landings. However, during each digging session sand got into their ears and eyes and became almost embedded in their armpits and scalp. With so little air below they panted as they worked, which brought sand into their mouth and up their nose. Dragging the sand back down the shaft virtually buried the digger's face as well, which only exacerbated the situation. It was surprisingly warm in the tunnel and as they worked each sweated freely, which allowed the sand to cake on the digger's body and face; it also left a horrible odour in the tunnel, due to the lack of fresh air. Following a session, it was important to have a scrub under a tap at the earliest possible convenience so as to not only work the sand off the body, but most especially out of the hair, where it tended to become ingrained into the scalp. Both men grew moustaches to help keep the sand out of their noses, and beards to help keep it out of their mouths. While each worked sessions both above and below ground, Codner spent the most time underground, while Williams seemed to have become the most fatigued by the scheme overall.

The work would have been simply exhausting under normal conditions, but on short rations the constant struggle of repeatedly climbing up and down the entry shaft made it even more so. At the end of each tunnelling session, the digger emerged from under the horse nearly spent. The Escape Committee, most of whom had worked in tunnels before, had some idea of how hard the work was, and had long before arranged to hold out a certain number of Red Cross parcels in reserve each week so as to provide tunnellers with extra rations to keep up their strength. While this was a boon to the tunnellers, on the wooden horse scheme it also served to cause a certain amount of resentment as the vaulters, who were certainly stretching their endurance to the limit, received no extra rations for their efforts.

As that first month of tunnelling went by and they gained more experience with their unorthodox scheme, they were heartened to hear the thump of the footfalls, on the circuit above through the sand, as they approached their goal. It meant that real progress was being made; were importantly, soon after they had begun digging forward it had become clear that the 'mole' method was probably not going to be the way they would continue digging. Enclosed in the hot, airless tunnel for up to 14 hours of continuous work with no way of escape was almost unthinkable.

Philpot was slowly gaining experience with the unorthodoxy of the scheme, though at first he quarreled frequently with Williams over details of security. To him, experienced in the conventional way of doing things where work only went forward when there were no Germans around at all, having an open hole in the ground covered simply by a box was a constant living nightmare. The vaulting horse could easily be pushed over by a clumsy vaulter when there were a number of 'Goons' in the immediate vicinity! In fact, this had already happened once, when it had been tipped over after a poor vault. Fortunately, Pilot Officer Leslie 'Sid' Sidwell, one of their mess mates who supported Williams and Codner fully and was a dedicated vaulter, had been very alert and immediately had the horse upright again before any 'Goon' noticed. 'Ferrets' in the compound, and especially in the area of the vaulting, caused Philpot no end of anxiety. From the duty pilot's seat in Hut 63, he signaled the 'danger' of any Germans entering the compound to the vaulting team by hanging a white towel out the window. It infuriated him when the signal was apparently ignored.

Williams and Codner, on the other hand, understood that work on the scheme only in a 'Goon' free environment would be impossible, and were willing to live with the apparent risks; such was their belief in the infallibility of their scheme. It all came to a head one afternoon when Williams and Philpot got into a heated argument over the subject after Williams had totally ignored an urgent danger signal. Not yet totally grasping the exact nature of the project, Philpot had not realized that it took around 15 minutes to close the trap, and that a vaulting session could not just simply cease because a number of 'Goons' had entered the camp and the situation looked to be getting 'hot'. Williams firmly, and in no uncertain terms, detailed the situation and in the end, they came to the conclusion that conventional security was of no value to the scheme. Risk was just going to be an inherent part. From then on Philpot did not watch from the window, but relied on a network of 'stooges', usually on duty around the camp anyway, to bring him reports of anything that might be important to the team. Meanwhile, he continued to line up to vault with the other athletes.

By the end of the month the horse had become firmly established as a part of normal camp routine. There were fewer spectators now and for the most part the 'Goons' largely ignored the sessions. Since it would be completely unnatural for the team to vault for 2½ hours continuously, variations in exercising had also been introduced. Tom Wilson later recorded, 'We managed to vault for about 30 minutes to begin with. Then we formed a ring round the horse and passed a medicine ball round the ring, or played some other game with it. That was followed by vaulting session number two. After that, individuals were timed running a lap of the circuit, with a final vaulting session before ending the tunnelling session. At the end I would do a head balance on the horse coached by the instructor (usually Williams), but he was actually talking to the tunneller, asking when to have the horse carried away.'

A low, running conversation was kept up between the instructor, always standing at one end of the horse encouraging and assisting the vaulters, and the digger below throughout the session to keep the latter aware of the time. When the digger was ready, the bearers would insert the carrying poles and then everyone would troop casually back into the cookhouse; the bearers trying hard not to stagger under the weight of the digger and spoil. The bearers always used one hand. Once the horse had been moved, it was not unusual for the 'Goon' in the centre tower on the east fence to raise his field glasses and inspect the ground where the horse had been placed. It was also not unusual for a few of the vaulters to shuffle along immediately behind the horse to disturb the earth.

From there it was carried up the three steps into the cookhouse, with the instructor ordering the bearers 'Down at the back!' in order that no snooping 'Goon' might see a sand-covered foot underneath as the horse lurched up the steps. Once in the passageway, with the rear of the horse practically scraping the floorboards, the digger would drop down and walk crouched-up inside to give the bearers a little assistance. When the vaulting horse was set down (with an audible sigh of relief) and the doors to the building closed, the instructor would go to the window and check with the 'stooges', to check that there were no wandering 'Goons' in the vicinity. If it was all clear, the horse would be tipped up on end and a naked, sweat and sand encrusted digger would crawl tiredly out from underneath. The kitbags of sand brought in would either be stuffed under the floorboards of the barber shop, or slung up above the ceiling through one of the 'Ferret' inspection traps until it could be dispersed. Then the digger would have a quick, initial brush down in the small cookhouse lavatory (which did not actually work) and, with the horse moved to one side and the bearer poles leant in a corner, the team dispersed out the door in twos and threes, while the digger went straight to one of the *Aborts* and had a quick wash under the tap before falling in for *Appell* at 5.00pm. Between the end of *Appell* and around 7.00pm, the spoil from the day's digging was dispersed.

One evening, soon after *Appell*, Williams and Philpot noticed a man standing above the position of the trap, digging his heel into the dirt. Hurrying over, they asked him what in hell he was playing at; he replied 'Oh, I just wanted to see how strong your trap was, is all. That's okay, is not it? Everyone walks on it all the time.' Williams, very angry, made the man agree to become a vaulter in atonement.

Among the prisoners, secrecy about the scheme was practically nil once the project had been going for a few weeks, as was the number of them who thought the idea had a chance. The project became the object of much head shaking and derision among 'serious' escapers and Philpot, as the guiding committee member, received the brunt of much of this comment. Nevertheless, there were occasionally those – usually new inmates – who approached one or the other of the three scheme handlers wondering if something could not be done with the vaulting horse: 'I'd like to try a tunnel from underneath there, if you've no objections …' Usually Philpot or another committee member would then take them quietly aside and inform them of the situation. Occasionally someone came of their own accord wondering if they might join the vaulting (always welcome), in hopes of getting on the scheme. In that case Williams and Codner would be quick to make it clear that it was a two-man show and nothing more, but the individual would be more than welcome to come and vault if he wanted to help. Most did, if for no other reason than it was the 'pukka' thing to do.

Williams and Codner were isolated from much of the talk going round the compound about the scheme. They lived in their own little world, wrapped-up totally in attending to their tunnel, often at times to the exclusion of what few official outside duties there were; a cardinal sin in a prison camp. This all came to a head one afternoon when their mess sat at the table waiting for a lunch which was not forthcoming, as that week's room 'stooge' – Codner – had again forgotten his duties for the umpteenth time. The unbroken mess rule was that only that week's room stooge, and him only, could go near the food locker; a very necessary rule in a situation where arguments arose if one man thought another received a slightly thicker slice of bread. Therefore, when Codner and Williams did finally arrive, with their hearty colleague Sidwell, a showdown with the rest of the mess ensued (Philpot was apparently excluded). The end result was that Williams, Codner, and Sidwell split from the group as a whole and messed separately, looking after their own needs, to their own schedule, and no longer participated in general mess arrangements. After this, although civility was maintained, the atmosphere in the room became decidedly cooler.

Shortly after the showdown, Philpot left the mess and moved into a room in Hut 65 with Tommy Calnan and Robert Kee (who had been Calnan's escape partner from Schubin); ostensibly to avoid any pretence of conflict of interest, in regard to the escape, between himself, Williams, Codner and Sidwell. However, there is also evidence to suggest that Philpot had quarreled badly with another member of the mess on several occasions and this was his reason for the move.

One morning Philpot, was taking a stroll following *Appell* and came across a most appalling site; around the area where the trap for the tunnel was buried, a group of men with spades, axes, and shovels were hacking away at the tree stumps dotted around the compound. He quickly ran back to collect Williams; at any moment they might break through the tunnel trap! On returning, the two spoke to the workers. They were the golfing fanatics, who were in the middle of finishing their carefully planned nine-hole golf course and this was where they had decided to locate the final hole and attending 'brown'. They also made it clear that they were unaware of the tunnel and did not care where it was located. Finally, after much persuasion – and a visit from Wing Commander Kayll – they agreed to slightly redesign the course. In a show of appreciation for both repositioning the hole and clearing away some of the stumps (that everyone seemed to be constantly tripping over during vaulting sessions) Williams, over the next few days, had the horse carefully lifted up a little to allow a few small kit bags of spoil to be passed out for the golfers to use to build the bunker for the 9th hole. Though it would not be the last encounter the escapers would have with the golfers, it would be the last cordial contact.

Chapter 9

'It *Cannot* Last, Old Boy …'

August 1943

Years after the war, Philpot once remarked, 'Any fool can build a tunnel, but it takes a genius to get rid of the sand. Well, we weren't geniuses, but we worked very hard at it!'

That is an understatement …

From the start, vast amounts of sand came out of the tunnel for disposal and it is doubtful whether Williams and Codner actually realized before they started the scheme, to what extent the tunnel was going to create spoil. Rare is the person who can accurately judge the volume of a space. They had worked on tunnels at Schubin, and even helped disperse soil from the Asselin dig. Dispersal from that tunnel had been relatively easy; simply carried in jugs then handed up to the latrine where it was poured through one of the seat holes slowly and evenly into the effluent below. Furthermore, matters were different at Sagan where the subsoil was sand, which has the very disagreeable aspect of taking up half again as much room once dug out as it did when firmly packed in the ground. All the sand had to go somewhere and Philpot, who not only had earlier experienced Sagan and its peculiarities, but also in his capacity as Escape Committee representative, but found himself saddled with the job of finding a disposal site which was unlikely to be discovered by the 'Ferrets'.

The spoil came in at the end of a digging session; filling first one, and then, as work progressed, two kit bags. In the first days of the project, when no-one except Williams and Codner thought it stood a chance and it was still expected it might become a 'mole'-type dig, Philpot had not put too much real thought into getting rid of the sand. At the end of a session people on the team were handed a cloth bag or Red Cross box filled with sand and simply told, 'Here! Get rid of this; pour it under your hut and cover it over, throw it in your garden, or dump it down in the shitter. I do not care what you do with it; just do not let the 'Goons' see you.' Each person would then stroll around the compound, perhaps with a shirt or battledress jacket draped over the 'offending' receptacle, to do as instructed. But as the project continued, and the amount of spoil increased, this method died the quick, and obviously inevitable, death.

The next method he thought up was sending it out in water jugs. Each room in the camp was issued with a large, aluminum, straight-sided *Humpen*

(Pitcher) with a capacity of 2½ litres. Every morning, it was the first duty for the room 'stooge' to take the *Humpen* to the cookhouse to collect hot water to make morning tea. He proposed that several of the vaulters bring their room's *Humpen* with them to a session, ostensibly to be filled with hot water at the cookhouse. As the 'Kitchen Goon' rarely remained in the compound following the issue of the prisoners mid-day meal (usually some form of thin, virtually inedible soup and some potatoes), no guard would be any the wiser if the aluminum pitchers were carried out containing spoil instead of water. The British officer responsible for the kitchen who shared his office with the German was Philpot's friend and fellow Escape Committee member Aidan Crawley.

This method 'dried up' early however (pun intended), when word of the activity got back to the 'Kitchen Goon' and he enquired of Crawley; why was there a sudden lack of prisoners collecting hot water in the afternoon? Crawley moved swiftly to alleviate his suspicions. It was the vaulters, he said, wanting to clean up after a session. 'Yes, but with HOT water … in the summer?' retorted the German.

Finally, Philpot resorted to a tried and trusted method. The spoil was first poured into smaller bags, made from the arms and legs of long woollen underwear, and then handed out to all the vaulters and others selected for dispersal duties by the committee. Flight Lieutenant W.J. 'Mike' Lewis, an RCAF pilot with No.207 Squadron whose Avro Manchester was shot down over the North Sea in 1941, recalled, 'I was involved with the dance band (at Sagan) and often we'd be rehearsing in the afternoon when they had to bring the wooden horse into the hall … The fellows got out and they had brought out the bags of sand to disperse it. People would take a bag of sand and you'd drop it down your trouser leg with a loose knot in the bottom end, and you'd go outside and walk around the camp and jiggle it loose and this would let the sand out … on the ground.'[1]

All it needed from there was a few surreptitious shuffles of the feet to blend the bright sand into the dirty top soil and – magic – the sand had 'disappeared'. Men engaged in this method of dispersal were generally referred to as 'penguins', as the weight and bulk of the sand bags in their trousers made them waddle with a slightly strange, rolling gait. Flight Lieutenant Ian Kirk and Pilot Officer Tom Hawthorn were just two others who remembered being involved in spoil dispersal for the project, others involved included virtually all of Williams and Codner's mess-mates; all hard feelings were forgotten. NCOs coming into the *Vorlager* from Centre Compound even carried some back.

But even that method soon proved to be unable to keep up with what was coming out of the tunnel. Finally, Philpot hit upon what seemed the perfect solution. Much of the cookhouse floor was brick and concrete, but there were several sections that were wood, mainly around the edges of the building. One of those was the floor of the room used as a barber shop. He collected Flight Lieutenant Douglas Cooper, one of the camp's skilled carpenters, and in no time they had lifted the floorboards. Plenty of space was found below and, most importantly, no way for the 'Goons' to get a good look at what might be under that section of floor, due to the construction of the foundations. A strong trap was made using the existing boards and dummy nails to give the appearance of solidity. When it was finished no one could tell that the floor had ever been touched.

After that, the procedure was simple: Lieutenant David Lubbock, RNVR, usually took up a place by the main window of the barber shop where he could clearly see one of the committee's well-informed 'stooges' standing at a strategic point in the compound. As soon as Lubbock came in, the horse would be brought back and if the signal that there were no 'Ferrets' in the immediate vicinity was received, the horse would be tipped up and the kitbags dragged into the barber shop. There they would be emptied quickly down the hole in the floor, where below was usually either Williams or Flight Lieutenant Robert G. Stark (also from No.75 Squadron, shot down in December 1940), ready to pack the sand into a corner. The diggers tools were then all gathered together for Codner or Williams to conceal in their room, while the floor was carefully swept with a handkerchief to remove any telltale trace of fresh sand before the trap was replaced. During it all, those who smoked puffed away enthusiastically as the fresh sand had a pungent, distinct smell, easily recognizable to anyone with experience of tunnels (as were most of the 'Ferrets') and it was imperative they disguise it as best they could.

During the operation, a running commentary was kept up by Lubbock at the window. With careful and alert attendance to detail, the procedure would take a maximum of 2 minutes and be completely finished before the digger emerged from his initial brush down over a blanket in the small lavatory. This sand was then emptied into the hole as well, and the trap firmly replaced. Then, when all was set, the team slowly drifted out of the cookhouse and went on their way, seemingly without a care in the world.

Then 'Charlie' (Karl Piltz) struck.

Exactly what made the Germans suspect that something was going on in the cookhouse remains a mystery. Perhaps the 'Kitchen Goon' had not been satisfied with Crawley's explanation for the use of hot water in the afternoons – and the subsequent halt of the need following their conversation. Perhaps a sentry in one of the guard towers had noticed something. Possibly the number of men entering and exiting the cookhouse during what had become regular dispersal hours (usually following evening *Appell* to around 7.00pm) did not appear as normal as Philpot and his team had tried to keep it. Maybe a 'Ferret' had found a minute amount of sand on the floor of the barber shop one day, or perhaps it was the trap; or it was a combination of reasons. Whatever it was

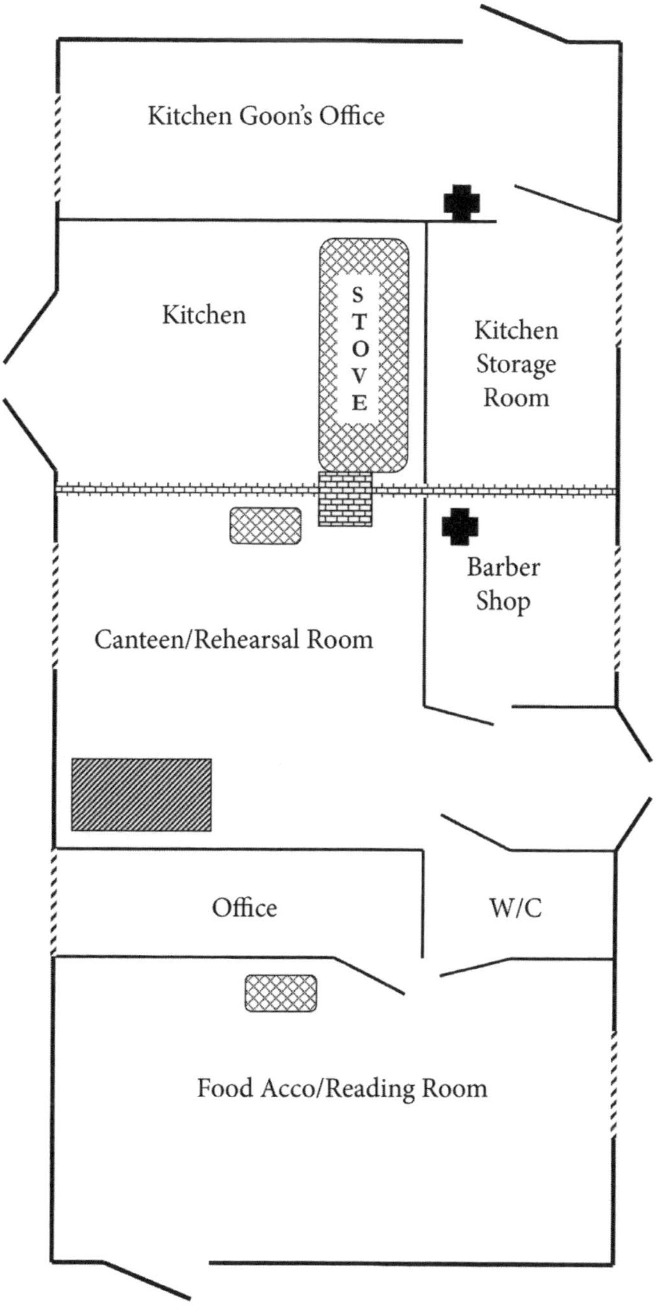

The Cookhouse.
All doors are shown ajar; windows as broken lines. Note the storage position of the wooden horse in the corner of the canteen, as well as the brick wall that separated the two portions of the building. The black crosses mark the spots where traps were cut in the floor for dispersal within the enclosed foundation that supported the kitchen stove, main chimney, and canteen stove.

must have made 'Charlie' suspect the cookhouse for some time, for he was not one to signal his punches and when the 'Ferrets' descended upon the building it was done with lightning speed and precision.

The raid came not too long after they started depositing sand under the barber shop floor. Williams was out on the circuit that morning when a truck load of 'Goons' came careering through the gate, pulled up in front of the cookhouse, threw everyone out, and set up a cordon of guards around the building.

Williams ran and fetched Philpot and together they walked over to join the meagre crowd watching the Germans tearing the cookhouse apart. Through the window they could see two 'Ferrets' in the barber shop, pulling up the floor boards, and then heard a shout. They had obviously found the tunnel sand. Soon Codner joined the pair. None of them spoke; what was there to say? Charlie might have suspected all along and had simply been biding his time for maximum damage to the morale of the prisoners. Who knew? Who cared? The attempt was obviously over.

There were a few quietly uttered 'tough luck' comments among the crowd before the three drifted away around the circuit, Williams and Codner sick at heart.

Later they returned, walking past the cookhouse as the Germans were leaving, and – miracle of miracles – there stood the horse; in much the same position it had been left! Could it be that the 'Goons' had *not* put two and two together? Or was it possibly a trap set by 'Charlie' to actually catch them in the act? At evening *Appell* that day there were no recriminations from the Germans concerning the sand the 'Ferrets' had found. Following *Appell*, they conferred with Philpot. Should the horse be taken out next day? Should they risk it? The next day, morning *Appell* came and went and still there was no hint from the Germans that anything was amiss. The escapers passed the word around to the vaulters: they would take the horse out as usual but empty, if merely to test the reaction of the Germans.

The horse was carried out under an air of tension and the session conducted in a normal fashion. A network of 'stooges' were covering every angle of the compound, watching for any signs of excessive observance from the Germans. So too were Williams, Codner and Philpot. The session ended and the horse was carried back indoors. Nothing had been reported amiss; nothing was found out of the ordinary from the 'Goon' standpoint. Strange, as the Germans liked to gloat on their little victories, and yet it was as if nothing had happened the day before.

For two more days they carried the empty horse out in the afternoon and vaulted to the normal schedule. Still there was no indication from the Germans that they had any more interest in the horse than normal. After three days without digging, they finally decided to try going underground. That session, too, was completed without a hitch, and they all began to breathe a little more easily again. When a few more days had passed and there was still no reaction from the Germans, the compound began to recognize that the impossible had happened: the horse was not suspect. It seemed incredible; the ridiculous project, as the more experienced escapers termed it, appeared to be blessed with most extraordinary good luck and Williams and Codner gained an epithet as 'the heavenly twins'.

For Philpot though, it was back to the continual challenge of where to hide the spoil. It was obvious that carrying it out of the building would be too risky an endeavour, for even if the horse was not suspect it had to be assumed that the cookhouse was. There was just no way in which the Germans could simply ignore sand found under the floor of the building. Therefore it must be presumed that careful attention was being paid to the men passing in and out. But where to hide the sand, after all, there are just a finite number of spaces available in any simple building?

The chimney was a possibility. The building was divided in two by a brick wall, separating the kitchen and the office from the rest of the building. Built against this wall on the cookhouse side was a brick-built chimney for a small tiled stove. Crawling up through one of the special inspection traps the 'Ferrets' had cut through the tongue and groove ceiling into the attic space, Philpot went to work on the chimney bricks with an improvised hammer and stolen chisel. After two days he managed to make a small hole in the hard concrete, which showed there would not be enough space inside to bother making the hole bigger.

Then Crawley suggested, as a temporary measure, perhaps carrying it out in the crates used for the potatoes issued by the Germans. Philpot thought that risky, as the 'Kitchen Goon' would no doubt want to know why the prisoners were collecting their ration so late in the day, instead of at noon as usual. Nevertheless they went forward with the idea for want of something better until, at last, they hit upon a better solution: under the floor of the 'Kitchen Goon's' office. What could be more perfect than hiding the sand under the very feet of the enemy?

To get into the German side of the building Philpot again crawled into the ceiling space through the 'Ferret' inspection trap. There were two nails holding the trap cover; one on the ceiling and one on the trap itself. Around them was wound a length of thread. He first memorized the pattern the thread was wound in as he removed it, slid the trap aside, then crawled up into the ceiling space and over to the German side, crouching low and balancing on the ceiling beams. Crawley then let him down through a 'Ferret' trap on the other side. Bringing the sand over proved far more difficult, as the kitbags weighed nearly 50lb each. In order to do it, the bags first had to be hoisted up into the roof space, with Philpot pulling from above, then swung forward a step at a time, carefully balanced at all times on the beams as the tongue and groove boarding of the ceiling could not stand any significant weight. On the other side Philpot carefully lowered the bags down to Crawley.

Flight Lieutenant Ken MacKenzie, a former Hurricane pilot from No.247 Squadron, who was highly skilled at making concealed traps, was brought in and did an excellent job on the 'Kitchen Goon's' office floor (in case it had been the trap that gave them away in the barber shop). When he had finished, it was impossible to tell the floor had been disturbed. Dispersal of tunnel sand, although somewhat physically strenuous, became easier once again. One day, Codner remarked to Philpot about the weight of the bags he was manhandling into the ceiling after a session when Williams had been the digger. He took the opportunity to complain that he should try swinging the bags along the length of the building. After that, Williams and Codner designed smaller bags, made from the legs of battledress trousers, that each held some 10lb of sand. Initially, they made twelve bags and found them easier to work with, both inside the horse as well as across the cookhouse ceiling. The only drawback to the scheme was knowing when the 'Kitchen Goon' would be away long enough to get the job done, but Crawley was unfailing in that regard.

Still difficulties arose, security failed on two occasions. One day, a 'Ferret' walked into the cookhouse while the ceiling trap was open and Philpot was in the attic space. Seeing the trap open and no doubt hearing something, he climbed onto the stove and managed to get a limited view inside. There was almost a wide alleyway down the centre of the ceiling, and to either side were fibreboard panels fitted vertically from ceiling to roof, nailed to upright studs that connected the roofing rafters to the ceiling beams. Philpot lay down and squeezed against a panel as flat as he could make himself when he saw the unfamiliar eyes peering into the attic. But it was extremely dark in the space, the only light was that which came through the open trap, and much of that was being blocked by the 'Ferret'. In any case, after a brief glance around, the 'Ferret' climbed down and, disturbingly, simply walked off.

Not long after, Flying Officer John Harris was in the 'Kitchen Goon's' office emptying sand into the trap there when he looked up and saw a 'Ferret' peering through the window across the room. But after a moment he too simply walked off. A mad scramble ensued to clear everything and shut the trap, but the 'Ferret' did not come into the building. Perhaps the bright sunshine that day had obscured his view into the room. Whatever the case, it was clear that the use of the office floor as a disposal site was over. Philpot noted that the space underneath was almost full anyway.

The next idea was the attic space. No one had ever wanted to dump sand there in the first place since the 'Ferrets' made a regular habit of inspecting all the attic spaces. But sand was being dug out of the tunnel daily and had to be dispersed. Philpot therefore decided to try and conceal it behind the fibreboard panels along the sides of the alleyway. Being hidden behind the panels, the 'Ferrets' should not be able to find the sand during a casual roof search, especially as there were no inspection traps in any of the panels. Prising the panels back close to the roof, all the while being careful not to split the cheap material, Philpot could pour the sand in through the narrow crack, but at a painfully slow rate.

However, the flimsy panels often sprung open at the bottom due to the weight of the sand, which flooded into the alleyway. It was then necessary to nail the panel back in place, but the sand would then spill out in another place.

Another hiding place was between the ceiling rafters in the dark, tight corners where the roof met the tops of the walls. To get there, he made a trap of one of the panels. When those areas were full, he then began to pour the sand between the rafters all over the ceiling area. First he covered the space by spreading out the pages of German newspapers, then he layered the sand as evenly as he could, raking it smooth by hand, then covered it with as many broken pieces of partition and other refuse as he could find in the attic. It was nerve-wracking to hear the nails holding the ceiling boards screech from time to time stressed by the weight of the tunnel spoil. This practice was soon dropped when the 'Kitchen Goon' complained to Crawley that the ceiling in his office appeared to be sagging. Crawley had also noticed it, and in other areas, and cheekily suggested to the the German that it was most likely due to the 'Ferrets' constant suspicion of everything and their heavy footed, never-ending snooping around in the attic space.

In desperation they went back to a modification of the plan of dumping sand under the floors. There was a passageway running from the kitchen office, through the cookhouse and into the storage room which looked to be relatively safe from view, if they were careful. MacKenzie was brought in again and performed another miracle with the floorboards. Underneath was a decent amount of space, once again hidden from 'Ferret' snooping by the hut's foundations. Once again they hoped that the dispersal problem was solved, at least in the short term.

Meanwhile, the tunnelling continued. One day, in a state of great excitement Williams and Codner reported to Philpot that they were now hearing the footfalls of the 'Circuit Bashers' *behind* them while underground and estimated they had dug a distance of some 40ft. That was some good news at least. Each Sunday evening the Escape Committee met and Wing Commander Kayll would receive updates from all the 'Little X' and 'Little S' on anything they had to report. Philpot's report was much anticipated, for the feelings of most of them had been summed up by one of their number earlier in the scheme; 'It *can not* last old boy. It simply *can not* …' Yet, week after week, it did, and he was able to report the scheme proceding forward nicely. First it had been 'Well, the entrance shaft is done …', and the smiles around him had been wide and many. Then it was, 'They have 10 feet done now …', and then 'They're 20 feet on …' and the smiles were starting to fade. After 40ft had been dug nobody was smiling anymore; most of them had dug before and knew what it took to dig a tunnel of that length.

Nevertheless, progress on the scheme, never fast to begin with, had slowed to a painfully slow crawl by mid-month. The number of bags the two would-be escapers were filling was becoming less and less as they no longer had the strength left to make the constant trips up and down the tunnel dragging sand. It took two trips to fill one of the twelve bags, and the more trips they took, each getting longer and longer as the days passed, the more quickly they became exhausted by the effort. Extra rations or not, they were not as fit as they needed to be. The work would have been difficult for an able-bodied man, let alone a prisoner. Often the digger would arrive back at his bunk, following his post *Appell* wash, effectively spent and uninterested even in an evening meal; a practically unheard of state for a prisoner.

Nor was the vaulting any easier. The effort required to keep up a 2½ hour session of virtually constant physical exertion, day after day, was taxing Williams' and Codner's wavering strength even further. The effort required was also simply beyond the physical capabilities of the general population of prisoners, and the turnover rate among the vaulters remained high. This, in turn, required a nearly constant search for additional vaulters to swell the small crowd of dedicated regulars, putting a further drain on their time and energy. The need to constantly replace vaulters and keep the sessions looking real and energetic, combined with the extreme physical demands underground, was stretching them both to the limit of their endurance.

Therefore, as the end of the month drew near, the project had virtually ground to a halt. It was all they could do to get six or eight men together to vault, and the digger was just managing to fill perhaps six bags in the 2½ hours. Obviously this situation could not continue or the scheme would simply end as it stood: partially finished.

What happened next is debatable. Wing Commander Kayll later recalled that it began to look as though Williams and Codner were becoming over arrogant. According to an interview the former Wing Commander gave in 1996, after some weeks the compound basically went on strike against the project, citing the attitude of the two would-be escapers. 'They got very arrogant,' he recalled, 'and started ordering people to do what they needed to complete the tunnel, and there was a fuss.' He stated people were coming to see him, basically saying 'we've had it with these two' and were not going to continue to participate in the project. Then, after a week had gone by with no vaulting, Kayll further alleges the two were forced to turn to the Escape Committee for help. Kayll then claims that it was at that point that the committee stepped in and offered to start organizing the vaulting from then on, in exchange for the two agreeing to allow a third member – one from the committee – into the escape attempt, which they thought would benefit from becoming a three-man operation. According to Kayll, the member they chose was Oliver Philpot, who had already done so much and was thus familiar with the attempt. The two were then given 24 hours to make their decision. In the end they decided to 'play the game' and gave the Escape Committee control, after which vaulting resumed and Philpot became a team member.

However, none of the above, as such, is documented anywhere else that the author could find in his research. It is not noted in any of the official paperwork from the camp, or the reports on the escape filed by the three escapers in person. Furthermore, no such detail has been recalled by any persons that were present at the time, who were interviewed by the author. Nor by those who left behind their own stories in written or other recorded form, including books by both Williams and Philpot. Certainly none recall there being an interval of 'a week with no vaulting', something which surely would have remained in *somebody's* mind, nor to the attitudes of Williams and Codner being anything worse than perhaps distant, and primarily focussed on the scheme.

That is not to say, however, that Wing Commander Kayll is wrong. Perhaps, it may simply be that after so many years, and in light of the completely successful nature of the escape, that other men may choose to forget the more distasteful aspects of the effort in not wishing to taint the memory of three such audaciously daring men. [Nor do I mean to do so here either.] There was, after all, an unspoken code of honour among the RAF of the time, and it is a very 'British Officer and a Gentleman' attitude to forget the disagreeable aspect of an action in the face of ultimate success during a shared difficult experience. Perhaps, it also could simply be that Wing Commander Kayll just remembered the situation to be worse than it actually was. Time has a way of adjusting memory and personal recollections.

But it must also be remembered that even given the 'all for one and one for all' attitude that has been heavily played upon concerning the image of the British officer prisoner of war of that time, that it was not necessarily as such in all situations. Certainly the attitude of East Compound was not as 'All Together Now, Chaps' as it was in North Compound during the summer and autumn of 1943, where the compound had united for a sole purpose – the massive escape scheme planned by Bushell. In East Compound, they did not have that sole purpose, nor was the wooden horse scheme likely to be such, as made clear by the number doubters who thought it ridiculous. A number of individuals, each with a different temperament and attitude, most of them young and half starved, trained for war and forced to suppress their vitality under an alien enemy authority, will all react differently. That many of East Compound would resist any participation in an activity that could sap what little strength they had in the face of almost certain failure can be understood.

However, there is probably more than just a seed of truth in what Kayll alleges. Indeed, it may have seemed to a number of the prisoners that Williams and Codner were becoming too pugnacious when it came to arranging the vaulting. Canvassing the compound constantly, or getting people to attend after an off-handed promise to vault, could not have been easy, and in doggedly pursuing their goals they could very likely have appeared as arrogant concerning the project, especially when so few others actually believed in it at first. This could also be true of how they may have jealously guarded their scheme and sought to protect it at almost any price, as they were firmly and unshakably convinced that it would succeed. Freedom – their freedom – was the prize, and who would not do what they could to regain that prize once taken? In fact, it is then entirely likely that the Escape Committee did have to get involved in order to help the project, although it is highly doubtful that it was quite as one-sided and to the great benevolence of the committee as Wing Commander Kayll makes it appear.

Either way, we do know this much as fact: As the end of the month drew nearer, Codner and Williams came to accept the fact that they had nearly destroyed their scheme; the number of active vaulters did improve as the summer wore on, mainly by members of the committee; and Philpot did join the team as a third.

However, although he may have been selected by the Escape Committee, Philpot was not the first choice of Williams and Codner. Even though he did have experience with tunnels and was their official representative with the committee, once Williams and Codner came to the conclusion that they needed help (however that conclusion was arrived at), they sought out someone who had specific experience in the 'mole' method. That someone was none other than Tommy Calnan, who had attempted a 'mole' escape from the bottom of the 'anti-mole' trench the Germans had initially dug in the warning strip area immediately after the Lamond/Best/Goldfinch attempt. He had also tried a 'mole' escape from Schubin when the tunnel had collapsed, almost suffocating him. Though he had been unsuccessful at these attempts, he had 'moled', and Williams and Codner still apparently had an idea about turning the wooden horse scheme into a possible 'mole' attempt at some point.

One morning, Williams went to meet Calnan in the *Vorlager*. At the time Calnan (of all people) had contrived to get himself the position British Book Censor for the camp, which was actually a cover for an escape he was planning. Williams asked him to walk round the circuit and, once away from eavesdropping 'Goons', Calnan asked casually how the tunnel was progressing. Williams got right to the point. They had come as far as they could as a pair, he said, and were thinking of now doing it as a 'mole' and needed a third set of hands, preferably those which had experience of 'moling'. Would Calnan be interested in joining the team?

Calnan hesitated. It was not that he did not think the effort had a chance; on the contrary, he said, he thought it stood a very good chance, actually making Calnan one of the few in East Compound that apparently did. He advised that 'moling' was risky and dangerous though, best left to the last few feet before actually breaking out. Also by sticking to a more traditional approach to get that far, he did not see them finishing before the onset of the harsh winter, and felt that the Germans were bound to discover the scheme. It was the same old problem: the longer it took to dig a tunnel, the greater the chances of it being found by the Germans. On top of that, Calnan already had a scheme underway to make an escape from the *Vorlager* before winter. He was also afraid that if he was to be caught on another tunnel scheme that he would be sent to Colditz *Straflager*, the home of the 'bad boys' who escaped too often and caused their captors too much trouble. In the end, though grateful for the offer, Calnan turned it down.[2]

Calnan did offer one important piece of help; he was in possession of a German railway timetable which was valid until the end of October. They were free to use it any time they wished, he said. Astounded by Calnan's unbounded resourcefulness, Williams told him they would definitely take him up on the offer.

Their next choice for the person to join them, one would assume, should have been Les Sidwell, the messmate of Williams and Codner and staunch supporter. Sidwell was a regular vaulter and had been from day one; was liked by both men; and had joined with them when the mess had split. For this he had been 'sent to Coventry' by the others in the mess, along with the two would-be escapers. However, exactly why Sidwell was not chosen by the Codner and Williams remains something of a mystery. Later when Williams wrote his book, he based the character 'Nigel' loosely on Sidwell; an enthusiastic vaulter and supporter of the scheme that had been wounded in the leg when shot down and really was not in any shape to go escaping, although the Williams and Codner characters in the book wanted to ask him. However the case is made that if he had to make a run for it he very likely could not and that could mean the recapture of all three. But in this regard, two points stand out: Firstly, 'Nigel' is actually known to be a compilation of at least two people that worked on the project; one was Sidwell and the other being John Stevens, who *was* wounded when shot down. Secondly, Sidwell was never wounded and was not lame in any way. Then why was he not asked? A possible answer might be that he was married and a little older than most of the men in camp, and therefore he may not have wanted to take the risk involved in an escape. Or he may have simply declined any offer made to him for some other unknown personal reason.[3]

Whatever the reasons, the only truly logical choice was Philpot. After all, he was familiar with the scheme – outside of Williams and Codner no one else even came close to understanding it – and had experience both with it and other tunnels. He was a born organizer and though he had never actually been enthusiastic about the success of the scheme he worked hard to make it successful. The only downside was that the two men did not always get along with him, Williams in particular. As an escape partner there could be problems. Williams and Codner had already decided that once outside the wire, though they had a plan it was far from rigid and they were more likely to adapt to the situation. Philpot was more likely to have a firm plan and stick with it to the end. It was apparent that it would be a good idea for them to travel separately, if Philpot agreed to come aboard.

It was Williams that approached Philpot, and while Philpot did not exactly jump at the chance immediately, he was flattered by the offer and only gave it a few minutes thought before agreeing on two conditions: Firstly, it would remain a three-man scheme, more would be likely to cause trouble, and in any case it did not seem possible that the scheme could possibly accommodate more than three. And secondly, there should be no waiting at the exit for each other on the night of the escape. Philpot's meaning was clear; he wished to journey alone. His persona 'Jon Jorgenson' was a lone traveller on business. Another (or two) with him would destroy the carefully prepared credibility that the 'Jorgenson' persona relied upon. Williams agreed, and Philpot became a fully-fledged member of the team.[4]

That is not to say that he suddenly became an advocate of the idea in its entirety. On the contrary; he remained as sceptical as ever. However, sceptical or not, he had to admit that the scheme was still in existence, where others, thought to be much better plans, had long since failed and faded into memory. Nor was it possible to escape the enthusiasm of Williams and Codner, who held absolute blind faith in the scheme and were determined to see it through, whatever the cost. The two had done a third of the work already through some very trying situations. Now all that was needed was a little more luck, and he might see the wire from the outside.

The next day, Philpot went out inside the horse for the first time. He refused to go down the tunnel naked though, as the others did, and arrived to dig wearing an undershirt and shorts. Annoyed, but willing to let it go, Codner warned him that the tunnel was narrow, and needed to stay so. Each bag of sand rubbed from the walls meant one less taken from the face and a longer task. Codner also gave him strict instructions on how to open the trap and what to watch out for once in the tunnel.

With no small effort he managed to uncover the tunnel and get in without caving in the sides of the entrance. But after just one trip into the narrow tunnel, with the horrifying roots dangling from above and no room to move or raise his head, Philpot was ready to quit. It was the most claustrophobic tunnel he had ever been in, and panic spread like a malaise through him as he lay, seemingly entombed, at the workface. Mustering all his courage, he hacked away a quantity of sand from the face ahead and began his backwards journey. Halfway along he became stuck, managed to free himself while just barely containing his terror, and arrived back at the entrance thoroughly exhausted and dreadfully anxious. Stuffing the sand into a bag he tried to think up a face-saving way to tell Williams he wanted no further part of the scheme. However, he could not very well do it through the side of the wooden horse so it would have to wait until after his session. Mustering up his courage again – he could not very well just sit there until the session was over – Philpot made another trip up and back. This time it was not quite as bad. Then another trip, and another, and before he knew it all twelve bags were full and he was on his way back into the cookhouse.

'Well what did you think of our tunnel, Ollie?' asked a grinning Williams. Philpot was utterly exhausted.

'Oh, pretty good, Bill! You've certainly worked on it! But it's not very big – the smallest I've been in. But the thing's quite workable. Not a bad *dienst* at all.'

Though Philpot may have had his own misgivings about the tunnel, the intrepid 'Jon Jorgenson' apparently did not.

The next crisis occurred at the end of the month. It was during a session when Codner was underground. The vaulters were lined up, each taking his turn to launch himself over the horse with plenty of gusto, when Les Sidwell noticed something unusual. On the other side of the horse, in the direction of the wire, a hole had suddenly appeared in the sand about the size of a man's arm. It was just past where the vaulters were landing, around two thirds of the way to the circuit. Thinking quickly, he leapt over the horse and executed a perfectly faked poor landing, collapsing on the ground and rolling over the

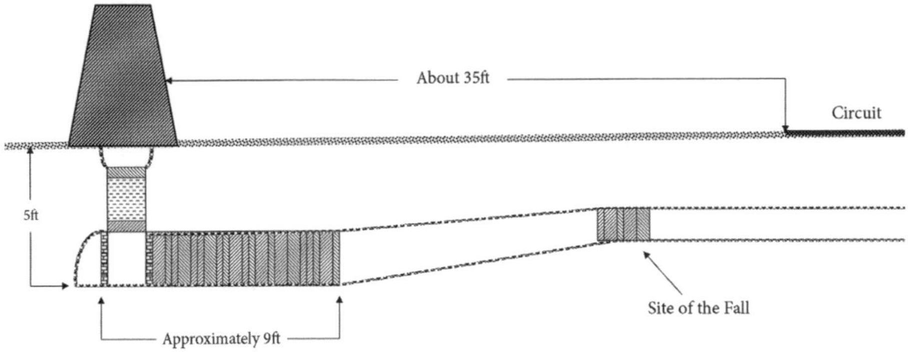

Side view of the tunnel's construction.
Note the entrance shaft of Red Cross packing crate plywood and bed boards set on the brick pilings; the rear alcove which allowed the men to crouch low enough to get into the tunnel; and the initial seven feet of 20in square box framing. Note also that the tunnel narrowed to just 18in in diameter after the box framing ended and then rose slightly once the 'landing zone' for the vaulters had been passed.

hole with a scream of angony. The others ran over to him and when Williams arrived Sidwell rolled over slightly and showed him the hole. Obviously there had been a fall in the tunnel, but what to do? Codner could be suffocating! Should they flip over the horse and go down after him, blowing the scheme? Or did they wait and hope for word from him? Sending someone for a stretcher, Williams pretended to look at Sidwell's leg while all the rest of the vaulters stood around in a circle. The 'Goon' in the nearest box had his field glasses on them, so they must make it look real. Meanwhile, Williams leaned in nearer Sidwell's leg and started to call low and urgently to Codner down the hole. After a short while he heard a faint voice coming through the hole; Codner was alright. There had indeed been a fall and he was going to take some shoring from the head of the shaft to support the roof. In five minutes or so they could try and fill from the top.

When the stretcher arrived with a first-aid kit, Williams made a big show of bandaging Sidwell's leg for the 'Goon' in the tower. Presently they heard a faint call from Codner, and cautiously some of those kneeling around Sid started to push the dirty top soil into the hole while others carefully loaded him onto the stretcher. In the end, Sidwell was carried away for effect, but not before the hole was pretty much full and levelled. Williams went back to his usual spot at the end of the horse and waited to hear from Codner while Philpot got the vaulters moving again. Williams kept trying to hail Codner as time neared for the end of the session, but with no luck. Had there been another fall? Was he trapped? The 'Goons' would be coming in for evening *Appell* soon.

Finally, Codner called from inside. The fall had made quite a mess in the tunnel, in an area just beyond the shored section around halfway between the location of the horse and the circuit. A tree root had worked loose, probably from the vibrations of both the vaulters and the 'Circuit Bashers', and had brought down a section of the roof. He had everything shored up temporarily and was closing the tunnel. Tom Wilson mounted the horse and got up on his head, as was usual for the end of a session, while the rest of the team gathered the gear. Finally, Codner's voice called out from inside that he was ready to go just as the 'Goons' marched through the gate for *Appell*. It had been a close call.

The next day, after a briefing by Codner on the damage, Williams went down with some more bedboards to carry out repairs. The sand was soft and shifting where the fall had occurred and he had to work fast. With little room to manoeuvre, the task was not easy and more sand continued to cascade down. Jamming the root up under the boards, he tightly packed sand behind the shoring to keep it rigid, and then installed more support. In the end he had repaired the fall exceptionally well but, as usual with sand that had been disturbed he was left with a pile of spoil that could not be put back in place. This he bagged up to be taken back and hung them the bags in the horse. The effort of lifting them up seemed almost impossible after all his hard work in the tunnel. As he was closing the trap, Codner signalled to him that he needed to hurry, as they were getting close to *Appell*. Williams, exhausted by what may have been the most strenuous two hours he had ever spent underground, worked feverishly to properly close the trap and then climbed onto the framework in the horse. The ride back into the cookhouse was a nightmare, and it was all he could do to hang on. Once back inside the building, when they lifted the horse, Williams collapsed onto the floor.

There was no time to lose. Grabbing the unconscious, sand covered Williams, several pairs of hands shoved him into the lavatory and started to clean him up, even as the 'Goon' whistles started blowing outside for *Appell*. Other men heaved the bags of sand and the gear up in the ceiling as a temporary measure. By the time everything else was cleaned up, Williams was starting to come round. Tom Wilson and Codner pulled a battledress jacket on him, fell in one on each side, and got him over to his hut area for *Appell* just in time. After parade was over, Williams was helped to the washhouse by Codner, where he cleaned himself thoroughly. Soon after, he went and reported to a 'Ferret', who escorted him to the Sick Quarters in the *Vorlager*.

For a second time that month, the tunnel came to a standstill.

Chapter 10

Exhaustion and Ingenuity

Interlude

The Sick Quarters for the East and Centre Compounds was located in the *Vorlager*, between the 'Cooler' and the coal shed. It was yet another dingey, greyish-green painted wooden building, virtually indistinguishable from any other in camp. Inside, however, was a clean and well kept twenty-four bed hospital divided into two bays, staffed by a German head doctor assisted by a British doctor, and a small group of German military personnel as orderlies. At one end of the building was the consulting room and office while at the other end was a large, clean lavatory. There were fresh sheets and blankets on the beds once a week, plenty of windows for light and fresh air, electric fans to keep it cool, and few guards. But, among the German orderlies were usually one or two of the lower ranking 'Ferrets', keeping an eye out for anyone who might be up to something involving the less well-guarded environment.

In charge was Dr Lechten, a captain of the Luftwaffe, who was a recently qualified and a dedicated young man. Like most ardent Nazi officers who were a product of Hitler's rise to power, he presented a very urbane bearing. His uniform was always immaculate, and he was as authoritative in English as he was in German. In all fairness, the man really did try to do his best for his patients with the limited resources available to him. However, he never forgot that he was also a German soldier, maintaining that only those in a truly bad way had a bed, and was known to have captured at least two escapees at Sagan's railway station. From time to time, he also worked in the much larger sick quarters in the North Compound.

The British doctor was an RAMC major who had been captured at St Valery, France in 1940 with the 51st Highland Division. Dr Edward 'Twee' Monteuis, was a Scotsman from Edinburgh and had worked at the Middlesex Hospital in west London before the war. He was unfailingly cheerful, very astute, and a deeply dedicated physician. He could not speak a word of German and was among that breed who believed of the 'Goons' that 'If one speaks English slowly enough, and loudly enough, the stupid bastards will understand one.' Because of this, he was often at odds with the refined Dr Lechten. At the same time, he was extremely popular with all the prisoners.

Williams was admitted that afternoon following *Appell*, given a clean pair of pyjamas, and immediately put to bed. In the morning, he was carefully examined by both doctors, who easily agreed he was suffering from both exhaustion and a severe case of hemorrhoids. The first could be explained to Lechten as caused by the strenuous vaulting, though Monteuis must have easily guessed what else was behind it since the tunnel was probably one of the worst kept secrets in the compound.

The second was a common enough ailment in prison camp, where the poor diet often led to severe constipation; the number two medical complaint a prisoner was likely to give when reporting sick. The third was followed by diarrhoea. The main cause of this was the German issue *Kriegsbrot* 'war bread', which provided (along with the potato) the bulk in a prisoner's diet. Breakfast, for instance, was usually a 'slice and a scrape' – a slice of the 'war bread' with a smear of Red Cross parcel margarine or jam – washed down with a mug of weak tea. This might not be considered to be too bad (though meagre) until it is noted that one of the main ingredients of the bread was up to 33 per cent of 'tree flour' (sawdust). When eaten in any significant amount, this bread had a nasty tendency to soak up fluid in the bowel which could lead to a very serious condition.

For the first problem treatment was simple; he needed plenty of rest; a week in bed would replace vaulting as his prime activity the immediate future. As for the second, much to Williams' horror, the medical prognosis was surgery.

The week of rest would be welcome, even if frustrating. It meant setting the schedule on the tunnel back by just that much time as it added to the workload of the others. But surgery would mean a delay of an indeterminate length, and that was not acceptable. Philpot reported sick, a day or so later, on the excuse of a shaving cut which had become septic in order to manage a few words with him, Williams told him what was happening and of his decision to not go through with the surgery and risk abandoning the tunnel. Philpot argued briefly with him, even going so far as to point out that the tunnel did not really have a chance and that there would be others. However, Williams was adamant; he would rest for a week, but then it was back to the tunnel. Philpot did not further dispute his decision.

On Sunday, Philpot reported the situation to the Escape Committee, whose reaction was largely noncommittal. They neither dismissed the idea anymore, nor enthusiastically supported it; instead assisting with the vaulting and taking a wait and see attitude. Meanwhile, he and Codner took the horse out every day as usual, although empty, in order to keep up appearances. They had all been pushing themselves pretty hard and though Philpot had not done nearly the same amount of digging as the other two (especially Codner), even he was feeling the strain. As the weather was not particularly hot in that late August, the two took the opportunity of Williams' enforced rest to ease the pace a little on the vaulting, do no digging, and scale down their own efforts.[1]

A few beds along from Williams, Pilot Officer Dallas Laskey, RCAF was nursing his aching temples and longing for his home in Canada. He and what remained of his crew had arrived at Sagan via Duisburg, which had been their target. It was their flight back in the small hours of 13 May 1943 that had put him in the sick quarters

The Germans had definitely been alert that night, and heavy Flak harassed them constantly, killing the rear gunner. Soon after that, a near direct hit blew a 6ft hole in the fuselage which killed the second pilot, damaged the control cables to the rudder, and fractured the petrol cocks to both engines. Starved of fuel, they stopped, and the No.426 Squadron Vickers Wellington quickly assumed the gliding angle of a brick. Thinking quickly, Flying Officer Gordon 'Moose' Miller, the navigator, calmly wrapped the leaking petrol cocks with the crew's silk escape maps, stemming much of the flow before making his way back through the aircraft and improvising a splice in the control cables. By then Sergeant Runciman, the pilot had managed to get the port engine started and reduce the rate of decent. Miller's ingenuity and bravery had temporarily solved their dilemma, and the pilot managed to fly to very near the Dutch border before the crew had to abandon the crippled aircraft.[2]

On his way out, Pilot Officer Laskey, the bomb-aimer, had struck the back of his head badly. He later recalled getting a glimpse of the dark shape of the Wellington falling through the night sky, but never remembered pulling his ripcord or hitting the ground. Sometime during the night he woke up in a pine forest, concussed and dazed with no idea where he was but otherwise unhurt. He gathered his parachute and 'Mae West' and concealed them under a bush but felt, 'it was like someone else was doing it.' After a while he pulled his escape kit from his battledress jacket, located the compass and began to walk. Time ceased to matter. 'We weren't far from the Dutch border when we jumped and I figured I had a pretty good chance at getting across,' he said. 'I wandered around behind German lines for about a week, I guess, living off one Horlicks tablet and a little bit from a fuzzy chocolate bar I found in my escape kit each day, drinking from streams. In fact, I may have been walking in circles. I know I did not get very far.'

Laskey was eventually found by some good natured German farmworkers, who fed him before turning him over to the local police. The next day he found himself in the back of a Luftwaffe truck heading for Dulag Luft, along with Runciman, Miller, and Sergeant Pennock, their wireless operator. The trip was a blur, and he was filthy and sick when they locked him into a detention cell at Dulag. He was still too fuddled to answer any questions. Also his condition and the dirty water he had drunk caused him to suffer from diarrhoea. His Dulag jailers were unsympathetic.

By July, Laskey had arrived in East Compound at Stalag Luft III, along with 'Moose' Miller, where he tried to get on as best he could, though still somewhat fuddled. He joined some language classes, read some books, learned to be a 'Kriegie', and wrote to his parents not to expect too many letters from him, as he was 'so very busy with things'. [He later remarked sadly to the author, 'That was something I always later regretted doing.']

Then, one morning in August, he woke up with a pounding headache and a severe swelling on the back of his head. When neither had subsided after a few days, he reported to sick call after evening *Appell* and was taken to the Sick Quarters. 'Twee had a good look at him, heard his bail out story, and tossed him into bed on a regimen of rest, regular doses of aspirin, and applications of topical *Fische Salbe* (Fish Salve) on his swelling. The name accurately describing the main ingredient, despite its atrocious smell, it was an excellent drawing salve and for whatever mysterious reason effectively reduced the swelling on Laskey's head.'

Within a few days, the salve and rest made him begin to feel better and take more of an interest in his surroundings and his fellow patients, especially a dark-haired chap named Williams, who kept quizzing an Australian, with a bullet in his shoulder, who had just been brought back after an escape attempt from North Compound. Laskey was immediately interested. 'I had not really thought about escape, but here were some guys talking about it. All of a sudden it occurred to me that maybe I should listen!'

Laskey came over to Williams and introduced himself, asking if he might listen. After he had detailed his background (proving he was not a 'Goon' plant to everyone's satisfaction) Williams agreed. He and the Australian were deep in a discussion over whether train travel was the way to get around Germany after an escape. The Australian, who had travelled on goods trains to the Baltic where he had been caught in the docks, did not agree. To travel openly among the German populace presented far too many difficulties to overcome; forged papers good enough to pass a check, correct clothing, at least a rudimentary knowledge of the language. It was far too dangerous, and there were far too many unknown problems involved. Checks on rail passengers were commonplace, especially on the faster, long-distance trains. And the slow, local trains which stopped at every station were a poor option. Hitching a ride on a goods train was a good way to travel, provided the escapee was careful and not seen.

Williams, however, had been gathering evidence in his own mind ever since the Schubin break that the railway was, in every way, the only way to travel. Yes, there were drawbacks but rail had tremendous advantages as well, not the least of which was that the escaper could be many kilometres away before the alarm was raised. As for the difficulties, they could be overcome, as they had been in the past and, in fact, were again as they continued their conversation.

All through the sultry July and August evenings, Codner, Philpot and Williams had turned their attentions to the details necessary for the second, and more difficult, aspect of their escape; that of crossing wartime Germany to freedom. Separately they mulled over their options and the intricacies of the journey; Williams and Codner working together, and Philpot on his own. He, as we have seen, was already well on his way to being prepared by the time he officially joined the scheme. Williams and Codner were far less organized.

The first order of business, however, was to decide on just where they were to get out of Germany. Sagan was a long way from any friendly border, so no matter which direction they travelled they would need to do so at speed, and that meant taking a train. When they had been selected at Schubin for the cookhouse tunnel, Williams and Codner had assembled a rather 'spur-of-the-moment' strategy for what they would do once outside the wire. Novice escapers that they were, at the time neither thought it possible to travel freely by train, even though both were aware it had been done in World War One. Instead, they had planned to travel on foot (commonly known as 'hard arseing it') down to Czechoslovakia, in order to try and get help from the Partisans, who were known to go to extraordinary lengths to help escapers. Both liked the idea of travelling on foot as they believed it offered the freedom of movement also the ability to revise their strategy as needed. They even contemplated getting out of the immediate area of the camp by having Codner, the slimmer of the two, pose as a woman, for which he had been letting his hair grow long ever since.

But the Schubin break had changed their line of thought in regards to the trains. After it, they gathered as much information from those who had escaped as they could find, or who otherwise had intimate knowledge of the requirements to travel through the Reich. After a time, they had a fairly accurate picture of what they would likely be up against in attempting to travel by train, and though it certainly looked to be a formidable task it did not seem altogether impossible. But it was the progress on the tunnel thus far (they would likely not be out until early autumn at the earliest) that had finally made up their minds. They had no desire to spend any freezing nights in ditches during the long walk to the Czechoslovak border. As for Philpot, he had long since come to the same conclusion, and had never even considered walking.

So travelling by train was the best option, but to just which destination should they travel? Switzerland was an obvious first point of discussion, being a neutral country and as close as any other to Sagan. Tales abounded of past prisoners on the run heading in that direction, and there were plenty of illicit maps available in camp detailing the German-Swiss border; most particularly the Schaffhausen Salient. However, it was also known that the border was heavily guarded and that it weaved back and forth in many narrow salients. Also that most of those tales had ended with the prisoner back in custody after having walked across one of those narrow areas of the Swiss border, without realizing it, and back into Germany. After careful consideration, all three decided that the risks in that direction were just too great.

Occupied France was certainly another option. If they could make it to a large French city and make contact with the underground forces there, they could be certain of being passed down an escape line that could quite possibly get them over the Pyrenees and into Spain. From there the British Embassy would arrange for their return to Great Britain. Yet there were risks here too; from time to time unsettling reports came into camp, through various devious means, that the Gestapo had infiltrated some of these escape routes, or that hard-pressed French partisans were handing over escapers in order to improve their own life under the German occupation. There was also no guarantee that contact could be made with the 'Underground', or that they would take an escaper for what he said he was, instead of shooting him out of hand as a potential German infiltrator. In the end, France was decided to be too uncertain and shelved as a destination.

That left north toward the Baltic coast, and the thought of stowing away on a ship bound for neutral Sweden. This was the route that Sergeant Wareing had taken from Schubin and seemed the only logical proposition. The idea was firmly settled for Williams and Codner when Philpot announced to them that he planned to head for the docks at Danzig, and that he also planned to travel to his destination in comfort and speed by train. For Philpot, the advantages were obvious. Speed, of course, was the main reason, as he could reasonably expect to be well away from the camp area long before the alarm was raised. Another was that he could keep looking respectable; important in a country where vagrants were routinely rounded up and 'dealt with' by the authorities. As he was posing as a businessman, he needed to continually look the part. Trekking on foot across of Germany and sleeping rough would rapidly affect his 'smart' business appearance. Of course, it also meant travelling openly among an ever suspicious German population, and submitting himself to scrutiny by the public and authorities. His appearance and papers had to meet this scrutiny and at times it would call for nerves of steel. However, the benefits certainly seemed to, at least, balance against the risks, giving him the best chance for his efforts.

Philpot had also made plans to stay at hotels if necessary; an idea which Williams and Codner looked at with no small measure of amazement and also took some inspiration. After some debate, they also agreed that hotels were best; the minute they started looking like an escaped prisoner of war, their chances of success would plummet. Therefore, they would need a base where they could maintain their clean and tidy persona and work to contact those who could help them once in a dock area. What could be a more perfect place where an escaper might hide than in a hotel as a guest? With Philpot's preparations seemingly impressive and 'watertight', they strove to make theirs equally as such, though perhaps a little less ambitious, and with more options for flexibility.

Deciding that the plan for Codner to escape as a woman as impractical, and their original plan to walk to Czechoslovakia in the cold of autumn was likely to be beaten by the weather, they instead turned their attentions to train travel and thoroughly explored this option. Just as it would be foolish to throw away their escape through an ill-conceived journey on foot, it would be equally foolish to do so through being unprepared to meet the risks of train travel. However, where Philpot's escape persona was 'designed' to mix on an even footing with his fellow travellers, Williams and Codner decided that they would rather their personas melded with the background of all situations and be as unremarkable and unobtrusive as possible. Just indistinguishable faces in a crowd, like any one of the millions of foreign workers then spread throughout the Reich.

To that end, Williams and Codner settled on becoming Frenchmen. Codner was quite fluent in the language which gave them an added advantage. Also there were a few French servicemen in the camp who had escaped to England when their country fell to fly with the RAF, and these they questioned for every detail of being French. However, they would pose as middle-class, skilled artisans volunteering for good jobs within the Reich. Such artisans would be much more likely to travel by train as need of their skills arose in distant locations, such as, Stettin – where there just happened to be docks that served neutral shipping.

In light of that decision Williams found his stay in the Sick Quarters a profitable one, as one of the 'Ferrets' that was on duty that week as a hospital orderly was a sallow fellow whom the prisoners had christened 'Dopey'. Dopey (his real name is long forgotten) was not exactly the finest specimen that the Third Reich had to offer. He was a dark haired, rather pallid young man who had fought on the Russian front, been badly wounded in the leg and left to die in the snow. Somehow he survived and was now listed as Class C physically and delegated to home-front duties only. It was widely rumoured among the 'Kriegies' that he was quite possibly the stupidest man alive (he had not gained the nickname 'Dopey' for nothing) and, very understandably in light of his experience in Russia, had a tendency to watch out for himself very closely. He was also both lazy and greedy, and that greed made him a soft target and easy to corrupt.

The Australian, seeing Williams had his mind set on train travel, introduced him to 'Dopey' one afternoon. Williams already had 'Dopey' under his influence, when for a few cigarettes (English cigarettes were like gold to the 'Goons') he was able to garner from the 'Ferret' some of the basics requirements of train travel for foreign workers in the Reich. After a few days of careful bribery Williams increased the pressure and asked 'Dopey' to bring in an example of a foreign workers travel permit.

'Dopey' balked; he was plainly horrified at getting caught which, for him, meant either going back to the Russia, or being shot as a collaborator. Williams, however, played his trump card. In a loud voice he announced to 'Dopey' that he had been a willing collaborator – there was a ward full of witnesses that would swear to it – so he would either provide what was requested, or Williams would turn him in. Doctor Lechten was just on the other side of the wall at the end of the room. 'Dopey' begged, pleaded but then agreed. A few days later, he brought in a permit and slipped it to Williams, who made a pencil sketch of the document, making detailed notes of the rubber stamps and their positions; also those of authorizing signatures and the identity photograph, before slipping it back to a very relieved 'Dopey', along with a generous number of cigarettes.

Dallas Laskey watched all of this, fascinated; listened to the conversations between Williams and the Australian; and then asked Williams about his scheme. Sensing a new vaulter still possessed of much of his pre-PoW vitality, Williams told him what was going on and asked him if he would be interested in vaulting. Laskey had of course seen the vaulting, but in his fuddled condition had not given it much thought. Now feeling better, also having once been a very gifted athlete while at university in New Brunswick, Canada before joining the RCAF, he was enthusiastic about the activity. It seemed a good way to stay fit and, having already seen the boredom that permeated prison life it would be, at the least, a very good way to pass the time.

Both were released from the Sick Quarters a few days later, Williams telling Laskey that he would call for him the next day. In the meantime, Codner met Williams at the gate and together they strolled around the circuit. It was obvious the tunnel could not continue as before. It was too difficult to get the sand back from the face; far too strenuous for one man. A new system had to be developed. What they required was a way to get the sand back from the face of the tunnel without it being dragged back by the digger. It was perfectly clear that what needed was a box on a sled moved by two ropes, to what they had used in the Schubin tunnel. There they had used a 'toboggan', which had worked well. But that would require two men to go down each time and it would be all the bearers could do to lift two men in the horse, let alone some 100lbs of sand or more. There had to be a different answer.

Then Codner had another inspiration. They would take the horse out for a morning session with two men inside, who would then dig as much as they could in the 2 hours available; the spoil packed into bags as usual. However at the end of the session, they would leave them behind stacked in the vertical shaft and then only the diggers would return in the horse. The afternoon session would go out with just one man in the horse and he would simply bring back the bags dug during the morning session. The next day they would repeat the process. Of course, it meant recruiting enough vaulters to arrange another daily vaulting session (always a headache, even with the help of the Escape Committee), and that the 'Goons' would have to get used to a second session each day. But it also meant that the afternoon session would be somewhat shorter, as it should not take as long to lift out twelve or forteen bags of sand

and close up the tunnel as it would to dig the same number of bags. It was obviously the solution and they immediately went to find Philpot.

That next day then, the horse went out at around 9.00am, following morning *Appell*, with both Williams and Codner inside. Along with them they carried an aluminum bowl some 18in in diameter and 8in deep that had been stolen from the cookhouse, and two long lengths of plaited cord, made from the twine that secured the British Red Cross parcel boxes. Nobody had been down for some days and they were apprehensive as to the condition of the tunnel.

They found that there had been a few minor falls along the sides, which they easily cleaned up, but otherwise the tunnel had held up nicely, and they quickly filled the twelve bags before the session was over. The new system worked well, the bowl easily glided between them over the sand of the tunnel floor. As for the 'Goons', they did not even seem to notice the extra session; to them the horse was now a regular feature of camp life.

There were only two difficulties: Firstly, since the tunnel was so cramped it became necessary that just short of the working face there should be a slightly larger area dug, into which the digger could wriggle back with his arm load of sand in order to fill the bowl. Then he would press himself up on hands and toes against the roof of the tunnel, pull the cord twice to signal the man in the entrance to haul away, and let the bowl slide under him and down the tunnel. The man in the entrance then tipped the sand out (which he packed in the sand bags) and pulled the cord twice as a signal for the digger to haul the bowl back. It took them 2 days to dig the loading area. As time went by that autumn and the tunnel became longer and longer, they filled in this loading area and dug another closer to the working face.

Secondly, the cord tended to snap where it was tied to the bowl. Originally they had punched two holes opposite each other in the lip of the bowl, through which they had then tied the cord securely. But the holes had been punched with a nail and had ragged edges, so one afternoon while Codner went out to retrieve the bags of sand, Williams made some hooks out of strong wire to connect the cord to the bowl.

Though it was not nearly as exhausting as it had been, digging was still difficult. Nor was hauling the bowls of sand back from the face an easy task in the strict confines of the entrance shaft, especially as the tunnel grew longer. Yet the new system worked so well that by around the third week in September they were digging twenty-four bags on a session (now called a digging session) and taking the next two sessions to get that sand in (called a lifting session). Still later that month, the numbers had increased to thirty-six bags over three lifting sessions. But this was the absolute maximum they could dig without exhausting themselves completely, which had happened before!

Another benefit they soon discovered was the quality of the air at the face became better with the use of the bowl. The constant movement of the bowl back and forth along the tunnel acted like a type of bellows, dragging fresh air into the tunnel with it, and the stale air back. Before, they had usually crawled out of the tunnel after a digging session with splitting headaches; a result of poor air quality at the face after a digger had been working for a short time. Now they found they had plenty of air, as long as the bowl kept moving. But if the bowl should stop for any reason the level began to drop again, and as the tunnel grew longer they found the situation could be very dangerous. Philpot suggested putting up an air hole under the warning rail, with a specially fitted cover that could be opened and closed just for sessions and camouflaged much in the same way as the tunnel entrance, but was vetoed by the other two. A 'Ferret' could easily stumble over the opening during the day, no matter how carefully hidden. At night there were the dog patrols. Covered over or not, the dogs might sniff it out. Therefore, it was deemed too dangerous.

By that time, Williams's new friend from the Sick Quarters, Dallas Laskey had become a regular member of the vaulting crowd. 'Oh, it was great fun, the vaulting,' Laskey later remembered, 'but damned hard work after a while. There were always new faces ... Some did not last long. I was in very good shape then, and happy to be helping [in the escape]. At least it was something to do.' Hurling himself over the horse with admirable skill, he soon proved himself a reliable and dedicated member of the team in other ways. Occaisionally, Philpot took him outside the cookhouse during dispersal times to toss a medicine ball back and forth. The two might keep up a steady conversation as they did, and the code if a 'Ferret' came too close for comfort was one of them stating in a loud voice, 'That's what I'd do if a policeman came.'

Also the 'Ferrets' continued to hang around the cookhouse with disturbing regularity. Obviously it was still a place of suspicion, and the three could never really be sure that the horse was not equally suspect. One evening a 'Ferret' positioned himself on the steps leading into the cookhouse, scowling at the vaulters and without showing any signs of moving any time soon. Codner was in the horse and the session (just a lifting one, fortunately) was ending, as it was getting close to *Appell*. The light fading, they needed to take the horse inside, but could they actually risk it with a 'Ferret' so close by; brushing past him with a 'loaded' horse? There was obviously no choice, and they did so with a brash *'Bitte, bitte'* (Please please) as they shoved past the sour-faced German, nearly pushing him off the steps. He hung around for a few more minutes before they re-emerged from the cookhouse and began tossing the medicine ball around until he finally wandered away. They then got Codner and his sand out from inside the horse, brushed him down and dressed him quickly before sauntering outside, only just in time for *Appell*; it had been another very close shave.[3]

Chapter 11

From Here to There

September 1943

On 8 September, all hell broke loose in the North Compound when the Germans discovered tunnel 'Tom', one of Roger Bushell's three major projects that had employed so much of the escape talent from East Compound. It was a most unfortunate state of affairs, in that all that had to be done to complete the 220ft tunnel was the construction of the exit shaft; success had been that close. However, even with the loss of one tunnel the North Compound 'X Committee' still had two cards up their sleeve. The *Abwehr* staff, temporarily placated by their discovery, displayed a certain satisfaction over the discovery but in East Compound, however, the event spurred on still further events.

Not long before the discovery of 'Tom', it became known among the escape-minded 'Kriegies' in East Compound that a tunnel was being tried from Hut 68 under the direction of Wing Commander Collard. Starting from what was regarded by the 'Goons' as the 'troublemakers hut', the attempt was to be an all out 'beitz' effort, simplicity was the byword, and the entire hut was involved. Immediately following the last thorough search of Hut 68 (as routine, one hut was searched every day, and then again after some 10 days), the tunnel was started from a simple trap cut through the floorboards under Collard's bunk. There was little regard for security, as it was believed that it would not be a need. The team worked virtually around the clock, either 'stooging' from the corner windows of the hut or digging some 20ft underground. The sand was dispersed inside the building, with virtually no thought of concealment. Sand went everywhere and anywhere; in the attic, in boxes under bunks, in kit bags stacked in the corners. The scheme operated on the theory that before the next search of the hut, all the occupants would have disappeared through the rapidly-dug tunnel and be scattered across the German countryside. It was a long distance to dig in a short time; over 200ft in a southerly direction to a ditch next to the road passing the south perimeter. All those in the camp were gripped with anticipation as the distance dug from Hut 68 rapidly increased. It was an entirely plausible idea that was working, and it overshadowed that ridiculously 'amateur' effort of the wooden horse, which was all but forgotten.

Williams and Codner were not happy about the situation though, despite the welcome lack of attention to their project. They argued with the 'X Committee' that if the scheme actually succeeded, then the furore that would be created across Germany would make their escape virtually impossible. Philpot tried to calm their fears, stating flatly that the Hut 68 tunnel had little real chance of success. Even if they did get out, most of those on the run were likely to be quickly recaptured and brought back and things returned to normal long before their tunnel was completed. Besides, since Bill White's escape effort from the *Waschrum* (Wash house) had ended in May, there had been nothing on except the wooden horse scheme, and German suspicion had been growing ever since the sand had been found under the barber shop floor the previous month. The longer the 'Goons' went without finding what had produced that sand, the stronger their suspicions of the cookhouse would likely grow, putting increasing pressure on the wooden horse effort. If the Hut 68 tunnel collapsed or was found, it would give the Germans what they expected and placate them for a while. One way or the other, the Hut 68 project could actually benefit their effort.

The timing of Philpot's judgment was uncanny. It was around three days after they had found 'Tom' in the North Compound that the *Abwehr* staff, flushed by that success, struck by springing another lightning search of the cookhouse in East Compound, which had indeed been suspect for nearly a month. With the North Compound triumph still fresh enough to make a point, 'Charlie' (Piltz) was determined not to allow there to be any 'problems' in his compound. To that end, once his 'Ferrets' descended upon the building, they began to tear the place to pieces in their zeal to find the tunnel.[1]

Philpot was in the *Abort* washing the sand out of his ears immediately following a morning lifting session when someone found him, demanding to know how the team knew about the search. Somewhat bemused, he asked the man what he was talking about, but with a sudden dread somehow he just knew. The fellow told him the cookhouse was being torn apart by some 'Ferrets'. How in the world had they known in advance that the search had been coming so they could stop work early? Their security system must be spot on! Philpot rushed over to the cookhouse, remembering dismally that they were not going to be able to dispose of the sand lifted that day until after *Appell*.

The building was cordoned off by a 'Goon squad' and the sounds of dedicated mayhem were coming from inside. Philpot joined the gathering crowd, as did Williams and Codner. By sheer chance the horse crew had indeed finished earlier than usual that afternoon. Everything was more or less tidied up and everyone dispersed to clean up by the time the truck load of Germans screeched to a halt outside the hut, rushed in, and cleared out the last few stragglers. With the search in progress, before long even Kommandant von Lindeiner was seen to stroll into the camp toward the cookhouse to witness what the 'Goons' obviously believed would be a certain victory. Almost immediately, there were excited shouts as the 'Ferrets' found the sand that had been deposited in between the rafters in the attic, along with the unemptied bags from that day's session which had been placed there less than 20 minutes earlier. Soon after, the sand under the passageway in the kitchen was found.

Frustratingly for the 'Goons', they did not find a tunnel. The watching prisoners began shouting ribald and taunting remarks at the Germans as the hours wore on, and after most of the day had been spent in fruitless searching, 'Charlie' and his 'Ferrets' retreated from the scene having been humiliated in front of the Kommandant. Piltz was a bad man to goad, and following on the heels of the discovery in the barber shop during the previous month, there could be no doubt as to what was coming next. Once 'Charlie' found sand, there would be no peace in the compound until he found the tunnel from where it had been dug.

That afternoon, opinion in the camp held that the Germans could now no longer fail to connect the horse with the sand found in the cookhouse; it seemed so patently obvious. Sand in the building (twice now, and some in convenient carrying bags) plus horse in the building equalled that the horse was possibly the source of tunnel, as no signs of a tunnel had been found in the cookhouse. 'The detractors of the scheme said, 'the project has obviously reached its inevitable end'.

However, Williams and Codner thought differently and that there was actually still a chance. Having found sand in the attic of a building in which no tunnel had been found, they expounded that the Germans would then naturally concentrate on all the attics in other huts first. If one was found to contain any unusual amount of sand they would tear that hut apart in the search for any sign of tunnelling activity. Realizing that there was no chance that the Hut 68 tunnel could now go undiscovered, the two saw an opportunity to divert suspicion from the cookhouse (and thus the horse) by throwing some of their empty sand bags, that they had in their room, up into the attic space in Hut 68. When found – as they surely would be – the bags should convince the Germans that the sand in the cookhouse was nothing more than overflow from Hut 68. The 'Ferrets' would then obviously concentrate their efforts there and forget about the cookhouse. Williams went to get permission from Wing Commander Collard and before lock up that evening the empty spare bags had been smuggled over to Hut 68 and tossed up into the attic space. The next day would tell the tale.

The next morning following *Appell*, the 'Ferrets' swarmed into the compound, and it took no time at all for them to find the sand, which was everywhere, in Hut 68. During the search, part of the ceiling collapsed on the searchers under the weight of sand, and the empty sand bags were quickly found. Not long after, the trap to the tunnel was found, after which the 'Ferrets' started work with shovels and a fire hose. Wing Commander Collard was marched off to serve a spell in the 'Cooler' as senior man in the hut. By the end of the day, all was routine again; German suspicions were satisfied for the time being and the prisoners looked on grimly as all the sand was carted out and away from Hut 68 in trucks. It was another failed effort and another win for the 'Goons'. Once again morale within the compound sank.

For the next few of days the cookhouse was closed as the 'Goons' cleared all the sand out of the attic, so there was no vaulting. But on the first day possible, the wooden horse was out in its usual location with the vaulters again hurling themselves over it in monotonous succession; its charmed existence remained intact.

Once everything got back to regular routine, they took the horse out every day for a week as usual, but suspended digging just in case the 'Goons' were not as satisfied as they seemed. Over the next few days they 'accidently' knocked the horse over a few times. One afternoon, they re-upholstered the padding on the top continuing their attempt to make everything look as natural as possible. They also had to make some new sand bags, and searched the compound for worn battledress trousers to cut up. When they opened the tunnel after a week off, again they found that the sand had dried and crumbled in spots, leaving several minor falls to remove and shore up, particularly under the circuit. Another week at least had passed before they were able to return to the face and make forward progress. It was another long delay they could ill afford; time was now getting short and they still had a long way to dig.

It was also back to the question of where to hide all that sand! The attic in the cookhouse was no longer of use. The 'Ferrets' would make a point to inspect it and all other attics far more regularly. The idea had never been a satisfactory answer anyway. Neither could they not risk carrying it away with the vaulters, as they could never tell if the 'Goons' were specifically watching the cookhouse. Where then? Oddly enough, the failed Hut 68 tunnel that had produced the problem, now gave them the answer. Perhaps they could hide the spoil openly, though not quite as obvious as in Hut 68. Why not put it discreetly where it had already been found – perhaps under the barber shop again? The floor did not look as though it had been touched by the 'Goons' in their last sweep, and the only way they could have inspected the space would have been to pull up the floorboards. Therefore, as long as the new nails the Germans had used to seal up the previous trap were not disturbed, there should be no reason why they would suspect the area again. It would be the perfect place; secure from inspection as it had already been inspected.

At least, the problem of finding vaulters had finally been solved. It had now fallen into a fairly routine schedule, organized after Philpot had formally joined the escape by a very bored, long-term inmate of Stalag Luft III, Pilot Officer Desmond Breed. One of the three would-be escapers, usually Philpot, was always in charge of the vaulting session. But with a team leader organizing a daily roster of vaulters for the two sessions, that side of the project became

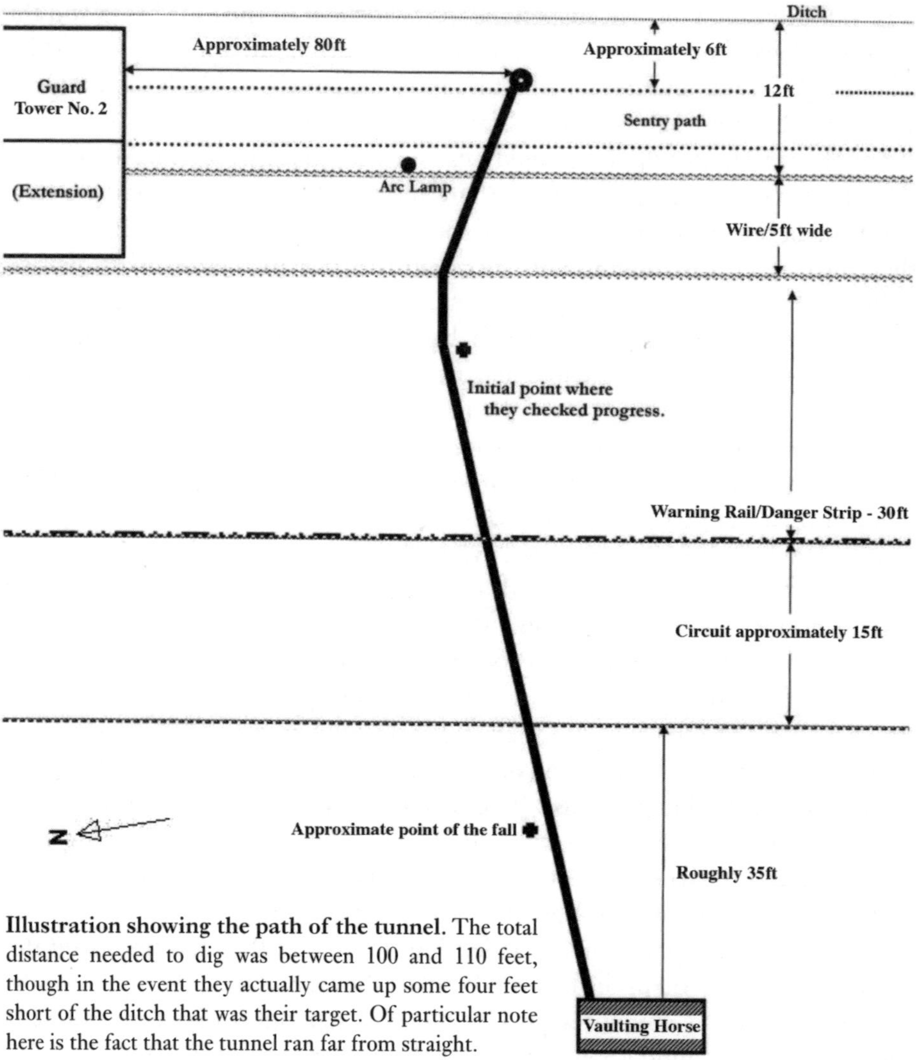

Illustration showing the path of the tunnel. The total distance needed to dig was between 100 and 110 feet, though in the event they actually came up some four feet short of the ditch that was their target. Of particular note here is the fact that the tunnel ran far from straight.

immensely easier. No longer was it necessary for any of the escapers to canvas the compound day-after-day looking for volunteers to vault. There were now enough regulars, rotated by days, to form a consistent schedule of sessions. A digging session still took 2½ hours, but only took place every third morning (or, more precisely, every fourth session) and only as needed. The lifting sessions were shorter, usually around 1½ hours, which allowed just enough time to get twelve bags into the horse and perhaps some time to do light maintenance on the tunnel. Everyone was grateful for these shorter sessions. Time blocks, adjusted as when necessary, were 9.00 to 11.30am and 2.00 to 4.30pm.[2]

Vaulters now generally fell into three categories: The committee members, as it was considered to be their duty (the many); those willing to help because they thought it a good idea worth supporting (the few); and those who vaulted because they found it a good exercise and an outlet for any surplus energy (the fewer). Pilot Officer Len Pearman, one of the committee men working for Dean & Dawson, was among the first group. Some 46 years later he remembers, with more than a little irony and much pride, 'We vaulted over their horse every day [but] laughed at them. "You'll never get it – you'll never make it. But, here goes; we'll do the vaulting, we'll do the carrying, and good luck to you." And they got out and all got home!'[3]

Dallas Laskey brought his navigator, 'Moose' Miller, onto the team. Miller, strong as an ox (or a Moose), usually carried one corner of the horse, with 'Pappy' Elliot, Ed Chapman and Ken Edwards as the other bearers. Joe Mennill was also a regular. 'I was one of the ones that was recruited … and used to go out there and jump quite religiously, every period we were scheduled. But they had quite a lot of different people, because it was not exactly all that exciting, vaulting that horse!'

Pilot Officer A.E.V. Oliver, the navigator of a Vickers Wellington shot down during a raid on Turin in August 1940, was another dedicated regular. Arriving at Sagan from Italy that summer of 1943, he was coerced almost immediately by Pilot Officer Tony Barber to become a vaulter. Oliver was there nearly every day, despite having two cracked vertebrae (the result of his bail-out) until he just could not get out of bed anymore and was taken to the Sick Quarters.[4]

By the end of September, Dallas Laskey being so dedicated to the project had taken over leading the vaulting team from Des Breed. 'I had barked my shins against the animal enough by then,' recalled Laskey. 'So when Ollie Philpot asked me to take over the scheduling of the vaulting teams, I 'jumped' at the chance!' Les Sidwell also remained as one of the dedicated regulars and another right-hand man. There were also Pilot Officers Aubrey Niner, William 'Tex' Ash (an American in the RAF), Tom Hawthorn, Peter Harding and A.G. Eperson, as well as Wing Commander John Barrett and Flight Lieutenant Colin Macfie. Problems with messing aside, Pilot Officer William 'Bill' Roe, another from Williams and Codner's room, also came on a regular basis, as did their other room mate, Lieutenant David Lubbock, who always vaulted with Aiden Crawley. Squadron Leaders 'Paddy' Barthropp (famous after the war as a 'high society man') and Ralph Bagshaw Ward, Clothing Officer on the Escape Committee, both frequently joined in the vaulting. Even the intrepid Tommy Calnan was seen launching himself over the horse on occasion, along with fellow No.1 PRU pilot, Flying Officer Alex Anderson and his partner for his escape from Schubin, Robert Kee (later a British television personality).

Another brief, but terrifying, crisis came during an afternoon session when someone tripped against the horse and knocked it over – with 'Charlie' standing not more than 10ft away and the open trap visible to all and sundry. In a flash, those closest to the horse crowded around and righted it immediately.

Fortunately, 'Charlie' was looking in the opposite direction and never saw a thing. Nor, apparently, did the 'Goons' in the towers overlooking the scene. Another disaster had been narrowly averted by good teamwork and dedication of those involved, whether they believed in the scheme or not. In the background, wiser heads in camp were again shaken in wonder at the luck.

The golfers had a distinct dislike of the horse. On a breezy afternoon, one of them demonstrated this dislike and sealed the fate of all golfers with one man on the horse crew. Tom Wilson later recalled, 'The 9th hole and its 'green' (only brushed sand) were very close to the horse in its digging position and actually made it easier for us to deposit the horse in its correct position. One afternoon a golfer made a bad approach-shot, his ball hit the horse and was deflected into the bunker beside the green. He lost his temper, shouted obscenities and rushed up to the horse and started kicking it. We had to intervene before he had it over. We took him prisoner and carted him off to our authorities for punishment. I have personally avoided golfers ever since!'

It was mid-month when Wilson's time as a vaulter came to an abrupt end. He had quickly progressed to become quite good, building up his strength and agility to a high degree and performing the most amazing flips and vaults. But one afternoon, on landing from a particularly demanding vault he tore the Achilles tendon in his right ankle. In excruciating pain, he collapsed on the sand and the stretcher was again sent for, this time for real. Once in the Sick Quarters, Dr Lechten examined him and then he was made comfortable in the bed that he would occupy for the foreseeable future. Though down, he was far from out and would be back at the beginning of October to play a new role in the scheme. While it would be tough to find someone as dedicated to the programme as Wilson, these days it was far easier than it ever had been to round up vaulters for the teams.

But, there were still those older 'Kriegies' who refused to help on the project on the grounds that one only helped on a tunnel for a chance at going through it upon completion. It was well known in camp that the three had no intentions of offering anyone else a place on a scheme that, if it succeeded, could not take more than three anyway. This almost detrimental attitude displayed by several of the 'Kriegie' toward the project had been, to one degree or another, standard operating procedure in the past. It was largely due to the number of independent projects that went forward in the early days before the firm, guiding hand of the Escape Committees organized and regulated escape. Nevertheless, committee policy or not, attitudes were not always quick to change. 'Why waste the effort? What will I get out of it?' the usual questions, of which Philpot, as 'X' representative to the scheme, were usually the recipient. The strongest questioners were the ones who lambasted the entire horse project the most; the ones who could only believe in a project that they themselves were part of, and then only if it looked an absolute certainty, which the horse certainly did not to most. Fortunately, they were the minority in the compound, and though they were far from quiet in expressing their views, those actually involved with the horse project (for whatever the reason) were able to largely ignore them.

The one obstacle which they could not ignore, however, was the weather. The coming of autumn over the Silesian plain brought with it showers and an occasional cold wind. Days that began warm and bright might suddenly cloud over before the first session of the day, threatening rain. If it did rain and they were out vaulting, they had to stop; nothing could be more bogus than vaulting in bad weather. Also the horse could not left out in the open. This had never been done before and surely the ever suspicious Germans would realize that it would not be such a burden for men already wet to get a little wetter carrying their equipment back inside. However, since it took 15 minutes on average to seal the trap, a sudden shower could possibly mean sudden death to the project.

The weather was watched very carefully and argued over as to whether the conditions would be suitable. More than once the team would gather, ready to go, when one of the three leaders would question the weather, starting an intense debate as to whether they should go underground or not. Vaulting was not the question; it was imperative that they should take the horse out as usual to maintain normality. That had to be done. But to open up the tunnel or not …. All important work days were lost and tempers flared when the decision not to open the tunnel was taken, only to see the threatening weather remain calm throughout a session. Philpot and Williams argued the most.

As the tunnel neared the wire, nerves began to fray on other matters. Williams and Codner still spent the most time underground, not completely trusting Philpot to maintain their simple standards on the project. They tried as much as possible to keep him involved, hauling the basin and filling sand bags, or organizing the dispersal and helping with the vaulting, rather than doing any digging. Occasionally Philpot would insist on doing a spell of digging. In that case, either Williams or Codner would carefully inspect his work during the next digging session.

Philpot did not mind being kept out of the tunnel. Never particularly fond of the hole from the outset, as it lengthened, work in the tunnel had taken on even more of a nightmarish quality than ever before. He was not alone in his assessments. Occasionally, they had found the need to use the committee's precious flashlight; a 'memento' stolen from a 'Ferret'. Seeing the tunnel with its eery weak light, illustrated the actual narrowness of the dig and the spidery tangle of roots dangling from the roof, gave a certain tomb like feel to everything that was not easily forgotten. Also when lit, the tunnel somehow appeared less sturdy. But darkness produced its own problems. As the tunnel lengthened, all three experienced becoming a little disorientated toward the end of a digging session. At times the digger might crawl back, convinced that the tunnel was going deeper. So the next man up to the face would check, only to find the tunnel appeared perfectly level. However, that man might then end his session insisting that the tunnel had veered left; or was actually getting smaller; or that the roots above seemed to be grabbing at him. They soon learned to contain these opinions.

Philpot again proposed an air-supply system, tried before in other shallow tunnels, which utilized a number of Nescafe tins joined together and fitted with a flip-up lid, opened and closed by an internal narrow rod. This could be put up safely once they got within the tangle of wire in between the fences. But, he was again overruled by the now ever watchful Williams and Codner, who were still concerned that the guard dogs would sniff out the vent. Each claimed that with the sand bowl moving they had no problems breathing. Philpot did not believe them. Nor did Williams and Codner really trust Philpot yet when it came to tunnel construction. Both were convinced that given the opportunity he would devise some sort of Heath-Robinson type of air pump, which to make would require time and effort they could ill afford. Though they were a team, they were still individuals and there were some tense moments.

'How do you know how far you've dug, and that you are indeed going straight?'

This was one of the many concerns, that each of them had heard recently. In fact, of late they had even begun to wonder about such things and by mid-month Codner was convinced that the tunnel was off course, veering to the left, while construction expert Williams was equally convinced that he was being silly. It was virtually the only time the two argued about anything, but they did argue. The length of string they used to measure underground showed they should be getting near the wire. But exactly how near? It was time to find out.

One afternoon session, Williams and Philpot went out in the horse armed with a thin, steel fire poker and a length of string. Once underground, Williams crawled to the end of the tunnel with the poker, and one end of the string (which promptly broke, necessitating him to wriggle back) tied to his ankle. At the face, he scooped a hole in the floor of the tunnel deep enough to accommodate the poker and then, using a careful corkscrew motion, drove it up through the roof. When he reached the end of the handle, he turned over and scooped out more of the roof and kept pushing. It was a tricky business, as he had to be careful not to bring the roof down on top of him. Sand cascaded down onto his chest and face, making him cough. When he felt the resistance slacken considerably, he stopped pushing and tugged gently twice on the string. He was through, and judging from the length of the poker and the hole in the roof he had carved, they were around 2ft 10in below the surface.

Crouching in the entrance shaft, Philpot felt the tugs and quickly stood up and gently knocked on the side of the horse. Codner, outside with the vaulters, called for a rest break and the vaulting team flopped down on the sand, or lounged against the horse. They gazed casually, showing no interest, toward the east fence and the wire; the 'Goon' in his box; the danger strip. The danger strip, just where the end of the poker should be sticking up above the sand, but it was not. The seconds ticked by like hours as they kept searching. Where the hell *was* that thing?

Under the horse the minutes ticked by and Philpot was beginning to wonder what was happening. How long could it take to see a poker?

Williams, sweating and caked in sand down at the end of the tunnel, wondered much the same thing and slowly began to carefully move the poker up and down.

Above, a dozen pairs of eyes frantically scanned the danger strip, trying hard not to look frantic, when a 'circuit basher' lazily altered his gait and wandered in their direction. It was Flight Lieutenant 'Freddie' McKay, a small New Zealander and photographic reconnaissance pilot shot down in 1942, one of the original vaulters, who was not on schedule for that session. Standing in the trap, Philpot could clearly hear his cheerful Kiwi voice as he approached.

'Hello you guys,' he said. 'What're you doing? You tired? You break your legs or something?'

Then he heard him exclaim with a loud shout, 'Say … what's that over there?'

This was quickly followed by a mild panic among the vaulters, quiet rapping on the side of the horse and insistent whispers from outside.

'Ollie! Ollie! Pull that poker down! Pull it down!'

Philpot immediately tugged on the string, signalling Williams.

Still the frantic whispers came.

'For God's sake Ollie; pull that bloody thing down!'

Philpot tugged again, this time a little harder.

Then he heard Codner's cultured, even voice, as cool and unconcerned in crisis as only the British can be:

'Ollie, you might pull that poker down now.'

Immediately after, there came the normal sound of the vaulters leaping over the horse and shortly a sweaty, peeved Williams came squirming back down the tunnel to close up.

Later, after the session and back in the cookhouse, there was a post mortem. Williams and Philpot emerged from under the horse somewhat piqued; what had taken so long? Codner broke the news: though the poker had come up rather more than halfway between the warning rail and the inner fence, they had not been able to locate it at first as it was some 15ft to the left of their intended line. The 'Goon' in the box that overlooked their sessions practically had a full view of the poker; all he would have to have done was turn his head a little and then he could not have missed the sun glinting off the end. Codner had been right.

When word got around among the crowd in the compound, the sceptics really had their day at the expense of the horse scheme. What sort of project had they got there? Almost 30 degrees off line; waving pokers at the 'Goons' … why not just invite the Germans in on the scheme?

Still Williams and Codner continued to ignore all the sceptics; despite the difficulties, the mistakes, and the odds. Remaining infinitely confident in their scheme, the next day the two quietly went about the business of correcting the problems and dug on.

For his part, Philpot had finally come to fully realize that a conventional way of thinking on this scheme was totally unworkable, and though the tunnel had so appalled him the first few times he had worked in it, he had now accepted it as a necessary evil. Much of the reason for this line of thought was caused by the attitude of the more experienced in the escape fraternity who continued to disparage the scheme. As time went by, in conjunction with those negative comments and the effort required, came the slow realization they had survived each near disaster, and that the project actually looked to have a real chance at success, due largely to the very irregular nature of the scheme that caused such comments in the first place. Earlier on it had seemed to him that only something truly unconventional would be likely to triumph in breaking out of East Compound. It could hardly be argued that unconventionality was the one thing the horse scheme had – in spades.

Now that they knew how close to the wire they were, the next question concerned the sound detectors. Everyone knew that the Germans had planted these in the ground outside the wire in order to discern any vibrations from tunnelling. These were wired to a receiver in the *Kommandantur*, where they were listened to by an operator. It was in deference to these detectors that tunnels dug at Sagan ran so deep underground. A tunnel at a depth of 20 or 30ft was not likely to be picked up by the detectors, but a tunnel at a depth of only 2ft 10in would be a prime target. Or so the sceptics said.

The trouble was, nobody in the compound was quite sure just where the detectors were or how deep they had been placed, as they had not been there when the camp was originally built. But there had been those volunteer working parties of 'Kriegies' who had gone to work on North Compound during its construction earlier in the year, and they might have some idea. Word was sent over to Bushell's people requesting information on the detectors, which was soon received: the detectors were sunk into the ground to a depth of 12ft and were some 15ft apart. By measuring from the corner fence posts of the compound, the committee was able to plot the approximate positions of all the detectors ringing East Compound by working on the assumption that the same spacing and depth had been used during the original construction. It also showed that the horse tunnel should be passing between two detectors. And though it did not occur to anyone (Williams and Codner included), until after the scheme had been going for a little while, that with the tunnel being so shallow any noise of digging that the detectors might pick up would likely be taken for nothing more than vibrations coming from the endless parade of 'circuit bashers' tramping around the camp and the efforts of the vaulters.

Providence had provided yet again.

One morning, as September gave its way to October, Williams uncovered something along one side of the tunnel which nearly drove him out. Emerging later, he described a stench unlike anything he had ever experienced. Consensus of opinion among the team was that most likely a cat or dog had been buried there at some time, though some of the old 'Kriegies' delighted in the (probably correct) observation that it might be a Russian prisoner who had died building the camp back in 1942 and been buried there by his comrades. Whatever it was, Williams had tightly walled it up again in the darkness. Considerably shaken by his experience, he then moved the tunnel slightly to avoid the area. But he was never able to pass that section of the tunnel comfortably again.

Chapter 12

'You're not thinking of *leaving us*, by any chance, are you?'

October 1943

By April 1943, the German High Command became exasperated at the number of PoWs escaping, and were alarmed at the ever increasing man hours and resources being spent in hunting for escapers. Following the Schubin escape, the Nazi hierarchy simply ripped up the rules book. A statement was issued from Berlin that month to the command staffs of PoW camps warning, in part, that:

> 'Each PoW must be informed that by escaping in civilian clothing or German uniform he is not only liable to disciplinary punishment, but runs the risk of being court martialled and committed for trial on suspicion of espionage and partisanship; in the affirmative he may even be sentenced to death.'

Throughout the summer, further additions and refinements were made to that original order. The text of some of these was made available to senior officers in some camps (mostly those run by the Luftwaffe), in the hope that they might caution, or perhaps even order, their men to give up the idea of escape. In the early autumn, these appeals were followed by the notorious 'Escaping Is No Longer A Sport' notices that were posted in virtually all PoW camps across the Reich. A portion of the text of this now infamous document used a quote from a captured British Commando handbook, which stated:

> 'For the time being, every soldier must be a political gangster and be prepared to adopt their methods whenever necessary. The sphere of operations should always include the enemy's own country, any occupied territory, and in certain circumstances such neutral countries as he is using as a source of supply.'

The Germans felt that this 'instituted illegal warfare in non-combat zones … even up to the frontier of Germany' and gave them complete freedom to institute whatever measures they felt necessary to safeguard their 'homeland and especially (their) industry and provisional centres for the fighting fronts.'

To that end, they had created a series of 'Death Zones' around the Reich, in which 'all unauthorized trespassers will be immediately shot on sight. Escaped prisoners of war entering such death zones will certainly lose their lives. They are therefore in constant danger of being mistaken for enemy agents or sabotage groups. Urgent warning is given against making future escapes. In plain English: Stay in the camp where you will be safe. Breaking out is now a dangerous act. The chances of preserving your life are small …'

Of course, all frontiers and coastal docks – the points for which a potential escaper would plan to go in order to reach neutral territory – were included among these 'Death Zones'.[1]

In East Compound/Stalag Luft III, that edict was supplemented by a letter issued by Kommandant von Lindeiner to Group Captain Kellett dated 6 October 1943; the content of which was posted openly for all prisoners to see alongside the original notice. It also stated, in plain detail, just how far the Germans were now prepared to remove themselves from the rules, and of the intention to send any PoW for summary court martial if he were caught; 'in civilian clothes or German uniform, or military uniform altered to resemble civilian clothes or German uniform; engaged in damage to Reich property in any way, including the use of bed boards for tunnelling, the theft of tools or materials, damage to Reich buildings and equipment, unjustified use of electricity in tunnels, etc …; forgery of official Reich paperwork and/or documentation or the possession of, or theft of, official Reich paperwork, including maps of forbidden zones.' The notice then went on to stress once again that any escaping prisoner caught in civilian clothing or German uniform could reasonably expect to face charges of 'espionage, sabotage or banditry' and if convicted could face civil penalties which, in Nazi Germany, usually meant death.[2]

The three would-be wooden horse escapers read these announcements grimly. The 'Goons' could hardly have made their intentions clearer. But were they bluffing? They were forever issuing warnings and various threats against escapers. But the Geneva Convention had laid down strict rules regarding treatment of prisoners of war, and these clearly dictated that escape was not an offence punishable by death. The prisoner had the right to try to escape, and unless actually caught in the act of 'sabotage or banditry' he was to be regarded as nothing more than a legitimate prisoner of war, even if he had altered his uniform to resemble clothing that would render him unobtrusive in a crowd.

However, it now appeared as if the Germans had decided to treat all escapers as not potential saboteurs, but as enemies of the state, proven or otherwise. If taken at face value, the edict could only mean that virtually everything to do with escape was now a punishable offense in one way or another. Even the activities of the wooden horse crew thus far, if discovered at that point, could have serious consequences, and they were still inside the camp. What might happen then if they were caught close to the Swiss border, or in the docks at

Stettin trying to stow away on a neutral ship? The thought was disquieting, to say the least.

But what was the alternative? Give up now; so close to apparent success? After all they had done thus far? Why, because the Germans had threatened them? Looked at from a strictly analytical point of view, the risks were essentially the same as they had faced in the air before capture, and the stakes remained unchanged. Only the manner of the risk had changed. Though the Germans liked to expound that for the 'Kriegies' the war was over, nothing could have been further from the truth. They were still officers in the service of His Britannic Majesty, duty bound to continue the fight by whatever means they could. Therefore, to just sit idly by and continue to do nothing simply because the Germans had threatened them, essentially amounted to surrendering yet again. Consequently, although the three talked it over briefly it was clear in what direction they would proceed, and their resolve was firmly set. Having come this far, it was unthinkable to abandon the tunnel.

At the beginning of October, Williams came upon the buried end of one of the fence poles during a digging session. That next day they again pushed the poker up next to the pole and there was no longer a doubt: they had finally reached the inner fence line. This fact had a very bracing effect on the three escapers, most particularly Philpot, as suddenly the project was not based on a big 'if' they could get beyond the wire anymore, but instead on a guardedly optimistic 'when' they would.

When the news got around the camp, the attitude of some toward the project began to change as well. No longer were the whispers concerned with what paltry distances had been dug, but instead with the few feet yet to go. Suddenly it was apparent that the three 'mad' men digging under that infernal horse might actually make it out, and the crowd gathering at the vaulting sessions swelled, as many sought to give what assistance they could.

'Rackets' Marsh, thirty years after the war remembered, 'As the weeks went by and the tunnel crept nearer and nearer to the wire, it began to dominate the minds of us all. Not that many of us would have wished to change places with the three men … Tunnelling is never very pleasant work, and remember that they were working in one so cramped that it was difficult to turn around … If the tunnel had ever caved in on them, there would have been very little chance of getting them out alive.'

Nevertheless, there were a number of people who suddenly wondered 'if there was room for one more' on the scheme. Of course there was not, but the Escape Committee did talk with the three about the possibility of covering the exit on the night of the break, in order that the tunnel might be used again. No one knew what the exit hole would entail, nor if they would have time to conceal it in some way. All things considered, the committee viewed the possibility very logically and calculated that if the tunnel were to survive, then immediately the hut doors were opened the next day three more men could be launched through it into the dense early morning fog that had been rolling in as of late and which did not burn off until just before *Appell*. For the intended attempt, they picked three deserving individuals who had given much to that particular scheme, or to escape in general: Dallas Laskey, who had taken over co-ordinating all the vaulting; Aiden Crawley, experienced escaper and who had helped Philpot enormously with dispersal; and Lieutenant David Lubbock.

Lubbock, an RNVR pilot shot down during a raid on Kirkenes, Norway in July 1941 flying a Fairey Albacore of No.828 NAS from the aircraft carrier HMS *Victorious*, was a messmate of Williams and Codner. The son-in-law of the renowned Scottish medical nutritionist Lord Boyd-Orr, Lubbock had attended Trinity College, Cambridge, before the war, receiving his degree in Nutrition and Economics. He had gained fame early in his time as a prisoner for concocting a recipe for an easily carried escape ration, usually referred to as 'Dog Food', made from porridge oats, chocolate, sugar, 'Bemax' (wheatgerm), raisins, and any other high-calorie items he could obtain. After mixing it was packed into used sardine tins and baked; it came out hard as a rock and far from tasty. However, a 1in square moistened in the mouth to a chewable state and swallowed had enough calories to keep a man going for half a day. If too much was ingested however (as sometimes happened, for even if it provided enough calories it could not fill that hollow feeling in the stomach), it caused severe stomach cramps. Nevertheless, all three escapers were taking some of the mixture with them, as had dozens of escapers before them. For this important contribution to the escape, as well as for his determined vaulting as Crawley's partner and great help during dispersal for the scheme, Lubbock was awarded a second chance at the tunnel.

With the reaching of the inner fence line, preparations for the escape were immediately stepped up. Though an exact date was yet to be decided, it would obviously have to be before the end of the month. Tommy Calnan's railway timetable expired on 31 October. The great question was whether they still had enough time to lengthen the tunnel to the small ditch next to the road. From the point at the inner fence, they still had 5ft of wire barrier to cross under in order to reach the far fence, and then a further estimated 12ft from the wire to the ditch, passing under the sentry path, and no cover whatsoever within that distance in which to safely emerge. The ditch, admittedly, did not offer much cover either, as it was only some 8 to 10in deep, and the pools of light thrown by the arc lamps spread for nearly 30ft. However it did provide some shadow and was the best place they could hope for – unless, of course, they wanted to dig under the road and into the trees beyond, which was clearly out of the question.

Williams and Codner again brought up the possibility of 'moling' those last remaining feet, as Tommy Calnan had earlier suggested. No hard and fast decisions were made concerning the prospect however, though Philpot let it be known that he was still not keen on the idea. The Escape Committee, of course, wanted an exit that could be used again, and if this could be concealed on the night of the escape, then so much the better. A 'mole' tunnel would not give the type of open exit desired, but if that was all that was available, then it would be better than nothing.

In the end, the three took a 'wait and see' attitude and started digging with renewed energy, in order to try and complete as much as they possibly could before the end of the month. They immediately moved the direction of the tunnel slightly to the right, in order to swing away from the 'Goon box' they were near, as much as they could. The number of bags of sand they dug increased, and during the lifting sessions the bearers found themselves staggering back with first fourteen and then sixteen bags in addition to the underground man. It was a tremendous strain for them, trying to make it look effortless, also the horse was beginning to creak and groan as they lurched up the steps into the cookhouse.

Tom Wilson came back to the scheme the first week in October, limping and under doctor's orders that he was not to begin vaulting in the near future. He broke the news to Williams, who heartened him immeasurably by announcing that, in that case, he had a new job for him; one that involved his violin. Wilson had obtained an old, battered violin which he had lovingly restored through the Germans not long after arriving in Sagan, a keen musician, anything to do with him playing his beloved instrument was welcome. Williams informed him that he would now be working security for dispersal. The barber shop, next to the cookhouse, was only open for business in the mornings. The Escape Committee then booked the shop, for Wilson to practice his violin, from 6.30 to 8.30 every evening in October. 'I had to play music I knew by heart,' he later recalled, 'for I had to keep my eyes fixed on my friend, Les Sidwell, standing by the trip wire before the barbed wire fence. He would be wearing his RAF officer's cap. If he took it off, that meant that a 'Ferret' or guard was approaching, who might see what was going on in the barber shop. I then had to warn the dispersal team, who would immediately [put] the floorboards down and join in singing sea shanties with me. We would just be a music group authorised to perform music in the barber shop in the evenings.' Wilson would continue this job until the day of the escape.

While October mellowed, with the birch trees among the pines around them changing colour, the three continued to work on their escape personas each evening. Some of the Schubin escapers had covered incredible distances by paying attention to details, thus making their cover as believable as possible in order that they might blend in. What weighed heavily against the Schubin men, however, was the nationwide furore in the wake of their mass escape (all escapes involving more than five men were considered mass escapes by the Germans). A huge number of people had been on the lookout for them, making blending in almost impossible when everyone was being considered a potential suspect.

Fortunately, that would not be likely in the case of an escape by three men. While the call would go out to be on the lookout for the escapers, that call would be a relatively minor one by comparison, and therefore blending in with the general public would be far easier – if the details of one's cover was convincing.

Perhaps the most important detail would be the proper credentials to support that cover. Travel around the Reich primarily involved the correct documentation, specific to the individual traveller, and all properly certified. In the years of escape activity leading up to the end of 1943, the 'X Organization' had been diligent in their collecting of examples of whatever up-to-date documentation was needed, and then perfecting the forging of that paperwork. Flight Lieutenant Mike Lewis would remember, 'We had a man who was a forgery expert with the Bank of England before he went in the air force during the war, and this man was fantastic. Give him a pen and ink and he could draw you anything. I mean, he could draw you passes which looked like they had been produced on a printing machine.'

However, there was no more difficult task than forgery. Both time consuming and meticulous, nearly all of the printing on the documents had to be drawn by hand, typescript included, on the correct weight and shade of paper. All this had to be achieved with only the minimum of necessary tools and materials. Also, all of the paperwork had to be properly arranged to fit the individual persona of the escaper, which was not an easy task in a country overrun with literally millions of foreign workers and a government living in official dread of subversion and sabotage. The Nazi way of keeping all those millions under control was by constant changing of the paperwork necessary for any foreigner to move around the country. Each pass was specific to that individual's travel needs and work situation. This problem was compounded by not only the excess of documentation issued by the Nazi government, but further by local documentation issued by employers and police for short distance travel. It was a dangerous area of escape and called for a high degree of attention to detail, for the easiest way to get picked up was through incorrect or poorly prepared paperwork; especially if one's escape persona was anything more than that of a local peasant.

'Jon Jorgenson' was already all but real on paper when Philpot joined the escape, and his documentation was well underway, thanks largely to the talents of 'Red' Hunter and the resolute Peter Stevens. These documents included a *Vorlaufausweise* (a temporary pass, in this case issued by the Dresden police), Philpot's was printed on a real blank, brought in by a corrupted 'Goon'; two *Urlaubscheine* (foreign workers permission to travel – one of these was again real); a *Bescheinigung* (confirmation of transfer from an employer); an *Arbeitskarte* (foreign workers identity card); a *Bestatigung* (a certificate confirming the issue of an *Arbeitsbuch*; a small booklet that detailed his work history and which, when travelling, was usually held by the issuing police service); a typed letter of introduction on the letterhead of the Margarine Sales Union he worked for; a typed letter from the National *Sammlung* (Norwegian Nazi Party), written in Norwegian courtesy Haldor Espelid, requesting that he go and hear Quisling speak about the reconstruction of Europe after the Nazi victory; a few calling cards for 'Jon Jorgenson'; and, finally, his membership card to the National *Sammlung*. The letters had been typed for him by Tommy Calnan. He kept everything in a large faux-leather wallet.

After further thought, since 'Jon Jorgenson' had decided to travel to the union at Danzig, Philpot decided that as an added back up it would do him well to have a second persona available that described him as a Swedish sailor. An employee of a Margarine Sales Union would hardly have cause to hang around in the docks. However, 'Jon Jorgenson, Swedish Sailor' would, and it might possibly be that part of his escape persona that would allow Philpot to board a neutral ship. In any case, it was better safe than sorry. The only true paperwork required for this persona was a Swedish sailor's identity card, which Philpot and Williams dreamed up together since nobody had any idea what a real one looked like. Nevertheless, although it looked suitably nautical when finished, it was not altogether the most convincing document, which both hoped they would not be forced to rely on.

If there was one problem with his papers – and this would extend to Williams and Codner – it was that the forgers had no way of providing real photographs for their documents. Instead, all three of them had to settle for existing photographs of men who had a similar appearance. In Philpot's case, it was fellow prisoner Squadron Leader 'Rusty' Wardell. Williams and Codner never knew who their 'doubles' were, but neither was a very accurate likeness, especially that for Codner.[3]

Although reasonably fluent in German, if with a noticeable accent, Philpot knew no Norwegian, though Espelid had made an attempt to teach him some during the weeks he coached him through his escape persona. But, preoccupied with the thousand and one details that demanded his attention first in his duties as 'Little X' on the horse scheme and then in being an active participant, Philpot had absorbed very little of what he had been taught. Considering that he was unlikely to run into any real Norwegians anyway, and believing that a little knowledge could be dangerous where a lot might be needed, he instead took up smoking a pipe in order to buy him time in lighting it during possible questioning by a suspicious official. It also gave him a reason for such poor diction in German, with the pipe firmly clenched between his teeth in the corner of his mouth. This, added to the fact he was supposed to be an *Auslander* (Foreigner) he reasoned, would be enough to quash any language suspicions.

The Men Who Made It Happen

Richard Michael Clinton Codner

Eric Ernest Williams

Oliver Laurence Spurling Philpot

An example of a standard stacking vaulting horse, of the type supplied to many schools in England before the war. This was Michael Codner's inspiration for perhaps the most ingenious escape of the Second World War. *(M/S Vinex Enterprises Pvt. Ltd. India)*

Schoolboy gymnast Tony Lynham vaulting over a stacking vaulting horse at Beechholme School, Banstead, England. Note the springboard (left), which the Sagan escapers did not have the luxury of using. *(Courtesy Beechholme School/Lewis Wood and Tony Lynham)*

Lieutenant Jack Millett (inset) and a view of the *Sportzplatz* at Oflag VI-B, Warburg. Though unknown to the three would-be escapers at Sagan, Millett and two others had tried a similar 'wooden horse' idea at Warburg in the summer of 1942, but were caught in the attempt almost immediately. *(Warburg.net)*

An exact replica of the 'Wooden Horse', constructed for this book. The original was made from stolen timber rafters and Red Cross packing crates and measured 5ft by 3ft, standing 4ft 6in high.

A front view of the horse, showing how four men carried it into position.

Four men carrying the horse with one side removed to reveal how a single individual was carried inside. Since the horse actually weighed little – and the Germans knew this – only the strongest men were used to carry it into position, as they would each use only one hand on the bearing poles in order to keep things looking natural. This was not an easy task, especially after a session when the horse was loaded with a man, 120lb of sand, and the bearers were tired after a strenuous session of vaulting. The empty area ahead of him inside would be where the sand bags were hung from the top boards once a session of digging was over.

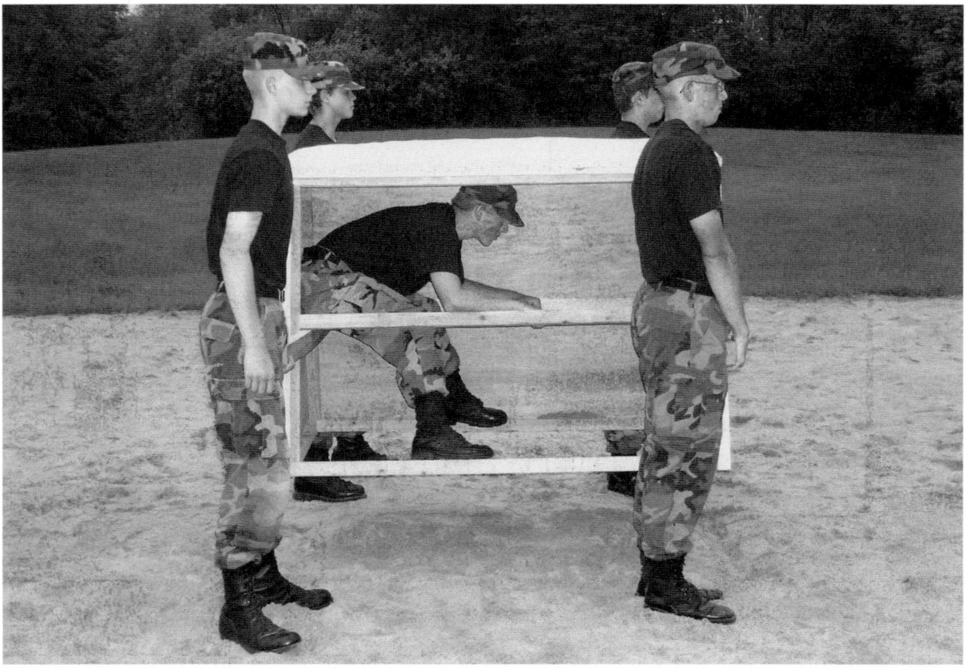

How two men rode in the horse.

This is how Williams, Philpot, and McKay were carried in the horse on the last day it was used. McKay, being the smallest was carried in the middle. Williams later said that under the weight of three, the horse seemed to sag in the middle and creaked badly. Uncovering the tunnel entrance proved a difficult task with so little room in the horse, but for once the bearers carried less going back inside.

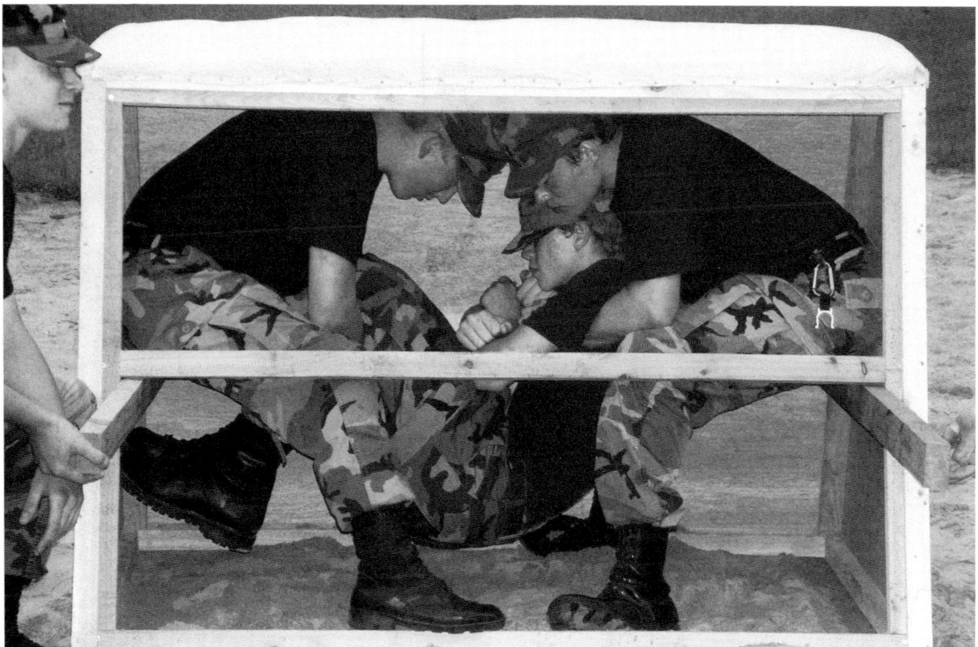

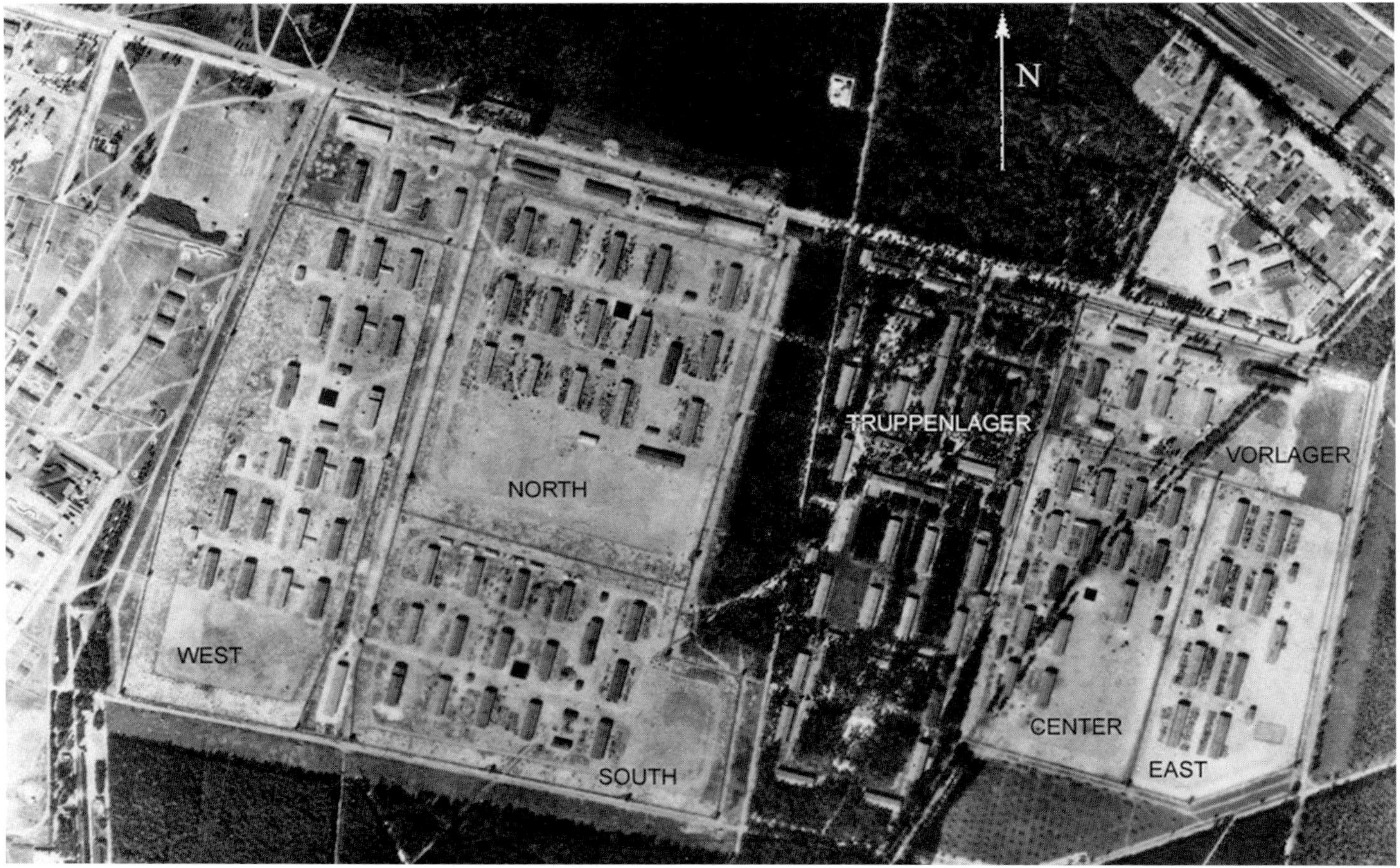

The entire Stalag Luft III complex as seen from the air in late 1944. East Compound is readily identified, as is the cookhouse and two *Aborts*, just to the left of the main cluster of buildings. Careful observation will also reveal the middle guard tower (No.2) along the east fence, on a northern angle from the cookhouse. *(US Air Force)*

The East Compound *Sportzplatz*, in the summer of 1943, as seen from up on the northeast corner of the north *Abort*. Just out of the photo to the left is 'Goon box' No.2, and to the right is the cookhouse, in front of which the line of men on the far right are standing. **A** – marks the spot where the vaulting horse was placed.

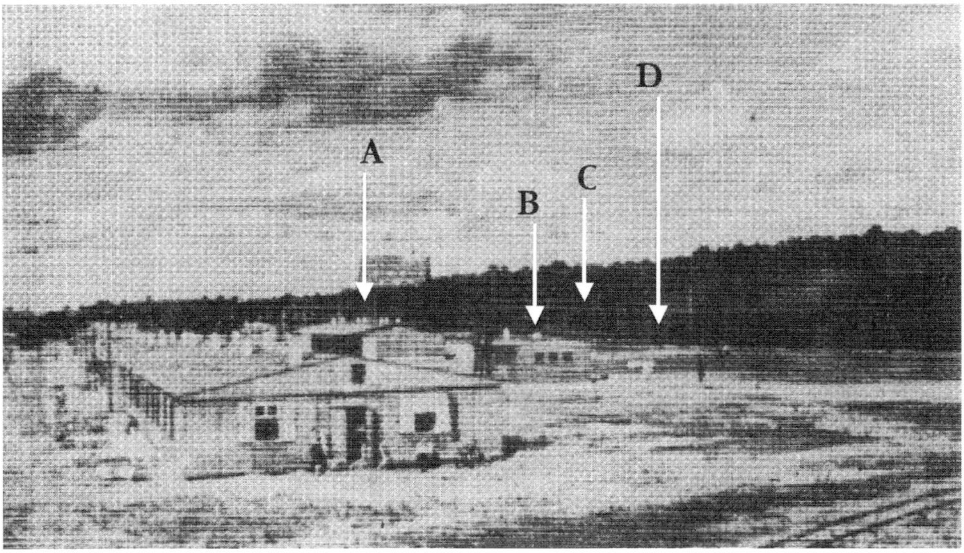

A view north and slightly east of the East Compound *Sportzplatz*, as seen from 'Goon box' No.4. In the foreground is Hut 69. Indicated in the photo are **A** – the cookhouse/canteen; **B** – the south *Abort*; **C** – a barely discernible 'Goon box' No.2; and **D** – the approximate spot where the wooden horse tunnel exited. The parade ground is in the right foreground. Note the granary in the distance.

The Tunnel, recreated

As it appears that no photos were taken of the original tunnel by the Germans following the escape, in order for the reader to better understand the actual effort, the author and his team recreated the first 9ft of it using authentic materials under authentic soil conditions.

At the bottom of the entrance shaft, facing away from the tunnel and showing the brick pilings, packing crate construction and rear 'alcove'.

The entrance shaft.

The first 7ft of the shored-up part of the tunnel.

The author, crawling out of the tunnel into the entrance shaft.

Williams in the recreation of the vaulting horse on the film set of 'The Wooden Horse' in Germany while his wife, Sybil, and director Ian Dalrymle look on. Gunter Wolter, who was an officer on the camp staff in 1943 and acted as German technical advisor on the film, is at the upper left.

[illegible] Polizeipraesident
in Breslau
Polizeirevier Nr. 8

Vorlaeufiger Ausweis

Nr. I./11278/43

Der Marcel Levasseur ..... Franzose ....
Name Nationalitaet

Inhaber dieses Ausweises erhaelt hiermit die Aufenthalts-erlaubnis fuer das Reichsgebiet. Dieser Ausweis ersetzt den rechtmaessigen Personalausweis. Er ist auf Verlangen vorzuzeigen. Der Verlust ist dem Polizeipraesidium Breslau umgehend zu melden. [illegible] der Geltungsdauer [illegible] der Ausweis an das Polizeipraesidium Breslau abzugeben.
Dieser Ausweis hat Gueltigkeit bis...30. November. 1943

Der Polizeipraesident
Im Auftrage
G. von. Blausmer
Unterschrift

Als richtige Abschrift beglaubigt
H. Bäumer
Unterschrift

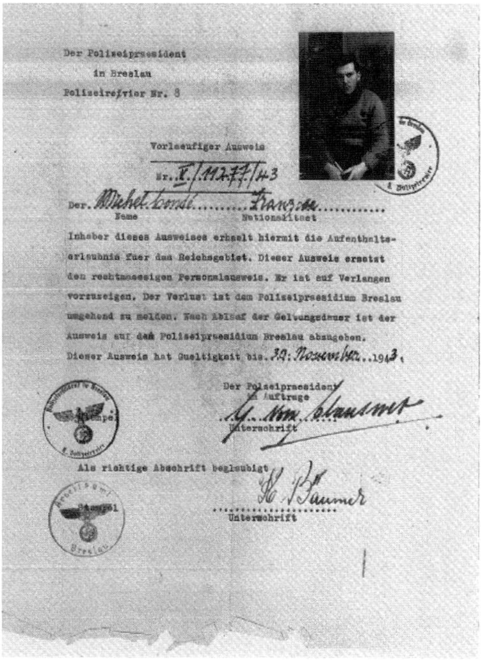

Der Polizeipraesident
in Breslau
Polizeirevier Nr. 8

Vorlaeufiger Ausweis

Nr. V./11277/43

Der. Michel Condé......... Franzose............
Name Nationalitaet

Inhaber dieses Ausweises erhaelt hiermit die Aufenthalts-erlaubnis fuer das Reichsgebiet. Dieser Ausweis ersetzt den rechtmaessigen Personalausweis. Er ist auf Verlangen vorzuzeigen. Der Verlust ist dem Polizeipraesidium Breslau umgehend zu melden. Nach Ablauf der Geltungsdauer ist der Ausweis auf dem Polizeipraesidium Breslau abzugeben.
Dieser Ausweis hat Gueltigkeit bis. 30. November..1943.

Der Polizeipraesident
Im Auftrage
G. Von. Blausmer
Unterschrift

Als richtige Abschrift beglaubigt
H. Bäumer
Unterschrift

Williams (left) and Codner's (right) original camp forged *Vorlaeufiger Ausweis. (Author's collection and the Codner family)*

Group Captain Richard 'Dickie' Kellett (right), the Senior British Officer for East Compound. The end of the war: Major Gustav Simoleit (left) surrenders the German command to him, while Lt Col Ron Johnson of the US Army, who liberated the prisoners, looks on. *(US National Archives)*

Wing Commander Joseph Kayll, the East Compound 'Big X', being led into captivity after having been shot down. *(Håkans Aviation)*

Flight Lieutenant Dudley Craig, the East Compound 'Big S'. *(Biplane Aces of WW2)*

Wing Commander Roger Maw (in later years), who designed the wooden horse and provided the illicit tools for its construction.

Wing Commander Richard Collard while at Sagan. *(Wartime Memories)*

A young Pilot Officer Tom Wilson; 'a guest of the Reich' and avid vaulter. *(Tom and Gabi Wilson)*

A recent photograph of Tom Wilson holding the violin he used while 'stooging'. This activity was featured in the 1950 film. *(Tom and Gabi Wilson)*

Lieutenant Haldor Espelid (left) was a Norwegian who served in the RAF; he was Philpot's coach in how to be 'Jon Jorgenson'. Espelid was among the fifty recaptured escapees murdered following the 'Great Escape'. *(Rob Davis)*

Pilot Officer James 'Red' Hunter (second left), who forged most of Philpot's papers. *(Allan Hunter)*

Flight Lieutenant Peter Stevens, who guided Philpot on what documents he would need in order to be 'Jon Jorgenson'. A German Jew, born George Hein, he and his family were living in England when the war broke out. Stevens hid his identity and changed his name in order to join the RAF. *(Marc Stevens)*

The *Kommandant*, Colonel Wilhelm von Lindeiner-Wildau with some of the camp staff. Major Gustav Simoleit, his assistant is on the far right.

Major Gustav Simoleit.

'Charlie' – Unteroffizier Karl Piltz – leader of the East Compound 'Ferrets', with his notorious water hose. Note the 'Ferret' in the background digging up a tunnel. *(US Air Force)*

A group of 'Ferrets' near the gate leading into South Compound. 'Dopey' is second from the right. 'Herman', who discovered tunnel 'Tom' in the North Compound in September 1943, is in the middle looking directly at the camera. *(US Air Force)*

The Danish ship, *J.C. Jacobsen* at sea. Her captain, E. Ostrup Olson and the First Mate may have been working for British intelligence. *(Varvshistoriska)*

The Swedish ship, *Aralizz* at dock. Note the three cranes on the wharf used for loading coal. *Aralizz* was launched in August 1943 and broken up at Savona, Italy in December 1967. *(Varvshistoriska)*

Railway Views Today

The booking hall at Sagan station. It has changed very little since the war. Note the notice board on the wall on the left; this is the one which Williams pretended to be looking at while Codner purchased their tickets. *(Michal Juran)*

The footings for the metal bridge over the tracks are all that now remain of the structure. *(Gavin J.F. Worrell)*

The Granary today; during the war it was used for storage of surplus Red Cross parcels. *(Marilyn Walton)*

The station platform for the 'Berlin Express', which continues to run today, albeit in a different form. Our model – in RAF kit – is Czech Filip Procházka. *(Michal Juran)*

The grave of R.M.C. Codner in Malaya (arrow) and a close up of the memorial stone. *(Codner family)*

Oliver Philpot

Behind the wire, 1942. Philpot (third from the left) reunited with his crew at Dulag Luft.

Basking in the continued glow of success in 1949 with (left to right) Leslie 'Sid' Sidwell, Eric Williams, Mike Codner and Oliver Philpot.

Gentleman, businessman, success … escaper.

The Intrepid Adventurer: Eric 'Bill' Williams

Aboard his motor yacht sailing the blue Mediterranean waters.

With his beloved Sybil, planning their 1956 expedition behind the Iron Curtain. Within 2 months they would be expelled by the Soviet authorities.

On the set of 'The Wooden Horse', second from left. Leo Genn, who played Williams, is third from left and Anthony Steel, who played Codner, is first on the left.

On the film set in 1950, Williams again digs into the sand of Germany for the cameras. Later he would dig a more authentic tunnel, but no one cared.

East Compound, Stalag Luft III today …

The *Appell* ground area for Hut 67. The entrance to 'Margaret' would be somewhere close to the centre of the photograph. In this, and the other illustrations on this page, it is plain to see how the forest is quickly reclaiming the former location of the camp. *(Gavin J.F. Worrell)*

The remains of the north *Abort* – site of the Bill White tunnel. Of particular notice is the remaining brick and concrete flooring in the centre of the photograph, and the concrete sections of the 'well' (left) that dropped down into the great pit. *(Gavin J.F. Worrell)*

The road that ran along the eastern fence of the East Compound, looking south and standing along the perimeter of the *Vorlager*. The East Compound would have been to the right of the road by the stand of trees. To the left of the road, the forest is much the same as it was during the escape, clearly illustrating the relative sparseness of the woods. *(Gavin J.F. Worrell)*

The general location of the 'Wooden Horse' tunnel exit would have been somewhere in the area just beyond the two trees in the centre of the photograph. Careful observation reveals the shallow ditch and the road beyond. *(Gavin J.F. Worrell)*

His clothing as 'Jon Jorgenson' had to match that of a person of his standing during wartime. Philpot chose a pair of Fleet Air Arm trousers, virtually new and kindly obtained from Lieutenant 'Johnny' Mercer, which were totally adequate. He had two RAF blue 'Viyella' shirts and collars from clothier Austin Reed, which did not become grubby that easily and were warm, also his black RAF tie, which one of the Fleet Air Arm pilots decorated for him with some white stitching to make it look more 'civilian'. Squadron Leader Ralph Ward, the Clothing Officer for the Escape Committee, issued him with a new pair of officer's black shoes recently delivered from England and fitted them with German laces. Also, he supplied a slightly-worn black Homburg hat which was obtained from a corrupted 'Goon'. For a jacket, Ward produced a genuine short, double-breasted civilian garment made from a strange, cheap material. A little worn and with a patch under one arm. While it was not top quality it certainly would be suitable for a mid-level salesman in wartime Germany. Rumour had it that the jacket had even been 'out' twice already. Perhaps a third time truly would prove to be lucky.

For an overcoat, Philpot had his own RAF officer's greatcoat, which Nathalie had sent out to him during the first year. One of the Czechoslovak officers in the camp was removing the epaulettes, belt loops and replacing the buttons with civilian ones for him. His gloves were brown RAF issue, virtually new. Des Breed had given him a small 'Vulcanite' case to carry, and into this he placed mainly items to keep himself looking as respectable as possible, the minute he started to look unkempt was the minute his persona became implausible. He carried his spare shirt and collar; spare socks; clean handkerchiefs; a German razor and blades; German soap; German matches; a plain hand towel; and cloth and German polish for his shoes. He also packed in several cakes of 'Dog Food' which he concealed in *Amada Margarine Werke zum Danzig* wrappers, ostensibly as 'samples' of a new food his company was working on; a small, unmarked bottle of Horlicks tablets; a small unmarked tin of Ovaltine tablets; and a small bottle for water. His samples were packed in a wooden box made by Wing Commander Maw, which had a special false bottom where he could hide his maps, and the 'Swedish mariner' ID card. A fellow officer agreed to loan him a Rolex watch just before he was about to leave, and he had a compass made by Pilot Officer Jerry Dawkins, the pilot of an Avro Manchester from Coventry. Also, to prove his identity in case he was picked up, he had glued his PoW identity tag between two small pieces of cardboard on which he had mounted a picture of Nathalie. This he hung around his neck on a piece of string under his shirt. He also had some mail addressed to him at the camp tucked into one of his maps.

Williams and Codner had decided to blend into the crowd as Frenchmen; Marcel Levasseur and Michel Conde respectively. Not forced labour, but volunteers, middle-class French artisans. Speaking to some of the French prisoners (who had escaped to England when France fell) in the camp, they gained something of a feel for French attitudes. Also, they quizzed those who had visited France and Germany before the war to gain further knowledge. Fortunately for Williams, Codner was more than reasonably fluent in French, and had enough German to get by (further supplemented by additional coaching from Philpot.) It was agreed that he would do all the talking. For his part, Williams knew no foreign language at all, except the slang German he had picked up in his nine months as a 'Kriegie', and the simple phrase that Codner had taught him in case he found himself being questioned– *'Ich bin Auslander; Nicht verstehen.'* ('I am a foreigner; I do not understand.') However, Williams was almost completely incapable of saying this without a heavy British accent, and he fervently hoped he would not be forced to speak. In fact, in later years Williams would remark, with no small measure of wonder, that he thought it remarkable he could have crossed Nazi-occupied Europe with that one poorly spoken phrase.

Their forged papers were fairly basic, uncomplicated, and virtually identical. Put together by the members of 'X', Flight Lieutenant Claude Frith and Pilot Officer Eric Shaw did much of the work. Frith said later, 'I only saw Williams three or four times while I was forging his papers, usually only when he came to the education room or to my room in Hut 68 to tell me what he wanted. He was very demanding and knew exactly what he wanted.' Much of the information Williams had obtained from 'Dopey' had proven to be just what was required. Posing as engineering draughtsmen who worked for the metallurgy company of Dr. Hoffman & Co. in Breslau, they were being transferred to the Arado Flugzeugwerke in Anklam, which just happened to be a short distance northwest of Stettin. The job was real, taken from a local German newspaper by a member of the 'X Organization', and Dean & Dawson were preparing their papers accordingly; a *Vorlaufweise*; a *Bescheinigung*; a *Polizeiliche Erlaubnis* (special police permission to travel); and an *Arbeitskarte* for each. On top of these official papers, for added authenticity, Williams also had prepared for himself two love letters, written in French in a beautiful hand and addressed to Marcel from his girlfriend, Jeanne, at home in France, along with a picture of an absolutely stunning girl inscribed. From 'Jeanne to Marcel'. Each also carried their own doubtful Swedish sailor's ID cards and maps (both hidden), while Codner had 50 Reichmarks and Williams 150. Both wore their PoW identity tags round their necks, under their shirts.[4]

Codner carried a small canvas valise, while Williams had a small leather attaché case. Both were made by the camp shoe repairer, Corporal Clive Nutting. In his, Codner carried washing, shaving, and shoe cleaning items (all of German origin), as well as five tins of 'Dog Food', a little chocolate (without label), some German cigarettes and matches, a spare pair of socks and a woollen toque (a distinctively French type of headwear). Hidden in the waist band of his trousers was a hand-drawn map. Williams carried in his case German cigarettes and matches, shaving and washing kit, a pack of hard biscuits (unlabelled), a small cloth sack of oatmeal, an empty food tin as a bowl, a spoon, a spare pair of socks and a black roll neck sweater, needle and thread, a penknife, some paper, also pens and ink for touching up documents). He also had the compass from his escape kit and a small bag of oatmeal sewn into the armpits of the raincoat he was going to wear, in case he got separated from Codner, as well as his silk escape map, which he had managed to secrete away through 9 months of searches, now sewn into the lining of his jacket.[5]

For clothing, Codner had a dark blue naval uniform jacket, donated by Aiden Crawley, and a pair of RAAF battledress trousers. Both were popular items with escapers due to their colour and the relative ease with which they could be converted to civilian styles. Wearing them he looked eminently respectable, although the cut of the jacket might have appeared a bit odd on anyone but a wartime Frenchman. The committee provided a German-made civilian shirt and collar, to which he added his own brown army tie, as well as his brown army officer's shoes (which had been sent out to him in a personal clothing parcel), tied with German laces. Over his suit he wore a converted RAF raincoat given to him by Squadron Leader Malcolm Strong. He also had plain woollen gloves and a beret which he had previously bought from the Pole who had driven the sewerage cart at Schubin.[6]

For Williams, the committee provided a black Royal Marine dress uniform jacket, without gold braid and buttons, and matching trousers. These had been sent out from England to an RM pilot. The uniform was not authentic but actually a good-quality civilian suit with braiding, buttons and extra pockets patched on. These would be removed just before Williams was to leave, as the committee had kept it hidden and Williams neither saw nor tried it on until the day before the escape. However, Ralph Ward had assured him on several occaisions that it would fit (which it did). He had his own RAF shirt, black RAF tie and a pair of black RAF officer's shoes with German laces. Over his 'suit' he wore a black ex-British Overseas Airways Corporation (BOAC) trench coat which he received from Phillip Tettenborn, a civilian pilot who had been in Paris when France fell, in exchange for the kit that he would leave behind in camp. To complete his 'French' appearance, Ward had given him a very nice beret, made from a German blanket by Flight Lieutenant Neville Smallwood.[7]

Williams and Codner would leave the camp more than reasonably well dressed and respectable for their 'new' identities, in clothing that would not attract any undue attention. In fact, by 'Kriegie' standards all three were exceptionally well dressed for their escape, and their attention to detail had been impeccable; well illustrated by the addition of German laces in their shoes, a simple detail that had already cost more than one escaper his chances. Philpot even discovered a small, unobtrusive 'Made in Britain' stamped on his travelling case; barely noticeable, but which he nonetheless had a friend erase with repeated coats of a thick paint. Even the British government depot and sizing stamps had been carefully scraped away from the inside their shoes

And, as the end of the month rapidly approached, one of the more important details of their actual escape from the camp was brought to their attention; the plan to get four men out into the compound under the horse – the three escapers and another to close the tunnel. Once again, it was Codner that thought up the solution. On the day of the escape, they would do a morning lifting session to clear away any last bags of sand. Then, on an afternoon session some 90 minutes before evening *Appell*, someone would go out with Codner and their baggage, sealing him in the tunnel before coming back in alone. Codner would then stay there for the next 2 hours. Following *Appell*, Williams and Philpot would go out on a third session, taking Freddie McKay (the smallest of the vaulters) along with them, who would then seal those two in before being carried back with the horse alone. The three would then await their decided breakout time underground.

It was obviously the solution, but it was fraught with danger; they had never before brought the horse out three times in one day. However, they figured that as the horse had become such an institution in the camp, and the 'Goons' already thought the vaulters were mad anyway, nobody was liable to notice and the gamble would come off without any suspicions being raised. In any case, the success of such a gamble would be in keeping with the luck of the scheme!

The three had also finally decided to go down the night of the escape wearing just shirts, trousers and shoes in order to enable them to crawl more easily through the narrow tunnel. At first Williams and Codner had considered going down naked, but were quickly talked out of that by Philpot; what if they had to run for it? To assist in keeping their clothes clean, Philpot arranged with John Paget for three sets of long woollen underwear to be dyed black for them to wear over their escape clothing on the night of the break. Black balaclavas would also be made to cover their faces, as well as black socks to cover their shoes. The majority of Williams and Codner's escape kit was packed in two small, black kitbags, while Philpot had his excess clothing wrapped up in his overcoat, which was wrapped in a long black undershirt. He carried his hat in his travel case packed with his essentials. The case was also wrapped in black dyed underwear.

In order to accommodate their baggage and still allow them to move through the tunnel on the night of the escape, it would be necessary to carve cavities in the sides somewhere near the end. Because of this necessity they came to the conclusion that it was likely that there would not be time to complete the tunnel as planned; they were going to have to 'mole' the last few remaining feet on the afternoon of the escape, as Calnan had suggested earlier. Codner would try and do this during the 2 hours he was to spend underground, and they agreed with the committee to send back as much of the sand as possible with McKay. They would also spread as much of the remainder as they could along the length of the tunnel, in order to leave the exit clear for possible use the next morning.

Desperately they hoped the distance to 'mole' would not be far. But this depended largely on their ability to dig which, in turn, depended on the weather. Again, fortune smiled on them, for in the last 12 days or so of the month, an 'Indian Summer' came to Sagan. The temperature, though cool at night, remained comfortably warm during the day, and there was not a drop of rain, so they were able to dig on rapidly and come very close to their goal.

One afternoon, as the end if the month approached, the 'Goons' marched in a group of Russian prisoners to clean up the compound. They collected all manner of refuse and stray leaves which they piled up in the danger strip. Escape Committee 'spies' found out that a German general was coming to inspect the camp the next day and all must be in order. Soon a pair of horses pulling a wagon swung through the gate and began to move round the perimeter inside the danger strip, stopping at each pile to let the Russians shovel in the refuse. It was just at *Appell* time and the three would be escapers watched in horror as the wagon moved along. If it kept on the same track, it must pass right over the spot where the tunnel ran and there was a chance that one of the horses would put a hoof through the thin layer of soil.

But with *Appell* came the gathering darkness, and a rush to get the job done and the danger strip raked over smooth. Just before it reached the spot over the tunnel, the cart was suddenly driven out of the danger strip and off through the gate. Instead, the Russians came along dragging spades and started to dig a hole very nearly where the tunnel would have run originally. They shovelled the refuse into the hole, back filled it, raked the area, and then marched back to their meagre quarters in the *Vorlager*.

It was a tense time for the escapers.

On the evening of the 26th, the three met to thrash out the final details for the 'off' date. Obviously, they wanted to go as late in the month as possible in light of the work still to be done on the tunnel. As it was, due to the many delays already endured, it looked like they were going to be cutting it rather fine. But before the end of the month it must be, as Calnan's railway timetable expired on the 31st. They would need to go in the evening, just as soon as full darkness had descended, and must be out and away before the night guard on duty along that stretch of wire came. (There were no guards along that part of the fence during the day.)

The Escape Committee had regularly recorded the movements of the guards in camp, and knew that at 7.30pm there was always a shift change, when fresh 'Goons' would occupy the towers, while those from the towers would relieve the guard along that stretch of the wire nearest their tower and patrol for 2 hours. Along the east fence, there were two guards patrolling at night; each walking from a far corner of the fence to the middle tower and then back. This made the escape window very brief, as it was not going to be completely dark until around 5.30pm. It would also help them if the tower guard closest to the exit could be distracted on that evening. To that end, Philpot agreed to arrange with the committee to put up some diversions at the right time on the night of the break for the 'Goons' benefit.

However, the exact time of the exit within that narrow window of opportunity would also be dictated by the schedule and availability of trains at Sagan station, just over a kilometre distant. The end of the October fell over a Friday, Saturday, and Sunday. The latter was ruled out immediately, as not only would there be far less travellers (far less chance of being unnoticed in a crowd), but that the remainder of the journey would be dictated by a train timetable they did not possess. Saturday night was vetoed as well, as Sagan station was more likely to be crowded with soldiers from the area with overnight or weekend passes, including many of the Luftwaffe guards from East Compound. The risk of being recognized was very obvious. That left Friday. The timetable showed only one fast train out of Sagan station that evening and that was the 'Berlin Express', which left at 7.00pm. This suited all three, as it not only took them in the right direction – and fast – but would also give them a full 30 minutes clear time ahead of any alarm. Time to break out of the tunnel, clean up in the woods and then walk to Sagan station, they estimated would take 45 minutes. Getting tickets as near the last minute as possible, meant not having to hang around on the platform, inviting questions. It also helped greatly that Bressey, the camp meteorologist, had told them that there would also be no moon that night. With the train schedule and those three additional factors taken into account, the break was set finally for 6.00pm on Friday, 29 October.

This made Philpot's route to Danzig both quick and reasonably direct. Leaving Sagan on the 'Berlin Express', he would take this as far as Frankfurt an der Oder. There he would get a slower 'local' train on to Küstrin. At Küstrin he would again get an express, this time for the town of Dirschau, which was just south of Danzig. From there he planned to catch the 'Breslau-Danzig Express' to Danzig. If all went to plan, he could be on the express away from Sagan at 7.00pm, and in Danzig looking for a ship before 8.30am the next morning. He carried 150 Reichmarks for train tickets, and for a stay in a cheaper hotel for a few of days, if necessary. He also had some coupons for free lunches at railway buffets.[8]

Williams and Codner's route was similar to Philpot's, in that they would also take the 'Berlin Express' to Frankfurt and from there a slow, local train to Küstrin. However, after Küstrin, they would take another local train onward to Stettin. They both reasoned that the slower trains would be far more crowded, making it easier for them to blend in and far less likely to have document checks. Once in Stettin, they were quietly confident they could find a neutral ship on which they would stowaway.

All the background details had been finalized. Now all they needed was to finish the tunnel to take them beyond the wire.

On the morning of the 27th, they held their last full digging session taking the tunnel as far as they could, and the afternoon session had been spent lifting sand. The morning of the 28th, they again lifted sand while that afternoon Codner went down to put the finishing touches to the tunnel. They had done all they could. The tunnel was as finished as they could make it. Codner came back that evening and estimated that they were perhaps 10ft short of their goal. This they would have to complete the next afternoon, before the actual break. Codner would be the one sealed down in the afternoon with their escape kit, and he would put up an air hole under the coiled wire between the fences and 'mole' as much of the remaining distance as he could, while his absence was covered at *Appell*. When the others came out following parade, they could bag and hang the sand he dug that afternoon for removal back into the cookhouse when the horse was taken back. They would then continue to dig until the last minute.

They had been lucky; the work had gone particularly well that last week, the weather had held beautifully, and the cavities for their luggage had been completed, along with some additional strengthening of weak spots along the tunnel. They could not afford any sort of accidents on the most important night of the tunnel's existence, and on that last day Codner had made doubly sure all was ready.

Bringing the horse in with the last load that afternoon of the 28th, it was hard for Williams and Codner to realize that it was nearly all over. The scheme had been their world for 4½ months, and the tunnel had filled their thoughts and every waking hour with its very existence. It had been a long and arduous road getting beyond the fence, and they had learned a lot about themselves and each other. Through it all both had remained dedicated and focused on their task, never giving up or losing faith. It had been trying and difficult much of the time, but now they stood on the very brink of success; poised to find out if all the pain, sweat, and exertion had truly been worth it after all. Although their own faith had never wavered, it amazed them that the horse – a mere box – had fooled the Germans (most particularly 'Charlie') for this long, a most incredible achievement. In fact, the whole project had been blessed with the most incredible luck! Now it only needed for that luck to continue for one more day and their dreams that lay beyond the wire could then have their chance.

The two placed the horse for the night in its usual spot in the cookhouse, dispersed the sand under the barber shop, and thanked Tom Wilson for his music as they dismissed him for the last time. Then they walked out of the building for a quick scrub and *Appell*; exhausted but elated.

Meanwhile, that afternoon in the *Vorlager*, Philpot had met with Hesse in his small office, to tell him that he would not be handling the hot shower duties for the compound anymore; there would be another officer taking the duty over next week. The fair-haired corporal simply eyed him carefully from across his desk for a moment before asking, 'You're not thinking of *leaving us* by any chance, are you?' The implications in the question seemed painfully obvious, and had Calnan and Marsh not had Hesse so thoroughly tamed, there is little doubt that the escape would never have happened the next day.

Philpot assured him that nothing could be further from the truth; it was simply common practice among the PoW leadership of the camp to rotate new officers into certain positions on a regular basis in order to spread the work around – even though no one but he had been shower officer since their re-arrival at Sagan 6 months earlier. Though Hesse accepted the answer (he had little choice), whether he believed it or not is in considerable doubt.

Aiden Crawley came over to Williams and Codner's room following *Appell* that evening to chat over the last details of the escape. The committee had organized two diversions for the next evening, one being a loud party in Hut 65, set to commence just before 6.00pm and with the sole purpose of drawing 'Goon' attention from along the east fence. Crawley was going to conduct the party and wanted to make sure one more time that all the details were set. He also mentioned that he had an address in Stettin of a brothel that was exclusively for foreign workers which, at one time, had been rumoured to help escapers get out of Germany. However, he hesitated to give them the contact details ('Don't you think we're old enough?' asked a grinning Williams.) because he had received it before the Schubin break, nearly a year ago, and he considered the information stale. The place might have since been raided by the Gestapo for all anyone knew. They discussed it for a while before he ultimately relented, making them commit the address to memory and warning them to use it only as a last resort.

During that last evening too, the committee was ready, and all of their escape gear was gathered together from the various hiding places around the camp and hidden in one centralized location, for ease of distribution the next day. That night Dean & Dawson worked late, putting the finishing touches to all the paperwork, and date stamps were cut and applied. For security purposes, their papers would not actually be delivered until the next day, along with the money. Both were too valuable to risk losing in a snap search, as 'Charlie' might still consider the horse and its creators suspect, although he had not shown any suspicion during the past few weeks. One could not underestimate Piltz.

At dinner in their respective rooms that night, their messmates cooked a large meal for the soon-to-be-escapers, stuffing them with as much as they could hold. Not all of the 'Kriegies' believed in escape but, personal feelings aside any escape attempt deserved the best wishes all could offer, and the very least that could be offered was a substantial meal on which to make the attempt. Then, after a quick wash in the *Abort* and perhaps a final check of their list of the next day's duties, the intrepid three settled down for what they fervently hoped would be their last night in Stalag Luft III.

The murmur in the rooms soon died down as darkness fell across the camp. The perimeter lights came on, and from the 'Goon' boxes the search lights beamed out, sweeping silently across the huts; the site of the unfinished bath house; the barren football pitch. The *Hundeführer* came through the gate and turned his dogs loose to roam the compound, their breaths sending silver clouds into the cool air. Stretching out into the dark void all around, the sombre pines loomed, casting silent shadows outside the glare around the fence. And away in the distance, across the top of the dark forest, the heavy stillness of the scene was broken briefly by the echoing, shrill sound of a locomotive's whistle from the Sagan railway yard.

Part III

Escape

Chapter 13

Through the Looking Glass

Friday, 29 October 1943

Dawn broke on the 29th as on any other Sagan morning. Doors were flung open at 6.00am, anxious 'Kriegies' bursting out to tramp round the circuit, now wearing greatcoats against the foggy morning chill, while room 'stooges' went for boiling water to brew tea. Tousled heads slowly came to life and the loud speaker over Wing Commander Maw's room shattered the peace with military German music, followed by the usual shouts of wrath from Maw inside. At 8.00am the guards began their rountine of stamping through the huts, shouting and bullying the inmates out for *Appell* and they were answered by the grumbling and testy prisoners shouting back with the usual abuse concerning the 'Goons' debatable ancestry and Hitler's questionable parentage. All was standard form; it was a very normal start to a very normal day in East Compound.

But the day was anything but normal. If the odds continued to favour the wooden horse, the 'Goons' would find themselves three prisonerss short at *Appell* on the next morning.

Waking up, Philpot was apprehensive, like before sitting an examination at school, or in the hours before a particularly important and dangerous sortie. With an effort, he focused his mind on what needed to be done that day and set about his tasks deliberately. He washed in the *Abort*, then went back to his room and carefully trimmed 'Jon Jorgenson's' moustache down to Hitler-like proportions for the escape ('Very Goon-like, Ollie. Very Goon-like …' Calnan had laconically remarked from his bunk), before eating his meagre breakfast, putting on his vaulting clothes and then his Polish greatcoat. Then he went to *Appell*; the morning was passing fast.

Williams and Codner had both shaved their beards and moustaches off the previous night. Codner, now looking young and fresh, was eagre to get started. There was tenseness in their room that morning, which the two largely detached themselves from while they went about their business. As stated, some people did not believe in escape; to them a successful escape only caused trouble in the form of petty reprisals by the Germans, which were a hardship on everyone. Fortunately, they were in the minority.[1]

Following *Appell*, the vaulting team met in the cookhouse as usual. Philpot was to go out and bring in the last bags of sand, while Codner would coach the vaulters. In the meantime, Williams went round to the Escape Committee to see about his and Codner's kit. To his great relief, and Ralph Ward's equally great satisfaction, the RM 'new' suit fitted excellently, and it took the tailors just a brief time to remove the embelishments. He gathered all the clothing up, wrapped in a greatcoat, and hustled it over to their room. Everything, except for shoes, shirts and trousers, was carefully folded into the two black kitbags. Once they were packed with their escape gear, both would be smuggled over to the cookhouse in a load of prisoners' dirty laundry, ostensibly meant for the kitchen boilers, just before the afternoon session went out.

Out in the compound, the session went by quickly. Philpot lifted the last twelve bags from the tunnel and then sealed the trap. He gave Codner the word he was nearly ready to go in and, as he was removing the little pieces of black sackcloth from the bearer pole slots, he noticed a 'Goon' bustling about in the barber shop, repairing a broken window. Today, of all days! But very quickly, Codner called one of the German speaking prisoners who persuaded the 'Goon' away on some pretext, and the horse was soon on its way back inside. Up the steps and in, where the sand bags were handed up to Pilot Officer G.A. Archer, an Australian from No.158 Squadron, who simply flung them up into the attic with little care. There would be no need for dispersal anymore; let the 'Goons' find all the sand they wanted.

Lunch came and Philpot's messmates again provided a large meal. Williams and Codner, for a second time, were also fed well in their mess. After lunch, Philpot bundled-up his escape kit and sent it over to the cookhouse as Williams had, hidden in with some dirty laundry. He then went and collected 'Jimmie' Sargeaunt's Rolex wristwatch which had a luminous dial. 'Give it to my father when you get back, won't you?' Sargeaunt had asked him as he handed it over. Williams had also borrowed a watch, and now he and Codner tramped endlessly round the circuit until time for the afternoon vaulting session. It was impossible to remain still.

When they finally gathered for the afternoon session at 1.00pm, it was Philpot who went out to seal Codner down, while Williams led one last round of vaulting. Codner's tall, lean figure stood away from the windows in the cookhouse, he looked slightly sinister dressed in his basic escape clothes with the black-dyed long underwear over them. He was focused on what lay ahead of him and that precluded any small talk. He and Philpot got under the horse, one at each end, and their baggage was passed under to them. The two kitbags were suspended from the top on sand bag hooks, while they each held one of Philpot's bundles. It was difficult to balance on the framework using only one hand. The horse, beginning to show its age, creaked as they moved down the steps and onto the *Sportzplatz* under the guidance of Williams. Once on the ground, the first act of their 'great drama' began.

Philpot hugged one end of the horse while Codner opened up and slipped below. He would be opening an air hole under the mass of coiled wire between the fences, which should make conditions in the tunnel bearable for the time he had to stay down. For this task he carried a piece of broom handle shaved to a point.

Codner crawled up the tunnel with the string from the sand bowl tied to his ankle, when he reached the end he tugged a signal to Philpot, who then attached a piece of luggage to the string and signalled for Codner to haul away. But the luggage did not slide as easily as the sand bowl, and consequently they spent much of their time unjamming it from the narrow or angled parts of the tunnel or repairing the string, which broke frequently and exasperatingly. Williams had chided Philpot for his bundles endlessly, but in point of fact it was the kitbags that jammed the most. When at last everything was in position in the cavities at the end, Codner crawled back for one last breath of air. Checking with Williams, they still had time on the session, he went back up and dug several bowls of sand and passed these back to Philpot to take in (the sand bags had always been stored in the entrance). When Williams gave the 15 minute warning, Philpot called up the tunnel to Codner that he was closing now, and then crawled out. 'It's like burying a man alive,' he thought as he dropped down first of the trap boards and then the 'anchor bags' of sand on top. He then tipped loose sand from the blanket over the bags, followed by the dirty sand from the pyjama bag, and realized with a start that this was the last time that he would have to seal the tunnel and that he only need go into the hated, dark hole one more time. It was 2.00pm.

Up the steps and back into the cookhouse again, where there was yet another delay and Philpot was again left under the horse. During the session, a grizzled little German civilian had come in to repair the porcelain stove (which had never worked) that the 'Kriegies' usually climbed on in order to get into the attic. Maddening! Two 'Goon' repairmen in one day! And on this day, of all days! Now he also had to be dealt with, and Williams ran off to see if Group Captain Kellett could draw the 'Goon' away – which he did, with Aiden Crawley's help, by fetching the repairman over to another hut to look at another stove. (Because of this, the cookhouse stove never would be repaired.) When Philpot finally emerged from under the horse, it was hard to tell whose nerves were more frazzled; his, or Williams. The sand was again flung up into the attic and the team dispersed. There was just one more session to go; arguably the most important one.

Both men scrubbed up in the washhouse and went off to wait for afternoon *Appell*. Their papers and money arrived from the Escape Committee to their respective rooms by special messenger and Williams, trying to relax, went through everything and then stuffed it all in the pocket of his escape trousers before hiding them back under his pillow. He lay down; he stood up. It was no use; he could not be still and went out on the circuit. David Lubbock fell in with him and they had a friendly chat. Lubbock told him he was one of those picked by the committee for the second attempt on the next morning and Williams wished him luck. After a while they walked on in thoughtful silence. More than once they passed over the spot where the tunnel ran under their feet, and Williams tried to imagine what Codner was going through alone in the dark. Had he made the air hole large enough? Would it be sufficient? What if there was a fall? He went to the *Abort* unnecessarily and tried to put the worries out of his mind, then went and double checked the time of the diversion with Philpot.

The afternoon was crawling by and Philpot paced in his room, dressed in his travelling clothes and afflicted with the same tension as Williams. He went through his wallet, making sure the papers he would need to buy his ticket at Sagan station were easily reachable, and answered Williams' questions robotically when he spoke. He checked his appearance in the mirror again; 'Jorgenson' wore a sombre expression behind the ridiculous toothbrush moustache; perfect for a pretend Norwegian Nazi. He looked at the dial on the Rolex. With any luck he would be in Danzig at this time tomorrow! Outside, a bugle blew and shortly there was the tramping of jackboots along the corridor and the familiar cry of 'Goon in the hut,' went up. At last it was 4.00pm and time for *Appell*. He quickly slipped into the large Polish greatcoat, pulled his cap down low over his forehead and went out to face act two of their great drama.

Outside it was growing chilly as the groups of prisoners formed up slowly into their straggling formations. The 'Goons' harangued them; the 'Kriegies' dawdled. Above, the sky was just starting to deepen to a purple hue, while from over in the *Kommandantur* the barking of the dogs floated indistinctly over the scene. Everything was as usual – except that there would be one man missing today. However, the Escape Committee had the answer. Only those holding the rank of Group Captain and above and the sick were allowed to miss standing to *Appell* and could be counted in their rooms. On this day, as Feldwebel Stuhlmeyer counted Hut 62, he did indeed find one man missing and sent a guard into the hut to check for the *krank im zimmer* (sick in bed). The guard returned after short while to report that there indeed was a prisoner curled up on his bunk under a blanket, sick. Stuhlmeyer made an entry in his notebook and moved on. Williams, standing next to the bed vacated by Codner, breathed again for the first time in minutes.

Soon after, Group Captain MacDonnell, adjutant for the British compound, strolled up; perhaps a little late but exercising a Group Captain's option to be counted when and where he chose. In this case MacDonnell had already just been counted indoors as sick, though not in his own bed; a fact the 'Goons' would never realize. Miraculously, he was suddenly well enough to leap out of a window, skirt round the buildings in order to arrive from the correct direction, and turn up at standing *Appell* to be counted. After all, for the 'Goons' to have an incorrect count today just would not do!

Stuhlmeyer came to an abrupt halt in front of Philpot's group. He was two or three rows back and saw Stuhlmeyer staring straight at him and instantly his face flushed. How could the he possibly know? Or had he taken offence at the moustache? But Stuhlmeyer, ever the systematic and professional 'Goon' soldier merely raised his hand and gave it a little sideways waving motion in Philpot's direction. From behind, he some heard a minor shuffling in the sand, after which Stuhlmeyer moved on. Philpot realized the Feldwebel had merely wanted a prisoner in a row behind to 'dress rank' on the man in front of him, in order to line up.

How typical of the 'Goons'! Concerned with a minor detail on formation, while completely oblivious to the fact that a virtually complete tunnel had been dug out of camp from beneath a vaulting horse, right under their noses … But it did not pay to get haughty; they were not out yet.

After *Appell*, the vaulting team gathered in the cookhouse for the last time. It was almost 4.20pm. Williams and Philpot quickly pulled on their black combinations, the dye from which was beginning to give off a foul odour. Freddie McKay was wearing only a pair of shorts. The atmosphere was very tense, and they avoided conversation. However, several 'Kreigies' did come up and asked them to 'go round and see my wife when you get back, won't you?' Incredulous, Philpot also noticed that one man was trying to teach Williams some phrases in German, even as they were climbing under the horse. Williams was paying him no attention whatsoever, but instead remained focused on what they must do next.

Then Lubbock, sitting at his usual spot by the window, called out firmly but quietly, 'Charlie's coming.'

Everyone froze. Damn! That was all they needed; 'Charlie's' highly-trained nose snooping around – now, of all times! Then there came yet another piece of good luck. From out of the blue, the church choir came trooping up the steps into the cookhouse to practice; completely oblivious to the fact that the horse was being taken out again and the escape was on. It was the perfect cover! Swiftly, the vaulting team and the two soon-to-be escapers (with greatcoats quickly thrown round their shoulders) melted into the group and fell into singing with them, while Lubbock called out 'Charlie's' progress. The hymn *Nearer, My God, to Thee* never had a heartier rendition. 'Charlie' pressed his sallow face up against the window briefly. But the choir had never given him any trouble, and so he moved on. As soon as Lubbock gave the 'all clear', the three crawled quickly under the horse, Williams and Philpot holding McKay between them by hooking their arms under his armpits and knees. They gave the signal that they were ready, up went the horse and Laskey had them moving out the door.

The horse gave out an ominous groan as the bearers lifted it, as did the bearers themselves, and Williams noticed that it seemed to be sagging in the middle. Going down the steps, one of the bearers slipped and very nearly dropped his corner. Again it creaked ominously. 'The old horse is falling to pieces. Hope it makes it through this last session' ran through Williams' mind as they went swaying across the dirt to the vaulting spot. Once there, Laskey quickly had the team vaulting in action. Inside the horse, Philpot climbed on McKay's back while Williams worked fast to open the trap then climbed down inside. McKay gasped at the size. 'Is it that small all the way?' he asked. 'Smaller,' Williams answered, then thanked him, and disappeared up the tunnel with the bowl and string.

At the face, Williams found a wall of sand that Codner had banked up behind him as he lengthened the tunnel that afternoon. He began to fill the bowl and send it back to the entrance for McKay to bag and take back. After some 3ft of progress he broke through to Codner and there was a rush of stale air from the forward area of the tunnel. Widening the hole he now saw Codner in the weak light of the borrowed flashlight, looking drawn and tired, with the sweat running down his face carving rivulets in the clinging sand. Thinking he had been down far longer than he really had and that something had gone wrong, he anxiously asked where in hell had they been. Williams assured him all was well and that they were moving along right on time. He passed up a small bottle of tea that Sidwell had sent thinking that after so long underground Codner would no doubt be very thirsty. He had thought right.

Philpot stayed in the horse and let McKay do the work while he instructed him on the closing procedure for the trap. McKay had already been instructed by Williams, but a recap never hurt. McKay passed up bag-after-bag of sand, which Philpot then hung up in the horse, until he heard Laskey call that it was time to finish. Then McKay called up the tunnel to Williams that it was time to close and swapped places with Philpot. It was difficult in the already confined space inside the horse, now partially filled with sand bags. Philpot wriggled down into the entrance shaft then McKay reached out and shook his hand. 'Good luck, boy. You'll be alright!' Philpot folded himself into the tunnel, grunted, 'Thanks Mac!' and then stretched himself out in the shored-up section. He lay there and listened as the boards of the trap were placed in position, one … two … three. Then the anchor bags thumped down and with them the distant prattle of the outside world was shut off as act three of the great drama began. It was 4.50pm.

At 5.15pm, as the vaulters carried the horse back, it creaked like an old barn door. Though it was chilly, there were still more than a few people out on the circuit. The boundary lights came on, throwing long shadows in the early evening. In the cookhouse, McKay emerged from under the horse as Les Sidwell and Bob Stark had the pleasure of flinging the last of the bags of sand up in the attic. That was the end of that duty. No more of that dreadful sand to get rid of! The equipment (blanket, sand bags, black clothes, etc …) was wrapped in a greatcoat, and surreptitiously returned to the Escape Committee. A few prisoners stayed around the horse to discuss the project, or just reminisce. It was hard to imagine that the project, so ridiculed, so dogged by near disaster, had actually survived to see fruition. The best wishes of everyone were with the three escapers, now sweating underground and about to face either success or disaster.

Down in the tunnel, Philpot kept pulling bowls of sand back from the face and dumping them in the entrance shaft. With the trap closed down it was pitch black and soon there was no air, while at the head of the tunnel Williams and Codner had the flashlight and an air hole under the wire. When he could no longer stand the lack of air, he crawled up to Williams. This was it; his last time in the hated and feared claustrophobic tube, and as he crawled up he gave a little spiteful kick to the wall at a spot that had given them particular trouble. It felt good to be a little reckless. Codner was still digging at the face, and Williams now started to push the sand back past his hips for Philpot to spread out on the tunnel floor. When he could no longer spread the sand, he started to bank it up. They began 'moling', much as the two had originally planned four months ago; sealed in a section of tunnel some 25ft long with a 3in hole driven through the roof to provide air. All three tried not to think what could happen if there was a fall now.

They worked steadily and automatically until 5.30pm, when Williams suggested that Codner start digging for the surface. Codner immediately started to dig the tunnel up hill, expecting any moment to break through. After all, 2ft 10in was not that deep. However, they must have taken an unnoticed downward dip toward the end of the dig, as the surface proved to be further away than anticipated. (Or were they merely underestimating the difficulties of 'moling', thinking they were making greater progress than they actually were?) Whatever the case, carefully and gradually, Codner continued to dig away the last layer of sand which was all that stood between them and freedom. For each this was the moment that would define their war and provide the adventure of a lifetime.

At around 5.40pm in the rapidly falling gloom, two officers walking the circuit suddenly got into a fist fight in front of the centre 'Goon box' along the eastern fence of the compound. The guard above yelled down to the two men as a crowd gathered round, and then ran to the back of the box and called the guardhouse. Soon a number of 'Ferrets' came hustling through the gate, broke up the fight, escorted the two culprits to the 'Cooler' and dispersed the crowd back to their huts. As soon as the doors of Hut 65 slammed shut, the beginning of what promised to be a loud party drew the continued attention of the guard in the centre 'Goon box'.

Meanwhile, in Hut 64, the camp theatre, former Spitfire pilot Squadron Leader Peter Tomlinson was producing and acting in the latest production, *French Without Tears*. Most of the German officers from the camp had been given invitations and were soon filing into the building, where they were seated in the front row. Off-duty sentries were also welcomed. The play got underway, amid much fanfare, at 6.00pm.

Codner worked steadily, waiting for the time to make its reluctant way to 6.00pm, gently scraping away at what would be the tunnel exit. Where was the surface? The air was thin and nauseating in the end of the tunnel; something must have blocked the air hole. Or was it that it was too small to cope with the three as they worked? Panting, he scraped at the uphill exit chamber when suddenly his fist punched through to the outside. The fresh, cool night air came gusting in through the small hole and cooled his sweaty, upturned face. He was through – through to the freedom side of the wire – and could see the dark sky above through the opening. He turned his head and whispered to Williams, but the fresh air had already told the tale.

There was just some 10 minutes to go until break-out time. Codner now quickly scraped out a hole in the floor of the exit slope to hold the excess sand. Then he paused, waiting for the word from Williams to open the tunnel completely. Their earlier, all consuming tiredness was now gone, replaced by the anticipation of what lay ahead and the fresh air. The next few minutes would tell the story: Were they to be successful, or had they just been wasting their time for 4 months? Perhaps the 'Goons' had known about the tunnel all along and would be waiting just outside the wire. It had happened before …

But such thoughts were unproductive. Better to focus instead on what lay ahead. Then, just when it seemed as if time had decided to stand permanently still, Williams was tapping him on the leg. Jerking his mask down and quickly adjusting it, Codner got to work with the trowel, attacking the exit hole in a near frenzy and squeezing himself off to one side to avoid the last of the sand and dirt.

The surface came away easily and he quickly widened the hole, the soft soil falling down to the floor of the exit hole with a dull, thumping sound. He clearly heard the noise of the diversion party in Hut 65, and he whispered back to Williams something to the effect that 'the silly bastards are going to get a bullet in there, if they're not careful.' He had finished and the hole was as wide as they had planned. It was lighter outside than they had anticipated; frighteningly so. Or was it nothing more than an optical illusion, created from being in the dark underground for so long, with only the weak light from the flashlight? Nevertheless, there were already some stars out, framed in the opening of the tunnel. They looked beautiful in the deep purple of the autumn evening sky. The stars of freedom!

The narrow hole was just wide enough to pass through and Codner cautiously raised his head, eyes wide open behind the sweaty, dark mask. A wind was rustling the trees on the far side of the road. That was good; it would help cover any noise they made. What he saw when he glanced around was not what they had expected.

They were short of their objective. Despite their best efforts, they had not dug quite enough that afternoon, and instead of coming out on the side of the shallow ditch in the shadows as they had planned, the tunnel exit had broken just at the far edge of the sentry path, still some 4ft short of the edge of the ditch! To his left, something less than 80ft away the 'Goon box' towered above standing out in clear relief against the brightness of the arc lamps along the fence line. Worse still, the tunnel exit was within a pool of light of an arc lamp. The outer fence was just some 8ft behind the hole and some 6 to 8ft in front, just beyond the ditch, was the road. The only way that the exit could have been in a worse position was if it had come up a 1ft or 2ft shorter, actually on the sentry path. As it was, when he came on at 7.30pm, there was absolutely no way that the sentry could possibly miss the hole and he would probably stumble into it if he were not careful. Either that, or the 'Goon' in the tower, visible only in silhouette through the glare of an arc lamp, who with only a casual turn of his head could easily spot the black hole in the ground, bathed as it was in the bright lamp light.

Codner assessed their situation in seconds. If this escape was going to succeed at all, they were going to have to act fast. Should he tell the others? But the decision was immediately taken from him by urgent whispering from Williams: 'Go on! Go! Now!'

Swiftly, Codner shoved his kitbag up and out and then he quickly scrambled out of the hole, rolling silently into the ditch with the heavy bag hugged in his arms. It was not as deep as they had estimated, and did not provide the shadow they had anticipated, and he suddenly felt naked after the confines of the tunnel. He lay just a moment, listening intently. Not a sound; he had not been spotted. Any idea of crawling across the road was now abandoned and he was up, dashing across the road and into the bushes on the other side. He pressed on for several yards into the forest before pausing to let Williams catch up.[2]

A forest, it barely seemed such! It was almost too tidy; the trees were widely spaced and there was very little undergrowth, giving minimal cover. It is strange how it had appeared denser from behind the wire. Breathing heavily, he crouched down and looked back in time to see Williams plunge quietly into the undergrowth, and presently he was beside him, down on all fours, kitbag at his side. Still breathing in heavy but quiet gasps, they both peered back at the camp for a moment.

The hole showed up clear as day in the light of the arc lamps and he was struck by the full realization of just how well the entire camp was illuminated. From the outside, it appeared every bit as bright as London in peacetime. The pools of light from the perimeter arc lamps shone brilliantly across the ground, even making the rusting wire appear clean and new, while the searchlights playing across the camp showed as arrow straight, glimmering shafts piercing the darkness. He had watched those beams repeatedly and with interest in all three of the camps he had been in; had tried to discover a pattern to the way they were swung the by guards. However, he had long since decided that there was none. Each guard might have his own way of doing things, until beams crossed. From inside the camp it had almost appeared playful, but watched now from the outside the beams appeared cold and ruthless and it suddenly occurred to him that while they had been inside planning, they had all obviously been looking at the light and shadow of the camp's perimeter with a truly optimistic eye.

Suddenly and clearly they saw Philpot's head pop-up, bathed in light and looking tiny in comparison to the menacing 'Goon box' – and then just as quickly it popped back down. A moment later, a searchlight swung in the direction of the exit and briefly bathed it with the edge of its light before passing on! Then, suddenly, two bundles appeared out of the hole, followed immediately by Philpot. With the hole in such an exposed position and so brilliantly lit, it was obvious there could be no possible chance of covering it over for further use. Once out of the hole, Philpot never stopped and sprinted off and away from the brightness of the lamps, crossed the road at an angle, and swiftly disappeared into the undergrowth.[3]

Codner tugged at Williams's sleeve and whispered hoarsely, 'It's a piece of cake. Come on! We're going to have to move if we're going to catch that train!' But Williams sat for just a moment more, taking one last look at the camp before he turned and quickly followed after Codner, who was already hurrying deeper into the forest in the direction of Sagan railway station. Gradually the sound of the diversion party faded into the night behind them.

Once in the undergrowth Philpot turned his gaze back for a last, long moment at the brilliantly lit camp. How many would ever get to see their prison camp from the outside as a free man before the end of the war? In the distance, from within the confines of the brightly lit wire, he could hear the sounds of the camp at night, as well as that of the diversion party; familiar sounds, but now somehow detatched from him. He had made his getaway and a great gulf now separated him from his fellows: He was free; they were not. Poor devils! He silently vowed to make the most of this rare opportunity that fate had granted him. Picking up his things, he turned deeper into the forest. Sagan was nearly a mile away and 'Jon Jorgenson' had a train to catch.

They had done it. Against all the odds the tunnel had been a success and they were now outside the wire, free to run as far and as fast as fate and their own exertions could carry them. Their captivity had effectively come to an end and all that was needed now was a certain amount of luck.

It was 6.10pm.

Chapter 14

Exhilaration

On the Berlin Express to Frankfurt

Cradling their kitbags in their arms, Williams and Codner walked quickly and deliberately deeper into the sparse forest, sweating in their foul-smelling black combinations and trying to keep as quiet as possible. Both desperately resisted a strong urge to run as fast as they could, and forced themselves to maintain a steady, even pace in the cool night. They needed to get deeper into the forest before they stripped and cleaned themselves, but they did not have time to waste. Their train was due to leave at 7.00pm, and they dare not be late. Missing it would ruin the minimal head start they had planned.

They had not gone too deeply into the forest when, Williams heard what he thought was suppressed giggling coming from somewhere in the darkness. Alert he turned his head, listening closely he discovered he was right – it was Codner. Then the giggle broke into a full laugh, low and just barely suppressed. Williams stopped.

Incredulous, he whispered to Codner 'What's the matter? What the hell are you laughing at?'

'You!' Codner replied barely suppressing his laughter. 'You look like some bloody great bear, mincing along like that!'

Williams, barely controlling a laugh, grabbed Codner by the arm and pulled him along.

'Come on you fool! Shut up before someone hears you!'

Some of the extreme tension of the break out was now draining away, and their nerves were obviously beginning to fray as a result. They were still keyed up, but that first full-blown impact of freedom, however brief it might turn out to be, was now descending on them, and the feeling was wonderful. Cold and trembling in their sweaty clothes, and although tired from the hard digging of the afternoon, all of that meant nothing next to that wonderful feeling of freedom!

Slowly they trudged on, taking care to remain as quiet as possible. Both knew that there were plenty of dangers awaiting them in the surrounding area. There was a Jewish labour camp somewhere close by, as well as a Russian camp and also a munitions dump, and who knew what odd paths there might be through the forest known only to, and made use of by, the camp staff. Sagan station was only less than a kilometre away at that point, but it was a dangerous distance so they talked little and kept moving, alert the whole time. When they assumed that they had put a reasonable distance between them and the camp, they stopped and stripped off the smelly black-dyed long underwear, then washed each others' face with a handkerchief before dressing in the darkness. The sand was the worst, and Codner had a difficult time getting it out of his hair and ears. Luckily, all they had worn under their escape clothing had been a shirt, trousers, and shoes; the dyed underwear had worked well, keeping most of the sand and dirt off everything. Pulling the rest of their escape gear out of the kitbags, they piled the combinations, balaclavas and bags under a bush. Williams sprinkled it with a tin of black pepper he had brought along, as well as the ground around, in order to throw off the dogs. Then, dressed and ready, they made one last quick check of each other before doubling back a little in a wide circle. A short time later, they carefully exited the forest onto a road running away from the camp. In the distance through the trees they could see a dim light of what they took to be Sagan station. It was just passing on 6.20pm.

They knew from their arrival at Sagan the previous April that there were two ways into the station: a metal footbridge passing over the railway and onto a road some distance along from the booking hall and platform, and a subway entrance that passed under the tracks and exited directly at the booking hall. As they would be coming from the correct direction, and it would be better for their sudden appearance out of the darkness, their intention was to head for the bridge. They had also been told in camp that it was the narrowest route, as opposed to the wider subway, and more likely to be safer from police checks.

Walking up to the footbridge, they found that a local train must have just arrived, for the roadway and the bridge was crowded. However, nobody paid them any attention, and that was encouraging since it was known in camp that the *Abwehr* had people who watched the station for suspected escapers. They crossed the bridge, turned left and, walking on the right-hand side of the road, found the booking hall with no problems and entered.

It was bright inside after the darkness of the forest walk, and thankfully crowded; just the perfect cover for a pair of escapers. Codner collected Williams' papers and went directly to the ticket office while Williams wandered over to the notice board and pretended to read the timetable. A glance at the station clock showed they had made it with plenty of time in hand; it was just 6.30pm. They would hopefully be on the train and gone before any search of the station commenced should the alarm be raised at the camp any time soon.

The Escape Committee had said that the first call the Kommandant was certain to make following the discovery of an escape would be to the railway station, warning them to check all papers carefully, and to look especially close at clothing. He glanced at Codner, who looked unconcerned enough even if the raincoat he was wearing appeared to be very obviously of military origin. Then

Williams saw him draw in his bottom lip as he neared the ticket office, revealing his nervousness, and for the first time he noticed that the darkly dressed, dignified-looking man wearing a black Homburg in line behind Codner was none other than Philpot.[1]

Once across the road, Philpot had rushed deeper into the pines for some 200yds before he stopped and stripped off the evil smelling black-dyed long underwear and balaclava. From his kitbag he drew out a small water bottle, rag and shaving mirror and proceeded to clean himself up as best he could in the dark. As with the others, the sand was everywhere and he struggled to get rid of as much of it as he could. Despite the hood he had worn, there were copious amounts of it in his hair that just would not comb out. Once he got to the station and bought his ticket, he could make for the lavatory and make a better job of it in the light, if there was time, but he had to at least look presentable to buy his ticket. By some small miracle, the black Homburg had not been damaged and his collar, folded into his shirt, had stayed clean and was free of any traces of the black dye. He finished dressing, quickly buried the underwear and kitbag under a nearby bush, ran the rag over his shoes, pulled on his greatcoat and hat, and set off again. It was 6.20pm.

Almost immediately he found a path and walked in what he thought was the right direction, but it was not. Soon lights and a 'Goon' box loomed out of the darkness and he realized his mistake. If he stayed on this path he would pass very close to the guard tower. Not good! Slightly befuddled, he left the path and after checking his watch he set off through the forest. He noted that there had been no guards patrolling the wire.

A short time later, he crossed the footbridge. There were a few people about and two women passed him without taking any notice. A good sign! After crossing, he then walked along the other side to a narrow road and then turned left. The station was ahead, as was as a policeman holding a small lamp. Sweat broke out on Philpot's forehead. Had the alarm been raised at the camp? Was this the end already? His stomach taught with anxiety, he passed the policeman expecting the familiar, guttural shout 'Halt!', but none came. Philpot then crossed the road as nonchalantly as his nerves would allow and trudged toward the station entrance, resisting any urge to run. Under a street lamp just outside the entrance he reached inside his coat for his wallet and extracted a 20 Reichsmark note before entering.

The preliminaries were over; it was now time for the real test. Inside, the booking hall was crowded and brilliantly lit. Philpot joined one of the queues moving slowly forward, toward the ticket booths. One way or another, the guessing shortly would be over.

He had been in line but a brief moment before he realized that the thin Frenchman in beret and blue raincoat just in front of him was none other than Codner. Weeks earlier they had worked together on what needed to be said in order to obtain tickets, with Philpot actually doing much of the teaching, and now it was time to see if Codner had learned his lessons well.

At the booth Codner asked for two tickets to Frankfurt, pushing his and Williams's papers through the slot, along with some money. His accent was magnificent. The figure behind the glass took the papers. This was it and Philpot, standing behind, bit his lip nervously. But the pretty young clerk barely glanced at the papers, issued the tickets and gave Codner his change. Making sure he had purchased the correct tickets for the express to Frankfurt, Codner again impressively spoke in German, and the girl behind the glass answered back without suspicion. Then he was thanking her and moving toward a strangely familiar figure, standing near the timetable boards wearing a black coat and beret that Philpot barely recognized as Williams. He doubted if Codner had ever been aware of just who was behind him in the queue.

At the booth, Philpot nervously fumbled his pronunciation while asking for his ticket to Frankfurt, with a connection to Küstrin, and was corrected on his pronunciation by the ticket clerk. Funny that he should be the one to make a slip with his language! Once he had collected his ticket and change, he turned toward the gate that led to the subway. His platform, he noted, was on the other side and he had some fifteen minutes to wait. But just then, a number of people came pushing through the gate after getting off a recently arrived train. He began pushing against the crowd to get on the platform. Among the arriving crowd, Philpot recognized a familiar figure coming towards him, and his blood ran cold ….

Once he had their tickets, Codner walked over and collected Williams and told him quietly that the girl in the booth had mentioned that their train was running late. It was now 6.45pm and their train was not now scheduled to leave until 7.05pm. It looked as though it was going to be close; far closer than comfort might allow! With time to kill, they headed for their platform; better to be out in the open and darkness than in the brightly-lit confines of the hall. That way if the alarm was raised and they saw a rush of guards arriving outside at least they could get off the platform and attempt to get away.

Moving toward the gate leading to their platform, Codner and Williams were met by a sudden rush of people and moved off to the side again, near the timetable. It was Williams that first saw the blue-uniformed figure of Dr Lechten coming directly at them through the crowd. When he had been in Sick Quarters, Williams had spoken to him nearly every day on a variety of subjects and so they would easily recognize one another. He also knew that Lechten had already been responsible, in the past, for apprehending a number of escapers at the station and, if he kept walking in the same direction, he would pass within a few feet of the escapers.

Disaster loomed and Williams' heart was in his mouth. What to do? It was impossible that he would not be noticed. Lechten was little more than 6ft away when he glanced in Williams' direction and actually stared directly at him for a moment … and then, incredibly, looked away and kept walking. Williams immediately turned towards the wall and looked into his small, attaché case, pretending to fumble with a stubborn latch, eyes closed tight and all the while waiting for the accented, urbane voice to hail him in English: 'Goot eefennink Meester Villiams. Please to come mit me …', but none came.

Codner had also seen Lechten and turned toward the timetable again, keeping his face away from the passing figure as he scrutinized the chart. The passing crowd of passengers was thinning now and when he had judged enough time had passed to be safe, Codner grabbed Williams' arm and hurried him through the turnstile and on to the platforms, neither daring to look back. It was a very close call; and a small miracle that Lechten had not recognized the now clean-shaven Williams.

Thinking fast Philpot, who once had his own dealings with Lechten, as well as when visiting Williams one day, suddenly stooped down and busied himself tying a shoelace. He resisted the urge to look up until he was sure Lechten had moved past him, and then he too was up and pushing his way through the turnstile. He never knew what Codner and Williams had done, and did not really care. All that mattered was that the odds still seemed to be working in their favour.

At 7.05pm, their train had still not arrived. The three escapers waited with the rest of the passengers on the platform, trying their best to look unconcerned, but they were becoming more anxious as the minutes ticked away. They would not truly be safe from the immediate danger of recapture until they were away from the station; and the further the better. Obviously, their exit hole had not been discovered, and that was pure luck considering that it had been open for around an hour. However, they would definitely need to be away before 7.30pm without fail. Yet, as the minutes agonizingly dragged by, there was still not a sound of alarm from beyond the dark trees that blocked the lights of the camp from the station.

Philpot had lit a cigar he had brought with him (removed of all traces of 'Britishness') and casually strolled along the length of the platform, coolly smoking but getting more and more anxious at every tick of the platform clock. Time rolled on, 7.10pm came and went, then 7.15. There was a basin at one end of the platform and he rinsed the sweat from his face and drank some water. If the alarm were raised he planned to jump off the platform when no one was looking and disappear into the night. Once or twice he passed Williams and Codner, also strolling along casually, but they paid him no attention whatsoever.

Williams and Codner also walked back and forth for a while before standing at one end of the main crowd, conversing in whispers about what they might do if they heard a siren in the distance; should they immediately run off and strike out on foot, or jump on the first moving train that came past?

However, their thoughts became irrelevant when, to the relief of all three, the signals changed and in the distance they heard a locomotive's whistle. It was 7.20pm when their train puffed into the station, wreathed in clouds of steam and smoke. Carriage doors opened and a number of people crowded out, while at the same time the crowd on the platform tried to push on board. There was a remarkable lack of cursing but the usual abundance of shouting without which Germans seemed unable to do anything. The train guard shouted out 'Frankfurt!' and 'Berlin!' while waving a coloured paddle and the loudspeaker crackled to life with an announcement in German. Philpot briefly saw Williams and Codner climb up and disappear into a third-class carriage and he never saw them again during his travels. Though he had considered travelling second class, he had decided that his clothes would not stand up to that kind of scrutiny and that third class would be the safer option. He mounted the steps to a third-class carriage, so crowded that he was forced to stand in the corridor. There he found a space between two large civilians and close to two soldiers standing near the door.

Meanwhile Codner and Williams, two carriages ahead, had been separated by the heaving crowd of passengers immediately they had boarded and were also standing in the corridor. Williams was very near the door, facing a window, and Codner was squeezed in between an old woman and a Wehrmacht soldier. There he had leaned back against the wall and closed his eyes.

The interior of the carriage was dark and uninviting, without the normal hum of conversation one would expect of a train, and smelled of dirt and unwashed humanity, giving the situation a slightly depressing atmosphere. However, after a shrill on the locomotive's whistle and a few sharp jerks, the train started to pull out of the station; the three tired and nervous escapers felt their confidence begin to return. They were on their way! They had escaped from the camp, and with that the first hurdle of their journey to freedom had well and truly been surmounted. Now they were being carried towards their second hurdle – that of getting out of Nazi Germany and back to England. From then on, each tick of the clock and clack of the rails was giving them precious time and distance.

That first part of their new found freedom was uneventful, tedious, but exhilarating; they had travelled 110km in 3 hours as the darkened countryside of Silesia rushed past the windows. Codner, worn by the afternoon spent in the tunnel and the tension of the escape, dozed lightly, wedged against the side of his carriage. Williams however, alert and aware of the language barrier that hampered him without Codner at his side to deflect any questions, stood alone in his spot still very anxious and too excited to sleep.

Philpot stood in his carriage also deep in thought. Robert Kee, (Calman's escape partner from Schubin), had told him only a few days earlier as he was making his preparations, 'Your first great moment is when you get out of your tunnel. Your second is when your train draws out of your starting station.' Indeed it was so, and inside he was elated as they drew away from Sagan. As they did, one of the passengers standing next to him remarked to another traveller at how late they were in leaving, and his companion agreed. Philpot also silently agreed that it was late – by one year, ten months and eighteen days to be exact.

There were several stops at small stations along the way, at each a few people would get on and off with little fuss. All three of them took careful note of the names of each stop, keeping track of their progress from their memorized route. With each stop came the possibility that the tunnel had been discovered and a message sent to all the railway stations, alerting police to board and search all trains. At each stop the escapers tensed at the prospect. But as the train left each station without incident, their confidence in success grew. Then, from out of the dark beyond the windows, glowed the dim lights of a larger station and the train guard struggled down the corridor announcing that they had arrived at Frankfurt an der Oder. It was 10.30pm.

Here was a true landmark for their journey, for here was where all three would get off and seek the correct connection for the next leg of their bid for freedom, meaning that they had actually made progress. It was 4½ hours since they had crawled out of the tunnel at Sagan, and if the escape had been discovered – as it surely must have been by then – then it would be here at a mainline station where the police would most likely be waiting. Consequently, all three waited until all the passengers had left their carriages before warily exiting, but expecting a special von Lindeiner reception committee to be waiting. But they all breathed easily again as they stepped out and saw nothing special or out of the ordinary was happening in the station. Except, of course, that there were now three escaped PoWs inside.

Seeing no one was being asked for papers, Williams boldly pushed his way through the crowd toward one of the barriers, but was pulled back by Codner and shoved in another direction. Once through the exit and into the well-lit booking hall, Williams furtively asked what the hell that had been all about.

'That gate was for soldiers only, you clot! Come on; let's get out of the station and find a hotel!'

Williams stayed close to him as they walked out into the open street and it was there that they truly felt it for the first time, alone in the chilly darkness: freedom. They stood for a moment on the cobbled street. The street signs were in gothic script and they recognized nothing as familiar, but they were free; out in the open, free to roam the streets and look in shop windows or buy a beer in a bar. There would be no *Appell* tomorrow morning; no queuing for water with a *Humpen*; no preparing to take the wooden horse out, or planning the dispersal of sand; no ring of confining barbed wire spoiling their view. A strange, exhilarating sense of nakedness, after the confines of a prison camp, now enveloped them which they found exciting. Through hard work and sheer tenacity they had gained their freedom; now all they needed to do was to remain free. Slowly they began walking toward a hotel sign glowing in the distance.

But the closer they approached the hotel, with its large, impressively lit sign 'VICTORIA', the more reluctant Williams became about booking a room, worried that they had pushed luck as far as they dared for one day. Codner, however, was determined to see their plan through and went in, but had no luck; all the rooms were full. He received the same response at the next hotel; and the next. Altogether they tried four hotels that night, but received the same reply at each. Apparently there were no rooms available in Frankfurt, and in the end they returned to the booking hall, tired and dejected. With no alternative, and their connection to Küstrin not leaving until 8.50am, they decided to walk into the countryside and look for a shelter for the remainder of the night; perhaps a barn or haystack.

After nearly two hours of walking, they settled down among the tall weeds near the dry entrance of a concrete drain running under a stretch of deserted road. Although tired they ate some corned beef sandwiches they had brought from the camp for this, their first meal of freedom, before settling down to try to sleep. It was now perhaps 3.00am and they were really exhausted, yet sleep proved fitful in the bitter cold. Nevertheless, the rest they did get made them feel better and they were soon up and heading back toward the station before dawn on 30 October, ready to face the next leg of their journey.

Once off the train and in the booking hall, Philpot immediately went over to the destinations board and found he would not be able to get a connection to Küstrin until 6.56am the next morning. The 9.56pm to Küstrin he had planned on catching, but had missed due to the late running of the train from Sagan, had been cancelled. But how was he to pass the time until next morning? Sleep of course … in a hotel, but firstly 'Jon Jorgenson' needed to tidy-up a little. Following a crowd, he made his way to the lavatory. But the cubicles were locked and there seemed no one in attendance. Making his way back furiously sucking his pipe, he watched for a few minutes before going to update his ticket for Küstrin to the 6.56am train. The girl behind the glass found it difficult to understand him until he removed the pipe from his mouth, then she was soon passing the replacement ticket through the slot. Philpot was elated. His pipe idea had worked.

Making his way back to the lavatory, he found an old female attendant letting people in and found himself an empty cubicle. There he destroyed his old Sagan ticket and Sagan area map and flushed them away. From out of the secret compartment in the bottom of his margarine samples box, he extracted the documents and maps necessary for the next stretch of the journey. He then stripped and removed as much sand from himself and his clothes as possible, changed his collar, brushed his hair, and ate some of Lubbock's 'Dog Food'. Emerging from the lavatory (though embarrassingly; the old lady had to come to let him out. When exiting the cubicle he had inadvertently allowed the door to close and half lock), 'Jon Jorgenson' then went out in search of a room for the night.

He tried two hotels, including the 'Victoria', but, also had no luck and had to walk into the countryside. Near the edge of town, he tramped along a narrow lane and crossed a wooden footbridge, there he found himself in what appeared to be a park on the bank of what he took to be the Oder River. Crawling in among some dense bushes he settled down, well wrapped in his heavy RAF greatcoat, and was quickly asleep. It had been a long day, and his exhaustion was such that not even the cold kept him awake. He only woke once; he dreamed that he was hearing the shouts of searchers, and as he woke he had first imagined that he saw their torches shining in his face. But the lights were the moon, and the shouts were from some men on a barge going down the river calling to people on the towpath. Upon realizing he was still safe, sleep again engulfed him; it was 3.00am of his first day of freedom.

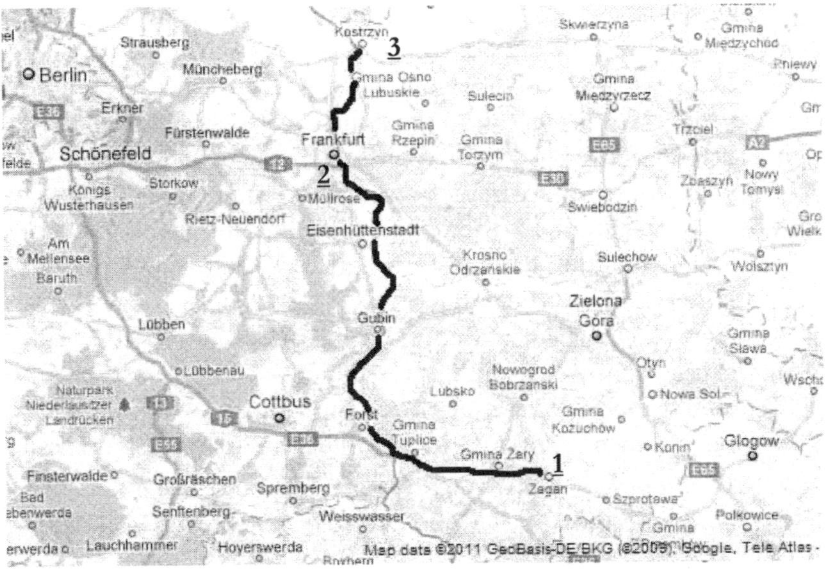

Sagan to Küstrin – the First Leg.
Williams & Codner and Philpot all caught the 7.00pm express to Berlin from (1) Sagan station, taking it as far as (2) Frankfurt an der Oder, a 137km journey. Williams and Codner travelled separate from Philpot, and after boarding the train at Sagan they did not see each other again for the length of their escape. After spending the night in Frankfurt, Philpot took an earlier train to (3) Küstrin (another 40km) than Williams and Codner, who left 2 hours later. As many of these locations are now with Polish territories, this map of the route contains today's Polish names for the towns they visited: Zagan (Sagan) and Kostyn (Küstrin), as well as Berlin for a reference point are shown, making it easy for the reader to follow along on any modern map.

Chapter 15

Meanwhile, back at Sagan …

Trouble visits Göring's 'Luxury Camp'

In later years, Flight Lieutenant Mike Lewis would recall that 'The night they left, the memourable thing is that nothing happened!'

Well, nothing happened until 8.30pm. After that, the Germans lost their collective minds.

Despite the palpable tension in the air that afternoon of 29 October, the day had ended as hundreds of others had for those imprisoned in the East Compound of the Reich's most 'luxurious' camp. The usual prison camp sounds during an autumn evening lent a general feeling of normality, except for the early party raging in Hut 65. And yet, hundreds of ears were cocked listening for a shout; a rifle shot; the barking of dogs; all signs that the escape had failed. Though it may not have been a popular scheme in its time, and the three may not have always been the most well-liked men in camp during the dig, now that the scheme was on the point of success and they had seen it through, nearly all wanted to see the three 'mad' men outside the wire, if only to 'muck up the Goons some'. In the event, no indication of failure was heard. The theatre closed at around 8.15pm, and as the autumn night slowly drew in and it became apparent they had succeeded, there was a certain sense of elation in camp, and in at least one room in particular.

Dallas Laskey had finished bathing and gone back to his mess that afternoon following the last vaulting session. He ate dinner, such as it was, got ready for bed, and turned in early. Nearly everyone in the compound did, as the next day was likely to be a long one and it would do to have as much rest as possible, in order to better enjoy it. In any case, all were certain that there would be plenty of 'fireworks'. Yet Dallas was feeling a little uneasy: 'I was not at all sure I wanted to go out that tunnel next morning, if it went undiscovered. You see, I was the junior officer as well as junior Kriegie on that escape, and that meant that I'd be the third one out. And laying there in the dark that night, I just had this reoccurring vision of poking my head out the hole and a German would be standing there with a machine pistol. So when the alarm went up that night, I was one relieved boy, I'll tell you. I let out a big sigh!'

Few eye witness reports from East Compound – and there are more than a few – seem to agree on exactly what time it was the 'Goons' discovered the exit hole, and most put it at or around 8.30pm. No fresh guard had come on duty at

7.30pm as was expected. Instead, the relief guard had been delayed that night due to his interest in the theatrical accomplishments of the prisoners. When the guard did come on duty and relieved the sentry in the 'Goon box' (who was to patrol the wire for a couple hours before going off duty) that sentry climbed down the ladder, began to walk his post, and promptly fell in the exit hole.

For a few minutes after, the air was filled with whistles and excited shouts before the camp alarm bell sounded in the *Vorlager*. Very soon after that, Feldwebel Stuhlmeyer turned out the guard to the exit site in full force, along with the dogs. There was much shouting by the time Major Gustav Simoleit, the camp adjutant, arrived. He then ordered the guard to fan-out into the surrounding dark forest, the beams of their flashlights spearing the darkness following the panting and barking dogs

'Charlie' Piltz, 'Lofty' and several other 'Ferrets' were soon seen arriving at the scene, along with the senior head of camp security, Hauptmann Broili. A Russian prisoner from the small slave-labour force kept in the *Vorlager* was brought forward and sent down the exit with a rope tied round his waist. He was soon back again, reporting that the tunnel was blocked with sand. 'Charlie' then entered the tunnel with a flashlight only to burst through the surface into the compound some minutes later, covered in sand and apparently looking exceptionally peeved. He no doubt knew that he would have some serious explaining to do, though it could hardly have taken him any time at all to put two and two together once he had initially arrived at the exit. Tom Wilson later remarked that "Charlie' must have kicked himself, but I also hope he thought it a brilliant exercise.'

It could not have been at all easy for him crawl through the tunnel from exit to entrance as the three escapers had left it blocked with sand. After all, even the Russian had reported it blocked. However, it may be that there was not quite as much sand crammed back into it after all, in light of the fact that the tunnel had actually come up short. Though Philpot had placed a certain quantity in the entrance shaft, he never did say how much, if he even truly realized the actual amount. Sealed in, short of air, and very keyed up at that point, he must have been in a hurry to get to the head of the tunnel with the others, which may have resulted in a relatively small amount actually packed into the entrance. At the face of the tunnel, he would have found Codner still digging, just as he had been for the better part of two hours in bad air and cramped conditions, which must have taken a toll on his strength. From then on, Williams later said they 'dug steadily' until 10 minutes before break-out time. It was during this time that they had 'moled'; a first experience for the three and one that must have produced what seemed to them like a huge quantity of sand, though it was in all probably not that much. It is very likely they only 'moled' for perhaps 2ft. On the day of the escape they had needed to dig some 10ft to enter the ditch, and they came up some 4ft short. Williams said that when he went up the tunnel that afternoon he found a wall of sand some 3ft thick that Codner had dug. One might then gather that once this sand was cleared up (which went back with McKay), that he and Codner dug perhaps a 1ft or so more. The spoil from their efforts would have been among what was sent back to Philpot in the entrance. This then would leave no more than 2ft of spoil that Philpot pushed behind him as they 'moled'.

Although it would have certainly been difficult for 'Charlie' to crawl through the tunnel, it would not have been that impossible. Once he did and came up in the compound, the wooden horse was quickly removed from the cookhouse and taken away to the escape museum in the *Kommandantur*.

Around the time when 'Charlie' emerged into the compound, Hauptmann Hellfachs arrived and was quickly briefed on the situation. This event in particular brought out the best in 'Kriegie' behaviour from behind the shuttered windows. Peering through cracks and knot holes in the shutters, a running commentary was kept up in the rooms, which brought forth howls of laughter and taunts from within the huts. Around 9.45pm, a large force of German troops was seen marching into the *Vorlager* from the direction of the *Kommandantur* and then through the gate into East Compound. They spread out, with several surrounding each hut, and the doors were then opened to allow several guards to enter. The lights were switched on and one by one the rooms were carefully searched and the occupants counted.

But as the count continued, several of the guards discovered that many of the prisoners did not appear to be in their assigned rooms, or even in their assigned huts for that matter. The Escape Committee, always alert, had taken the extra precaution of re-arranging the sleeping arrangements of a number of the men that night.

The Germans now became highly agitated, and demanded that the compound's adjutant be brought forward. Reports quickly came back that Wing Commander McDonnell was not in his room and was, in fact, nowhere to be found. Could McDonnell be among the escapers? They could not know until an accurate count of the prisoners was made! The *Kriegsgefangenerkartes* (PoW Identity Cards) were sent for and, Hauptmann Broili and the 'Photographic Goons' started to slowly make their way through the huts in an effort to find out who was still there and who had 'gone away'. Each 'Kriegie' was to come forward and produce his identity disc that had been given to him when he became a prisoner. The number on the disc was then matched with a card in the file, and the photograph on the card matched to the face illuminated in the glow of a flashlight. Perhaps it should not be thought strange to find that in some instances, the face did not match the image!

Meanwhile, continued shouting by the Germans followed in the compound until McDonnell's assistant adjutant, none other than escape clothing officer Ralph Ward, was found and brought before Hauptmann Hellfachs to explain why a number of prisoners were not located in their correct huts. Ward, assuming the attitude of an officious, indignant, British officer, carefully explained that there was no regulation, he was aware of, that forced the prisoners to always sleep in the same room. Bemused by the lack of any reasonable answer to this challenge, as well as by Ward's attitude, the Germans were grudgingly forced to agree with him and calmed down.

By that time, it was nearing 11.00pm and Broili and his 'Photographic Goons', through no small effort, had made their way through most of the huts, except for Huts 68 and 69. That, reasoned Wing Commander Collard, was the perfect time to fuse the lighting circuits for the huts – which he duly did, plunging the already dim interiors into total darkness. The 'Kriegies' roared with delight. The Germans simply roared.

Regrouping in the compound, the German staff conferred. It could be dangerous to send anyone into the two darkened huts to continue the count with nothing more than flashlights. Who knew what nefarious activities the wily and excited prisoners might get up to, especially within Hut 68, home of the troublemakers? The decision was made (and certainly a sensible one, under the circumstances) to let things be for the night, lock the huts securely, and continue the count in the light of the morning. The dogs were out in the forest, the railway station was placed on high alert, and the initial search orders had already gone out in all directions. There was little more to be done until it was known for sure just how many and exactly who had escaped. The 'Kriegies' were all marched back to their huts and locked in for the night.

By 11.30am, a tense stillness had settled over the camp, only punctuated at intervals by the distant barking of the dogs and harsh shouts of guards searching in the surrounding forest.

That next morning started off just as badly for the 'Goons'. 'The Germans,' said Flying Officer Hugh Lynch-Blosse, ever the master of understatement, 'were very, very angry.'

The 'bush telegraph' had flashed the news of the break over to the Centre Compound as quick as lightning, making it general knowledge among the prisoners there by morning *Appell*. Success always brought out the best in radical PoW behavior, and so it was as the sun came up on 30 October that the guards unlocking the hut doors in the compound found most of the prisoners already up, dressed, and waiting to flood out for parade. That morning, a German force of some fifty fully-armed troops assembled in front of the night guard's hut, and prepared to attempt an accurate head count in the East Compound. The prisoners of Centre Compound quickly gathered by the northern fence and started jeering their captors. The Germans, already agitated after the previous night and and having had little sleep, became even more angry at the abuse. As Flight Lieutenant David Codd later recalled, 'They were clearly furious at being made to look stupid, and we onlookers did what we could to increase their discomfiture. However, when some of the troops started pointing their rifles in our direction, we decided enough was enough. By then the three escapers were on their way to freedom.' With no further interference from the Centre Compound prisoners, the ill-tempered German garrison then entered East Compound, spread out and unlocked the doors. However, in divergence to usual routine, instead of dispersing until *Appell* the unusually large number of guards maintained their presence in the compound. What became known as 'Black Saturday' in East Compound had begun.[1]

In sharp contrast to those in Centre, those prisoners in East were not awake early and waiting to be let out; except for the room 'stooges', who went about their usual duties. At the cookhouse while waiting for hot water, Tom Wilson and a few others had a furtive look in the passageway by the barber shop, but the wooden horse had been removed. The 'Kitchen Goon' was impassive as always, giving no indication he was even aware anything had occurred in the compound overnight. But there was no avoiding the overlying tension, only heightened by the number of 'Goons' milling about throughout the camp. Two were standing guard over the entrance to the tunnel, which was open; the trap boards and anchor bags lying in a dismal heap alongside the hole.

Following on from breakfast, the call for *Appell* blew as usual and, the 'Kriegies' had to be ushered from their huts as on nearly every other day. Except today, they dawdled even more than usual; even as the guards tramped through each hut, their hoarse shouts shattering the morning, each 'Little X' circulated among the straggling prisoners, quietly urging them to take their time so as to give the escapers that much more time. This, understandably, caused German tempers to become frayed again.

Once outside, the prisoners' formed ragged ranks and should their usual indifference, but the count went ahead as usual. Hauptmann Broili was there again, alongside Hauptmann Hellfachs, to take the count. Ralph Ward stood in again for McDonnell, although the Wing Commander he had been counted in his room and confirmed as present this time. There was no longer any need to cover for the three; the Germans would know who they were soon enough.

Indeed the count showed three missing; ostensibly two from Hut 62 and one from Hut 67. Yet as the prisoners had already been shuffling around between rooms and huts the night before, the missing men might have actually come from any one of the huts. To that end, another attempt at checking each 'Kriegie' against his *Kriegsgefangenerkarte* would be necessary, and the Germans were prepared with the presence of the extra guards.

The count completed, the 'Kriegies' waited to be dismissed; but this did not happen. Instead, they watched as a table was brought out and set up in the centre of the *Sportzplatz*, along with several chairs. The extra guards then formed a line behind the table effectively dividing the area into an east section, which contained the milling ranks of prisoners, and an empty west section.

Soon, the 'Photographic Goons' appeared again with their boxes of cards and sat down at the table. Broili, Hellfachs, and 'Charlie' Piltz, all looking very angry and very tired, were also present.

There was some debate among the Germans as to where they should begin the count; at Huts 68 and 69, where it had ended last night when the lights went out, or to start afresh? They eventually decided to start with the two neglected huts. Major Simoleit and Feldwebel Stuhlmeyer began to call forward prisoners one at a time by hut number, name and number to be individually checked. Once that prisoner was positively identified, he was ushered into the west section, as Tom Wilson put it, 'to separate the sheep from the goats'.

It was a long and tedious process, giving the prisoners plenty of time to find additional ways to make trouble, even with such a seemingly efficient system in place. Some men appeared not to hear their name called out until several others had been called, in which case they would then rush up to the table with three or four others, all talking at once and creating considerable confusion. The 'Photographic Goons' apparently spoke no English and several English voices at once quickly overwhelmed them. Some men answered for others and some men apparently could not understand their name through Stuhlmeyer's accent. Others simply did not answer at all and at the end of the counting for a hut, there would still be a small group of men standing in the dirty sand who steadfastly insisted their names had not been called.

These distractions compounded the fact that many of the prisoners had neglected to wear their tags, while others had lost them. The negligent had to be escorted back to his room to collect it, while those who had 'lost' theirs had their names taken by Stuhlmeyer for a later spell in 'Cooler'. A number of the older 'Kriegies' did not look as they did when shot down, many having grown beards and longer hair while losing considerable weight, making positive identification difficult. There was a constant stream of 'Kriegies' needing to use the *Abort*, each had to be escorted, and though they had added extra guards for the count the Germans soon found they were still under strength. The chaos increased as time passed, German tempers again reaching boiling point in the process, and there was a great deal of shouting around the table. Meanwhile both the checked prisoners and the guards along the separation line grew increasingly bored with the whole process.

Next to Tom Wilson's hut stood eight of the army orderlies who performed services in the camp, waiting to be counted. One of them had carried a football on parade with him, and they now started to boot it back and forth in an effort to keep warm. Wing Commander Maw, seeing this, asked if he might borrow the ball and it was duly kicked over to him. Soon the ball was being passed up and down among the ranks of the men in Hut 64. Everything was going well until someone kicked it too hard and sent it bouncing across the *Sportzplatz*. At this, Feldwebel Stuhlmeyer, already flustered by them being uncooperative at the identity check, lost all patience and sense of reason. Pointing out the bouncing ball to one of the guards on the demarcation line, he shouted *'Arrest zat ball!'* at which all the 'Kriegies' of Hut 64 howled with laughter. This was followed by more shouting from Stuhlmeyer at the guard as he failed to move, followed by the ludicrous sight of the guard, in full winter uniform, chasing the ball, gave weight to the derisive term 'Goon'.

Just as the guard had gathered it, Tom Wilson suddenly darted out and snatched the ball from his grasp, tossing it over to a friend in the ranks, who then tossed it back, as the 'Goon' ran back and forth. However the guard, seeing that Stuhlmeyer was now otherwise occupied yelling at some other malicious 'Kriegie' activity somewhere else, quickly gave up and wandered back to his place in the line.

It was then that the real trouble started, Wing Commander Collard, whose Hut 68 had been among the first counted, appeared through the crowd. He had used his rank and privilege to bully his way back through the guards and into the area of uncounted prisoners. Seeing the football he now issued Wing Commander Maw a rousing challenge: 'Roger, I'll bet your chaps can not score a try behind our lines!'

It was all that was needed.

With a roar, and moving almost as one, the prisoners of Hut 64 now surged forward, the ball passing efficiently up and down their ranks, heading directly for those of Hut 68 standing behind the line of guards. And, moving almost as one, they rushed toward the line as well, in order to defend against the Block 64 attack. With these two moves, complete pandemonium broke out.

The inmates of Hut 68 easily broke through the thin line of guards, and the end result was that the two groups met at the table. In the ensuing clash the table was overturned and the cards scattereded over the dirty sand, effectively mixing the counted with the uncounted. The Germans, leaped out of their chairs in the midst of the scrum, shouted and jumped around impotently, while the football was tossed around with 'Kriegies' in enthusiastic persuit. The rest of the counted prisoners, seeing their chance, also barged through the guards. Perfect anarchy reigned.[2]

For a while there was nothing the Germans could do and, much to their credit, there was no shooting. The compound was overrun by rampaging 'Kreigies' and it was only after some time and a lot of shouting and brandishing of weaponry that the 'Goons' managed to herd the prisoners back into their huts, which were then locked. On his way to report to Kommandant von Lindeiner, Major Simoleit met Ralph Ward and warned him that now there would be 'very great trouble'. Ward later recalled that Simoleit looked 'very afraid'. For a second time, the Germans had failed to establish how many had escaped or any idea to the identity of the escapers

There then followed a curious 'peace', during which time the Kommandant sent for Group Captain Kellett. The prisoners, said von Lindeiner, were not acting as proper officers with their flagrant disregard of camp rules. If such an attitude were to continue, serious consequences would be the result. Kellett was ordered to control his troops. Kellett, realizing that reprisals were already being planned, responded, 'I thought your chaps were doing that,' and then returned to the compound. Once there, he sent Ralph Ward, under German escort, to see the commander of each hut with the instruction: 'While the inmates were not to exactly co-operate at next parade, they were at least to make an effort toward not pushing the 'Goons' to quite the limit they had previously'. It was obvious the Germans were not going to take much more, and they had given the three escapers about as much lead time as they could. More could mean pushing matters too far in the compound.

The instructions came at precisely the right time. Just after noon, Tom Wilson eating his lunch, while watching from the window of the library, spied the same fifty troops from the morning formed up again in the *Vorlager*. Then a number of German trucks came through the outer gate carrying some 200 fully-armed Luftwaffe troops, effectively doubling the compound garrison. Among them was the Kommandant and most of the camp's officers. The original fifty marched through the gate and dispersed in squads to each hut once again just before the call to *Appell*. Throwing open the doors, they tramped through each hut with bayonets fixed, turning everyone out in a display of forceful determination.

Wing Commander Collard and the troublemakers of Hut 68 remained obstinately uncoopertive. Dragging their feet and arguing with the 'Goons' at every turn, the hut still had not completely cleared by the time the other prisoners were already standing on parade. An exasperated von Lindeiner ordered the guards out of the hut before another 'Goon' walked up and fired off a few bursts from his machine pistol into the doorway and front windows and walls. After that, the hut emptied rapidly with the inmates leaping out of windows and door, and as they sprinted away, many made diparaging remarks and gestures at the guards. Seeing this, Ralph Ward went and had a brief word with Wing Commander Collard, asking him to have his men behave, for their own sake.[3]

In the ranks on the *Sportzplatz* the episode was proof that the Germans had reached the end of their patience; the fun was obviously over. The extra garrison of troops marched into the compound and formed a solid line behind the ranks, machine pistols at the ready, while an Oberfeldwebel from another compound, who was helping to supervise the count, arrested anyone who was not presenting a military bearing and sent them to the 'Cooler'. Once the physical count was over, the identification parade began again in earnest. This time there was no thin line of guards dividing the compound but a solid barrier and strict enforcement of separation. Once or twice, a few 'Kriegies' tried to get through the line and cause further trouble, but a few shots in the air from the guards quickly dissuaded them and the practice came to an abrupt halt.[4]

The parade took a long time and slowly dragged on as the afternoon ended. Two of Tom Wilson's fellow inmates, from Hut 64, brought a chess set and decided to sit down on the ground and play as they waited. But the Oberfeldwebel, seeing this, charged over, kicked away the board and sent the two to the 'Cooler' for a week. Finally, the 'Photographic Goons' announced they were finished and able to report the identities of the three escapers to the Kommandant. Reportedly, von Lindeiner showed no emotion whatsoever at the news.

The prisoners were again assembled in their ranks and called to attention. Through Major Simoleit, von Lindeiner announced that as a result of the escape and the method used, the golf course was to be completely levelled; indeed even as the 'Kriegies' paraded, around them the 'Ferrets' were already destroying the carefully constructed bunkers and browns. This news was greeted with both cheers and boos. The Kommandant went on; Red Cross parcels would not be issued for three weeks. More cheers and boos. There would be three *Appell* a day until further notice and all prisoners would be locked in the huts from 5.00pm. More cheers and boos, only louder this time. The International Red Cross was also visiting a number of PoW camps around the Reich with a portable cinema for the prisoners' benefit – they would not be visiting East Compound, Stalag Luft III. Still more cheers and boos. The prisoners remained unrepentant, and finally, as the last light of the incredible day quickly faded, they were dismissed back to their huts and locked in. As they were, a red-faced 'Charlie' Piltz was fixing a hose to the camp fire appliance and getting ready to collapse the tunnel.

So ended what Flying Officer Hugh Lynch-Blosse later remembered as 'rather a nerve wracking day, but worth it!'

The next day, the Kommandant arranged an interview in his office with Group Captains Kellett and Willetts (who was soon to take over as SBO in East Compound); Wing Commanders Collard and Maw; Pilot Officers Poulton, Ruffel, and Walters; and First Lieutenant Haller (all leaders in the previous days disruption), where he issued a statement, translated again by Major Simoleit:

> "On the morning of Saturday, 30th October, 1943, incidents took place in the East camp which could have easily led to serious consequences. The cause of these incidents was that the PoWs did not behave in the manner which must be required of them.
>
> 'Professional soldiers do not tolerate provocative and mocking behaviour. On Saturday, the German soldiers showed extraordinary self control

when they were greeted as they marched into the camp with extremely improper shouts. Certain PoWs tried to mock us on our own soil. This behaviour shows a totally wrong-headed outlook. I expect neither liking nor sympathy, but I do expect a military bearing, and respect for German soldiers and for the German uniform. In his own mind, each one of you may think as he likes, but in his behaviour he must conduct himself respectfully and in accordance with his circumstances.

'I cannot understand how senior staff officers can encourage their junior comrades to play football during Appell or to run across the parade ground from one hut to another. Wing Commanders Collard and Maw may hate us Germans and our country as much as they like, but that does not interest me in the slightest; I do not seek their friendship, nor do I need it. But while they are prisoners of war they will learn what we Germans expect, above all from an officer: namely correct, respectable behavior in accordance with the German ideals of officership.

'On Saturday we arrested seven men who expressed their bravery, their heroism, and their good up-bringing by grinning, shouting, and whistling. Behaviour of this kind is only possible if their attitude is totally misguided. I believe that I can be certain that at least 95% of the officers in this camp have the same officer-like attitude as we have. But a small proportion appear to desire to make their relations between the detaining power and the PoWs as strained as possible. I wish to warn these gentlemen and to advise them for the last time to avoid stirring up trouble amongst their comrades.

'After the attempted escape on Friday, we discovered that the entrance to the tunnel was on the sports field in the golf course and that sand had been dispersed on the golf course. The tunnel had to be filled in as quickly as possible and the leveling of the ground was absolutely essential in order to maintain security.

'I myself saw as we entered Huts 68 and 69 that the lights were extinguished and that they came back on again as we left the barracks. In order to prevent this kind of mockery during the night, I had the light bulbs removed from both barracks.[5]

'The escape on Friday took place on the northern part of the sports field between 1920 and 2120 hours. The PoWs must therefore have been outside the permitted area at this time, having left their barracks by a route not allowed. As a result I must take all security measures to see that no one leaves the barracks after dark or climbs out of the windows. I therefore gave the order forbidding all movement outside the huts after the circuit lighting is switched on, and having the window shutters closed all night.

'I will now repeat the quintessence of my remarks:

'I urgently advise the avoidance of any stirring up by underhand propaganda on the part of some of the prisoners, and any sympathetic reception of it by the rest.

'I expect no sympathy and I will use all the force at my command to ensure that due respect as well as absolute obedience is paid to the detaining power and its representatives."

Von Lindeiner
Oberst and Kommandant'[5]

In all fairness, the Germans had shown remarkable restraint in the light of the day's activities, and much of that needs to be attributed to the leadership of von Lindeiner; a truly humane and professional soldier. No lover of the Nazis by any stretch of the imagination, von Lindeiner had resisted joining the Nazi struggle as long as he could, retiring from a lifetime of military service to Germany before the war in order to avoid having to directly participate in Hitler's madness. But, as an experienced military man, he was highly valued by the Nazi High Command and as such was ordered back into service, certainly against his will. He chose the Luftwaffe, the least Nazi-fied of the military services, and called in favours in order to get himself appointed to Göring's staff. They had been personal friends ever since serving together in World War One. It was Göring himself, knowing his friend's sense of fairness and soldierly respect, who appointed him to run Stalag Luft III. But von Lindeiner was an officer of the 'old school', who perhaps expected far more of the 'old world' respect and honesty from his charges than they were willing to give to a representative of the Nazi regime. Nevertheless, he was well aware of the High Command's attitude toward escape, and he truly believed that escapers were taking too great a risk when free in the Reich. This attitude he tried hard to impress upon the senior officers in the camp, but to no avail. He would, of course, be proven right following the 'Great Escape' by the tunnel from North Compound in March of the next year. In any event, in the case of the aftermath of the wooden horse escape it is entirely likely that under any other Kommandant in Germany, the behaviour of the prisoners that Saturday would most probably have led to bloodshed.

With the tunnel filled in and the wooden horse locked in the *Kommandantur*, the excitement of 'Black Saturday' was over. The compound quickly settled back into the usual routine again as night arrived that Sunday. It looked as though it was going to be a long winter; already there was not enough coal to keep the stoves in the rooms going, and similarly those in the 'Cooler' shivered under the thin blankets in the semi-darkness of the cells. Outside, the first flurries of snow gently fell from under a leaden sky and the last of the 'circuit bashers', wrapped in their greatcoats, stepped over the long depression in the ground left by the tunnel, awhile fondly remembering the shouts and yells of the vaulters that summer.

During *Appell* the next morning, Hauptmann Hellfachs announced that all three of the escapers had already been caught and sent off to Colditz Castle.

Chapter 16

'Jon Jorgenson' Takes a Trip

30 October–4 November 1943

Philpot woke in the park at 5.00am and set out for Frankfurt station. He brushed himself down thoroughly before taking to the streets and was amazed at the number of people around at that early hour. Also at the station which was very busy. Making his way to double check his ticket against the departure board, he saw he had some time to spare and made his way to the small grooming cubicle next to the lavatory in order to give himself a final clean. Just as he was about to enter, a fat German pushed in ahead of him and occupied the cubicle for 25 minutes. Philpot entered and was out in around 15 minutes. He emerged with a clean-shaven face (done with a brand new blade to celebrate the first day out), a clean collar, hair and clothes brushed. He had also managed to polish his shoes. Ready to face the world he made his way toward the platform and was through the turnstile with hardly as much as a glance by the ticket collector. Philpot entered a third-class carriage which was occupied by only a handful of people and found a seat in a compartment where he laid his head back and pretended to be asleep. He recalled that the man who had given them their one and only rather 'fact austere' evasion lecture back on his squadron had said that pretending to be asleep on a train or bus was an excellent dodge to deflect unwanted attention. In truth he was very tired anyway; the night before had hardly lent itself to a good night's rest. Perhaps it would make the hours pass quickly if he dozed.

The train left for Küstrin at 6.56am, but by the time it pulled out, Philpot was no longer alone in his compartment, although there was still considerable room throughout the carriage. A man had entered and deliberately sat down facing him. He looked exceptionally bright and alert for the time of day and Philpot sensed danger. Sure enough, after taking his seat the man said something which Philpot did not immediately catch, but which was obviously directed at him. Still feigning sleep, but peeking at the man through half-closed eyes, he saw that he was looking directly at him with a smile. Again he said something. It was clear that the man wanted to talk and was not going to go away. Philpot woke up, yawned, stretched, and apologized for not completely understanding what the man said. 'You see, I am a foreigner.'

'So, a foreigner?' The man showed a definate interest.

'Yes. I am Norwegian.' Philpot explained.

The man brightened considerably – if that were possible – and exclaimed, 'Ooohhhh, a Norwegian! My son is in Norway!'

Alert now, with all the tiredness drained away in an instant, Philpot needed to be very careful. Norway was known to this man; But, just how much?

'Or at least he is off Norway,' the man continued cheerfully. 'You see, he is in the Kriegsmarine operating off of the coast there.'

Philpot politely inquired if the fellow had ever had occasion to visit his country. He needed to feign interest to get out of this with care.

'Unfortunately, no; I've never had the opportunity.'

Relief immediately flooded over Philpot; there would be no prying questions – questions that it would be unlikely he would be able to answer satisfactorily.

'And what brings you to Germany?' the man was leaning forward with interest.

Philpot thought hard. Here was the opportunity for him to extract himself from a possibly dangerous situation. It would depend on attitude.

'Me? I am here on a business trip; an important one.' He replied haughtily and slightly severely, with a serious, hard look at his companion that he hoped would warn him against asking further questions. It was patently obvious that his 'companion' was on Reich business, so the less questions the better as any German knew that internal Reich business was not discussed in the open.

'Oh …' The man sank back. Philpot turned his head away and again feigned sleep. Possible disaster had been averted.[1]

The kilometres raced by, and before long the train guard was passing down the corridor shouting out the stops for Küstrin ahead (there were three). Suddenly the man looked inquisitive again and tapped Philpot on the knee. Quietly he asked if he might know which of the Küstrin stops might be best for him, as he had never been to the town. Might the first one be the best? It was a only a platform on the edge of the town, as was common in continental cities of the time. Philpot replied he thought it might indeed be the best one – for him – and the man made ready to leave. Only the fear of an unknown traveller on apparent Reich business kept the man from the formal politeness of a handshake as he left the carriage.

A short time after the first stop, the train drew into Küstrin. Philpot went directly to the departure board to confirm the time of his connection, purchased his ticket to Danzig without any problems and no check on papers, and walked out of the station into the town. It was not yet 8.00am and he had almost 2½ hours to spend before departure time.

He found the town bleak and boring but walked briskly around, occasionally stopping to look in mainly empty shop windows, all the while trying to make himself look as if he had a purpose in his travels. Before too long, he entered a park near the town centre, and comfortably tucked himself away from prying eyes until it was time to head back to the station. Around him were the sounds

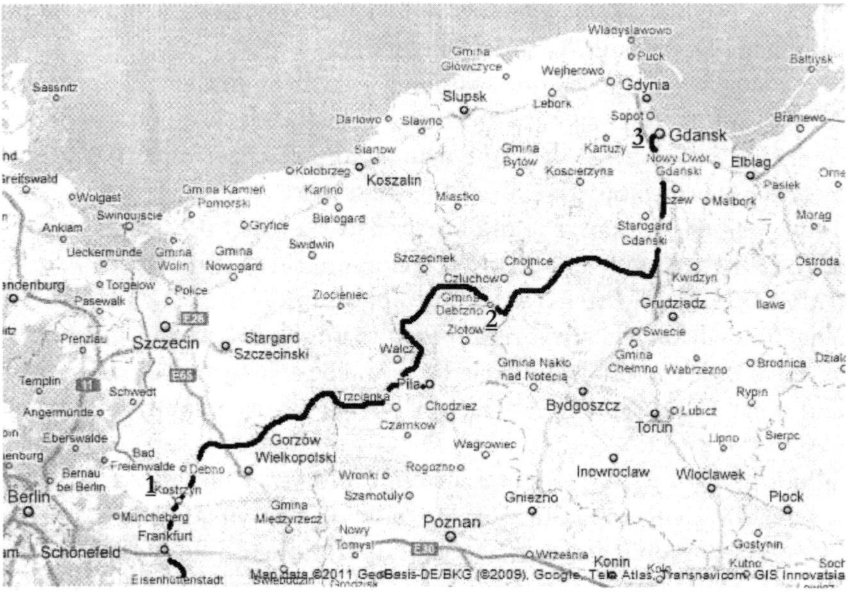

From Küstrin to Danzig – Perfection.

From (1) Küstrin, Philpot caught the 'Königsberg Express' to (2) Dirchau, and then the Breslau Express to (3) Danzig, a distance of about 400km. The train made few stops, thus he was in Danzig within 24 hours of crawling out of the tunnel at Sagan. It was from Danzig the he was ultimately successful, and today his may be considered the nearly perfect escape. As many of these locations are now within Polish territories, this map of his route contains today's Polish names for the towns he visited: Kostzyn (Küstrin), Debinzo (Dirschau), and Gdansk (Danzig), as well as Berlin for a reference point, making it easy for the reader to follow along on any modern map.

of true civilization, which he enjoyed immensely. He was wide awake and alert now and the sounds brought a sense of normality to the situation, and for a few moments he was able to truly relax. What caught his attention most though was the crying of a baby. It had been nearly two years since he had heard the sound, Anne and Alison his daughters were crying on the morning he had taken-off for the last time in O for 'Orange', and it brought a certain sadness and urgency to him. Checking the Rolex, he restlessly got up to walk around again and would note later in his escape report on the remarkable lack of civilian motorized traffic in the town.

After passing a policeman who looked at him suspiciously, he finally returned to the station seeking a crowd to melt into, so as to be as unobtrusive as possible. At the turnstile, he showed his ticket and was waved through to his platform. He immediately headed for the lavatory, which he was rapidly discovering to be the escaper's best office of operations. Locking himself in a cubicle, he again sorted out his papers, ate a little of his 'Dog Food', and brushed his shoes. At the basin he washed his face and hands. Continuing to remain eminently respectable, after a cup of acorn coffee in the station buffet, he made his way out to the platform. The crowd was dense and when the large locomotive steamed in he had to elbow his way onto the 'D-1/Königsberg Express', which would take him to Dirschau. The 'Königsberg Express' was an impressive looking train and when he boarded he felt that he was now making real progress.

The express pulled out promptly at 10.29am. The train was very crowded and he was once again forced to stand in the corridor, occupying a spot along the side near a door. Despite his fear of being drawn into conversation, mixing with the general German citizenry made him feel strangely safe and secure. In order to ensure he was left alone, Philpot quickly adopted what he felt to be a continental attitude and attempted to adopt a superior, aloof manner. It helped that Philpot had been associated with several high-ranking British officers during his military career and could clearly remember their superior attitudes toward subordinates. To his fellow travellers, his neatly groomed and clean shaven appearance, combined with his well dressed, erect stance and superior attitude. This perhaps gave the impression that he could be, a minor Nazi Party member not to be trifled with, or at least some other kind of official best left alone. In any case, no one made any attempt to speak to him as he settled in for the long journey.

The express made a few stops, and after one or two, Philpot found there was sufficient room in the corridor to place his case down and make a seat. The hours since Sagan, with what little sleep he had managed, and the initial rush of excitement which had now worn off, were beginning to tell. He placed his chin in hands, and resting his elbows on his knees, he was soon dozing comfortably in the warmth of the gently rocking train. The situation around him was slowly fading into oblivion when, dimly, he felt himself sliding sideways off the case and onto the floor, uttering 'Damn!' as he did so! Abruptly, he was wide awake and aware of what had happened and quickly sat up amid the general laughter among the civilians and soldiers. Standing again, with the case placed between his feet, he made a show of being unruffled and again adopted a superior stance, ignoring the amusement caused at his expense. Luckily, no one had apparently heard what he said, or if they had they most likely mistook it for the German, *V'damnt*.

The train stopped just outside of Schneidemuhl due to an air raid ahead. Several people groaned about the delay, but there was one traveller among the group at Philpot's end of the carriage who was soon grumbling louder than all the rest about how much more appalling were conditions in the west of Germany, where he was from, than here in the east. In the west, he complained, the number and frequency of air raids was intolerable. Day and night they came, giving nobody any peace and disrupting the lives of thousands. It was all so very dreadful. Personally Philpot was elated at hearing this, while his persona 'Jorgenson' pretended to listen with a disapproving air to one spreading such obvious subversion within the 'Glorious Reich'.

But the grumbler soon silenced himself as the blue-uniformed ticket collector came into the carriage and started making his way down the corridor. Philpot handed his ticket over for punching, relieved there was no request for papers. Relaxing again, it all seemed to be too easy. Then from behind, he heard the polite voice of the plain-clothes *Kriminalpolizei* officer asking to see his *Ausweis*. He turned, saw the identity badge in the man's hand and, with no apparent alarm, reached into his overcoat for his leather wallet. This was it! When it was opened, it showed the correct document. Philpot remained calm, but alert, and carefully watched the man for any sign of suspicion. The officer was a fleshy, middle-aged man, not unkind of features, and he studied the document with little apparent concern. He inquired of his movements and questioned the granting of the *Ausweis* to a foreign national. 'Jorgenson' explained that the Dresden police had issued the document for his temporary travel purposes in place of his Norwegian passport, which they had kept. '*Herr* Jorgensen would be returning to Dresden soon? ' the officer asked. 'Why yes, he would; his trips were for training purposes only.' The official studied the document for just a moment more before pointing out that had the Dresden police stamped the document across the corner of the photograph – which they had not – then all would be in proper order. Philpot chilled a little and his knees suddenly grew weak. However, the man continued, as everything else seemed to be correct there was no sense worrying over such a trivial matter. He wished 'Jon Jorgensen' safe journey then handed the wallet back and moved on. Dry mouthed but elated, Philpot let out an imperceptible sigh, and not long after found an empty seat in a compartment; he needed to sit down after that episode! He dozed for the rest of the journey with a slight smile on his lips. 'Jon Jorgenson' had come under the scrutiny of a hardened Nazi professional from the much vaunted *Kriminalpolizei* and passed with flying colours.[2]

A few hours later, just before 4.00pm, the train pulled into Dirschau, where Philpot changed to the fast 'Breslau Express' without any trouble. This would take him straight through the rest of the journey to Danzig. He was very pleased at reaching this landmark along his route. If he were to be recaptured anywhere beyond this point, it would be a most respectable achievement; Sagan to Dirschau was nearly 400km. No one could fault his effort in any way.

The 'Breslau Express' pulled into Dirschau at soon after 5.00pm on 30 October and Philpot stepped down onto the platform. Elated, he noted that it was just 22 hours and 50 minutes after he had emerged from the tunnel at Sagan. He had originally planned to arrive that morning instead of in the evening, but the cancelled connection between Frankfurt and Küstrin had ruined that plan. Nevertheless, his progress thus far had been amazing, and he recognized that to arrive at his target destination in less than 24 hours was nothing less than phenomenal. Phase one of the escape – leaving the camp successfully – was complete. Phase two – reaching his border destination from where he had a chance to make for neutral Sweden – was now complete. Now all that remained was phase three – reaching neutral Sweden, and then to England. From here, there would be room (indeed a need) for a certain amount of luck. Perhaps luck might even still be with him that evening and he could find a neutral ship. What a true success that would be!

Philpot drank a beer in the station buffet to celebrate his success so far, during which he noticed the same plain-clothes officer from the train standing against the far wall of the room, watching everything and nothing. He once again retreated to a lavatory and rang for the attendant. No one came until another German entered, rang the bell and shouted for service. The ageing attendant arrived and let them each into a cubicle, and Philpot immediately began to dispose of unrequired papers and anything else that might indentify him in any way as an escaper. Outside of his identity tag, still well-hidden under his shirt sealed in the cardboard backing of Nathalie's photograph he must show no signs of ever having been associated with Sagan. From the secret compartment of his sample box, he also destroyed all maps of everywhere but Danzig and also threw away his old train ticket. Studying the Danzig map for a while, he saw where he must go, and then put it aside before getting out his 'Dog Food' to eat. Was he becoming dangerously overconfident? He was in Danzig, locked in a lavatory cubicle, feeling safe from the world and on his way home. Sweden then England beckoned.

Suddenly came the sounds of footsteps on the tiled floor, followed by the rattle on his door, which was suddenly flung open, as he sat fully clothed with his case opened across his knees, and ready to eat his concentrated food. He looked up to see the old attendant staring down at him. He thought 'This Was It'; his escape was over and he would soon be back in a cell at Sagan and then returned to the hated compound, to again stare out through the wire at the endless vista of depressing gaunt pines … all after such good and careful preparation and terrific progress.

'Ten Pfennigs, please' requested the old man. He continued to stare with indifference at Philpot and held out a gnarled hand for the money.

Philpot found a coin in his pocket, paid the attendant who then shut the door. Dejected, he carefully scanned his map of Danzig before stowing it away safely. He then left the lavatory to check the route timetable for the local tram system.

Danzig harbour is where the River Vistula meets the Baltic Sea. The river snakes in a westerly direction north of Danzig, and makes a final loop north to northeast, then a sharp turn west again before gently turning north and entering the Baltic. Completing the circle half-formed by the loop north of Danzig is a man-made canal along the east, which was then called the Kaiserhafen. The island this created in the middle of the loop was known as the Holm, and its primary function was as a docking and supply depot for U-boats. The land area to the west of the loop was the Schellmuhl and Lauental; industrial suburbs that supported the docks, along with fuel storage tanks. North of this, where the Vistula veers sharply west before its gentle turn into the Baltic was what was known as the Neufahrwasser suburb. This was a large area of docks supported by a railway running on lines that came through Danzig. This was also the area where civilian shipping docked.

Along the east bank of the Kaiserhafen is what was once known as Troyl suburb. Besides two large fuel storage facilities, this area was also the location of a substantial PoW camp for slave labourers brought in to work the docks; mostly French, but also a large number of Eastern Europeans brought in to do the dirtiest work. South of Troyl was the suburb of Heubude, surrounded by disused farmland and forests. North of Troyl was the suburb of Weichselmunde, another area of docks primarily for civilian shipping. Most importantly (for 'Jon Jorgensen' anyway) was the fact that the two suburbs were separated by a wide sea inlet, with access by rail and surrounded by barbed-wire fencing. This was where Swedish ships docked.

However, his camp-drawn map of Danzig did not show exactly where the Swedish ships docked; only that the main docks for civilian shipping was in the Neufahrwasser area. That is where his search for a ship to freedom would begin. He found that a No.8 tram went to Neufahrwasser, and purchased a ticket in order to investigate the area. Considering his luck had been so good this far, 'Jorgenson' might even find his ship that night!

The tram was noisy and rickety and he found a seat near the door. The conductress came around to punch his ticket, expressionless, and opposite him sat two sailors of the Kriegsmarine in uniform. Over their heads, stapled to the wall, was a large poster. It depicted a menacing looking man in civilian clothing, listening intently; the caption read, 'Keep Quiet! The Enemy Is Listening!' Under the poster, the two sailors were talking openly about military matters, the docks and their ship. 'Jon Jorgenson' merely smiled to himself.

He did not wait to arrive at the tram station, but instead stepped off at a point he considered close enough to the banks of the Vistula in order to get a good, but safe, look at the docks. He had no idea what guards there might be, or any other security measures, but the word at Sagan was that security in Danzig harbour was considerable.

In the darkness he found himself at the end of a residential area, walked a few streets east toward the river, and came upon a flat open expanse. Across it, he could see the outline of ships and cranes illuminated by the dock arc lamps. He walked on quickly covering some 200yds before, somewhere close ahead, a dog began barking and he froze. Listening carefully, he heard a car engine start up in the same direction he had come from and immediately turned briskly walking away in another direction. He walked down a side street and then around a corner. The car sped down the road he had originally walked down, obviously looking for something or someone.

Striding down the streets as close to the river bank as he could, he soon came upon the downward slope of a ferry crossing. This had been marked on his map, and crossed the river to Weichselmunde. Boarding, he paid the fare of 5 Pfennig and shortly after arrived near what he was delighted to discover were the civilian docks. Boldly walking into Weichselmunde, he found a pathway that came nearer the docks and discovered they were surrounded by barbed-wire fencing. Briskly striding up and down the path and the streets that gave a clear view of the docks, he scanned every vessel he could see for any signs of a Swedish flag. But he was disappointed to discover that in the dark, and with the numerous cranes and buildings in the way, he could not identify which ships were neutral. He was moving openly now, and though his suitcase and businessman appearance made him eminently respectable if anyone should see him, but there did not appear to be anyone around. This made him nervous; by then 'Jon Jorgenson' was a man for crowds to blend into, and he was also unsure about curfews for foreigners.

He was just on the verge of giving up for the night when a well lit building came into sight, which he instantly recognized as a guard hut. This was certainly something to be avoided! Turning to go back, he saw an elderly, blue-coated railway official heading towards him. Determined to help the situation along as much as possible, he immediately fell back on his 'nationality' and boldly asked, 'Where was the ferry?' He explained that he was a foreigner and completely lost. The railway man took pity on him, and escorted him back to the ferry, gave him explicit directions on getting to the railway station once he had crossed the river. Then, with a friendly wave, bade him farewell as he boarded the ferry.

Once back at the railway station, he went into the buffet, ordered a *Stammgericht,* (Dish of the Day) free with a coupon, and a beer, then thought about all that had happened in the last 3 hours. He decided that he had been foolish to push his luck as he had. There had been too many close shaves since he had arrived in Danzig, and there was no sense throwing his escape away at this point. What he needed was a good night's sleep to freshen his outlook.

First things first, 'Jon Jorgenson' had come to Danzig to visit the Amada Margarine Works. This he had obviously done, as he was now in Danzig and it was late. Logically, his next visit would be to the works in Dirschau tomorrow, and so he went to the booking hall and purchased a ticket to Dirschau. He now had a valid reason to stay the night in Danzig and just outside the station, across the main street, was the Hotel Continentale. On entering the reception area a clerk told him that the hotel was full. But, wait! Would Herr Jorgensen mind sharing a room with another gentleman? Why no, Herr Jorgensen would not, Philpot lied. The hotel register was in three languages, one of them English, which made it easy to fill in. Tiredness upon him like a draped blanket, he began to write 'J – O – *H* …' then caught himself, altering the H to an N and then writing 'Jorgensen' a little shakily as well for effect. Then there was the question of his documents. Why had he only a temporary passport and did not have an actual travel permit. Again he used the same explanation he had given the railway official. It was all perfectly legal, and to back up the story he produced his *Erlaubnis*. The clerk studied the documents thoroughly, while 'Jorgenson' sweated trying to appear calm, and eventually the clerk accepted them. He asked for a paynment of 5.80 Reichmarks then handed 'Jorgenson' the key to Room 220. The documents had passed scrutiny again. 'Red' Hunter would have been proud.

He took a hot bath and then slipped between the clean, white sheets and had the most restful night he had ever spent in Germany. 'Jorgenson' was asleep long before the other man arrived. After his roommate left at 7.40 the next morning, 'Jorgenson' washed and shaved then put on a clean shirt and collar. He was walking down the hall a short time later when a maid stopped him and asked if he would be staying that night.

He replied 'No, not tonight, thank you.'

The morning of 31 October was a typical Sunday in Danzig and there was little going on, except for people attending church and some children playing. Philpot walked with the crowd, trying to decide his next move. Weichselmunde had been difficult, and it would seem suspicious if he were caught looking around there again. Therefore, perhaps a different approach was necessary. Having studied his map before leaving the hotel, he settled on having a look at the Kaiserhafen where, he had been told, Swedish ships also docked. At a tram stop there was a map of the town on the wall, which he studied closely. First east toward the River Mottlau, which skirted the town along the eastern side; then north toward the harbour. It was a long distance, but all the months of vaulting had built up his fitness and he walked on happily.

But he was disappointed; everything was too far out in the harbour and he could see nothing with any clarity. He retraced his journey; strolling along enjoying the sunshine, with little plan or purpose in mind. Slightly dejected, his morale was taking another plunge and he thought to himself that what 'Jon Jorgenson' needed was some kind of advice or intervention; a starting point. How did one get information as to where the Swedish docks actually were? All around him were Germans (he would later remark, 'I had never seen such a German looking lot.') Perhaps Crawley had been correct back in East Compound that summer when he had suggested going to Switzerland. It was the only route one need not rely on others for help.

Then, proving that wishes did occasionally come true, even in the Reich, Philpot saw a little crowd of people near a waterway under a sign offering '*Hafenrundfahrt*' ('Round the Harbour' boat trip) and tied to the jetty there was a small passenger vessel.

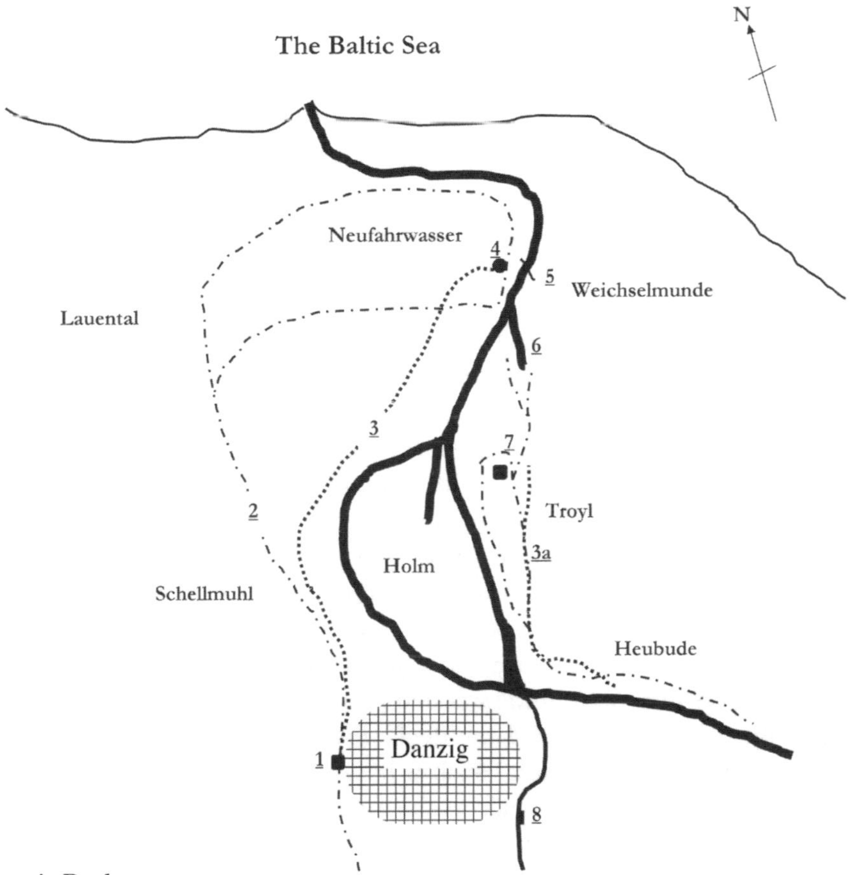

Danzig Docks

The heavy black lines represent the River Vistula and the Kaiserhafen. (1) Danzig Hauptbahnhof; (2) Railway lines; (3) No.8 Tram line; (3a) No.4 Tram line (4) Neufahrwasser Tram station; (5) Ferry crossing; (6) Docks for Swedish ships; (7) PoW camp; (8) The start of the Hafenrundfahrt on the River Mottlau.

Goodness! Were the Germans actually allowing tours around a military harbour, in wartime! Here was just the thing he needed! For 40 Pfennigs he purchased a ticket to the mouth of the Vistula and back and joined the passengers. As he boarded he glanced at a notice posted near the gangway stating, 'Passengers who take these boats are warned that they must have special permits to enter the dock area'. It was signed by the Danzig Harbour Police. Still, nobody asked him for any permit or pass or papers of any kind and he went on board, and sat on one side of the vessel so that he could 'get a good squint at things'[3]

The boat trip was incredible, during which he was presented with splendid views of U-boats in their pens, their depot ships close by taking on supplies, and the harbour defences. Next, they were escorted down a line of German freighters taking on supplies and cargo. Trying hard to memorize what he could in case he got home, Philpot paid careful attention. Did the British Secret Service know this boat trip existed? It was a 'goldmine' of information, and he wished for a moment he was flying overhead with a load of bombs.

Then they were approaching the docks at Weichselmunde, but were still too far out to see anything clearly. But providence again proved that patience is rewarded, and their boat chugged its way toward what turned out to be the Swedish docks! Soon they were within 100ft of the stern of a large ship. Philpot allowed himself to look up and there it was, in white, block letters against the black-painted stern, *Aralizz* and under that Stockholm. He could scarcely believe it! The Germans had actually taken him to see a Swedish ship! As they motored around the ship he saw that there were two thick mooring ropes running from the stern to the dock. He also noted that the vessel was sitting high in the water; obviously still waiting to be loaded and would not be leaving soon. Excellent! With the eye of a professional observer, and as excited as he had ever been on any sortie when flying, he then studied the route he would need to take in order to reach the ship. Along a pathway leading to a fence; over that and along the far end of the landing stage, where their boat was now pausing – giving him extra time to study; then along the dock wall, which had some fenders jutting from the wooden pilings, making it possible to reach another fence which surrounded the dock. The main dock was mostly bare, only railway tracks and a few items such as boxes and barrels lying around. But there should be enough cover to access the mooring ropes.[4]

Their boat pulled away and they continued on the trip. At the turning point of the tour, it stopped at Seefer's Hotel where a number of passengers alighted and others boarded. Philpot, however, sat tight, noticing little; too deep in thought of what could happen that night, willing himself to be successful. Only when a group of Russian PoWs were boarded to be taken to another dock did he come out of his reverie. He also noticed the PoW camp on the docks at Troyl. Its sight merely strengthened his resolve.

It was after noon when the trip ended. His plan set, he went about the business of killing time until dark, when he must be in position to make his attempt. All must be ready. Nothing must be left to chance. He made his way back to the tram stop with the city map that he had consulted earlier that day. It would be easier to use that map than to find a suitable hiding place to look at his escape map, and it was better detailed in any case. By 1.00pm he had settled on his route. Never mind the western approach of tram and ferry that he had taken the previous night, where he might be noticed as a repeat offender. The boat tour had shown him the way. Tonight he would approach from the east, coming up from Heubude, where there were woods in which he could await the darkness before moving on to Weichselmunde. Yes, there were variables of which he had no knowledge. But the basics of the plan had been presented for him. The variables could be dealt with. It became clear to him, as he walked through town, that 'Jon Jorgensen' was nearing the end of his useful life, and what a wonderful travelling companion he had been.

He began his walk to Heubude, keeping to the quietest of roads. Passing over a bridge he found it unguarded, dispelling another myth generated at Sagan that all bridges had sentries. After the bridge, he began moving over flat farmland, with the railway tracks heading out to Weichselmunde to his left. The small, yellow-painted trams passed on separate lines with the numeral 4 painted on them, and of this he made note. The walk had taken longer than he thought until finally he came to a fork in the road; left to Weichselmunde, 5km distant, and right to Heubude, the outskirts of which were visible. Turning right and passing the town cemetery, he went down a path into some woods and after some distance left the path. Pushing deeper into the undergrowth, he found a small clearing, laid down his overcoat and stretched out in the fading sunlight. Sawing off a piece of 'Dog Food', he got out his water bottle and ate a late lunch. Hopefully, dinner would be provided aboard 'his' ship.

After a brief rest, he dug two holes in the ground. It was time to begin disassociating himself from 'Jon Jorgensen'. Into one hole he folded his greatcoat; a souvenir of all he had been through in his service life, from commission, through imprisonment and now his escape. He hated to leave the old and comforting friend, but could see it now only as a hinderance to climbing aboard a ship. Into the other hole went his case, with the Homburg hat. In his pockets he kept only his papers in their wallet, 100 Reichmarks, and his smoking items; his pipe which he had puffed almost constantly throughout his escape, and which had lent that air of respectability when it was needed. He kept his gloves too, knowing the mooring ropes of a ship would be rough should he be forced to climb. Covering the holes over, he broke a branch and left it as an unobtrusive marker, in case things did not go as planned and he had to resume his escape persona. In that event, provided he was still free, he had plans to make for Lubeck, where there were other docks to explore.

It was 6.00pm when he walked out of the woods and back to the road. In the distance, across an open field, he could see a lighthouse flashing at the mouth of the Vistula, seemingly beckoning him on. Making his way past the cemetery, he passed by an elderly couple and heard the old man comment to his wife that it was remarkable how young people could be seen walking about at that time of year without a top coat.

Looking to save some time, he made for Heubude, where he quickly found the tram station and purchased a ticket for the No.4. The easiest ticket to get was to the railway station, even though it cost twice as much. So be it; there would be little need for money from here on. The tram rattled off and soon he alighted in the outskirts of Weichselmunde. Walking into town, he passed several Luftwaffe soldiers and once thought a civilian was following him, whom he managed to lose down a series of side streets. At last he arrived in the area he had been in the previous night and found the main gate to the Swedish dock; well guarded. Skirting the gate, he found a bridge from where he could study the area, but was thwarted when a guard shouted to him. He hurried off into the night and then, completely by accident, stumbled on the narrow road leading to the landing stage he had been on that afternoon.

He was now creeping along, keeping alert, and truly feeling like an escaped prisoner. Slipping down to the landing stage, he scrambled onto the fenders jutting from the pilings, walking carefully along them to where the wire fence separating the Swedish dock hung down, grabbed the wire and swung up with ease. Carefully, he climbed the fence trying not to make any noise or get snagged on the barbed wire. Then he was over and in the dock, and again standing on the fenders. He stood on his toes and carefully poked his head above the edge of the dock and saw 'his ship' being loaded with coal. A searchlight illuminated the grab as it lifted coal from railway waggons next to the ship over to the coal bunker. The ship's gangway was patrolled by a German sentry. The dock was illuminated by arc lamps which threw out large pools of light, but in between left large areas of total darkness. None of these shone on the mooring ropes, though the searchlight was occasionally swung in that direction.

Then, behind him, he heard a vessel approaching. He was in an exposed position with nowhere to go. A light was switched on and began to play along the fenders, looking for the mooring bollards. Panic swept over him; any minute he could be illuminated. Then his hand sank into a void, and he realized that there was space between the pilings and the concrete of the main dock. Quickly he slipped behind a piling, straddling it with his feet on the very ends of the fender and clinging on with his fingers, just as the light swept over where he had been standing. He hung there for several minutes as the passengers alighted. The vessel then departed.

Continuing his crawl along the dockside, he came to a section where it curved and the wooden pilings and fenders ended. At the end was a steel ladder, extending down to the water from the dock. He climbed up it and saw the stern of the *Aralizz* looming above him. Again he heard a noise behind him, smaller this time but unmistakable. It was the engine of a small motor boat, and another light began to be shone in his direction. This was not good. There was no time to get back to the fenders, or to climb down the ladder into the water. With no other option, he decided to take his chance on the dockside.

Silently, he climbed up but was alarmed to see that the sentry from the gate was marching deliberately in the direction of the ladder, waving his flashlight around. Obviously he had been seen climbing along the fenders of the dock and reported. The boat in the harbour could only be the harbour police.

The sentry was coming on, stabbing the darkness ahead of him on his way to the ladder. The boat had now pulled up to the ladder and the deck light was playing along the dockside. Philpot crouched in the dark out of site, but with nowhere to go on the dockside. He noticed a large crate standing nearby, the markings on the side indicated that it contained sand to put out fires from incendiarics, behind which he would hide. As the sentry passed him, he moved around the crate to keep hidden. The sentry stopped at the ladder, where he stood for a few minutes talking to the men in the boat, and then turned back to his post. Philpot's eyes, now adjusted to the dim light, saw the sentry was going to pass the opposite side of the box and moved accordingly. The sentry passed and returned to his post at the gate and Philpot breathed freely again for the first time in five minutes.

Off to the side was the stern of the ship, just 30ft away. The mooring ropes and bollards were in almost total darkness. It was now or never; the escape hung in the balance. He could dimly see the sentry at the gangway, perhaps some 100ft away, and waited until he had his back turned before making a move. Crouched down low and moving slowly and deliberately, he set off for the bollard, trying to keep his face away from the glare of the light following the coal grab. Although noise was not problem, his movement perhaps might be seen by the sentry at the gate, the one at the gangway, or someone in a nearby boat. Nor would the bollard give him any concealment once he was there; he would have to move up the rope immediately.

Halfway across, he spotted two guards coming his way, strolling along and laughing, obviously going off duty. Again there was nowhere to go; if he moved quickly, it would definitely draw attention, and without speed there was no time to get to the bollard, the crate, or back to the ladder. With no other option, he did the only thing he could; he lay down flat next to a railway track and covered his face with his hands. Between him and the sentries was nothing more than that track; just 4ft 8in of darkness. It could not possibly be enough, but that was his only option.

But then, unbelievably, the sentries simply strolled past. When he carefully looked around, some 30 seconds later, he was more than surprised to find that he was alone. But as there was no time to marvel at his luck and that it continued to hold, he was quickly on his feet again. Now he was at the bollard where the two ropes held the ship to the dock. Which one? Both stretched off into the darkness, up to the stern of the ship. Picking one, he swung down and was hanging from the bottom, legs wrapped around, and then moving hand over hand up the rope. It became steeper, and steeper; the climb became harder and harder. The vaulting had helped strengthen his legs, but unfortunately had done little for his arms. Sweating, he continued to pull himself up, his muscles straining at the effort. He passed through a patch where the glare of the searchlight covered the rope. Still there were no shouts – he had not been seen – then again into the black darkness. Where was the deck? He was now climbing almost vertically.

Then he felt the steel plating. At last! But something was wrong; terribly wrong. Instead of going through the side plating and attaching to a bollard on deck, the rope passed around the stern, possibly to the other side of the ship. The deck was still some 5ft above him, and there was no way to climb any higher. Dimly, he could see the other rope several feet away as it disappeared through a scupper in the plating. There was nothing for it but to go back down and climb the other rope.

On his way down, he spotted a darkened port hole and rapped on the glass. There was, of course, no response. Well, at least if there was a sentry waiting for him at the bottom of the rope, he could tell them back at Sagan that he had knocked on the window of his Swedish ship; he had been that close ….

Going down was much easier than going up, despite the thrill of escape and the promise of freedom that had driven him on initially. To his surprise, there was no one waiting below, and after a brief rest, he began the climb once again. It was worse this time; the rope seeming steeper, the lighted area larger and brighter. He moved slower. Sweat poured from him freely. Somewhere in the darkness ahead the deck loomed. The angle increased. He could hardly pull himself up any higher. Above, the rope disappeared through the hole in the side plating. Then he was there, reaching to grab the mooring bollard and then pulling himself onto the damp deck.

There was not a sound, not a shout, not a shot. He had not been seen, nor heard. His breath came in gasps at first, burning his lungs and then gradually eased. He simply had to rest for a few minutes, until the escaper inside whispered insistently that he must get moving again; he was not free yet. Getting labouriously to his feet, he was at a complete loss. It had been said in camp that the Germans always searched neutral ships very carefully before they sailed, using dogs and sometimes even tear gas. With that in mind, it suddenly occurred to him that he had no idea where to hide on board a ship; he had never thought that far ahead. What he needed then was advice again, and who better to ask than a crew member. True, there would be severe consequences if any of them were caught aiding an escaper. But intelligence at Sagan had told him that there was a good chance the Swedes would be the ones to help, if anybody were to, although he really could not see a crew member of a neutral ship risking his life to help a German escape from England.

Then his escaper's 'voice' whispered in his mind again: Inaction was useless and dangerous. He could stand and debate the question all night and get nowhere; stop dithering and get on with it. He stepped quickly over to a door near the stern, but found it locked. Then moving silently along the darkened side of the ship, he came to another door with a light shining behind a small window. It was unlocked and he went in, entering a passage that led deeper into the ship. Another door led off to a small galley, where he saw a small heating stove. Warmth! Suddenly he realized just how cold he was and paused a moment. There was some sort of chocolate-type beverage simmering in a saucepan and, using a ladle as a cup, he sampled it several times. Delicious!

Warm inside and out now, he moved down the passageway until he came to a small lighted cabin, the door of which was partially open. Taking a deep breath, he knocked and then walked in. Inside was a steward wearing a clean, white coat. He was perhaps in his mid-fifties and stood up from the table he was sitting at, looking very surprised. Philpot held his finger to his lips.

'Do not be alarmed. I am a British flyer … escaped. No one knows I'm here,' he said in English, and then repeated the statement in German.

The steward did not say or do anything, but looked very frightened. Finally he spoke in halting, stammering English.

'No. I can do nothing. You must leave this ship.'

Philpot was appalled.

'That's impossible. Surely it's safe enough for you to take me to Sweden in this ship?'

'No.' The man's jaw was firmly set.

'But no one has seen me come on board I tell you.' But Philpot was cut off by the arrival of another man. He was older, and was wearing a dark-blue cap and jacket with gold rings on the sleeve. Surprised by Philpot's presence, he looked inquisitively at the steward and there was a rapid exchange of Swedish. The second man looked at Philpot as he was about to begin his story again, when a third man walked in; younger and taller than the other two. Another exchange in Swedish followed. He was the chief engineer, and the other man was the first mate; now, what was the story? Philpot explained it all again and there was a short argument amongst the four in a mixture of Swedish, German and English. The conclusion was that none of them could give him the okay to stay on the ship. It must be the captain's decision, and he was unlikely to agree.

It was then, as if by providence, that the captain appeared. He was a large man with a rugged face and heavy, bushy eyebrows. Aged around fifty he seemed the type to get things done. Everyone stopped talking when he walked in, eyeing Philpot with suspicion.

'Who are you?' His voice was rough, but not unkind.

Philpot went through the tale again. There was the briefest of pauses.

'You cannot stay here.' He said it flatly, as a man does who is used to being obeyed at all times.

Yet Philpot persisted, arguing his case with him in a mixture of German and English. He had been a prisoner for nearly two years; had not seen his wife and daughters in all that time. The captain was sorry for him, but could not help. But Philpot continued that he had heard that the Swedes were most kind and generous in helping the English get out of Germany so they could fight the Nazis again. The captain was unmoved. The war would be over soon;

the British were in Rome, so why chance it now? He was walking away when Philpot played his last card.[5]

'The British government will reward you if you take me. They will give you two hundred pounds, sterling.' he said.

The captain looked back but shook his head.

'It is not worth it.'

'Well, they will give you five hundred pounds,' Philpot said, going to the limit the Crown had authorized officers to offer for their safe return. He said it again with slow emphasis.

'Five … Hundred … Pounds.'

The captain again shook his head.

'No.'

The others stared at the floor.

'But that is a lot of money!'

'Yes, but it is not worth my while to be hanged by the Gestapo for five hundred pounds.'

Still he continued to argue his point; that no one else had seen him thus far; that no one else need know, as he would stay out of sight … but it was no use.

'You must leave this ship. There is another ship five hundred yards further down the dock that leaves before we do. They sail tomorrow; we do not go until Tuesday morning. It is now Sunday evening.'

'Look captain, you just forget about me. You have never seen me. I will disappear, I tell you!'

'No.'

He continued the argument for several more minutes, but it was plain the captain was not going to budge. Nor would any of the small group intercede on his behalf. The captain, after all, gave the orders.

The captain walked away, as did the engineer and first mate. The steward and Philpot simply stared at one another. There was no point in continuing the argument; the captain's word was final. Philpot went to the door and listened to hear if the captain had walked to the rail of the ship and was hailing the sentry at the gangway, but heard nothing. If he was indeed calling to the guard, he was doing it very quietly.

Determined not give up at this critical juncture, after all he had done to get that far, he walked out on deck. The coal bunker is where he would hide. He could hear the rumble as each load was deposited in the coal bunker. But how was he to get there? He looked around for a hatchway or ladder of some kind and noticed a movement in the shadows. The engineer emerged, looked at him meaningfully and pointed to a box-like structure surrounding a ladder which went down through a hole in the deck. Then he again disappeared into the shadows.

Thankful, Philpot went down the ladder and arrived somewhere in the middle of the ship. He could hear the crash of the coal, louder now and knew where he was. To one side was a smaller bunker, nearly full. He climbed in, hoping that that bunker was full to capacity. He was in the act of trying to bury himself in amongst the coal (unsuccessfully) when a flashlight began to play around the bunker, and then on him. A small Swedish sailor came up to him and grinned. He could not tell if the engineer had sent him, as they had no language in common, but the sailor introduced himself as Gustafson. He indicated that Philpot should continue to cover himself, and then left.

But covering one's self with coal lumps ranging from fist sized to pumpkin sized is harder than might be imagined, as he soon discovered. The weight of just a single layer over the body quickly brought a throbbing, crushing pain within minutes, and stacking the coal in a sort of den was impossible; the more-rounded lumps simply collapsed. He felt for the largest lumps and managed to form a sort of wall against the slope of the pile and the sides of the bunker in which he could lay down and just cover his shape. In the event of a cursory search, with a flashlight shone around the bunker through the doorway, he might be missed. In the event of a thorough search, he was finished.

It had been around 9.00pm of 31 October when Philpot had entered the bunker. It was some 9 hours later when Gustafson reappeared, in the early hours of 1 November. He managed to convey to the sailor how impossible it was for him to cover himself with the coal and the Swede, looking thoughtful for a moment, signalled for Philpot to follow him. He led Philpot through the ship; going down, past the engine room, past the boiler room, always avoiding other crew members, until they emerged through a small door set in a grimy metal wall. There on the floor was an oval metal plate, held down by several large nuts. Gustafson produced a wrench, undid the nuts and motioned Philpot in the hole.

At one time, it had obviously been some sort of storage tank, as it still stank of oil. It certainly seemed a good hiding spot. What German was going to go so far as to unbolt the plate and climb down inside? More importantly, what about the air? Would there be enough? He looked at the Swede.

'Air … Luft … Good?' He took several deep breaths and pointed to the tank.

Gustafson nodded encouragingly. 'OK! OK!' he said.

Philpot looked doubtful, wanting to be sure the man understood.

'Air … Luft … OK?' he said, and took several more deep breaths.

'Air, OK!' the Swede repeated, and nodded again.

And with that he had to be satisfied.

As he climbed into the tank he looked up at Gustafson, tapped the borrowed Rolex on his wrist and wagged a finger at the man. Smiling reassuringly, the Swede nodded reassuringly; he would not forget to come back! Then the lid was in place and Philpot listened as the nuts were replaced. Silence filled the darkness all around him. He was now truly in another man's hands …

He found the tank was large enough to crawl in, but not to stand. There was a film of water on the floor and, as it was in the bilges of the ship, it was dreadfully cold. The tank had baffle plates, dividing it into several smaller compartments and at the far end the ceiling went upward to a relief vent for trapped air. He found that it was large enough for him to climb up into and hold himself up in by bracing his knees against one wall and his back against the other. In such a position, the only way a searcher could find him would be if he climbed down the length of the tank and shone a flashlight directly at him, and he felt that was extremely unlikely. This was a good hiding spot, safe and secure.

It was too cold to sleep, and he had to keep moving to generate enough warmth to stay alert. At least the air was decent; it had been worse in the tunnel, which now seemed to have been a thousand years ago. When he heard the nuts being undone, hours later, he squeezed up into his hiding place and waited. Then Gustafson was calling out to him and he came forward, standing up and stretching in the entrance. The sailor had brought sandwiches and water. They would sail soon, he said. But until then he must remain there, and he was quickly shut in once again.

It was many hours later when he heard the ring of the engine-room telegraph somewhere nearby, jarring him out of a semi-frozen torpor. At first he thought he was dreaming, but the ringing was quickly followed by the slow thump-thump as the engines began to turn. Could it be …? Were they really on their way? Soon the heavy vibrations shaking the ship settled into a steady rhythm and he felt the movement as the ship cut through the water. It was true – they were moving – he was on his way to Sweden – he had done it! He had escaped! And in that cramped, smelly tank Philpot shivered with excitement and let out with a wild yell of triumph. Their crazy 'horse' scheme had worked after all!

It seemed an eternity before Gustafson appeared to let him out, after 28 hours in the tank. It was 10.00am on 2 November 1943, just 87 hours and 50 minutes after he had emerged from the tunnel at Sagan. The sailor took him to a spot behind some machinery a few decks above and there he sat hidden for a further several hours, lunching on more sandwiches and water. Eventually Gustafson brought him up to hide in a small storage cabin, full of brooms and paint cans and such, where he was met by the engineer. He told him his name was Monson, and that while it was not safe to come out yet, as only he and Gustafson knew he was aboard, he was definitely free of Germany and on his way to Sweden. He must, however, tell no one the truth of his activities while on the ship, including the captain, who he would be meeting soon. He must say instead that he had hidden under his own initiative in the coal bunker, and that after they had been underway a suitable time he had knocked on the bulkhead to be let out. Gustafson had heard him and fetched Monson. No mention must be made of the tank in the bilges.

At around midnight on 2 November, Monson brought him to the bridge to see the captain, reminding him to tell the agreed story.

'Hello', the captain said genially when Philpot entered 'You still here?' and immediately he launched into his story, but doubted if the captain was convinced.

Once word got around, he became something of a celebrity on the ship. Later, Monson took him to his cabin and allowed Philpot to clean himself. After his time amongst the coal and in the tank he was filthy and he spent an hour with some rags and a small can of parafin removing the grime. Monson loaned him some clothes and they put his escape suit out on the deck to air. They then chatted about the many joys of having twin daughters, before Philpot fell asleep on the comfortable settee in the warm, snug cabin.

Next day, as he spent the hours trying to clean his clothes again, a small package was left in the cabin for him, anonymously. It came from a group among the crew and contained Camel cigarettes, sweets and 45 Kroner 'For the brave British flyer who has escaped from Germany'. Touched by their generosity, Philpot gave his remaining 100 Reichmarks to Monson to treat the men.

At midnight of the 3 November, they docked at Södertälje, a town just south of Stockholm. Soon after he looked up from his seat in Monson's cabin to see two Swedish policemen, nodding politely at him. They said something to Monson in Swedish. The sailor lowered his eyes.

'You must go with them.' He looked apologetic, but Philpot had known it would be so, and thanked Monson for all he had done, and shook his hand warmly. At the bottom of the gangway, the captain shook his hand and grinned. It was obvious that he had not been fooled in any way by the coal bunker story.

The policemen took him to their station, where he spent the night locked in a cell, much to his dismay. It was all too familiar but, as he had heard the 'Goons' say so often, *'Befuhl ist Befuhl'*' ('Orders are Orders') so he just managed to contain his temper.

The next day there was a hearty breakfast and an interminable delay as the police waited to hear what they were to do with him. Philpot asked if he could call the British Legation in Stockholm, but that had apparently already been done. Other members of the police force came in from time to time to talk to him, but he refused to give details of the escape until he had been debriefed by British officials. A detective had brought him a clean white collar, and a senior policeman told him that following lunch he would be going to the British Legation in Stockholm. After lunch, the policeman arrived dressed in civilian clothes and drove him to an office building in the suburbs of Södertälje. There he signed some release papers and was put into a taxi, which sped him through the streets of the town and on to Stockholm.

It was like entering another world; a world of plenty, where shop windows bulged with tempting items, bright lights shone and well-dressed people walked happily about. He looked at his own shabby appearance, which had fitted in so well with the German people and thought of the depressing atmosphere and general emptiness of Frankfurt and Küstrin.

The taxi pulled up at the kerb and, as if in a dream, he was gliding through a door next to the plaque that read 'British Legation' and into a finely-furnished foyer. Inside was a well-dressed porter, and without preamble Oliver L.S. Philpot, former PoW, walked up to him and announced, 'I'm in the RAF. I've just come from Germany … from a prison camp; from Stalag Luft III …'

It was 4.42pm on 4 November 1943, exactly 5 days, 22 hours and 30 minutes since his exit from the tunnel.

Group Captain Maycock, the Air Attaché, did his initial debriefing in the legation. Over the next few weeks there would be many more debriefings, but for now it was enough that Philpot had proved to be who he had said he was; the first man to make it back from Stalag Luft III. Afterwards, Group Captain Maycock passed him over to Mr Stairs, his office manager. The Air Attaché ordered Stairs to take him out and get him properly fitted out with everything he needed as regards to clothes and toiletries. It was with no small measure of shame that he noticed that wherever his escape suit touched it left a black, oily patch.

At the Nordiska department store, basking in his success Philpot spared himself no luxury, seeing as how the British Legation had the 'honour' of paying. After all, he had earned it, had he not? All the toiletries he needed; silk pyjamas; shirts; handkerchiefs; reindeer-skin gloves; shoes; bedroom slippers; socks; undergarments; a fine, grey top coat with a herringbone weave; and, to top it all off, a beautiful, dark grey, pinstripe suit.

'And where shall we send it all, Mr Philpot?' he was asked.

Stairs, alarmed at the final total, stammered, 'Excelsior … Hotel Excelsior.' The available credit arranged by London for such circumstances had been taken to the limit, and Stairs was relieved when it was over.

At the Excelsior, Philpot signed the register with a flourish. His escape persona, 'Jon Jorgensen' was already becoming a fond memory as he wrote. Name: Oliver L.S. Philpot Nationality: British Occupation: RAF From: Germany.

After a bath and a shave, an Assistant Air Attaché Squadron Leader Fleet, took him to dinner that evening. Later he sent a telegram home to Nathalie: 'Arrived in Sweden. Safe and well. Home soon.'

The legation put him on the list to fly home with the BOAC and he waited for an available seat. In the meantime, there were parties to go to where he was an honoured guest, also the cinema, and tours of factories and Swedish tourist sites. His stomach had to get used to rich foods again, but adjusted quickly.

Fine wine and good spirits replaced the rancid 'Kriegie Brew' they had made in camp. He visited an internment centre, where aircrew who had landed in Swedish territory in uniform on active duty were kept; free to wander about and live a life, with parties and girlfriends, but not technically free as they could not leave the country until the war had ended. Philpot noted that the men there had little concept of what real prison camp life was like.

Time went on and there was no word about Williams or Codner, and he was forced to accept the likelihood that they had not made it. The thought saddened him, as they had both worked so very hard, and it had been their idea that had seen them all escape.

At the same time, warm congratulations came from home with a list of things to bring when he came back. He bought silk stockings for Nathalie, and little matching ski suits for the daughters; wrote long, uncensored, letters to his wife and father; listened freely to the BBC; and at night slept on the floor sometimes because the bed was too soft. Elated at his freedom, and surrounded by well-wishers and people that showed concern for him after all he had been through, he nevertheless quite often felt alone in the world. He was the only one of his kind then in Sweden – an escaped British officer. To those around him, his was an exciting story, full of adventure and daring. But there was no one who really understood all it had taken to pull it off; no one to talk to who understood about the camp … the boredom, the danger and the fear on both sides of the wire … and what it really meant to be free.

He had been in Sweden for 9 days when the telephone in his room rang one morning and he answered to hear the Military Attaché, Colonel Reggie Sutton-Pratt on the line.

'Are you up yet?'

'More or less.' Philpot replied.

'You might like to come down to the legation.'

'Yes sir. Certainly.'

'There are a couple of friends of yours here who want to see you.'

'I'll come as soon as I can. Thank you.'

He dressed quickly and went down to the legation, never imagining who might be in Sweden that he would know. After knocking on the door to the attachés' office, he walked in to find the Colonel smiling broadly and waving a hand over in the direction of the far side of the office.

'I think you may have met before,' he said expansively.

And there, looking rather 'coal bunker-ish', sat Williams and Codner.

Chapter 17

The Varied Adventures of 'Marcel Lavasuer' and 'Michel Conde'

30 October–11 November 1943

Williams and Codner walked back into Frankfurt in the cold, pre-dawn darkness of Saturday, 30 October, numb from their night in the drain but reasonably rested. It was hard to imagine that 24 hours earlier they had been in their bunks at Sagan wondering what that fateful day would bring. Now here they were; some 100km from the camp and greeting their first dawn on the run. It was an intoxicating feeling, being out of the confines of the camp and making progress, but the feeling was tempered by the thought that there was still much ground to be covered.

As they slowly made their way back to the railway station, all around them the Germans were already up and about in relatively large numbers. Both were relieved to notice that their own clothing did not appear to stand out among the crowds. Most of the civilians around them looked to be a little ragged and unkempt in general. No one was strolling; everyone seemed to be moving with purpose, though there was little conversation or the normal noise one expected from a city, even in the early morning hours.

They easily found the station, having memorized landmarks along their walk the night before, and arrived just as the sun was coming up. The booking hall was very crowded and Codner forced his way through the crowd with Williams following toward the destinations board. For a few minutes he scanned the train timetable before dragging Williams back through the crowd to a secluded spot near a wall. They had struck lucky; the next train for Küstrin, a local passenger train, would leave in about an hour. With no other way to kill time, they made their way to the station buffet to buy a cup of coffee or tea. Inside it was warm and smelled strongly of pungent German tobacco. They sat down at a dirty, deserted table and looked around. Most of the people around them were in some form of uniform or another and nearly all, as well as the civilians, looked down-trodden and tired. There did not seem to be any life or morale among them. The 'Master Race' indeed … Rubbing his hand along the stubble on his chin, Williams noticed that many of them also looked as if they had missed their morning shave.

Williams casually pulled out a packet of cigarettes, took one and offered them to Codner, who thanked him in French. When no one arrived to take their order, it occurred to him that the place was a self-service. Grabbing an abandoned newspaper, he took a pencil from his pocket and wrote along an edge 'No waiters – Help yourself' and passed it to Codner, who read it, tore the slip off, stuffed it in his pocket and got up, muttering something in French as he did. There was a busy coffee counter where they each bought a cup of ersatz coffee, the same as they had drunk in the camp. It was as unsatisfying as ever, but warm and somehow comforting.

After they had finished, Williams waited as Codner purchased their tickets. There was no real check on their papers with Codner's *Ausweis* being acceptable enough to get both tickets. They immediately went to their platform and at the turnstile Codner handed their tickets to the inspector, who said something in German and handed them back. Codner made some sort of appeal to the German that Williams could not understand and the inspector yelled at them, pointing to Küstrin on the destination board then again at the tickets. Once they were again alone, Williams asked what the problem had been, Codner had received the wrong tickets; he had been given those for Berlin instead of Küstrin. Flustered, Codner simply pocketed the wrong tickets and went and purchased two correct tickets, rather than try and explain the situation to the girl at the booth in his limited German.

They passed through the turnstile where the inspector was busy shouting at someone else. He hardly glanced at their tickets, let alone their faces or papers. Climbing into a third-class carriage that appeared more like a cattle truck than not, they found themselves alone. They were looking through the glass of the sliding door into the next carriage which was completely full, when a German railway official came in and shouted at them to get out onto the platform. The two had inadvertently boarded a carriage reserved for Russian prisoners of war; certainly not the place for them! Slipping into another carriage, which was packed with civilians and soldiers, they found a space to stand together at one end and blended into the crowd.

Their train pulled out of Frankfurt at 8.50am, and the journey soon became tedious. The train stopped at every small station along the way, letting people on and off. Soon they were able to get seats, and they leant their heads back and pretended to be sleeping to avoid any questions or conversation with their fellow travellers, though they need not have worried. There was little conversation in the carriage; only the rhythmic thrumming of the track which was taking them further from Sagan with each passing minute. At each stop they expected the *Bahnhofpolizei* (Railway police) to enter their carriage, as there could be no chance that word had not been sent out about the escape now, but they were left untroubled for the length of the trip. When the train pulled into Küstrin there were no checks on papers at the exit barrier, and they left the station after checking the destination board and noting the time of their connecting train to Stettin. It was now 10.00am; just 16 hours after they had crawled from the tunnel outside the wire at Sagan.

Küstrin was small; too small for their liking, and felt dangerous. It was little more than a railway junction, yet it was busy; everyone walking with a purpose and direction. The two escapers stood in the sunlight perplexed. Their connection did not leave until 5.00pm. There was a lot of time to kill and their morale was beginning to sag. Undecided, they set out to walk round the town, looking into shop windows and trying to appear as if they had some purpose. But, being young, obviously healthy men of military age not in uniform, everywhere they went they seemed to attract attention. Finally they headed for a park, where they sat on a bench and ate some 'Dog Food' and Canadian biscuits. Afterwards, they brushed their hair and then dusted each other down before deciding to go back to walking. As they were about to go, they noticed a policeman walking slowly down the path they had taken into the park. Without appearing to hurry, the two stood and walked past him, Codner making conversation in French while Williams appeared to look interested. They were not followed.

They decided that what they really needed to spur their sagging morale was a beer and a proper meal. In their travels through the small town they had passed a number of *Gasthaus* (a type of restaurant/bar/overnight hotel) and now searched for one. Sitting down in the comfortable atmosphere at about noon, they ordered two beers and a *Stammgericht* (Dish of the Day). The meal was warm and filling and most enjoyable, while the beer was weak but satisfying. But their appearance made a few older men at the bar appear inordinately curious, so they finished their meal and came out into the sunlight.

With more than four hours still to wait, they decided to hide in a cinema they had noticed. What better place to pass time than hidden in the dark of a cinema? Inside, the auditorium was shabby and had a strange smell. The film was uninteresting to Williams, as he did not understand anything the actors were saying. He had not realized he had fallen asleep until Codner was gently shaking him awake. It was 4.30pm and time to get back to the station.

At the ticket booth, the two stood together in line. Here was potentially the most dangerous part of the trip; that of asking for tickets to a border area. Surely the officials would want to see their papers, and these were the people who were experts at spotting forgeries. Both held their breath. The girl behind the grille was stern and demanding. She looked bored and was impatient, like most Germans. Codner asked for the two tickets to Stettin and she demanded their *Ausweis* and permission to travel. Codner pushed the papers through the slot with the money. The girl glanced at them briefly before sliding them back through with the two tickets and his change. He thanked her and the two moved off, elated. If it was all going to be that easy, then they were as good as home. But neither believed it would be.

Some 23 hours after they had crawled out of the tunnel, they now boldly stepped onto the train for Stettin. It was a local train, with a corridor carriage and the compartments were all full by the time they boarded. However, they found a spot to stand together near the back of the carriage and at 5.10pm they rolled out of Küstrin. An hour later, the train stopped at a large station (the name of which they never learned) and most of the people in the corridor got off, leaving them room to squat-down on their cases. Before long, heads leaning against the side of the swaying carriage, they were asleep.

The shouts of the ticket collector entering the carriage woke them up with a start. He was moving down the corridor demanding tickets and behind him were two members of the *Bahnhofpolizei* inspecting papers at random. It did not seem a search as such, meaning that it was unlikely they were looking for anyone in particular, but appeared more like a normal random check that they had been warned about. Wide awake now, their hearts pounded as they slowly stood up as they got their tickets and papers ready.

Near them an old woman, with a large sack of potatoes at her feet, fidgeted nervously. The nearer the officials came, the more agitated she became. When the ticket collector saw this he shouted at her, demanding her papers. She dug them from her tattered handbag and thrust it meekly forward. He glanced at it, brushed it aside, and again shouted at her for her papers. She merely tried to hand him the same grubby paper again, now clearly and utterly terrified. Red faced and now puffed-up with his own importance, the ticket collector gestured to the *Polizei* who collected the now sobbing old lady and pushed her bag down the corridor.

The collector then turned to Codner and demanded their tickets, merely glancing at them before handing them back without a word before he moved on. It was the most incredible luck, and both men were left somewhat shaken by the experience.

It was raining when the train pulled into Stettin at 10.00pm. They had arrived at the destination which they had dreamed of back in the camp. It seemed incredible! But they were tiring fast and now needed a solid base of operations and a good night's sleep. All together they tried four hotels that night, but all were full for the weekend. Their confidence seriously sagging at this point, they decided to set out for the countryside once again and trust to luck. Williams got out his escape compass, which he had managed to get through every search since Dulag Luft, and they studied it carefully in the dim light of the torch the committee had given them for use in the tunnel. Walking in the direction of what they hoped would be the suburbs, they saw a policeman on the other side of the street suddenly alter course to intercept them. It was nearly midnight and neither knew if there was a curfew for foreigners in Stettin, but guessed it was a probability. As they passed the policeman, Codner again chatted in French as Williams looked interested, then turned down the first side street they came to. Listening closely, they heard his footsteps hurrying after them and they quickly walked through the gate of a house and up the path. The policeman was still coming. They leapt over the back fence, into a huge garden. Hurrying along a path that skirted behind the row of houses, they came upon a series of simply constructed, air-raid shelters set in the ground. Soaked to the skin, tired and frightened, they chose a roomy, comfortable looking one filled with fresh straw, burrowed deep into it and were soon fast asleep.

They woke the morning of Sunday, just as dawn was breaking. They had a quick meal of oatmeal, made with rainwater they had collected over night, and then moved off cautiously toward town. People were everywhere; shifts of workers from the docks, families heading to church, soldiers in their last hours of weekend leave. It was easy to blend into the crowd. They found a public lavatory and were able to clean up, though not shave, before beginning to search again for a hotel. Still they had no luck; all of them remained full for the weekend. Slightly dejected, they walked along the river front through town until the docks came into view. They saw plenty of German ships and several with no name or flag flying, but not one that was obviously Swedish. Worse, none were moored at the quays. In fact, the only ships they found moored there were

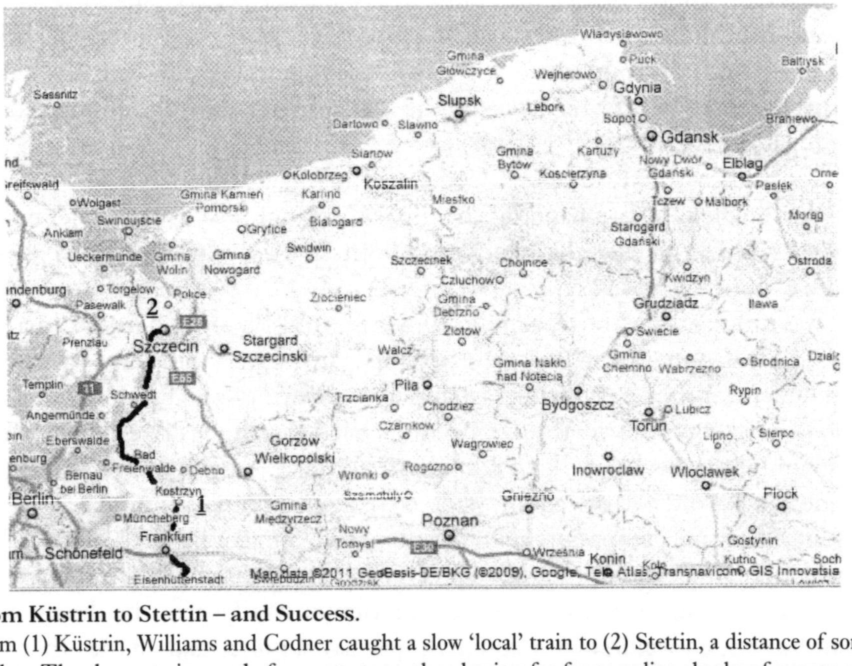

From Küstrin to Stettin – and Success.
From (1) Küstrin, Williams and Codner caught a slow 'local' train to (2) Stettin, a distance of some 119km. The slower trains made frequent stops, thus having far fewer police checks of papers and making them safer to travel on, though harder to put distance to ones heels. It was from Stettin that they were ultimately successful. As many of these locations are now within Polish territories, this map of their route contains today's Polish names for the towns they visited: Kostyn (Küstrin), and Szczecin (Stettin), as well as Berlin for a reference point, making it easy for the reader to follow along on any modern map.

smaller fishing vessels; all the large freighters were anchored further out in the harbour, out of reach save for a strenuous and very cold swim. Disappointed, they turned back toward town, found a café and had another *Stammgericht* and a beer.

Deciding that what they really needed was information, after lunch Codner tried talking to several French PoWs they saw out on working parties, but all refused to talk to him. It was obvious by his accent and Williams' figure constantly skulking in the background that he was not French, and the prisoners were clearly concerned that he could be a Gestapo agent or similar. On the verge of giving it up as a bad job, they approached one last Frenchman who looked more at ease and amiable than the others they had tried. Codner approached him while Williams waited on a corner. There was a long protracted conversation, after which the Frenchman shook Codner's hand warmly and, after waving to Williams, strode away with smiling happily. It was obvious he had guessed what they were, though Codner had said nothing. Most importantly, he gave them the address and directions to the Hotel Schobel, near the docks, which would most likely have an empty room.

The Hotel Schobel was a shabby, typical dock-area hotel, run by a German veteran of the last war. The registration papers were printed in German, French and English, making them easier to fill out, and they had to produce their papers to book the room. The Frenchman had warned them not to stay for longer than three nights, for if they did the manager had to send their papers to the police. Codner booked a double room for two nights, explaining that they were to visit the Arado works in Stettin before moving on to Anklam, but that the work's manager would not see them on a Sunday. They then paid in advance and were soon upstairs behind a locked door.

After they had washed and shaved, Williams got out their map of Stettin docks, and found they had been looking at the wrong docks that morning. They had found the docks for the fishing fleet, when what they actually wanted was the *Friehaven* docks. If there were any Swedish ships to be found in Stettin, then that was where they would be docked. Barring that, 4km along the coast from the *Freihaven* was the Reiherwerder coaling station. And, if all else failed, there was always the brothel address on Kleine Oder Strasse that Crawley had given them, though that was the last resort. While nibbling Canadian biscuits and chocolate, they planned their next move.

That afternoon they first scouted the *Freihaven*, but were unable to actually get into the docks as the bridge was guarded by police. In any case, they saw no Swedish flags and moved on to the Reiherwerder, but had no luck there either. Again they spoke with several French prisoners, but none were able to provide any advice or help. Returning to their hotel, they had a quick meal from their quickly diminishing rations and went out at 7.00pm to some dock-side cafés to drink beer and try to make contact with someone who might be able to help.

Finding no one, and still unsure about a curfew, they were back in their room by 11.00pm.

Williams woke the next morning (Monday, 1 November) to find Codner standing in their room already dressed. He had been up and out before dawn, talking to more French labourers, having reasoned, correctly as it turned out, that the main reason most of them appeared unwilling to talk was the presence of Williams hanging about in the background. He had learned that morning that there were indeed Swedish ships in the *Freihaven*, though none of the prisoners he had talked to had any ideas of how to get on board one. They had told him, however, that the majority of the Swedish sailors in port spent their time and money in bars along the Grosse Lastadie Strasse. Perhaps contact could be made there. Encouraged by Codner's success, Williams quickly dressed and the two hurried down in the direction of the *Freihaven*. Mixing with the French labourers heading in to work, they successfully shuffled across the bridge and through the gate among the crowd. Walking cautiously around the docks, they soon spotted a Swedish coastal defence ship named *Sverige*. Moored nearby was the *Walter*, a large German trawler. Fixing the position of the *Sverige*, they located a place from where to climb into the docks and agreed that if they had not made contact with any Swedish sailors by that evening, then they would climb into the docks and attempt to stowaway.

Lunch was another *Stammgericht* and beer in a café on the Grosse Lastadie Strasse, and then they spent the remainder of the afternoon again at the cinema. When it was dark, they went back to their room at the Schobel, filled their pockets with what food they had and set out, leaving their cases behind but insuring that their PoW identity tags were still round their necks. If they found a ship, their baggage would not be needed anymore, but their tags were very necessary. For several hours they visited the bars on the Grosse Lastadie Strasse, but had no success.

Finally, they set out for *Freihaven* again. Locating the spot they had found earlier, they climbed on the top of a railway waggon then over the 12ft fence and dropped down quietly into the docks. Moving carefully through the darkness, they made their way to the quay where the *Sverige* had been tied up only to find the ship had gone and the place taken by a German vessel. Thinking they may be at the wrong quay, they got out the flashlight and began checking the names of other vessels in the darkness. No, they were in the right place all right. But, the *Sverige* had sailed, leaving them bitterly disappointed. Slowly they began to search the other quays, hoping to find another neutral ship. Though it was really fading, the light from the flashlight helped greatly.

Suddenly the darkness was cut by another flashlight, shining at them from further along the quay. They had been spotted and, sprinting off, the night air was filled with whistles and shouts of 'Halt!' from behind. Running to the other side of a large warehouse, they saw another flashlight coming toward them from the opposite direction. Trapped between the sentries, the two ducked down and rolled under a railway platform, where they lay in the darkness trying to control their heavy breathing, and listened to their pounding hearts. After all that work to get out of the camp and all the way to Stettin, this could be the end of their escape.

The two lights converged nearby and there was muffled conversation in the darkness. The lights swivelled here and there, this way and that. Boots walked past the platform several times. Thankfully the sentries did not have dogs with them.

They lay there in the cold for over an hour before they dared to crawl out. When they did, they found that they were completely lost in the darkness and could not find the exact spot where they had planned to exit. Instead, most of the area ahead of them appeared to be brilliantly lit; an area they would have to cross in order to gain the fence, as they saw no future in prowling around the docks any further in light of recent events! With no hope for it, they boldly stepped out of the shadows and walked across the area as if they were workers. They had almost made it when out of the shadows stepped an armed sentry, demanding to know who they were and their papers. Producing their *Ausweis*, the guard studied them under the light of a dim German army flashlight and seemed satisfied. He asked if they knew what all the commotion had been a while ago, and Codner told him that a drunken sailor had fallen into the dock and had to be fished out. Laughing, the guard went on his way. Shortly after, the two climbed over the fence and made their way back to their hotel, agreeing that climbing into the docks was far too risky, and the future of any success for them relied on contacting Swedish sailors outside the docks. And in order to do this, they were going to have to enlist the aid of the French labourers in the area, who appeared well informed.

Up until then, the two had agreed to keep their identity a secret from everyone, including the French, as one could never tell who was truly willing to work with them, and who might turn them in for a reward. However, it was obvious that without assistance they were not going to get anywhere, and in order to gain that help they were going to have to instill confidence among those who might be ready to help. In order to do that, they must confide in them. That night they sat up planning an intensive campaign toward the French.

The next morning, they packed their things and checked out of the Hotel Schobel, as their two day safe period had ended. It was a cold, damp morning, and they followed the tram lines to the Reiherwerder coaling station, where the French also worked, to try their luck. There were many docks and coaling stations off the mainline and everywhere were prisoner labourers, most were from either Poland, with a bright yellow 'P' painted on their clothing, or from Eastern European countries, distinguishable by the OST. At Reiherwerder they found the French, as they expected, and had immediate success. Codner sidled up to one and started asking questions. The Frenchman spoke a dialect Codner did not altogether understand, but told him that he should come to their camp that evening, as there was a man among them who spoke English and might be able to help. He gave detailed instructions on how to enter the camp and then boarded a tram and went into the coal yards. Thrilled to have made some progress at last, the two made their way back into town, had their usual *Stammgericht* and beer for lunch and visited the bars on Grosse Lastadie Strasse before settling down in a cinema for the remainder of the afternoon.

With the darkness, they made their way to the camp; a smaller one than they had occupied, with only a single, bored sentry at the gate. Otherwise, there were no guards at all, and they climbed the wire into the camp at the spot they had been told and from there easily found the correct hut. When they entered, their contact was eating but got up and went out of the door and down the hallway. The room they were in was very much like theirs had been at Sagan; the same smells, the same dirty clothing, and the same wooden clogs under the beds. However this room was dirtier and more squalid and they did not feel welcome by the French occupants. Presently their contact was back with a man he introduced as 'Jo-Jo' le Corse (Jo-Jo the Corsican), the camp barber. He, in turn, took them to his room. Through the course of conversation, they learned that while he could not help them directly, as he did not work on the docks, but he did have many friends who loaded cargo on the ships and would ask their advice. As for the Reiherwerder, this was only used by coal barges heading for the rivers of Germany. Codner and Williams traded cigarettes for some black bread. As they made to leave they mentioned that there could be a reward for those who would help them. The Corsican brushed the offer aside and told them he would talk to the right people and send someone to fetch them if he had news. The Corsican told them that from then on they were to take their *Stammgericht* each evening at 8.00pm at the Café Schiff, opposite the main entrance to the *Freihaven*. That way he would know where they were to be found.

Hurrying back to town, they booked a room for two nights at the Hotel Gust, where they had to pay in advance again, and settled down for another good night's sleep. They were satisfied in the knowledge that they were getting somewhere and their morale was ran high that night.

The morning of Wednesday, started off with an alarm. Deciding to have coffee in the dining room for breakfast with the bread they had been given by the French, they sat at a table in the far corner of the room. It was only half full at that hour and quiet. Williams saw them coming first; three German officers, a Major and two Captains, and they were entering the dining room for breakfast. Both escapers watched in mild horror as the three crossed the room and sat down opposite them at the same table, ordered coffee and then pulled bread out of their briefcases to eat as they started a meeting. For a few minutes they all sat together, the Germans conversing normally and Williams and Codner not saying anything. Then Codner, as cool as always, finished his bread, looked over at Williams and merely raised his eyebrows. Then they finished their coffee and got up to leave.

They visited the cafés near the *Freihaven* that morning, paying a late visit to the Café Schiff. There they met two young Frenchmen who initially thought the two escapers were Gestapo agents, but once shown their prisoner identity discs began speaking and told them they were planning to stowaway on a coal barge due for France. They had a dock pass borrowed from a friend who worked there and regularly lent it to them to get into the docks. They, in turn, offered to loan it to the two escapers the next afternoon to copy. Codner made an appointment to get it and he and Williams then left and had lunch and beer before heading to the cinema to while away the rest of the afternoon. There were only a few cinemas in Stettin, and just one of them was comfortable. They were to know them all before they left, and they had watched the same film four times, though neither one could later recall any of them.

In the early evening, they looked up the address of the brothel Crawley had given them and it was indeed still in operation. However they decided to still keep it as a last resort, and by 8.00pm they were eating in the Café Schiff as instructed. Though there was no word from 'Jo-Jo', the two did observe another Frenchman who seemed an affable type; extrovert with his companions and enthusiastic. Determined to make contact, when he got up to leave, the two followed him and Codner told him who they were. He took them back inside, and had a long and hushed conversation with Codner while Williams sweated out the furtiveness of the situation. The Frenchman was definitely drawing attention. When he suggested taking them to another café which was sympathetic to foreigners, they both readily agreed, if only to make it possible to show up in the Schiff again to await word from 'Jo-Jo' and not be the object of suspicion.

The Frenchman led them through a winding series of streets to a well-lit, busy café, occupied by several women and more than one German soldier. Codner and the Frenchman were deep into a conversation when four military policemen walked in, who went straight to the soldiers at another table. It was all getting to be too much for Williams, who made his way into the lavatory and unfastened the window just in case they had to escape.

This came sooner than expected. A plan was agreed between Codner and the Frenchman and they were to meet the next night at the Café Schiff. The Frenchman got up to leave, as he did he grabbed a waitress and told her in a loud voice that his friends were Swedes and that if any other Swedes were to come in to send them to this table. Then he rushed out of the door. It was a foolish thing to do, for no sooner had the Frenchman left than a German woman got up, walked over to the two and started chatting in Swedish. Williams finished the remainder of his beer, got up and excused himself to go to the lavatory. Shocked, the woman said something to Codner but he answered by saying that while his friend was Swedish, he was French and did not understand, and his friend was very drunk. He then followed Williams into the lavatory where they locked the door and climbed out of the window. It had been a very close shave.

On the morning of 4 November, they made their usual rounds of the docks and, finding nothing new, headed for a café the 'furtive' Frenchman from the night before had recommended, but it was full of Germans. They then returned to the Hotel Gust, where they packed and checked out, then walked a short distance to the Hotel Sack. But here they could only get a room for one night. At lunch, they kept an appointment at the Schiff to meet the young Frenchmen and borrow his dock pass. Back in their hotel room, Williams got out his pens, inks and paper he had brought from camp and got to work making copies. At 5.00pm, he was still at it and Codner went out to meet their 'Furtive Frenchman'. By 8.00pm Williams had finished, and the two young Frenchmen came to collect the original. Also Codner had returned, and was full of news.

He had indeed met the 'Furtive Frenchman', who had taken him to a place called the Café de l'Accordian which, he said, was a favourite haunt of Swedish sailors. There they met two members of the Communist underground in France, who gave him food and 100 Reichmarks, neither promising nor discounting further help. Just as the three were leaving him, Codner turned and was surprised to find 'Jo-Jo' sitting at a table close by, extremely angry that he had missed their rendezvous at the Schiff. He warned him to be wary of the Communists and the 'Furtive Frenchman' as although they had plenty of enthusiasm, they were inexperienced in the sort of subterfuge necessary to get the two escapers out of Germany. With 'Jo-Jo' was a man he introduced simply as Pierre, who had some news.

Pierre told Codner that he worked in the docks, and in his camp was a fellow worker; a former sergeant of the French army named Andre Henri Daix who was going to Sweden on a ship the day after tomorrow. Codner went with him back to his camp where he met Daix, who spoke with him about the possibilities of them joining him. Unfortunately, he thought that it was unlikely that the two would be able to come along at that time. It was tantalizing, if perhaps disappointing, news, but did hold out some hope. After all, Daix had only thought it unlikely; not completely out of the question.

By the morning of 5 November, things were beginning to look grim for Codner and Williams. Had it not been for the 100 Reichmarks donated by the Communists, they would have been virtually out of money. As it was, the food they had brought with them from Sagan was nearly all gone and they had used all the available hotels in town that were open to foreign workers, except for the Hotel Timm. But, they had been warned against staying there as the owner spoke fluent French. Checking out of the Hotel Sack that day, the two sat in serious discussion. Along with their food supply and their money, their morale was beginning to dwindle as well; despite the contacts they had formed, they appeared to be getting nowhere fast. And yet, both felt that the word was definitely out there for them, and that if the French were possibly able to help then they surely would. As for accommodation, they made a plan to return to the air-raid shelter they had hidden in previously. They also began to seriously think about perhaps boarding a freight train to Danzig to try their luck there if nothing happened in Stettin within the next day or two.

That day, with little else to do, they wandered around the town, checking both the *Freihaven* and Reiherwerder before visiting most of the bars that were open during the day. They had a meal at noon, and as darkness fell they began to make another round of the bars.

However, during the late afternoon Williams began to get the impression that they were being followed. It did not take long to confirm the fact and, afraid they might have been sold out by the 'Furtive Frenchman' or his Communist associates, they split up, agreeing to meet at one of the cinemas. At a fork in the road, each turned in a different direction. Their 'tail' followed Williams, who led him a merry chase around town before finally jumping on a tram and losing him completely. Meeting Codner later at the cinema as arranged, the two returned to the Grosse Lastadie Strasse and went to the Café de l'Accordian, where they encountered a very drunk, very large Danish sailor talking in a mixture of English, Norwegian and German. Williams, sensing an opportunity, boldly (and somewhat desperately) took him aside and questioned him hurriedly in English. But before he was able to get anywhere, the sailor passed out and Williams departed in a hurry.

Codner was annoyed, but Williams brushed it aside and suggested on a hunch that Codner speak to a confdent-looking Frenchman sitting at a nearby table. Codner took the chance, walked over and introduced himself. A fast and animated exchange followed, after which the Frenchman came and sat at their table. Codner explained his name was Rene, and that he was a friend of Pierre; in fact he was in the same camp. On hearing that the two had no place to sleep, he offered to put them up for the night at his camp. As they were getting up to leave, Williams noticed their 'tail' from the afternoon standing at the bar, watching them. Codner indicated him to Rene, who walked over and confronted the man. He returned with him following and smiled as he introduced him as the brother of 'Jo-Jo'. After seeing Codner with the Communists, 'Jo-Jo' had sent him to follow the two escapers; first, to ensure that they were not Gestapo agents and second, to make sure they kept out of trouble.

The camp was several kilometres outside the town and was not a proper prison camp, but had been a training camp for Hitler Youth before the war.

Now it had been converted for minimum security prisoners, and the three walked boldly through the front gate, unchecked, and into a hut. Rene took them to his room, where they had a meal and shared his bunk, while Rene shared a bunk with a fellow inmate. It was strange and slightly unnerving, to be back sleeping in a prison camp again.

At 7.30 the next morning, 6 November, Rene shook the two awake with the news that 'Jo-Jo' had arrived with exciting news. He had walked the long distance from his own camp that morning to tell them that he had found a Danish sailor, involved with helping Daix, who had agreed to take them on board the same ship which was bound for Copenhagen. Hurried goodbyes were followed by a rapid walk back to town, where 'Jo-Jo' led them to the Café Schiff and presented them to a 19 year-old, fair-haired Dane who introduced himself as Sigmund Hjelm-Jensen. He explained that Andre Daix had informed the ship's Bosun, Olaf Pedersen, that there were two escaped British officers looking to get out of the Germany. Pedersen, in turn, had made the decision to send Hjelm-Jensen to collect Codner and Williams. They were to sail that afternoon. The young Dane had a forged dock pass in the name of Daix and said he would take them into the docks one at a time to board the ship. While Codner and 'Jo-Jo' went into the Café Schiff for a final beer together, Williams set off following Helm-Jensen to the docks, the forged pass in his sweating palm.

It was a short walk, and Williams followed the Dane through the gate. Rounding a corner, he dimly recognized as one that he and Codner had run past on the night they were almost caught in the docks; then he saw a small, black-hulled cargo ship moored to the quay named *J. C. Jacobsen* with Denmark underneath painted on the stern in white lettering. He watched Hjelm-Jensen stride up the narrow gangway and onto the deck and then, with his heart racing, quickly followed. He went down a companionway and into a small V-shaped cabin in the bow of the ship, where the Dane took the pass from him and hurried out. Williams stood in the semi-darkness of the cabin, trembling with excitement. Along the two the sides of the hull were bunks, and in a top one a body stirred and rolled over. 'Ah – c'est toi, mon vieux. And just where is the good Michel?' a voice said.

Williams looked up at the bunk and saw the smiling face of Andre Daix.

Codner came aboard the same way as Williams had, and soon after they were all gathered in the cabin, when a huge, half-drunk figure stumbled in. Immediately, they recognized him as the sailor Williams had been trying to speak to in the Café de l'Accordian. He was Olaf Pedersen the Bosun, and behind him came several others from the crew, who changed into their working clothes then disappeared out the door. No questions were asked of the two strangers and Daix had remained in his bunk. Pedersen spoke seriously with them while the cabin boy fried ham and eggs for them to eat, with soft white bread, real coffee and schnapps. The ship carried passengers, he said, including some Germans among them, so they must remain hidden at all times. Also, the ship would be searched, and they must be prepared; the Germans sometimes used dogs. After they had eaten he urged them to get some sleep. He would come for them when the ship was ready to sail. Wrapped in warm blankets in their bunks, the cabin resounded to their deep snores.

A few hours later, Pedersen woke them and gave them thick jam sandwiches. He then slid open a panel near the very top of the cabin, sent them down into a storage locker some 6ft deep. He warned them not to make any noise under any circumstances, nor smoke, as the Germans had arrived to search the ship and did indeed have some dogs, but he was confident he could take care of them. It was cold and damp in the locker with very little room. The walls of the locker were formed by the bow of the ship and were running with condensation. Pedersen had given them a bottle of water to share, as well as a funnel and another bottle to use if they needed to urinate, also a weak flashlight that he warned them not to use once they heard noises. Daix immediately rolled himself in a blanket and went back to sleep, while Williams and Codner found several coils of rope and settled down on them to wait. They sat on the rope listening tensely to the muffled shouts of the Germans and before long heard the tramp of jackboots and the clicking of dog claws on the steel deck. There were German voices, joined by the big, booming voice of Pedersen; laughter and the sound of a bottle against glasses. They heard more spoken German and then the panel was slid back, and an arm clothed in field grey reached in and waved around aimlessly. Williams and Codner pressed back against the hull. The arm was withdrawn and the panel slid back. There were footsteps and then … silence. A few moments later hurried footsteps across the floor were followed by Pedersen's smiling face framed in the opening, and soon they were back in the cabin.

But they were still not safe from German eyes. They had to get beyond Swinemunde, the last checkpoint for the Germans and where the the German pilot would get off and be replaced by one from Sweden. Until that had happened, they were still in much danger. In order to ensure their safety, they must remain hidden, but in a more comfortable place. Hurrying now, as the ship was about to sail, Pedersen hustled the three out of of the cabin and down deeper into the ship. As he did, Williams got a last fleeting glimpse of the *Freihaven* out a porthole and saw a German sentry standing guard at the bottom of the gangway. Then he was shuffling down the narrow ladders and through the hatchways behind Pedersen's big frame. Finally the Bosun stopped and opened another hatch that led into a locker deep in the bilges of the ship. They would have to stay in there until the ship had cleared Swinemunde. Pedersen, before locking them in gave them his assurance that they would be all right, and backed it with his huge smile.

It took some 4 hours to make Swinemunde. They knew they were there when they heard the engine stop. Shortly they heard the pilot boat bumping on the side of the ship followed by some shouting. The ship was stationary and all they heard was the lap of the waves against the hull. Daix, asleep again, did not even wake up; it would indeed appear he had been through all this before. Codner and Williams breathed freely again when they heard the engine start. Soon after, Pedersen appeared at the hatch and jokingly offered them a choice of two meals: bacon and eggs, or eggs and bacon. That night they slept well in their bunks.[1]

They docked in Copenhagen on the morning of 7 November and Sigmund Hjelm-Jensen took them to his stepbrother's second-floor flat in the city, while Daix stayed on the ship, acting as one of the crew. The flat was supposed to be empty, as the step-brother was a fisherman and away somewhere in the North Sea. But his wife, who was staying with her parents in his absence, had taken the opportunity to come home and clean the flat that day. She was delighted to see her brother-in-law, but froze in terror when she saw Codner and Williams. The young Dane explained the situation to her, though she had obviously already guessed something of what was going on, and she made them as welcome as her fear would allow. He then left, but gave strict instructions to the two escapers to keep quiet, not answer the door, and not leave the flat under any circumstances. He would be back in a day or so, when he would take them back to the ship to continue the voyage.

They stayed in the flat for the rest of that day and the next. The sister-in-law fed them, but otherwise stayed away much of the time. She was taking a huge risk and was well aware of it. Outside the window on the street below, the two escapers could see German soldiers strolling along. Occasionally she would wind up the gramophone and play records at maximum volume then tune the radio so that they could listen to the BBC with their ears pressed up to the speaker. Home … so close, yet so far! With luck they may yet be home by Christmas.[2]

On 9 November, the young Dane picked them up that evening and they went to meet Pedersen at a café ready to go back to the ship. But by the time they arrived, Pedersen was very drunk, and quite beyond reason. He hailed the two jovially and loudly in the crowded café in English and refused to speak to them in any other language. The three hauled him out into the street, where he grew belligerent and even louder until Williams threatened to punch him if he did not shut up. Quiet and morose after that, he steadfastly refused to acknowledge them further and stumbled back into the bar. Hjelm-Jensen wisely decided to take them to another café, where they ordered a meal and charged it to Pedersen!

After eating, he took them back to the ship and was just preparing to hide them aboard when the cabin boy brought word that the Captain, E. Ostrup

Olson, had become aware of the escapers presence on board, knew what was going on, and wanted to talk to them all. Hjelm-Jensen then took them over to Olson's house in town. This was it; the captain held all the cards. He could turn them in, in which case Codner and Williams would likely be detained by the Gestapo, as they would surely want to know how the two escapers had made it as far as Copenhagen. Or he could refuse them safe passage, and they would find themselves in the unenviable position of being in occupied Denmark with no money, no food, no contacts, and no closer to freedom than at Stettin. In that case, it would only be a matter of time and survival before they would be forced to surrender. Or – and here is where hope played such a large part – he could agree to help.

This is exactly what he did; although he warned his crewman to be wary of the pro-German sailors on the ship as well as the German passengers. He also warned him to keep clear of Pedersen who, though he had helped greatly so far, was far too unpredictable when drunk, which he was much of the time. Hjelm-Jensen then returned the two to the flat, telling them he would collect them the next day just before the ship was about sail. Captain Olson had said they were to be taken as far as Göteborg (Gothenburg); although the end of the voyage was Oslo. The Swedish pilot would leave the ship at either Strømstad or Göteborg. Sometimes, depending on who was running the boat, the Pilot might ask if there were any others on board who wished to 'exit unannounced'. If the skipper of the pilot boat was a Swede or Dane, then all was well. If he was a Norwegian Quisling, there could be trouble. Hearing this, Williams and Codner thought the end could finally be in sight, but they tempered any enthusiasm they might have felt by reminding themselves that they were still quite a distance from Sweden.

At midday on 10 November, they were safely on the ship and were ushered with Daix down into the chain locker at the bottom of the bow compartment by Hjelm-Jensen. They were given a paraffin lantern and told them to be as silent and still as possible until they were under way, and he apologized to them in advance for having to lock them in. The locker was a cavernous place, with slimy bilge water sloshing around in the bottom. It smelled horrible and was very dank. Then they heard the engine begin to turn and the anchor was hauled in, the wet, heavy chain clanking loudly into one corner of the locker. At last they were underway. The three found a pile of mouldy canvas, climbed onto it and make themselves as comfortable as possible. Daix was again asleep instantly, but the other two were still far too excited for that.

All too soon time ceased to exist as the hours below passed by. It soon became clear that they had reached a new level of discomfort that none could have imagined. The *J. C. Jacobsen* ran through a storm that night, and the old ship pitched and rolled heavily; the hull creaking and groaning. The motion, combined with the foul-smelling bilge water in the locker, had made all three of them sick, which added to the slime sluicing around their feet. Williams remembered being airsick over a target on more than one occasion, but that had been nothing compared to this unrelenting nightmare. The paraffin in the lantern soon ran out, and all they had left was Pedersen's flashlight. But, the batteries were now virtually dead. Their watches stopped; there was no ideal place to relieve one's self. Their 'comfortable' seat on the pile of damp canvas became a place of unequalled discomfort.

When the engine stopped some time later, Daix suddenly leapt up and quickly pulled the other two over into a corner just before the anchor dropped; the chain, thrashing wildly, spattered them with muck which completed their misery. Not long after, the young Dane's face appeared in an opened hatchway above, beckoning them to climb up the ladder. It was noon on 11 November. They had been in the locker for some 24 hours.

Hjelm-Jensen took them up to see Captain Olson, who told them that the pilot boat would be arriving at Strømstad that evening, and all three should plan to depart when it left. There was time, and they were sick, so he took them back to their cabin to wash, then gave each a thick, woollen sweater and something light to eat. They each climbed into a bunk and slept until it was time to leave.

The young Danish seaman came for them at 5.00pm. Outside it was raining again and a rope ladder had been let down to a small pilot boat pitching and swaying next to the ship. The skipper of the pilot boat was one who could be trusted, so they were to leave as quickly as possible. All the German passengers and pro-German crew members were being kept occupied on the opposite side of the ship, but there was not much time. A spotlight from the pilot boat illuminated each of them as they made their way slowly down through the sea spray, before dropping heavily onto the plunging deck below. As soon as they were all on deck the pilot boat was cast-off and chugged away into the darkness. A last glimpse of Sigmund Hjelm-Jensen in his oilskins waving from the side of the ship as they slipped out of sight was replaced by the smiling face and assurances in English by the pilot boat skipper as they chugged along quietly through the rain and into the darkened quay. When they arrived they were taken quickly and silently to the police station in town.

At the police station, they answered all questions with nothing but their name, rank, and number, amid the smiles of the police chief and his men, who expected nothing less from their new British charges. Daix, who had remained silent through the whole experience, was mysteriously whisked away in a car by a waiting Frenchman, and Williams and Codner never saw him again. The police chief rang the British Legation in Stockholm for instructions. The two escapers were taken to the municipal baths in town, where a large blond woman scrubbed 13 days worth of accumulated filth from their bodies, and had their clothing thoroughly washed. After they were clean and dressed again, they returned to the police station where both were toasted with schnapps and cold beer and given sandwiches before being put in the cells for the night.' Vitriolic protests by Williams succeeded in keeping the doors unlocked.

Taken to Göteborg on the morning of Friday, 12 November they were met there and interviewed by a representative of the British Legation, who requested that the Strømstad police chief escort the two escapers on the 500km journey to Stockholm. The police chief changed into civilian clothing, so as to not cause the two any undue embarrassment, and they caught the overnight express. The chief slept most of the way, leaving the two the option of attempting to jump train and escape all over again, if it had seemed necessary. But it obviously was not any longer, and both agreed somewhat gleefully that the police chief would have made a rotten 'Goon' guard.

On arrival in Stockholm on the morning of 13 November they were taken to see the British Military Attaché, Colonel Reggie Sutton-Pratt, who was delighted to accept them and listened to their story in detail. Afterwards, he made a telephone call to the Excelsior Hotel before informing the two that they were to be presented to the British Ambassador at dinner that evening, but not in their escape clothes. Arrangements had to be made. Sutton-Pratt picked up the telephone again and ordered in Mr Stairs, the office manager. The two would each need complete outfits. 'You mean the same as …' Stairs began, and Sutton-Pratt cut him off with a quick 'Yes, just like that.' Stairs rushed out to get a car. While he was gone and the two were lounging comfortably in the office, still in the dirty sailor's sweaters Hjelm-Jensen had given them, the door quietly opened and in strode Philpot, all smiles and freshly scrubbed wearing new clothes.

Williams immediately laughed with delight and Codner slowly got up and went over to Philpot with all the confident swagger of success. Looking him up and down for a moment, the grubby young man fingered the lapel of Philpot's jacket and asked, 'Where did you get that suit?'

Chapter 18

Complete and Free

Once outfitted by Stairs, Williams and Codner hit Stockholm with a vengeance. After nearly a year locked-up in Germany, the strenuous efforts of the previous summer with the wooden horse, and the tension of the escape, they had an overwhelming urge to celebrate their victory. This they did with enthusiasm and their antics in Sweden over the 6 weeks might best be described as 'Men Behaving Badly'. Philpot also joined in some of this schoolboyish activity. But for the most part he managed to maintain much of the bearing required of a British Officer that had been drilled into him during his long association with the military. Not so the unconventional Williams and college age Codner who, likely as not, were just as apt to be found jumping on their beds in the room they shared in the Excelsior, as whooping it up at a party across town with a girl in one hand and a drink in the other. They were the toast of the town, and knew it, and intended to take advantage of it, which they did.

Both had been placed on the list to fly home, as had Philpot, and had to be content to wait for a BOAC seat to become available. However the authorities in England were not sure exactly what to do with the three. True, they were not the first to get back from Germany. But that did not mean that a definite policy had yet been thought up to deal with returning prisoners. And so the British military did what most military organizations the world over do when faced with a minor dilemma at a point when major things are begging for their attention.

They did nothing.

So the three waited – and waited, and waited and waited …

Both men had sent cables home the day they had arrived at the Legation, just as had Philpot. Each read exactly the same:

> 'Have arrived in Sweden under own steam in excellent health and looking forward to seeing you before Christmas.'

On 18 November, Codner wrote home to his mother: 'This is the sort of letter I have been wanting to write you for ages. Something that I hope the Germans will never set eyes on. After some months of hard work, of which I could tell nothing at the time, I managed to get out of that bloody camp and over to a neutral country …'

Later in the letter, he mentions the chances of retrieving the personal items sent out to him from home which he had left behind in Germany as 'infinitely remote' but, '… they are an extremely small price to pay for Liberty (CAPITAL 'L' for Liberty; I have only just learnt what the word means) …

From your loving FREE son,

Michael'

Williams wrote home as well, saying in part: 'Just a line to let you know that I have escaped the 'Nazi Hell Camp' and am in Sweden. I am quite fit and shall be in England, I hope, in about a week. Do not worry if I am a bit longer, as transport is unreliable …'

Sharing a room at the Excelsior both quickly found, as Philpot had, that the beds were too soft, and they had considerably startled the maid one morning when she found them both curled up on the floor, 'cocooned' in their blankets just as at Sagan. They both also caught themselves looking for suitable hiding places for personal items that were *streng verboten* (strictly forbidden) in camp, and neither found they could initially sleep past *Appell* time, though this quickly changed as their amount of alchohol consumption escalated each night. Each was secretly appalled when they caught themselves sneaking food from a smörgasbord into their pockets to eat later.

Initially, during the day there were debriefings with Colonel Sutton-Pratt and Group Captain Maycock. After these were over, it only remained for each to write a report on their 'adventures' to be sent to London. Philpot had already completed his before the other two had arrived in Stockholm, spending ten hours on his report, which he showed to Codner and Williams. Both of them agreed that it was an excellent depiction of the events in camp. Williams and Codner had decided that as they had spent their entire time behind the wire together and escaped together, that they would write the report together. And instead of repeating, as far as the details of what had happened in camp, they simply agreed to make reference to Philpot's report, to which he agreed. True, they all had not always got along, nor had the entire camp been behind them, or had co-operation always been given by every quarter. But that was all so much side story which did not need to be delved into and could now be forgotten in the glow of success. But, how they had succeeded, and what had happened was what the authorities wanted to know about, not the social aspects of camp life.[1]

However, when their official work was over the partying continued; November melted into December, and as December dragged on, and they stayed put, the restlessness building in the three began to reach destructive levels. One night Codner mentioned to Williams, in all seriousness, the possibility of escaping again, this time from Stockholm to England, or possibly to Norway to join partisans there. It was he, more so than the others, who had enjoyed the actual escape; a fact he had alluded to more than once. Young and as impetuous as he had always been in the camp, he now wanted to get back into uniform and rid himself of the dishonour of surrender, and was seemingly willing to go to almost any lengths to achieve that goal. It was with a certain amount of difficulty that Williams was able to harness and control his impetuosity.

Although he also wanted to get back to England, Williams was more content; taking life as it came and willing to bask a bit more in the 'glow' of success. With time to think, he began to realize exactly what they had done and how it was truly spectacular. He had also found a female companion to spend some time with, and that helped.

Philpot was also anxious. He had a wife and twin daughters waiting for him, who he had not seen in two years. The girls would not even know him; and what of Nathalie? Surely there would be a certain length of readjustment needed for them to get back into the 'groove' of their marriage. How much had he changed? What would she think if he dragged his mattress down on the floor, in order to get comfortable?

One day, Philpot stopped at a jeweller's shop and purchased a cheap Swedish watch. On the back he had engraved a smiling horse with three tails, all pointing straight up. A member of the hotel staff assured him that he would post it, via the Red Cross, to a certain watch lender in Sagan. He fervently hoped that Jimmy would understand when it arrived.

Meanwhile, Group Captain Maycock had sent a short message on a postcard to his friend, Squadron Leader Peter Tomlinson a prisoner in Stalag Luft III. The message read, 'We had three friends of yours here yesterday. They are well and send you their regards …'

Day-after-day they filled their time with trips to sauna baths; the cinema; hiking in the mountains; shopping excursions, while each afternoon they would telephone the BOAC station manager at Bromma airfield to see if they were to fly that night. Every day they received the same reply – 'Sorry, not tonight, old man …' – and were forced to find another way to fill their time. While this was not nearly as difficult a prospect as it had been at Sagan, it was still a trying exercise which usually involved copious amounts of alcohol.

Part of the problem was the way the BOAC was forced to operate. As a service of the British Empire, the Germans saw their aircraft as any other target. The airline's inventory was mainly military; Consolidated B-24 Liberator, Douglas C-47 'Dakota', DeHavilland Mosquito and Lockheed 14 Super Electra/Hudson aircraft. However, in order to land in neutral Sweden, they were not allowed to be armed, and without guns they were an easy target for the Luftwaffe. The safest way to avoid the German fighters was to operate the flights at night and they relied on having moonless and misty nights, which naturally limited the number of flights that could be operated. Their tactics were always the same; fly out from Leuchars, Scotland, climb as high as possible, make the run over the North Sea as fast as possible, and then rapidly descend into Swedish (neutral) air space. Returning they climbed high over Sweden and, if there was no nightfighter activity, made a long straight shallow (high-speed) descent back to Leuchars always by a different route. Many flights were successfully completed; but a few did fall to the guns of German nightfighters.

More than once they had orders to fly that night, only to arrive at Bromma and be told there was no room, or that the weather was too bad. Williams and some of the BOAC pilots quarrelled badly on several occasions; he usually remarking, cuttingly, that 'Bomber Command would be up tonight'. In one incident, he actually challenged a pilot to a fight, and the Air Attaché had to officially admonish him more than once for his attitude with the BOAC men. And each time they were cancelled they grew more irritated.

Christmas came and went, but on Boxing Day, Philpot was told at 4.00pm to get ready, and this time there were no hitches. The first to be shot down and the first to arrive in Sweden, he was now the first to leave, going home in a Consolidated B-24 Liberator registered G-AGFO. By that evening he had landed at his old station, Leuchars in Scotland. Walking into the Operations Room, he startled an airman who had been the one to post him 'Missing' on the station board in 1941. Outside of this airman though, there was no one else on the station that he knew; time had indeed marched on. After checking in with the Intelligence Officer, he then wandered over to the BOAC office, feeling more like 'Rip Van Winkle' than anything else and unsure of what to do next. There, a kind air hostess made a telephone call to his home for him (his family had moved during his absence) and very soon he was hearing Nathalie's voice fill his ear. He had been gone two years and thirteen days.

Two days after Philpot left, Williams and Codner escalated their antics in a truly 'heroic' finale. That evening, after they had been refused a flight out of Bromma yet again, they returned to Stockholm and gatecrashed a party at the German Embassy, started a fight and left a trail of chaos and broken glassware in their drunken wake. And, as if that were not enough, they stole the German national flag from the front of the embassy. By the time an Assistant Air Attaché caught up with them by telephone at the Excelsior later that night, the Germans had worked themselves up into a typical ranting hysteria, formally complaining to the British Ambassador, who had immediately telephoned the British Military Attaché about the incident. Colonel Sutton-Pratt did not have to think for long who the perpetrators were, as these two difficult escapers had been a thorn in his side almost since they had arrived. He, in turn, contacted Group Captain Maycock and told him to either get the two under control or get them out of Sweden. Before midnight, the Group Captain had them booked on a flight out-of-Bromma – on Liberator G-AGFO, the same aircraft that had carried Philpot – the flag well hidden in Williams' luggage and they landed at Leuchars in the misty early morning hours of 29 December 1943.

Once firmly re-integrated into the British military system, all three were granted extended leave until an actual decision could be made about their futures. Home – real home – reached out its welcome, and as the doors closed behind and embraces enfolded them, all the risk and danger melted away. The fruits of success were certainly sweet indeed.

The New Year began, promising that whatever it might bring it was a certainty that 1944 would not contain the challenges for the three that they had experienced in 1943, or so they thought. Yet challenges there were. Although they were only three among an extremely select category (the successful escapers), and what one would think a very useful commodity, the military actually had little idea what to do with them once the initial interrogations had been completed. It was policy not to send escaped personnel back into the Theatre of Operations where they had been captured in case they were shot down again, recognized and tortured into divulging details of how they had been able to escape. That left either assignment to another theatre, or home-front duties.

The initial enquiry by the military came from MI9, the PoW/Resistance Assistance section of British secret services, asking if they might be interested in helping establish escape lines to assist the return of downed aircrew. The appointment at first caught their attention, until it was revealed that the work involved little more than sitting behind a desk in London. Williams and Codner immediately lost complete interest, but Philpot gave it some thought. The SOE (the famous Special Operations Executive; the clandestine warfare section of the British Intelligence Service) also made an approach, but their style of warfare was not to their tastes. Escaping from Stalag Luft III had apparently been enough clandestine excitement for one lifetime, even for the hard living Codner.

The three did fulfill a requests by the Air Ministry to lecture on the subject of their escape, and the conditions aircrew might expect if downed behind enemy lines. Codner, after mistakenly having had to spend all his prison time billeted with the RAF due to a German administrative error, now actually did find himself temporarily seconded to the RAF for this duty. Billeted with Williams initially, the two spent their days answering questions from various departments of the military and lecturing aircrew. But they 'relaxed' at night in much the same way they had in Sweden.

Before long the duty began to bore Codner; eager to get back to his unit and active duty. One night he confided to Williams, 'Y'know, I enjoyed myself when we were escaping. There was something about it. We were really living then. People do not live half the time, y'know. I think it's only when you're being hunted that you really live. I liked being hunted … the feeling that every minute was important; that everything you did would sway the balance. We lived.'

Codner applied for transfer back to his unit and before long was sent to Italy and once again in combat. He was awarded a Military Cross (gazetted on 27 April 1944) and was soon after promoted to the rank of Captain. His men greatly respected and admired him when they learned his story, and he in turn went to great pains to see that they were well cared for. At the front, he gained the affectionate name of 'Wicked Captain Black Gloves' from some of his Indian troops, as he wore gauntlets when riding his horse and would tap them on a soldier's chest to make a point.

At the end of the war he was in Malaya with the liberating forces, and he was able to spend a few months with his family before going back to England to be demobilized. He returned to Exeter College and finished his degree in Colonial Administration. On 25 September 1948, he married Florence Isobel Rosemary Mosely-Leigh at Westminster, and after graduating he applied for duty in Malaya with the Colonial Service. He was, of course, selected and in April 1949 was made Assistant District Officer for Tanjong Malim, Perak State. He had control of some 20,000 Malayans and Chinese, and he did his best to be fair and just, but he joined the Colonial Service near the height of what became known as the 'Malayan Emergency'. The area around Tanjong Malim was a hot spot in the then on-going war between the British and the Malayan Communists, and the village in which he and Rosemary lived was – ironically, for him – surrounded by barbed wire. Nevertheless, the adventurer in Codner was very much at home in the tense atmosphere. His only son, Peter, was born there in 1951.

On 6 October 1951, communist guerrillas killed the area High Commissioner, Sir Henry Gurney, while on his way to a conference. However, his replacement, General Sir Gerald Templar, who would be forever known as the man who solved the Malayan problem, would not take command of the area until January 1952, and then it would be some time before his policies would have any real effect on the region. On 23 March 1952, when the main-water pipeline into Tanjong Malim was damaged by terrorists, Assistant District Officer Codner quickly assembled a maintenance party, and on the afternoon of 25 March set out into the jungle to attempt repairs. It was a particularly bad time in the area; just a week before seven members of the Gordon Highlanders had been killed nearby in an ambush while on a routine patrol, so the repair party was on high alert. They had not gone far, when they were ambushed by guerrillas armed with automatic weapons. One of the lightly wounded was sent back to Tanjong Malim for help, but by the time help arrived the attack was over and fourteen of the repair party lay dead, and the remaining eight wounded. One of those killed was Richard Michael Clinton Codner. He had been wounded and crawled under a bush for cover, where he had been shot again at point blank range.

Upon hearing of Codner's death Williams sank into a depression over the loss of his friend from which he never truly recovered. Until his death, he would hail Codner as the true genius behind their escape and gave him never-ending praise, even going so far as to point out that their journey once outside the wire could never have been accomplished without his bravery, nerve and boldness. 'He was quite the bravest, the most gifted and the most unassuming man I've ever met,' he later said.

Philpot, on hearing the news, was more to the point; 'It's appalling, but it's the way you might have expected him to die.'

Oliver Philpot never flew on operations again. In early 1944, he was appointed as one of the Senior Scientific Officers at the Air Ministry. The job involved helping to devise escape aids, through MI9, that could be smuggled into PoW camps through personal parcels, and lecturing extensively on his escape to aircrew. He was also awarded a Military Cross (gazetted on 16 May 1944) for the escape. For the remainder of the war, he spent his time trying to prepare others for the possibility of capture, just as he had done years before when he made his crew engage in dinghy drill when on squadron.

He was demobilized in 1946 and initially joined the Maypole Company, in the dairy division. Two years later he was appointed chairman of Trufood. After that, he served in a variety of posts, always moving up, almost always in the food industry – in 1950, he was office manager at Unilever House; in 1951, general manager at T. Walls & Sons; in 1954, a director at Arthur Woollcott & Rappings; in 1956, joining the Spirella Corporation, where he was first marketing director and then managing director until 1958; from there as managing director of Benesta Foils, until he joined Union International in 1962, and from their head office ran 8 other companies. From 1965 to 1967 he was chief executive at Fropax Eskimo Food (later to become Findus), and finally, from 1974 until his retirement in 1978, he was managing director of Remploy, the government-backed company that provided (and still does) employment and other services for disabled people.

Of all his appointments, his service with Remploy was perhaps the most satisfying to him, for throughout his life, Philpot gave unstintingly of himself to a variety of charities. Prominent among these was serving for many years on the National Advisory Council on Employment for Disabled People; as overseas administrator for Help the Aged; as advisory council member for the International Bar Association; and manager for the St Bride Foundation Institute.

He was also, for many, many years, chairman of the RAF Escaping Society, and never failed to respond when asked to relate his story. Once, at a meeting of the society in Esher, Surrey, he was able to meet again with 'Red' Hunter, the man who had forged his nearly flawless papers.

Though his daughters with Nathalie were followed by a son, the war, his imprisonment, and their separation had apparently changed the couple too much, and the marriage was dissolved in 1951. However, he was married again, in September 1954, to Rosl Widhalm, and with her had another son and daughter.

In 1948, Eric Williams contacted Philpot to tell him that he had received Crown permission to publish a book concerning the escape. Williams had published a short novel, before the war had ended, loosely based on his own experiences as a PoW. However, this new effort would detail the complete escape from his and Codner's viewpoint. Like his earlier work, it would be told in the third person with substitutions for all names and other characters. Williams at the time was working as a book buyer for Lewis's, and had connections within the publishing industry. Philpot, who was also writing his own book at the time, decided that it would be a good idea to stop and wait until after the publication of Williams' book.

Philpot's book, called *Stolen Journey*, would be published in October 1950, but only after Williams' *The Wooden Horse*, published in 1949, had become a best seller and the film of the same name was made the following year. In both Williams' book and the film, Oliver Philpot appears as 'Philip Rowe'. The fact that *Stolen Journey* became somewhat eclipsed by the popularity of *The Wooden Horse* is tragic, for his is a classic of escape storytelling; well written and certainly one of the best. [This author's copy is inscribed by Oliver Philpot to Bill White; the very same Bill White who attempted the tunnel out of the north *Abort* at Sagan.]

Until his death, on 6 May 1993, Oliver Philpot remained one of the shining examples of the 'classic' RAF officer; a man who had faced war in order to defeat one of the greatest evils of all time and lived an adventure that few could barely dream of, and then lived a full, rich life.

In 2006 Philpot's widow, Dr Rosl Philpot, and his daughter Diana Henfrey, collected together all his escape kit, which he had held onto all those years, and donated them to the Imperial War Museum in London for an exhibition called, 'Great Escapes'. His daughter explained, 'My father kept the kit in the attic – it was just part of our household. He was very modest about it.' When they delivered the kit, his wife related to museum staff how when the family originally opened the box the items were stored in, they could still smell the paraffin and oil on the jacket, even after 63 years.

Certainly neither of the other two escapers gained as much popularity from the adventure as did Eric Ernest Williams. His book, and the subsequent film, cemented the escape in the public imagination and gave him the impetus to begin a career as a writer. While Codner never really had a chance to fully enjoy the fruits of their success and Philpot remained modest about it for much of his life, Williams remained connected to the story for much of his life and never seems to have lost his sense of awe over the episode. Ten years after the event he wrote, 'It seems to me scarcely believable that a mere plywood box could have fooled the Germans for so long. Nor does it seem possible that I, or my younger self, could have crossed wartime Germany as I did, knowing so little of that country or its language.' But cross it he did and then shared the experience with generations to come.

Following his post-escape return from leave, Williams was put to work by MI9 giving lectures, travelling from airfield to airfield talking about his experiences. As a Canadian pilot later remembered, 'Sixteen of us were posted to No.19 Operational Training Unit at Kinloss, Northern Scotland, to be crewed up for flying heavy bombers. On March 21, 1944 … flying was cancelled for the morning and the new crews were told to assemble at the lecture hall by 9.00am. The Commanding Officer of the station introduced the speaker; Eric Williams…who had escaped from Germany using a wooden vaulting horse.'

Initially, Williams enjoyed the freedom of lecturing at different locations. He did his lectures, sometimes as many as twelve a week, in hangers, on airfields and in the squadron mess. He even managed to make a few 'unofficial' flights over Germany on raids. He really felt he was making a difference until, one day, he advised the crews on how to tie their flying boots properly in order to avoid having the jerk of the parachute opening pull them off. After the lecture, when the crews were heading out to their aircraft for that nights mission, he noticed that not one man had tied his boots as he had been suggested. After that, he began to feel his lectures were not really doing any good and, with the 'nomadic' lifestyle beginning to tire him, he applied for what he had always wanted but had been told years before he was too old for: pilot training.

By the time he was accepted for the pilot course, he had met the woman who was destined to become his lifelong companion and supporter, Elsie Sybil Margaret Grain. They met while she was a Second Officer in the Women's Royal Naval Reserve and personal secretary to an admiral (for which she was later awarded the MBE). He was lecturing to the Fleet Air Arm at the time. The attraction was immediate. Soon they were a couple and, having heard his whole exciting story, she began urging him to write his experiences down on paper. He took her advice, and as he moved from airfield to airfield, began to write down the beginnings of his adventures, working in the squadron mess and sometimes even by torchlight in a bed in some draughty Nissan huts. He would then send the result off to Sybil and she would type them up at night on her Admiralty-issued typewriter at Submarine Headquarters.[1]

Soon, however, he had his orders and was sent to Canada for training, and then on operations in Italy. He was there when the war in Europe ended and, now redundant as a pilot, found himself again in much the same situation as he had been in Sweden, unsure of what role he might still have to fill. When he returned to England, he applied to do welfare work with PoWs returning from the Pacific Theatre and was soon sent to Manila. While there, he continued to work on his writing but was very moved at the poor state of the prisoners once held by the Japanese. He often told the men he helped care for that he had been a prisoner in Europe and, if they asked, might tell them of his escape; But not in a boastful way. Eventually, he had seen enough of the human 'wreckage' left by the Japanese and requested to be sent home. 'I had chosen Welfare (work) as perhaps the least boring, the most entertaining way of finishing the war,' he later said. 'I had not found it entertaining.'

He finished his book sailing home on the RMS *Queen Mary*, and Sybil soon had a manuscript completed. He gave it the title *Goon in the Block*, and it was a little short in content. He had to apply for permission from the Crown before he could submit it to a publisher, as it contained service matters and Great Britain had the Official Secrets Act, in which those items deemed to be of national importance were classified and not allowed to be made public. Escape matters were such and, as the war in the Pacific was still going when he was writing the book, the escape was still a national secret. Therefore *Goon in the Block* contained nothing about the escape. Instead it merely told of his being shot down, captured and something of his imprisonment. However, in order to gain more literary freedom, as well as to disguise anything that might be interpreted as a secret concerning his fellow prisoners being accidentally made public, he wrote the story in the third person, changed all the names, and sometimes combined events, while compressing the time line. In it, he called himself 'Peter Howard' and Codner became 'John Clinton'. The book was based on fact, but written as more of a novel. Nevertheless, Jonathan Cape in London published the book in 1945 and the print run of 5,000 copies sold out in the first week. Wartime rationing of paper prevented further printing.

By that time, Williams had returned to Germany to take a skiing trip. While he was there, he went back to Dulag Luft, by then an Allied interrogation centre for any enemy forces suspected of war crimes, and visited the cell where he had been held. He also went back to Steinbild, where he had made his first escape attempt, thanking the proprietors of the hotel for their hospitality. The old forester, whose drunkenness had allowed him to escape, did not even get into trouble over the matter. They all had simply faked the times and dates on the arrest report to show Williams had run off before they had got him back to town.

He was demobilized in 1946 as a Squadron Leader and went back to work at Lewis's, where he was welcomed with open arms. Within months he was managing the book buying department for all seven of the company's stores, based on his writing experience. (He was by then a published author, after all!) Here he was introduced to many publishers and promotional people, attended book launch parties and fairs, and built a thorough feel for the business of books and writing. Before he left the service, his Commanding Officer had read *Goon in the Block* and was outraged to learn that Williams was contemplating writing a book on the escape along the same lines. In fact, it had been the Air Ministry that had approached him with the idea about that same time. Sybil also thought it a good idea. With his new-found publishing knowledge, he felt he might be successful and started writing. Only one literary agent gave him any advice, and that was to wait; in the man's opinion Williams was still too close in time to when it had happened to be able to see the escape objectively. He also suggested dropping the novel-type approach and request permission from the Crown to tell the true story.

But, Williams enjoyed the freedom that the style he had used for *Goon in the Block* had given him, and therefore continued in that vein. He received permission from the Air Ministry to tell the details of the escape, on the understanding that he would continue with the third person/novel approach. He wrote an article on the escape for an RAF magazine, which had raised great interest among the service personnel who read it, encouraging him still further. By the time he and Sybil went to France for a vacation in 1947 (during which he asked her to marry him and she accepted) he was well advanced with the manuscript for the book which he had entitled *The Sagan Horse*. By the time they married, on 1 April 1948, he had begun sending the manuscript to publishers. Each time he did, it came back rejected, always with the same excuse; 'War books are not selling, old man.' Each time it was returned, he worked on it making improvements before sending it out again. In all, the manuscript was rejected nineteen times.

Then, one day Williams went to lunch with Ronald Politzer the publicity manager of William Collins & Sons. As with most in those immediate post-war years, they got to talking about what each had done in the war. Politzer had been an intelligence officer in Cairo and had many stories to tell. He then asked about the escape, and Williams, who had already been rejected by Collins but now saw a glimmer of opportunity, said it was a long story and he would send him the manuscript.

When he read it, Politzer was stunned by what Williams had written and immediately recommended it for publication, but with three changes. Firstly, it needed to be shortened; the manuscript incorporated nearly all of *Goon in the Block*, which had begun with Williams being shot down. Instead, the book needed to begin in the camp and then quickly move onto the escape. Secondly, he wanted to change the title from *The Sagan Horse*, to *The Wooden Horse*; as the latter sounded better, and would conjure familiarity within the public mind when the publicity department tied it to the classic tale of the 'Trojan Horse'. Thirdly, there needed to be a much more dramatic ending; they could not simply step off the boat into neutral territory as indeed they had. It would leave the reader feeling flat, not actually being able to experience the thrill of freedom after having lived the experience of captivity.

Williams agreed to the title change, though was not at all enthusiastic about the other two requests. Nevertheless, anxious to oblige in order to get the book into print and become a published novelist, he cut the first half of the manuscript and invented an ending where 'his' character kills a German guard, the final obstacle between the main characters and their freedom. The changes suited Collins, and the book was published in February 1949.

The day before publication, eleven Sunday newspapers carried a feature or a review of the book and one carried a leading article about the event, introducing the world to the escape. Tom Wilson, who had just accepted a position with Royal Liberty School in Romford, Essex, was on the train travelling to school that Monday morning when he noticed an advertisement for Williams' book in the centre section of the newspaper. 'I had not got round to reading the [news] papers that Sunday, but took the Observer to scan on my way to school. A pupil had joined me only to hear me call out, when I reached the centre page with its picture of the Wooden Horse, 'How many, many times have I jumped over that contraption?' 'I think that the first print-run sold out that first day.'[2]

Wilson was almost correct. The book was an instant hit, selling the first printing in under a week, and then a second before the first month was out, and then into a third. Soon Williams was attending book signings all over the country, sometimes accompanied by Codner and Philpot. The heady atmosphere made him burn with ambition and he thought of resigning from Lewis's and become a full-time author. Prudence, however, dictated otherwise. Post-war Britain was still in a serious recession, and work was at a premium. He was lucky to be employed, and by an employer that had stood by him for so long, and stayed.

He received a telephone call from London Films who wanted to adapt the book for the screen. British Lion Film Corporation would make the film, and it would be directed by Jack Lee. Would Mr Williams care to be an advisor and work on the script? Lewis's generously gave him six months' leave to do the film.

Three months later, the script had been completeded and he and Sybil were taking a leisurely week-long journey to Germany, where the film was to be shot. During the trip, Williams received permission to visit the American military retention facility where Kommandant von Lindeiner was being detained by the US Army. But the man he found there was not the straight-backed, immaculately uniformed Prussian officer he remembered. He was now just a stooped old man wearing a bathrobe, and looking defeated. He remembered Williams and the escape very well and asked about the other two escapers, as well as Wing Commander Day. The wooden horse escape had been the beginning of the end for him and the 'Great Escape' which happened only five months later sealed his fate. He had been arrested and court martialled for dereliction of duty. Williams felt desperately sad for von Lindeiner; he had not been a harsh or cruel Kommandant. In fact, he had been eminently fair and just, and had done his duty well. He could hardly be held to blame for the escape. Williams soon left and, getting back into the car with Sybil, told her he wished he had not come. It had been too much like kicking a man when he was down, though he had not meant it to be that way at all.

Although it would have been ironically pleasurable to shoot the film there, Stalag Luft III was now within the Polish zone, and inaccessible to Williams and the film crew, while all the other original camps still in existence in Western Germany were being used as relocation centres for bombed out civilians. Therefore, a specially recreated camp was built from German war surplus materials. It really did look like the original camp, if perhaps appearing to be too neat and clean. Williams arrived in plenty of time to supervise the building of a replica wooden horse, and made sure it was as close to the original as possible. He was very active on the set, coaching the actors that played his and Codner's characters – Leo Genn and Anthony Steele respectively – in how things really were during the escape, and helping to dig the initial entrance shaft for the 'tunnel'.

Overall however, filming did not go smoothly, being plagued by bad weather and indecision from the start. The director, Jack Lee, and producer, Ian Dalrymple, had not liked Williams' ending and could not agree on one of their own. Nor did they reportedly work well together in other aspects. Further, many of the cast were, for the most part, amateurs as the production budget was small. A good many of the 'extras' came from nearby RAF stations for the scenes where many bodies were needed, and these were hard to direct. However among them was Ralph Ward, the man that had been clothing officer for the Escape Committee in East Compound, who managed to get leave from the RAF to play the part of compound adjutant. At least that was one step in the right direction. Another who wanted to appear was Peter Butterworth, who was at the beginning of his career as a professional actor. He applied to be one of the vaulters in the film, and why not? He had been one of the 'original' vaulters after all. However he was turned down, as the producer did not feel he looked 'convincingly heroic and athletic enough.'

Perhaps the worst moment came during the filming of scenes in the 'tunnel'. Williams was appalled at the size, as it was much larger than the original. He complained to both Lee and Dalrymple, but to little effect. Actually there was not much they could do, as the tunnel needed to be a certain size in order to suit the camera they were using. Disgusted nonetheless, Williams disappeared one afternoon and was missing at dinner that evening and that night as well. He only reappeared the next morning, during breakfast, covered in sand and inviting everyone to come have a look at what the real tunnel had looked like.

The incurable adventurer had spent the night under the earth of Germany again, digging a 'true' reproduction of the tunnel that they had dug seven years earlier. Pathetically, no one – not one – of the cast or crew went to see his effort.

In the end, director Lee left the production, which was by then over budget, leaving Dalrymple to clean up the mess. Dalrymple, in turn, quickly finished the filming in Germany, and returned to England, still without an ending. They did not complete the final scenes until after their return.

However, problems of production aside, when the film was released in 1950 it, like the book, was an instant success. Previously, there had been only one film made concerning prisoners during World War Two; a partial love story called *The Captive Heart*, which had been released in 1946 and been filmed at the *Marlag* naval prison camp in Bremen. That one had only done moderately well. *The Wooden Horse*, however, set the tone for many PoW films to follow and became an instant classic. Though actual prisoners remarked at the time (and still do) that the camp was too clean, the prisoners and their clothing too clean and neat, and everyone looked too well fed and healthy, the film is still hailed as authentically documenting the escape. Even if it failed from a authentic detail point of view, it did very well illustrate the attitude of Williams and Codner toward the escape and told their side of the story reasonably well.

During the earlier showings of the film, Tom Wilson managed to view it in a special way. Tom was commander of the Combined Cadet Force at his school. During a visit to RAF Hornchurch with some of his cadets, it just so happened that the Duchess of Gloucester wished to see the film and Hornchurch was called on to provide the guard of honour. However, there were no airmen available for the duty at the time so, without hesitating, Wilson volunteered to lead a group of London area Air Training Corps cadets. That evening, Tom managed to watch the film as part of the party who came with the Duchess. He enjoyed it very much, though he kept it to himself at the time that he had been part of the original scheme.

When the film premiered in Paris, the French Air Force flew several of the men involved in the event over as honoured guests of the French Prime Minister (whom they all met). Among other guests brought to France was Les Sidwell; the honour partially making up for being ostracized by his former messmates following the escape.

Williams' life following the production of the film was largely the one for which he had dreamed. There had been a small 'spark' of adventure in Williams before the war, but he had not understood what to do with it. The visit back to Germany with Sybil had shown him what he needed. The escape and its retelling had made that initial 'spark' a burning desire and he now knew that it was adventure he sought – needed – to give him the inspiration to write. By the time they made their way back to England, Sybil had agreed that he needed to resign from Lewis's and write. Therefore, when he got back home, he gave in his notice and never looked back.

With the ever faithful and encouraging Sybil by his side, he became the adventurer and author he was destined to be, eventually publishing eleven books in total. His next book was entitled *The Tunnel*. Basically a reworking of *Goon in the Block*, it was a prequel to *The Wooden Horse*, starting with his being shot down and taking up the story until he walked through the gates of Stalag Luft III. Three further books centred around chronicling escapes throughout history, and he became something of an escape 'expert', with a personal library of over 300 books all dealing with escape. In 1957, he told the story of going back to Germany to make the film *Complete and Free: A Modern Idyll.* The cover illustration was a painting by the eccentric artist Stanley Spencer, which Williams had commissioned in 1954. The work had taken two weeks to paint, and it is said that the most time was spent detailing the stitches on Williams' sweater. Spencer also completed a portrait of Sybil at the same time, of which Williams was very fond.

In 1956 he and Sybil also set out on an overland tour through Hungary, Rumania, Bulgaria, and Yugoslavia in a specially equipped Land Rover; a highly unusual event during the Cold War. Two months later, British newspapers were reporting that the two had been expelled from Eastern Europe by the Communists. Though he never told exactly what had happened, the tour later became the inspiration behind his books *Dragoman Pass* (1959) and *The Borders of Barbarism* (1961). He spent 1962 in Denmark supervising the construction of a motor/sail yacht, after which he and Sybil sailed the Mediterranean extensively. They settled in Porto Cheli, Greece, though occasionally spending time in Turkey and also home in England. He occasionally talked with those who sought him out and agreed to some interviews, and fulfilled every request to autograph First Day Covers (special postage stamps and envelope) sent in honour of the escape or activities of his fellow ex-prisoners, usually in co-operation with Philpot.

The last strong contact he would have with his escape, however, was when he rewrote *The Wooden Horse* in 1979 for a 30th Anniversary Edition. This time, he was able to steer the book toward a much stronger resemblance to his original manuscript and he set the record straight in several areas where changes had been made for commercial reasons. The scene of killing the German guard had bothered him for years, for he saw it as a particularly terrible thing to have done toward an army and people that had largely treated him with correct adherence to the rules, and even a certain amount of respect. When the newly-edited book was published Williams, by all accounts, was far more pleased with the result than he had been in 1949. However, the book still remained more of a novel rather than the true story of their escape, and by then some were beginning to see it as a dated work. The detractors he brushed aside; it was the story that mattered to the novelist in him, and it was that story which he had told, in a truly entertaining way. To this day it remains one of the most clearly written examples of escape literature to emerge from the war, unclouded by personal opinion, and has sold over two million copies, in more than twenty-five editions and in many languages.

Eric Williams died peacefully at his home in Porto Cheli, Greece, on 24 December 1983 at the age of 72 – truly satisfied with life and free.

Postscript: 'Margaret'

November 1943–May 1945

Flying Officer John Harvie tramped slowly around the circuit along with Ed Beaton, one of his new messmates in Hut 67. It was October 1944 and Harvie had only just arrived in East Compound the day before. He had received harsh treatment in Nazi hands thus far. Betrayed by a traitor in the escape line he was slowly being moved along. Following his being shot down, Harvie had first spent a month under Gestapo 'care' at the notorious Fresnes prison in Paris. There, he had been 'welcomed' into the world of a PoW as only the Gestapo was capable. Following his time in Fresnes, his captors had decided that he need not live anymore and sent him to a concentration camp at Buchenwald. There he languished under appalling conditions for three months, sleeping in a filthy hole scratched out of the ground and slowly wasting away, until official intervention arrived only just in time, and he was sent to Stalag Luft III.

On arrival, during induction even his new Luftwaffe captors were disgusted at his condition. His uniform was little more than a filthy rag; he was crawling with lice and fleas and suffering greatly from malnutrition and dehydration. Once cleaned and fed and deloused, with a shaved head and fresh uniform and brushed teeth for the first time since he was shot down, the young man was quickly and quietly handed over to the British staff in the compound. They, in turn, were aghast when they heard his tale, and understood why the camp 'Goons' had slunk away so quickly. They were too ashamed to face him.

For Harvie, it was strange to admit that it was heaven to be in a true PoW camp. Here he now found himself in relatively good health and vermin free, with enough to eat and drink, and people around him that cared. His messmates, once they heard his story, were gentle and kindness personified, asking little of him and listening to only what he cared to tell them of his experiences; never pressing him for detail. They were horrified by what they heard and went out of their way to make him feel he was truly 'home'. Buchenwald had been a nightmare; Sagan was safe, and for that he was grateful.

Escape, therefore, was the farthest thing from Harvie's mind as he and Beaton slowly strolled round the circuit. Then Beaton casually pointed to one side and said, with great pride, 'Do you see that shallow depression in the ground slanting out through the barbed wire? That is where three Kriegies, hidden inside a vaulting box, slowly tunnelled their way to freedom while PoW gymnasts practiced on top. Within a few weeks they made it back to England via Sweden. After the 'Goons' discovered the 'wooden horse' tunnel, they collapsed it by pumping it full of water from the fire hoses.'

Such was the legacy of the only completely successful escape from East Compound during the war; just a depression in the ground, and 800 or so proud prisoners.

A few weeks later, Beaton and Harvie were out on the circuit again. By this time Harvie was feeling much stronger and was full of escape questions, the story of the wooden horse having fascinated him. Beaton had been a 'Kriegie' for some time and had seen escapes progress. Having gained Harvie's interest, he said cryptically, 'Has anyone confided to you about the tunnel our hut dug which is ready to 'Go'? No? Well ...' and with that, he related a most incredible story ...

Despite the general malaise common to PoW camp, a new feeling seemed to have descended on East Compound as the autumn of 1943 finally faded and winter took firm hold. The three 'mad horsemen' had made it out, and as such had proven once again that it could be done from Sagan. And as time passed and the three did not return, hope was held high that they had made the coveted 'home run'. No one believed it when the Germans had announced that the three had been caught within two days of the escape. Certainly no one wanted to believe it, at any rate. And the two facts of both their successful exit and apparent evasion from recapture had had the double effect of bolstering general morale within the compound, and re-energizing escape plans.

Proof positive of the escaper's complete success, arrived at Sagan that December, in the form of a small package addressed to Squadron Leader 'Jimmie' Sargeaunt and postmarked from the Excelsior Hotel in Stockholm, Sweden. There was no name or note in the package, however when Sargeaunt opened it he found that it contained a cheap, Swedish-made watch. Engraved on the back was a horse with three tails, standing up straight. Combined with the postmark, there could be no doubt what it meant. The Escape Committee was euphoric, and Group Captain Kellett announced the news at the end of evening *Appell* to a mighty cheer.

By that time, however, a successor to the wooden horse effort had already been underway for nearly a month. It was code-named 'Margaret' by the committee, and was the brainchild of Freddie McKay. So inspired had he been by the tunnel when he had sealed Williams and Philpot in on the afternoon of 29 October, that McKay had conceived the idea of using the same general plan that Williams and Codner had first dreamed up, only with a different scheme for a cover to the entrance, and still closer to the wire.

Having been one of the first vaulters, and thus having seen how the best place to hide something from the 'Goons' was apparently in plain sight right under their noses, McKay went to the Escape Committee with a plan to start a tunnel from the parade area where his hut (67) stood for *Appell.* The entrance to the tunnel would be of the same type as the wooden horse; a sand-covered trap door dug in an open area. The difference would be the method. McKay proposed to use members of his hut for *Appell* as his cover. Following both morning and afternoon *Appell*, a group would linger on the parade ground, as was common, in the middle of which the entrance would be excavated and the trap made sturdy. Once enough headway had been made and there was room enough inside the hole for him, McKay would then enter following morning *Appell* with a collection of empty trouser leg bags. There he would stay all day, tunnelling until just before afternoon *Appell*, when a group would again gather together at the site of the entrance, as though preparing for parade, and extricate him and his bags of sand. Only a relatively small amount of sand would be dug each day, but seeing as winter was setting in there would be no hurry to actually finish the project until spring, the start of the escape season, by which time they could have all the necessary escape materials ready. A hidden air hole would be made under the warning rail, such as Philpot had suggested to Williams and Codner, and the frozen ground would help hold the roof in place along the tunnel's length during construction. Upon completion and once a suitable camouflaged exit could be thought up, they could keep sending men out during each evening *Appell.*

Having already witnessed the incredible events of the previous summer, the committee needed little convincing before giving McKay their go ahead and full backing.

They started the project late in November and at first it was indeed very slow going, excavating the entrance shaft. Only so much could be done in the brief time before *Appell.* Had Philpot still been around it might well have reminded him of the accordion stunt of 1942, as McKay dug away in the middle of the tight gathering of 'Kriegies' before each parade and passed bags of sand around for everyone to take away. Earlier in the war, the inmates from the huts had paraded in a loose formation, with the men widely spaced, which would have made the project impossible. Now, however sad to say, the Germans had been shooting down increasing numbers of Allied aircrew during that summer and autumn, and thus the hut parades had got far tighter, actually necessitating the prisoners to begin arriving early for parade. However, they had to be extremely careful. The men from Hut 67 paraded in the far south-eastern corner of the *Sportzplatz*, overlooked by a 'Goon box' No.4, making security around McKay's effort to dig the trap of special concern. Furthermore, a watch had to be kept for the arrival of the 'Goon' who took up a position behind the hut as they paraded. Each hut had a back-door 'Goon' who completed the count from the rear of the formation, while Feldwebel Stuhlmeyer did the count from the front. Then the two would meet and compare figures for each hut. If they agreed, all was well; if not a second, more thorough, count was taken again. Such a count might bring notice to the many strange bulges that appeared to be emerging under some of the 'Kriegies' greatcoats and thus Hut 67 attempted to be a model of efficiency on parade.

Then weather was also a problem. Fresh snow on the ground just before an *Appell* would prevent the trap from being opened; a large bare, dirty patch in the trampled snow would give the game away. Also the cold weather had to be dealt with, as the Germans frequently called *Appell* indoors if it was exceptionally bad. Christmas came and went, then the New Year. It was well into January 1944 before the entrance shaft was complete and McKay began operating underground.

At the bottom of the shaft, McKay constructed a small chamber, large enough for two men to be in the tunnel when the time came. The initial length of the tunnel (some 25ft) had to be securely shored, as it passed not only under where the parading prisoners stood, but also under the circuit on the way toward the eastern fence. From there it was aimed again for the small ditch by the side of the road. Initially it was to run without shoring for the majority of its length, but the Escape Committee stepped in and insisted that it be solidly constructed and shored the whole way, in case it could indeed be reused. This time, however, it was far easier to get everyone to give up a bedboard for the project, as the complete success of the wooden horse tunnel had raised escape hopes. Tom Wilson assigned by the committee as one of McKay's main above-ground assistants, made an example and gave up the remainder of his boards, making a sort of hammock for his palliasse out of Red Cross string. He also helped sew sandbags with McKay for the project and was instrumental in helping him in and out of the trap.[1]

The first major crisis for the scheme came in February 1944. On that day, morning *Appell* was held as usual, and McKay was lowered into the shaft as the Germans counted another hut. But before the 'Kriegies' were dismissed, Hauptmann Hellfachs announced that there was to be an immediate individual identity check, which would be held indoors due to the severity of the weather. Directly after the announcement, guards fanned out and quickly ushered everyone back into their huts, which were then locked while sentries ringed each to prevent anyone from leaving.

The trouble was that McKay was underground, and there was no way for Hut 67 to get him out for the check. Finding one man short and knowing who that man was, the 'Goons' would search the whole camp. Not finding McKay anywhere above ground, 'Charlie' Piltz would naturally suspect tunnelling activity. This following on the wooden horse scheme might, in turn, lead him to carefully inspect the only place where there was any reasonable PoW activity in the compound in winter; the football pitch, which was also where the 'Kriegies' paraded for *Appell*. Not likely to be fooled a second time, he would probably find the tunnel. All this would also mean keeping everyone locked in, and as such who knew when, or if, they would be able to get McKay out, if 'Charlie' did not discover the hole first. Either way, a count and a search would take up serious time, and McKay certainly could not last for long underground in the dead of winter. Something needed to be done, and fast.

The Escape Committee quickly assessed the situation as everyone was being ushered inside. What they must do is try to find a way to force the *Appell* to be made outside in order to recover McKay. And the easiest method of doing that would be to confuse the count.

The committee called on Tom Wilson and two others – none of them from Hut 67 – to 'disappear' during the indoor count, banking on the probability that the 'Goons' would herd them all back outside during an initial search of the huts for the missing men. Wilson, in turn, headed for the *Abort*, telling the guard that stopped him that it was an emergency. There he settled down in a dark corner for what he hoped would not be a long wait in the cold. He did not know where the other two were hiding.

It all worked out just as the committee hoped. Once the Germans had the names of the four missing men, they indeed marched everyone back out on parade. Once there, they quickly extracted McKay while runners went to tell the hidden men that he was out and that they could once again rejoin the parade. Meanwhile the searches of the rooms began, while Feldwebel Stuhlmeyer counted again. This time, however, the numbers added up. Plenty of head scratching by the Germans followed, and in the end the missing four were called out of formation by name. When all had appeared, they were asked as to where each had been and then admonished. Despite their plausible explanations, each was sent to the 'Cooler' for a week. Disaster for 'Margaret' had been avoided.

The second crisis occurred when McKay and Pilot Officer J.A.C. 'Flash' Gordon (an Australian from No.455 Squadron shot down over Cologne on 7 November 1941) went down the tunnel together one morning; by that time there was a need for two below ground. But during that particular day, both temperatures and plenty of snow began to fall, causing the 'Goons' to announce an indoor *Appell* for the afternoon. Now, there was a real problem: without afternoon parade what other innocent diversion could the 'Kriegies' use in order to get the two tunnellers out? Oddly enough, it was sports that again provided the answer, as two groups of men from Hut 67 appeared on the *Sportzplatz* following lunch that afternoon with a rugby football. Soon the game was on, and a rousing game it was too, with plenty of the violent action rugby is famous for, as well as several perfectly outrageous scrums. One in particular, close to the southeast corner of the field proved to be exceptionally physical, for when it broke up it had produced two additional players.

After that, rugby was played on a fairly regular basis in bad weather, just to keep the 'Goons' satisfied in case the method should be needed again. As events evolved, it was indeed used a few more times, to get the men into the tunnel as well as out.

Perhaps the greatest crisis for the scheme came one afternoon at the beginning of April, when the news of the shooting of the escapers from the North Compound ('Harry') tunnel that had broken at the end of March was announced by Group Captain Kellett. Though this forced a reassessment of escape by the committee, the discussion was short. They were obviously in the hands of murderers who would stop at nothing, ignoring whatever rules they wished, in order to achieve their ends. For weeks some of those more humane among the camp staff were penitent when they met with the British staff, being as disgusted as their prisoners at what had been done in the name of Germany. But the staff was not the Gestapo, and it was decided that work on 'Margaret' should be suspended.

One main event further supported the Escape Committee's decision as a beautiful spring gave way to the momentous summer of 1944. In June came the invasion, and invasion equalled liberation to the prisoners. In a matter of weeks, the gates would be opened by British or US forces and they would all be on their way back to England in no time (or so they thought). Therefore, with the war now obviously drawing to a close, 'Margaret' would not be needed. Escape was just not worth the risk anymore.[2]

However, as that summer turned to the beginning of another Sagan autumn, frustration mounted in camp at the slow pace of the Allied advance, and McKay began to argue for his tunnel to be reopened. Certainly there was no definite policy toward escape, but it would be good to have an exit in case of emergency. As the Allies – in particular the Russians – advanced ever closer to Sagan that autumn, and the Allied bombing campaign had virtually destroyed German industry and infrastructure, it became more and more clear to their guards that they were going to lose another war. At this, several of them began dropping hints that if that were the case, then Hitler would have no problem disposing of his prisoners.

Consequently, McKay was guardedly given permission by the Escape Committee and he got back to work until a strongly shored-up tunnel, running from the parade ground to beyond the wire, which might at any moment be driven into the ditch. It had taken a year to construct; a year that had seen many changes in the attitudes of the prisoners, their captors, and the direction of the war. By the time McKay semi-permanently sealed the tunnel that autumn, the camp was on half rations, as the allied bombing campaign had destroyed the German road and rail network, making the delivery of Red Cross parcels very difficult. Fortunately, 'Rackets' Marsh had quite a surplus stored away and it was this that would carry them through. But no one was hoarding anything for escape rations.

And there 'Margaret' was left as yet another winter swept down the Silesian plain, enveloping Stalag Luft III in a blanket of snow.

John Harvie strolled slowly alongside Ed Beaton and listened with interest to the whole disturbing tale. A perfect, undiscovered ruse had successfully fooled the 'Goons' once again; a ready-made tunnel, just waiting to be used was just over there, almost beneath their feet! But a brutal captor, who thought nothing of murdering escapers, had proved the ultimate escape preventative, no matter how ingenious the idea. The irony was almost too much to bear.

In the falling darkness, Harvie and Beaton went back into Hut 67 as the perimeter lights came on, leaving 'Margaret' to once again sleep another night; unused but unforgotten …

'Margaret' never was used. At the end of January 1945, with the Russians less than 40km from Sagan, the Germans announced the immediate evacuation of the camp. The Escape Committee hurriedly met to discuss the possibility of putting a few men down 'Margaret' and take their chances when the Russians had overrun the area. Ultimately, however, it was decided that the risks of such an act were just too great, there were too many variables. A day later the Germans marched all the prisoners out into a blinding snowstorm on what became known as the infamous 'Black March'.

Hitler, knowing that the end had indeed come, instead of exterminating them as planned, had ordered that all PoWs be marched back into Germany, where their lives would be used as a bargaining tool to dictate better peace terms. All across Germany, camps were being evacuated ahead of the advancing Allies and the 'Kriegies' marched some hundreds of kilometres, under appalling conditions, with only the food they could carry and practically no shelter. Hundreds died along the way of disease or exhaustion, or at the hands of sadistic guards about to lose their war. Their eventual destination usually turned out to be an already overcrowded, sometimes condemned, older camp where food and sanitary conditions was virtually nonexistent. Some were herded into makeshift, open barbed-wire enclosures set up in forests, where they had to make do with whatever shelter they could fabricate for themselves and what food could be foraged from around the area by indifferent guards who were usually as hungry as their prisoners.

For most, on both sides, those last weeks of the war were the worst in so many ways. It was obvious the war was over. And yet the Nazi war machine kept grinding insanely on; refusing to admit defeat and terrified at the dicscovery of what had been done in the name of the Third Reich. There were weeks of starvation and deprivation which many had never witnessed before, and would pray to never see again; anxious weeks of waiting and expectation in the knowledge that liberation – freedom – was just around the corner. For them it could not come fast enough; when it did – Oh! That feeling of utter joy.

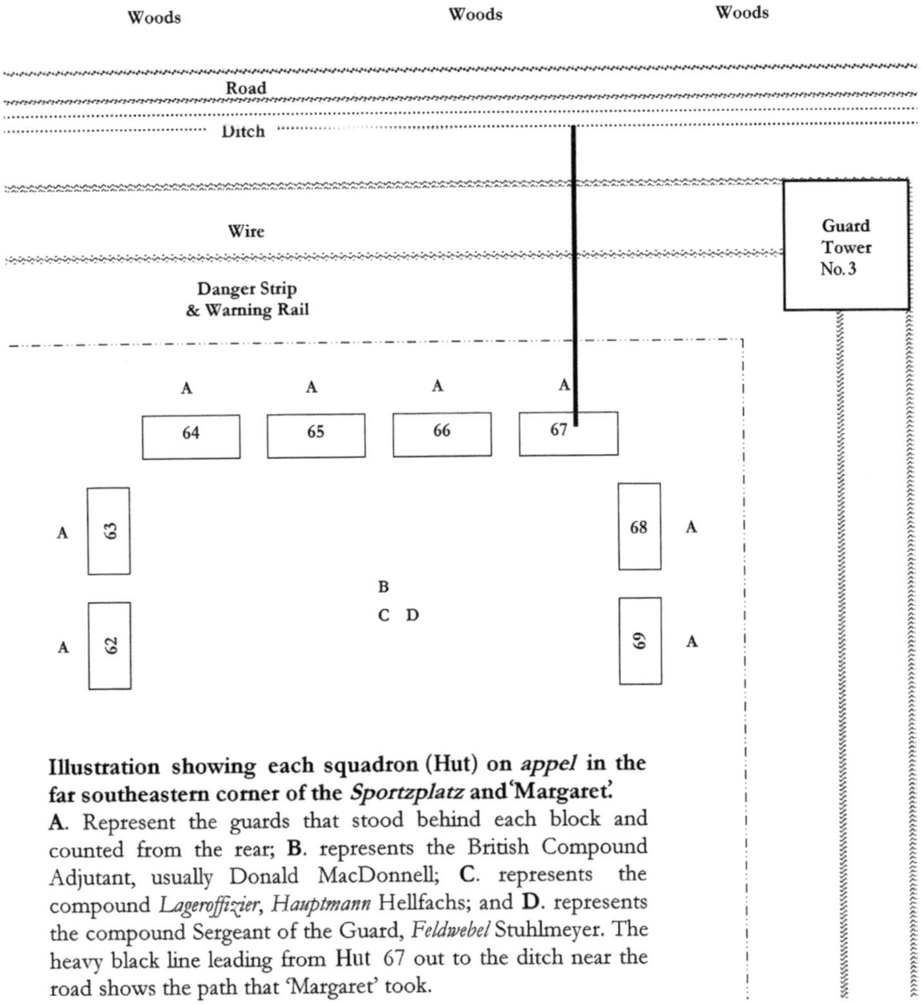

Illustration showing each squadron (Hut) on *appel* in the far southeastern corner of the *Sportzplatz* and 'Margaret'.

A. Represent the guards that stood behind each block and counted from the rear; **B**. represents the British Compound Adjutant, usually Donald MacDonnell; **C**. represents the compound *Lageroffizier*, *Hauptmann* Hellfachs; and **D**. represents the compound Sergeant of the Guard, *Feldwebel* Stuhlmeyer. The heavy black line leading from Hut 67 out to the ditch near the road shows the path that 'Margaret' took.

Notes

Chapter 1: The Demise of O for 'Orange'

1. Squadron Leader (later Wing Commander) Thomas Daniel Calnan was captured on 30 December 1941 flying a Supermarine Spitfire of No.1 Photographic Reconnaissance Unit, and was on a mission to film the results of a bombing raid on Brest. Badly burned about the face when his aircraft went down, he nevertheless became one of the war's most determined escapers.
2. That evening, however, Tommy Calnan managed to wriggle out of a lavatory window in his third-class carriage and get clear away. He was not discovered to be missing until some hours later, when the train made a stop to feed the prisoners a 'meal' of thin soup. He had been looking for a partner among his fellow 'third-class men', but had found no takers. He detailed his adventures during this escape in his autobiography *Free as a Running Fox*. Once recaptured some days later (as he would be on all his subsequent escapes), he would again join Philpot and the rest of the Spangenburg contingent in Stalag Luft III.
3. With typical inter-service rivalry, when their Wehrmacht guards turned the prisoners over to the Luftwaffe guards at Sagan station that night, the Luftwaffe NCO taking charge said, with a grin, 'So, I hear you lost one along the way!' (Tommy Calnan), to which the Wehrmacht NCO could only feebly reply, 'Yes, but he won't be loose long in the glorious Reich.'

Chapter 2: Sagan

1. Despite beliefs to the contrary, the distance between the warning wire, or warning rail, and the main fence line in both compounds varied depending on which side of the compound one was on. In East Compound, along the western boundary with Centre Compound and the northern boundary with the *Vorlager*, the distance of the 'no man's land' was no more than 10ft; along the open eastern and southern boundaries the distance was almost 30ft.
2. Weir had been badly burned when the main petrol tank in his Spitfire exploded after it was hit. While his oxygen mask and flying helmet had saved most of his face, the skin around his eyes had healed a red and purple colour as he had not been wearing goggles. He was a quiet, determined man and much admired by all that knew him. Weir died in 2009.

   'Wally' Floody, who died in 1989, is the more well known of the pair, largely due to Paul Brickhill's book *The Great Escape* and his involvement with the film made in 1963 about the event, on which he was a technical advisor. Buried many, many times in the tunnels he dug, at dinner with the director one evening Floody mentioned that he felt the crew was definitely getting the tunnel scenes right because, 'I'm having nightmares about it all'.
3. The huts in East and Centre Compounds were of slightly different construction than those of the later North Compound (of the 'Great Escape' fame), as well as those in South and West Compounds. While the huts in the later compounds were set on brick and mortar pilings which provided another route for a tunnel entrance, the huts in East Compound were set up on a number of of 4in by 4in stilts, the only brick and mortar pilings being under the stoves and washrooms.

   Searching the huts was a joy for the 'Goons', who would take a hut almost to pieces in the process; rapping on walls and floors looking for loose boards or hollow sounds under the concrete in the washrooms and around the chimneys, as well as breaking, ripping, tearing and smashing anything belonging to the prisoners.

4. This project became eternally famous among those who were at Sagan that summer as ‘Colonel Clark’s Crap in Comfort Campaign – Keep the smell in and the flies out!’ Indeed, even after 65 years, men interviewed by the author had still not forgotten the efforts of Colonel Clark; one even went so far as to write to him thanking him after the war!

Chapter 3: ‘One of Our Aircraft Failed to Return …’

1. Flight Sergeant Dunmall eventually set the burning Shorts Stirling down into a small lake (the Westeinderplassen, near the town of Kudelstaart) he had glimpsed in the searchlight glare, on the off chance that he might just survive. However, luck was with him during that long descent, and he did indeed survive the ditching with barely a scratch, soon passing into captivity believing – as always afterward – that he actually had landed in Holland. Interestingly, in 1981, a group of amateur Dutch divers discovered the remains of the Stirling (the Germans had removed much of it in 1942) recovering one of the aircraft’s propellers, the rear gun turret, and several other parts that had not been destroyed on the way down. The propeller is today on display as a memorial near the lake. Dunmall later received the Distinguished Flying Medal for his bravery.

Chapter 4: Under the North African Stars

1. For the supply of forces in the Tunisian campaign, the German Air Transport Service (*Lufttransport Mittelmeer*, or LTM) was organized under a central headquarters at Rome. Wings were located at Capodichino near Naples and Trapani, Sicily, with control officers at the Tunisian airfields of Sidi Ahmed (Bizerte) and El Aouïna (Tunis), also at some airfields in the Naples area and Catania, Sicily. One round trip from Naples and two from Sicily were made each day. In his escape report, Codner wrote Tuapani meaning Trapani.
2. The Dulag in Rome was initially located at and administered by PG 122.
3. Royal Army Medical Corps (RAMC)
4. Apparently this had much to do with the fact that he walked off with a book of Latin verse he found in the Dulag Luft library; he had taken it because no one else apparently had been able to get any use out of it! Later, at Stalag Luft III, it would be the only book anyone ever remembered him reading, and many frequently recall him having it tucked under his arm when he was out on the circuit.

Chapter 5: ‘A Rum Sort of Place …’

1. In point of fact, when the Luftwaffe *Abwehr* sergeant that had accompanied the ‘Kriegies’ to Schubin from Sagan – an old and well-respected opponent of the escapers– had tried to warn the Wehrmacht staff that the RAF men were trouble, he was brushed off as an incompetent. This so infuriated him that upon emerging from the camp staff office he gathered as many ‘Kriegies’ around him as he could and actually urged them to ‘Escape, escape, escape!’ In a strange sort of turnabout that can only be brought on by war the Kriegies response actually applauded their wily foe in.
2. There would be additional moves from Sagan as well; a second in early October and a small third in November. Added to this were regular moves that arrived from Dulag Luft. By the time the camp was evacuated in April 1943, and the RAF men were moved back to Sagan in order to make space for captured US Army officers, overcrowding had reached a critical point.
3. A ‘Stooge’ was the PoW equivalent of the ‘Ferret’; doomed to hours of silent watchfulness observing any Germans that entered the camp, and be ready to warn those engaged in illicit activities should a ‘Goon’ get too close. Though ‘stooging’ was the lowest and most monotonous of jobs in an escape organization, it was nonetheless one of the most important, providing the needed security screen.

4. Before *Appell*, on the morning following the escape, seeing that the hole had not yet been found, a quick thinking Squadron Leader gathered up his escape equipment and disappeared down the *Abort*. Witnesses saw him emerge from the tunnel exit a short time later and sprint off across the field – behind the back of the German sentry facing the wire.

Chapter 6: Back in the 'Sandpit'

1. Writer and journalist Aidan Crawley was already a Royal Auxiliary Air Force pilot at the beginning of the war. His first post was as Assistant Air Attaché to Ankara, Turkey and included responsibilities in Belgrade and Sofia, where he may have been involved in covert operations. He barely escaped capture there and managed to get himself transferred to active operations. He was shot down over Italy in 1941, and was being taken by train to his initial interrogation when he saw an article about himself on the back page of a German newspaper a passenger was reading, labelling him a spy and saboteur. In order to protect himself from the Germans, he gave his first name as 'Stafford' (a family name) and was thereafter known by that name. After escaping from Schubin, he had travelled to Innsbruck – the furthest of any of the escapers – surviving nine checks on his papers, only to be eventually noted as suspicious because (as his captors later told him) he 'just looked so exhausted,' rendering him worth a second glance. On that second look, it was his English shoe laces that gave him away.
2. Wing Commander Joseph Robert Kayll, DSO, DFC, MBE, was an ace with twelve victories, and had fought throughout the Battle of Britain before being shot down in July 1941. It is rumoured he once downed a German bomber by sawing off a portion of its tail surface with his propeller when he had run out of ammunition. William 'Tex' Ash, a good friend and fellow prisoner of Kayll, described him as 'a quiet, gentle man of remarkable courage.' In September 1942, he had participated in a tunnel escape out of Oflag VI-B at Warburg and, with a companion, walked 90km in 7 days before being arrested by a forester near the town of Fulda. After spending time at Oflag XXI-B at Schubin, Poland, where he headed the Escape Committee after Jimmy Buckley's death, he was sent to East Compound, Stalag Luft III, where he again assumed the role of 'Big X'.

   Squadron Leader Dudley 'Dud' Craig, OBE, was shot down by anti-aircraft fire on 4 November 1941, over the French coast, when flying a Hawker Hurricane from No.607 Squadron. At Stalag Luft I, on 15 January 1942, he and another pilot attempted to walk out of the camp disguised as guards, but were apprehended before they got outside the fence. Then, as partner to Wing Commander Harry Day, he escaped from the Schubin latrine tunnel in early March 1943. The two were recaptured two days later near Gneisen and returned to camp, and then sent to Stalag Luft III. Assigned to East Compound, Craig helped to devise the security and intelligence systems for the compound.
3. Lieutenant Haldor Espelid, RNAF, was shot down 27 August 1942, when flying a Supermarine Spitfire from No.331 (Norwegian) Squadron, RAF. He would soon transfer to the North Compound and together with another RNAF officer, Nils Fuglesang, participate in the 'Great Escape' the following March. Both were among the fifty officers who were recaptured and then murdered.
4. Stevens was born Georg Franz Hein in Hanover, Germany in 1919 into a wealthy German-Jewish family. In 1934, alarmed at the rise of Naziism, his widowed mother sent him to England, where he remained after finishing school. Following Great Britain's declaration of war on Germany, he should have reported to a police station for internment as an enemy alien but instead assumed the identity of a deceased school friend, Peter Stevens, and joined the RAF. He was shot down on 8 September 1941, flying a Handley Page Hampden of No.144 Squadron, and would attempt escape eight times before the end of the war (including the Schubin tunnel), and as a natural German speaker, his skills were frequently in demand by other escapers.

5. A World War One pilot, Group Captain Herbert Massey was due to be promoted to the rank of Air Commodore and go to the United States on a command exchange scheme, but felt he needed the experience of at least flying on one bombing raid before he did. That raid turned out to be the second 'Thousand Bomber Raid' of the war, against the Krupp Works at Essen during the night of 2 June 1942 – during which the Shorts Stirling he was flying in was shot down. The only permanent camp he entered was Stalag Luft III until he was repatriated due to ill health in mid-1944.
6. By the end of the summer Maw, had become exasperated and confronted the German *Lageroffizier* after *Appell* one morning and told him to either move the speaker or he would chop the pole down on which it was mounted. In deference to the Wing Commander's rank, the Germans compromised and agreed to turn the speaker on only after *Appell.*
7. It was the diffidence of the prisoners on *Appell* this summer that led the Germans to issue orders that autumn stating that from then on each man was required to show up dressed in at least trousers or shorts and a shirt. Anyone ignoring this order would earn a spell in the 'Cooler'. After that, the *Appell* looked much more orderly – even if immediately after, in warm weather, the more disreputable prisoners would quickly disrobe to the barest of essentials – occasionally right in front of their guards.
8. Hauptmann Hellfachs was another Hungarian in the German staff, like Feldwebel Stuhlmeyer, and generally known to the 'Kriegies' as either 'Halifax' or, the more ribald, 'Hellfucks'. He was a rather tired looking man approaching middle age, of medium height and rather overweight. In his off-duty hours he was often seen when the weather was fair, dressed as a racing cyclist, riding his bicycle along the sandy road that bordered the eastern side of the camp, waving genially to the 'Kriegies'. It was widely rumoured in the camp that he was homosexual.

Chapter 7: Inspiration

1. Rupert John Stevens was born in London in 1919, but his parents almost immediately moved the family to Cape Town, South Africa, where John (as he was generally known) spent a normal South African childhood, excelling in sports while at school. He might even have had a future in that direction, but for the war. Recruited into the Royal South African Air Force in November 1939, he was soon on operations in the Western Desert with No.12 Squadron. In November 1941, he and his crew were returning from a bombing mission when their aircraft was hit by Flak, which punctured the main fuel tank. Stevens decidied to land at an emergency strip near Tobruk, but mistook the landscape and instead brought them down over enemy occupied Bardia, where they were hit by Flak again. Stevens, wounded severely in the crash, was immediately taken to a German hospital. There he was poorly patched up by a German doctor, which left him with a limp. Arriving at Sagan a few months later mostly healed but still very stiff, he sought relief in exercise, quickly organizing a small, but dedicated, group each morning. Sent to Schubin and then back to Sagan again, he continued his classes, no matter the weather, earning him a reputation as somewhat eccentric, for the weather at Sagan could be very unpredictable. A natural German speaker, Stevens would eventually become one of the fifty officers murdered following the 'Great Escape'.
2. What exactly happened next has always been in some debate. Sudden inspiration is rarely as clear cut as people like to believe. Often a variety of elements play a part, making it difficult to later define exactly what it was that triggered a singularly brilliant thought or idea. Then too, time and talent have a way of playing a part over the passage of years to help cloud facts. The description presented is based on the best available information from the only reliable sources privy to the initial event – Eric Williams and Oliver Philpot – as, so far as is known, Codner never recorded his side of the story. The description here is a composite of those two depictions.

3. Years later, Kayll would make it clear that he was, at the time, nonplussed about handing the project over to two men he did not consider worthy of such a idea, and assumed that faced with the challenge of building a vaulting horse, the two 'non-escaping types' would likely give up – at which time the Escape Committee could take full control and 'get it done right'. In at least two interviews, Kayll describes Williams and Codner as 'unpopular men', and 'loners' who had never attempted to help anyone else on an escape. He paints a wholly unflattering picture of the two which, while it may have some basis in minor fact, almost certainly is not to the extent that Kayll makes it out to be. This subject will shortly be addressed again in the story.
4. Pilot Officer Kenneth McIntosh, No.12 Squadron, shot down on 12 May 1940, became famous as an actor and director with the National Theatre after the war.
5. Wing Commander Roger Maw, commanding officer of No.108 Squadron was shot down leading a bombing attack on Tobruk in August 1942, and without doubt was the strangest-dressed man the 'Goons' ever imprisoned. When shot down he had been wearing a pair of Egyptian sandals and rose-coloured socks, grey flannel trousers, a bright yellow shirt and a large red paisley handkerchief tied round his neck. Over this he had worn his flight overalls and a pair of oversized flying boots. 'I thought I'd dress like a foreigner,' he later explained, 'Then I shouldn't be noticed if I had to bail out. But I think I must have dressed as the wrong sort of foreigner because I was arrested quite soon!'
6. Wilson could hardly be blamed for falling into enemy hands. Knocked out when he bailed from his stricken Vickers Wellington, he woke hours later lying across a drainage ditch, missing one flying boot. Dazed, he was picked up almost immediately by some Dutch dairy workers who quickly handed him over to searching Germans, in order to save others hiding in the area from being sent to forced labour camps in Germany.
7. 'Food Acco' – sometimes referred to as 'The Mart' – was a food exchange programme. The basic unit of value was a cigarette.
8. Tom Wilson later stated, 'The horse had been built as large as possible, without arousing the suspicion of the 'Ferrets', to give the tunnellers the space they needed. So it was higher than any vaulting box we had ever used at school. We were all in our twenties (mostly) and should have been pretty fit, but on the German rationing system we came into the lowest category.' Naturally all this made it difficult for some vaulters.

Chapter 8: First Steps

1. 'Pappy' Elliot was reluctant to admit to the author that he had indeed been one of those to initially knock the horse over. Whether it was athletic pride, or just a general reluctance to 'shoot a line' regarding the part he played in the affair, one cannot say. Several years earlier, however, he gave an interview to the History Channel where he had admitted as much, which is where the quote used here is from. In any case, Mr Elliot was a truly remarkable man and was wonderful to interview!
2. The 'duty pilot' was the Escape Committee's answer to the 'Ferrets'. It was a job taken in shifts by a man seated where he could keep a steady watch on the main gate, and who then noted in a log book every German that came in or out of the compound. Each German entering the compound was watched closely and the 'duty pilot', warned of any special 'Kriegie' activities would keep them informed of each German's movements. In this way the escape organization always knew how many Germans were in the compound at any given time, who and where they were. In order to avoid the 'duty pilot' at times when they were sure the 'Kriegies' were up to something, the 'Ferrets' sometimes climbed over the fence to get in when no one was around.
3. After helping organize and instigate the vaulting regime, the 'fanatical physical jerks wallah' John Stevens had managed to be transferred to the new North Compound, in order to participate in the 'Great Escape' and would be among the fifty recaptured and murdered.

Chapter 9: 'It *cannot* last, old boy …'

1. Lewis was a dedicated escaper who had been 'out' three times already, once on the run with Peter Stevens (who was helping Philpot prepare his forged papers) but also from the Schubin tunnel.
2. Calnan did make an escape from the *Vorlager* – but only after the wooden horse tunnel was closed. Again, this was with Robert Kee, his old escaping partner from the Schubin tunnel, but the two were eventually picked up near Kottbus through a defect in Kee's forged papers. However, Calnan never expressed any regret about not having joined with Williams and Codner, instead praising them thoroughly in his excellent wartime autobiography *Free as a Running Fox*. Perhaps the veteran escaper had had his fill of 'moles'.
3. RAF slang for a person to cast out the 'farthest reaches of the realm', with whom there was no contact; in short, to be ostracized by one's fellows.
4. These are the version of events as generally presented by Philpot and Williams, and as remembered by others. But are they simply the events as played out in accordance with what Wing Commander Kayll later recalled? After all, Tommy Calnan was on the Escape Committee at the time, as 'Little S' for Hut 67, and so asking him to join the team would have satisfied the needs of both Williams and Codner, as well as satisfying any possible committee demand that a deserving member be included on the scheme. Nor was Sidwell on the committee. Furthermore, it is known that virtually everyone on the committee participated in vaulting and, as the all-powerful committee they had the authority to 'persuade' others to vault as well. As we shall see, soon after Philpot had joined the team a vaulting co-ordinator also joined the scheme, and while he was not a member of the committee, he was a long-term prisoner, and as such would have been a committee favourite. The selection of a third also fits in with the 24-hour time frame. It is therefore possible that what Kyall remembered was something of the way it happened, and that perhaps no one outside of the committee knew or ever mentioned the true facts, for reasons already stated in the text. It should be noted, however, that this does not account for his claim of 'a week without any vaulting' that nobody seems to remember.

Chapter 10: Exhaustion and Ingenuity

1. Although there is conflicting evidence, Codner may indeed have gone down the tunnel in the first few days of Williams' rest in order to finish the strengthening work in the area of the fall where Williams had been working the day he collapsed. In fact, it is very likely he did. During the whole of the scheme, Williams was considered to be the 'construction engineer', as his earlier architectural experience gave him an insight into building practice, while the younger Codner was the 'brawn' of the project, doing the majority of the digging and heavy work. Philpot was the 'man behind the scenes' making sure it all went as smooth as possible. The arrangement worked very well, although Williams would later credit Codner with doing the most on the entire scheme.
2. For this action Miller would receive the DFC.
3. German for either 'please', 'thank you', or 'excuse me'

Chapter 11: From Here to There

1. The only 'Ferrets' who were brave enough to go down 'Tom' and crawl the entire length of the tunnel – as well as 'Harry', the tunnel from North Compound – was 'Charlie' Piltz and his number two, 'Lofty'. Piltz was definitely the 'go to' man when it came to tunnels. One wonders what his thoughts were of the expertly constructed 'Tom'.
2. Pilot Officer Desmond E. Breed had been with No.1651 Squadron, which was designated a Heavy Conversion Unit, training 'two-engine types' to fly the new, heavier four-engine aircraft. Though officially a training unit, No.1651 flew forty-nine operations for Bomber Command during 1942, for a loss of five aircraft. On 28 July 1942, one of these was a Shorts

Sterling flown by Breed during a raid on Hamburg. He would be among those who had not been sent to Schubin and was destined to spend his entire imprisonment at Sagan. One can only assume he became bored with the place in a relatively short time.

3. Pearman was the pilot of a DeHavilland Mosquito shot down on 31 May 1942, during a photographic reconnaissance of the results from the first 'Thousand Bomber Raid'. Following the war, he went on to international acclaim as a wildlife artist, painting some of the most incredibly vivid and life-like images put on canvas of tigers in the wild ever.
4. Anthony Perrinott Lysberg Barber, originally served in the Territorial Army (Royal Artillery), went to France in 1940 and was evacuated from Dunkirk. Later, he was selected for pilot training with the RAF, and served with Tommy Calnan in No.1 Photographic Reconnaissance Unit. On 25 January 1942, Barber was forced to bail out of his Supermarine Spitfire after he became lost on an operation and ran out of fuel. He escaped on the Asselin scheme, was recaptured and sent to Sagan. He took over as 'Little X' in Hut 62 from Philpot when he joined the wooden horse scheme. He studied for a law degree through the International Red Cross, and graduated with honours. After the war he became a lawyer before turning to politics, and joined the House of Commons before becoming Chancellor of the Exchequer from 1970 to 1974. He died in 2005.

Chapter 12: 'You're not thinking of *leaving us*, by any chance, are you?'

1. It is, of course, ludicrous for the Nazis to have cried 'Unfair' to any position the British may have taken against them, in light of their own activities, re: the concentration camps and the 'Final Solution'; Lidice; the gross atrocities conducted in occupied Poland; the forcing millions into slave labour for the Reich; etc. The situation is similar to that of the German population crying out against the 'savage' bombing campaign conducted by the 'Luftgangsters' from 1943 on, after having apparently forgotten what their own forces did to Great Britain during the 'Blitz'.
2. This letter to Kellett from von Lindeiner is here paraphrased. It would take up too much space to reprint in its entirity and unnecessarily divert from the content of the text, as it contained many sub-paragraphs: A to E. The basic content of each is covered in this passage.
3. Squadron Leader R.N. Wardell, from No.82 Squadron was shot down on 13 August 1940.
4. It was common practice for German speakers to read all the German newspapers issued to the 'Kriegies' in order to gain information such as this, as well as the actual names of local Nazi officials who might sign papers and numerous other handy items useful when 'designing' an authentic escape persona. The 'X Organization' arranged all this and carefully catalogued it for use when needed. Had any of these secret files survived the war, they would have certainly made for fascinating reading!
5. Corporal Nutting, of the Royal Signals, was captured at Dunkirk in 1940. He helped in dispersing sand for the horse scheme as well vaulting, in between his duties as an orderly.
6. RAAF: Royal Australian Air Force. Codner had swapped his last decent army battledress for a pair of these.
7. This was most likely Lieutenant Guy B.K. Griffiths, Royal Marines. The pilot of a Blackburn Skua of No.803 Naval Air Squadron from HMS *Ark Royal*, he was shot down on 14 September 1939 and was one of only thirty-four Royal Marine pilots to serve with the Fleet Air Arm during the war. Griffiths, along with Lieutenant Commander Richard Thurstan, another No.803 pilot shot down on the same raid, became the first British naval officers to be taken prisoner in the war and would spend nearly 6 years behind the wire.
8. Though it would have saved time and been more direct, the reason he did not take the express straight to Danzig from Breslau (which was very near Sagan) was because it passed through Posen, rumoured to be a very dangerous place, full of police and a particularly nasty group of the Gestapo.

Chapter 13: Through the Looking Glass

1. The mess which was home to Williams and Codner has been variously described as anything from 'distant' or 'standoff-ish', to 'cold' and 'seemingly unhappy'. Of the men I talked to who had visited there (none for any great length of time), few felt particularly comfortable among the group, yet could not definitely say exactly what the problem was, except that it likely had much to do with tunnelling activities of Williams and Codner (as well as Les Sidwell). The split over the scheme had definitely formed a clear divide within the mess that could not normally be crossed.
2. They had earlier discussed and agreed that crawling across the road 'commando style' in order to minimize the danger of being seen was the best way to get from the exit to the forest.
3. As many a disappointed escaper was to find out, many German forests were often park like, as many were usually current or ex-hunting preserves, or replanting projects carried out by the Nazis. They took forestry very seriously, and their Forestry Service was practically a branch of the Wehrmacht, and Forest Wardens kept a close watch on their assigned areas.

Chapter 14: Exhilaration

1. Indeed, upon the initial discovery of an escape, what was known in German as *Allgemeine Fahndung* (manhunt) was immediately launched, and the first order of business was for the Kommandant of the camp to alert all the local foresters and police stations in the area to set up a general cordon within a 5km radius. The call would also include all the local Landwacht and Landwehr units in the area. These institutions in turn then called on the local elements of the Hitler Youth. Then, on bicycle, foot, or horseback, and along with volunteers and others pressed into helping, all together they immediately began searching the fields, the forests, and setting up security check points at crossroads and bridges, while also keeping watch at easy crossing points over rivers and streams. Meanwhile, a detachment of guards from the camp would search the immediate area near the escape exit and then, with the dogs, would begin a pattern search of the entire area within a 15km radius. If this produced no result, the search area would then be increased to 25km.

   The second call made by the Kommandant would be to the local railway station, where security police would immediately be placed on high alert and then telephone the news to other railway stations, and newspapers. How people were dressed would be examined much more closely. In fact, during the search following the 'Great Escape', one of the escapers was arrested after a German railway policeman noticed his RAF-issue blue trousers. It was not that the trousers were suspicious but that the same policeman had, just an hour earlier, arrested another one of the escapers on a technicality who had been wearing the same kind and colour of trousers.

   The third call the Kommandant made followed an identity parade to find out just who was missing from camp. That call would be to the area Headquarters of the *Kriminalpolizei* (Criminal Police), who had jurisdiction over local military criminal matters. Their headquarters would have copies of the identity cards for every PoW in the camp and, upon finding out who was on the run, would issue a special edition of the 'Criminal Police Gazette', complete with 'Wanted' posters and descriptions of the escapers, as well as known details of the actual escape.

   It was all very efficient and highly effective, therefore timing was everything. If an escaper had a good start and could put plenty of time and distance between him and the camp before the escape was discovered, then his chances of freedom increased substantially.

Chapter 15: Meanwhile, Back at the Ranch …

1. It is likely, but unconfirmed, that word was flashed from one compound to the next by Morse code using a flashlight shone between two huts opposite each other with a clear line of sight through a gap in the fencing separating the compounds.

2. ‘Paddy’ Barthropp later recalled being one of the leading lights in the Hut 64, along with ‘Tex’ Ash. In his memoirs he recounts how he and Ash were spurred into action by Douglas Bader, and that after they were arrested and marched into the woods where the Germans gave them some tense moments forcing them down on their knees with their hands on their heads before removing them to the ‘Cooler’ for 14 days. Barthropp’s story has a few errors; in that by that time Ash had swapped places with a New Zealand sergeant from Centre Compound named Don Fair he was already at a camp in Lithuania, and that Douglas Bader had left Sagan during the previous summer. Ash, moreover, does not mention the incident at all in his excellent autobiography. It is because of these inconsistencies that I have deferred from using Barthopp’s story in the main text and only mention it briefly as a footnote.
3. Ward, as Acting Compound Adjutant, actually had charge of the officers during *Appell* and might well have ordered the men of Hut 68 to comply with his wishes – Wing Commander Collard included – even though he was a Squadron Leader. However, such an act would most likely have had the effect on the inmates of the hut to become even more ‘bolshie’ than before. Yet something had to be done, especially once the firing started. Thinking that that might be about to happen he hurried to find Group Captain Kellett, but Ward was stopped by a tight-lipped von Lindeiner shouting in English, ‘Get back on parade or I will have you shot!’ Ward need not have bothered; at the first shots into Hut 68, Kellett was already on his way.
4. Oberfeldwebel (Senior Sergeant): a non-commissioned rank which held a great deal of power. The Oberfeldwebel in this case was Herman Glemnitz, chief of security for South Compound and probably the keenest of all the ‘Ferrets’. He was an experienced campaigner, having served in the trenches in World War One, and every bit a correct soldier, though he held no illusions about the Nazis. He was most efficient and very well respected by the ‘Kriegies’, both for his skill as a ‘Ferret’ and his humanity. Having served in East Compound in the summer of 1942, he moved to the new North Compound when it opened, where he was partly responsible for finding tunnel ‘Tom’ before again being transferred; this time to the fresh South Compound containing US personnel in September 1943. Glemnitz spoke good English and was not unknown to sympathize with his charges at their lot in life. For example, to ‘Kriegies’ who were suffering depression caused by being held behind the wire away from home and family he would say something like, ‘Try not to be too down. You are locked up – this is true. But we are both in the same boat, for I am locked up the same as you, and it’s my barbed wire!’

   Glemnitz was held briefly by the RAF after the war in its investigation into the murders following the ‘Great Escape’, and on his release went to work for them in several different capacities. Late in life, he was several times a special guest during annual meetings of Stalag Luft III societies in the UK and USA.
5. Another reprisal was that the electric light in all the huts was shut off from 7.00pm each night for three weeks; a measure that merely increased the already mind-numbing boredom of the long evenings.
6. Previously, it was the custom of many messes to open the shutters to the rooms after dark, at 11.00pm. In the winter time the circuit lighting might be switched on as early as immediately following afternoon *Appell*, forcing the ‘Kriegies’ inside early endure some long nights.

Chapter 16: ‘Jon Jorgenson’ Takes a Trip

1. Philpot later mentioned the thought had briefly passed through his mind that perhaps the man’s son was the one that had shot out his aircraft’s starboard engine all those months ago; a thought he struggled to rid from his mind.
2. The same mistake made by Dean & Dawson on the *Ausweis* of escaper Robert Kee would cost him and Tommy Calnan their short won freedom the next month after they made a brilliant escape from the *Vorlager* of East Compound.

3. Outside of his one experience on the train, and during check-in at the Hotel Continentale, only one ticket clerk at a railway station ever asked to see his paperwork.
4. In his escape report, Philpot named the ship as the *Björn*, while in his book and ever thereafter he called it the *Aralizz*. Exactly why is unknown as *Aralizz* was correct.
5. In fact the first allied elements would not enter the 'Eternal City' until members of the 88th Infantry Division US Army did on 4 June 1944.

Chapter 17: The Varied Adventures of 'Marcel Lavasuer' and 'Michel Conde'

1. Indeed it appears that Andre Henri Daix actually was a saboteur, working with the French resistance, and had been in and out of Germany several times. It is believed that he sailed on the *J.C. Jacobsen* at least twice. However, the intelligence and clandestine operations of the French resistance are not fully known – even at this distance in time – and it is unfortunate that more of Daix's story cannot be found.

   It is also believed that Olaf Pederson and Captain Olson were both working with British Intelligence, photographing German shipping, but the veracity of this claim is also unsubstantiated. In any case, the escape of the three was betrayed to the Germans and the two sailors were arrested when they reached Copenhagen, along with Sigmund Hjelm-Jensen. All three served sentences, but survived the war. Years later, Williams met Hjelm-Jensen again in his travels and stayed in contact with him for the rest of their lives.
2. In the wartime journal of Talbot Rothwell, kept during his time as a PoW, there is a postcard of a Danish dock scene pasted in with the title written above it 'From unknown Friends in Denmark,' discovered a few years ago by Tyler Butterworth, son of Rothwell's close friend and actor Peter Butterworth. Nothing else is written on it, and there is a very good chance that Williams, who, as already related, worked in the camp theatre and probably knew both actors well, most likely sent it from Copenhagen to their fellow 'Kriegies' in order to let them know the two were making progress. Both Rothwell and Butterworth vaulted regularly as a pair when their theatre duties permitted.

Chapter 18: Complete and Free

1. A member of the Most Excellent Order of the British Empire.
2. Years later, a former pupil said of Wilson as a headmaster: 'Tom Wilson ran a fine school. I think we all thought him eccentric but he commanded immense respect and there were few who felt any real antipathy towards him … For his time, some of his ideas were extremely avant garde. He introduced Russian into the curriculum 20 years before the fall of the Iron Curtain (and) he supervised skiing trips - an almost unheard of activity for state school pupils in those days - to mention but two. During the war he had been a PoW and was a peripheral character in Eric Williams' book *The Wooden Horse.*'

   Wilson also led exchange programmes to Germany and Russia in order to broaden young people's horizons, who would then better understand different cultures – all of which might help prevent another world catastrophe such as his generation had witnessed. In a taped letter to Freddie McKay, Les Sidwell joked about Wilson – by then headmaster at Coleshill Grammar School, Warwickshire – as having 'his own prison camp', and remarking that his 'inmates' were far from happy, as he knew all the 'tricks of the trade' already!

Postscript: 'Margaret'

1. So dedicated was McKay to spending his time underground that he earned the nickname 'The Weasel'. Those who had worked on the wooden horse scheme were particularly appalled by 'Margaret' simply because of the unknowns involved, mainly due to the weather. On the other hand, security, except for entrance and extraction, was not a high priority, making the scheme particularly attractive!
2. It was not until early October that word was received relieving British officers of their duty to escape, once the murders had become known to the British government.

Glossary

Abort – The German word for the pit latrines.

Abwehr – The German intelligence and clandestine warfare office. They were responsible for ensuring against escape from PoW camps.

Appell – The German word for counting parade, or roll call.

Cooler – Prisoner's name for the solitary confinement cells.

Dulag – The German for *Durchgangslager* (reception camp). Adding *Luft* to the end made it an air force reception camp.

Ferret – Prisoner's term for a German who was charged with uncovering the various nefarious activities of the prisoners in camp.

Feldwebel – Sergeant. OberFeldwebel was a Senior or First Sergeant; StabsFeldwebel was a Staff Sergeant.

Gestapo – Hitler's personal body guards and terror enforcement organization. Very powerful and much feared unit that did not let rules or morals get in their way.

Goon – Prisoner's term for a German or anything to do with the Germans. For example, 'Goon skins' were camp made replicas of German uniforms.

Hauptmann – Captain.

Hitler Jugend – The Hitler Youth. When the Nazis came to power they closed all youth organizations except those authorized by the state.

Hundeführer – Prisoner's term for a German dog handler in camp. The correct German term was *Hundmeister (*Hound master).

Komandantur – Administrative compound which governed the entire camp.

Kriegie – Prisoner's slang term for *Kriegsgefangener* (Prisoner of War).

Kriegsmarine – German Navy.

Lageroffizier – Officer in charge of a compound.

Landwehr/Landwacht – The two German 'home-guard' organizations, made up of the over aged, under aged (who were not in the *Hitler Jugend* for whatever reason) and those unfit for normal military service.

Luftwaffe – The German Air Force; the least 'Nazi-fied' of the German military; strange in that Reichmarshall Göring was second in command of the Nazi empire.

Mole – Method of tunnelling where the sand excavated from the face of the tunnel is used to fill in the back of the tunnel as digging moved forward; a terrifying way of tunnelling.

Oberst – Colonel.

Oflag – The German *Offizier Lager* (Officer's camp).

Posten – The standard German words for a soldier doing sentry duty.

Pukka – A British army slang term meaning everything is as it should be; all is well. The term was derived from a Hindustani word.

Sportzplatz – Outdoor recreation and sports area of a camp. The Germans constantly encouraged sport as a way for prisoners to be kept busy, as busy 'Kriegies' did not try to escape.

Stalag – The German acronym for *Stammlager* (Non-comissioned camp). The Luftwaffe was liberal in its use of the term.

Stooge/Stooging – Words used by prisoners for a man on watch duty or snooping. Stooges did all the daily work in a camp, both legal and illegal. Stooging was the performance of those duties.

Straflager – A punishment camp. The most famous – and feared, though largely unnecessarily – was Colditz Castle.
The Form or Gen – Substantiated information, or general information.
Trap – Short for trap door; covering for a tunnel.
Verboten – German word for 'forbidden'.
Vorlager – Fore-camp, the front compound. The *Vorlager* was the administrative section of a compound.

Sources

Internet

http://426sqdn.ca/remembrances/honour_roll_i.html
http://airforce.ca/uploads/airforce/2009/07/ALPHA-AA.html
http://www.acesofww2.com/UK/aces/kayll.htm
http://surfcity.kund.dalnet.se/commonwealth_craig2.htm
http://www.militaryresearchon.com/
http://www.torontoaircrew.com/Navigators/Mennill_1/mennill_1.html
http://www.torontoaircrew.com/Navigators/Elliott_D_1/elliott_d_1.html
http://www.vinexshop.com/
http://www.bansteadhistory.com/beechholme_feature.html
http://www.rafcommands.com/Air%20Force%20PoWs/RAF%20POWs%20Query%20W_1.html http://www.talkingproud.us/Retired/Retired/Oflag64_files/page118-introduction-of-oflag-64-in-sczubin002c-poland.pdf
http://www.muzeum.eline2.serwery.pl/index.php?id=61&lng=eng http://www.warburg.net/doessel/expo/eoflag.htm
http://www.wartimememories.co.uk/pow/stalagluft3.html
http://www.independent.co.uk/news/people/obituary-wing-commander-roger-maw-1550739.html http://www.acesofww2.com/UK/aces/kayll.htm
http://brantford.library.on.ca/genealogy/pdfs/albumhonour.pdf
http://www.varvshistoriska.com/?p=visa-nyhetartikel&n=71-aralizz
http://www.lib.unb.ca/archives/UNBComposites/
http://www.kwantes.com/SSG%20website/current-exhibition.html
http://www.lgchf.com/files/INSIGHT_Winter_2005.pdf
http://newspapers.nl.sg/Digitised/Page/straitstimes19490508.1.1.aspx
http://genforum.genealogy.com/codner/messages/83.html
http://www.lancs-fusiliers.co.uk/gallerynew/WW2/2ndBn/ThebattleofMedjez-el-bar/BattleofMedjez.htm
http://www.ibiblio.org/hyperwar/USA/USA-MTO-NWA/USA-MTO-NWA-19.html
http://www.swalwelluk.co.uk/memstwo.html
http://www.rafcommands.com/forum/showthread.php?1632-Collard-Kellett
http://travel.poland.com/texts/en/t-ap-2.php
http://lubbock.co.uk/david-lubbock.html
http://www.24hourmuseum.org.uk/nwh_gfx_en/ART29411.html
http://www.lgchf.com/files/INSIGHT_Winter_2005.pdf
http://www.familymaw.co.uk/database/getperson.php?personID=14880&tree=Maw
http://www.bbc.co.uk/ww2peopleswar/stories/63/a5283263.shtml
http://www.awm.gov.au/blog/2008/01/30/colditz-collection/
http://www.rootsweb.ancestry.com/~nbpennfi/penn8b2Miller_G.htm
http://www.flensted.eu.com/
http://www.corsetiere.net/Spirella/History.htm
http://www.trasksdad.com/PopsProgress/chaptrs2.htm#Chapters
http://www.rafinfo.org.uk/rafexpow/

http://homepage.ntlworld.com/r_m_g.varley/Strategic_Air_Offensive.pdf
http://www.unithistories.com/officers/RAF_officers_A01.html
http://www.militaryresearchon.com/
http://www.conscript-heroes.com/escapelines/index.htm
http://www.214squadron.org.uk/Personnel_M.htm
http://www.fleetairarmarchive.net/rollofhonour/pow/POW_Index.html
http://articles.sun-sentinel.com/1990-01-14/news/9001190170_1_german-pow-stalag-luft-iii-tunnels
http://www.elsham.pwp.blueyonder.co.uk/gt_esc/
http://www.ww2escapelines.co.uk/youngelms/history-escape/
http://www.field-studies-council.org/fieldstudies/documents/vol9.4_263.pdf
http://www.nla.gov.au/pub/nlanews/1997/aug97/story-2.pdf
http://www.49squadron.co.uk/Files/POW%20Story.pdf
http://silveropossum.homestead.com/House/Marple/Said/Butterworth/Butterworth.html
http://www.cgca.org.uk/downloads/imperialengineer_issue4_full_peter_harding.pdf
http://www.findagrave.com/cgi-bin/fg.cgi?page=gr&GRid=74054465
http://www.express.co.uk/posts/view/144427/Bravery-of-the-German-Jew-who-flew-RAF-bombers-over-his-homeland/
http://www.memorialgrove.org.uk/specialidentificationgrouplionsofjudahhistory3.htm
http://article.wn.com/view/2011/11/28/The_Great_Escape_the_sequel_Historian_recreates_the_astoundi/
http://news.stv.tv/scotland/195429-veterans-poignant-trip-back-to-leuchars-raf-base/
http://news.google.com/newspapers?nid=2507&dat=19520326&id=UFBAAAAAIBAJ&sjid=MZIMAAAAIBAJ&pg=4618,2354675
http://news.google.com/newspapers?nid=1301&dat=19500701&id=nKAQAAAAIBAJ&sjid=LJMDAAAAIBAJ&pg=7158,53034
http://www.aircrewremembrancesociety.com/obituaries/mackenzie.html
http://www.militaryimages.net/photopost/showphoto.php/photo/24256
http://www.findmypast.co.uk/search/military/wwii/wwii-escapers
http://www.nationalarchives.gov.uk/records/research-guides/prisoners-war-1939-1953.htm
http://www.ww2escapelines.co.uk/
http://www.conscript-heroes.com/escapelines/index.htm

Published books

Ash, William and Foley, Brendan, *Under the Wire* (St Martin's Press, New York, 2005)
Barthropp, Patrick, *Paddy* (Howard Baker, London, 1987)
Brickhill, Paul and Norton, Conrad, *Escape To Danger* (Faber & Faber Limited, London, 1946)
Brickhill, Paul, *The Great Escape* (W.W. Norton & Co., New York, NY, 1950)
Brown, Kingsley, *Bonds of Wire* (Collins Publishers, Toronto, Canada, 1989)
Burgess, Colin, *'Bush' Parker* (Australian Military History Publications, NSW, 2007)
Burgess, Colin and Champ, Jack, *The Diggers of Colditz* (George Allen & Unwin, Sydney, Australia, 1985)
Calnan, Thomas D, *Free As a Running Fox* (McDonald & Co. Ltd, London/The Dial Press, New York, 1970)
Carroll, Tim, *The Great Escape From Stalag Luft III* (Pocket Books, New York, 2005)
Chisel, O.M, *Clipped Wings* (R.W. Kimball, 1948)
Clark, Albert P, *33 Months As A POW in Stalag Luft III* (Fulcrum Publishing, Golden, Connecticut, 2004)
Clutton-Brock, Oliver, *Footprints on the Sands of Time* (Grub Street, London, 2003)
Codd, David A, *Blue Job-Brown Job* (Exlibris Press, 2000)
Conrad, Peter, *Canadian Wartime Prison Escapes* (Lone Pine Publishing, Edmonton, Alberta, Canada, 2007)

Crawley, Aidan, *Escape From Germany* (Dorset Press, New York, 1987)
Crawley, Aidan, *Leap Before You Look* (William Collins & Sons, London, 1988)
Durand, Arthur. *Stalag Luft III: The Secret Story* (Louisiana State University, Baton Rouge, 1988)
Eggers, Reinhold, *Colditz: The German Story* (Pen & Sword Books Ltd, Barnsley, 2007)
Fancy, John, *Tunnelling To Freedom* (Panther Books, London, 1957)
Franks, Norman L, *RAF Fighter Command Losses Vol. 1 1939-1941* (Ian Allan Publishing Ltd, Shepperton, 1997/2003)
Franks, Norman L, *RAF Fighter Command Losses Vol. 2 1942-1943* (Ian Allan Publishing Ltd, Shepperton, 1998)
Gammon, Vic, *Not All Glory!* (Arms & Armour Press Ltd, London, 1996)
Gammon, Vic, *No Time For Fear* (Arms & Armour Press Ltd, London, 1998)
Harvie, John D, *Missing In Action* (McGill-Queen's University Press, Montreal & Kingston, 1995)
Haugland, Vern, *Caged Eagles* (Tab Aero, Blue Ridge Summit, Pennsylvania, 1992)
Hayes, Helen, *Beyond the Great Escape* (Possum Publishing, Queensland, Australia, 2004)
Hunter, William J, *From Coastal Command to Captivity* (Leo Cooper/Pen & Sword Books Ltd, Barnsley, 2003)
James, B.A, *Moonless Night* (Pen & Sword Books Ltd, Barnsley, 2006)
Kee, Robert, *A Crowd Is Not Company* (Phoenix Press, London, 1947/1982)
Lynch-Blosse, Hugh, *Wings - And Other Things* (Square One Publications, Worcester, 1990)
MacDonell, Donald, *From Dogfight to Diplomacy* (Pen & Sword Books Ltd, Barnsley, 2005)
MacKenzie, K.W, *Hurricane Combat* (Grenville Publishing Co. Ltd, London, 1987)
Marsh, Marcus, *Racing With the Gods* (A.S. Barnes & Co., Cranbury, New Jersey, 1970)
Martin, Gwyn, *Up and Under* (Gwyn Martin, 1989)
McNeill, Ross, *RAF Coastal Command Losses 1939-1941* (Ian Allan Publishing Ltd, Shepperton, 2003)
Morison, Walter, *Flak and 'Ferrets'* (Sentinel Publishing, London, 1995)
Oliver, A.E.V, *Kriegie* (George Mann Books, Maidstone, 1998)
Philpot, Oliver L.S, *Stolen Journey* (Hodder & Stoughton, London, 1950)
Rees, Ken with Arrandale, Karen, *Lie in the Dark and Listen* (Grub Street, London, 2006)
Rollings, Charles, *Wire and Walls* (Ian Allan Publishing Ltd, Shepperton, 2003)
Rollings, Charles, *Wire and Worse* (Ian Allan Publishing Ltd, Shepperton, 2004)
Sidwell, Leslie R, *Wingless Journey* (Merlin Books, Braunton, Devon, 1995)
Slack, Tom, *Happy is the Day* (United Writers, Cornwall, 1987)
Smith, Martin, *What A Bloody Arrival* (The Book Guild Ltd, Sussex, 1997)
Smith, Sydney, *Wings Day* (William Collins & Sons Ltd, London, 1968)
Sniders, Edward, *Flying In – Walking Out* (Leo Cooper/Pen & Sword Books Ltd, Barnsley, 1999)
Stevens, Marc H, *Escape, Evasion and Revenge* (Pen & Sword Books Ltd, Barnsley, 2009)
Vance, Jonathan F, *A Gallant Company* (iBooks, New York, 2000)
Vanderstock, Bram, *War Pilot of Orange* (Pictorial Histories Publishing, Missoula, Montana, 1987)
Ward-Thomas, Pat, *Not Only Golf* (Hodder & Stoughton, London, 1981)
Williams, Eric E, *Complete and Free* (Eyre & Spottiswoode, London, 1957)
Williams, Eric E, *'Goon' in the Block* (Jonathan Cape Ltd, London, 1945)
Williams, Eric E, *The Escapers* (William Collins, with Eyre & Spottiswoode, London, 1953)
Williams, Eric E, *The Tunnel* (Coward-McCann Inc, New York, 1952)
Williams, Eric E, *The Wooden Horse* (William Collins & Sons Ltd, London, 1949 and Revised 1979)
Wilson, Thomas and Gabriele, *In the Shadow of the Wooden Horse* (Gabriele Wilson, 2009)

Magazine articles/Newspaper articles

After The Battle (No.87, 1985)
Time (Vol. LIX No.14, 7 April 1952)
Flight (p.613, 26 May 1949)
Flight (p.375, 4 April 1952)
World War II (Vol.18, No.6, February 2004)
The Straits Times (Kuala, Lampur, 8 May 1949)
The South African Military History Society Newsletter (March 2007)
Courage, Perseverance and Artistry in Stalag Luft III (The Times Online, 9 September 2006)
Great Escaper Sees His Own Past In A Museum (The Times Online, 13 October 2004)
The Great Escapes: The Harsh Reality and True Heroism Behind the Hollywood Prison Camp Epics (The Independent Online, 13 October 2007)
The Third Man in the "Wooden Horse" Escape Tells This Exciting Story (The Sydney Morning Herald, 1 July 1950)
Obituary: Roger Maw (The Independent Online, 11 September 1992)
Obituary: Oliver Philpot (The Telegraph Online, 6 May 1993)
Obituary: Aubrey Niner (The Telegraph Online, 9 January 2011)
Obituary: Joseph Kayll (The Guardian Online, 25 April 2000)
Obituary: Leonard Pearman (The Sunday Times, 14 August 2003)
Obituary: John Fancy (The Mail Online, 2 October 2008)
Obituary: Harry S. Crease (Sun Sentinel Online, 14 January 1990)
Obituary: Peter Harding (The Imperial College Online, 27 January 2006)
Obituary: Anthony Barber (The Sunday Times, 8 December 2005)
Obituary: Donald MacDonnell, (Scottish Daily Record & Sunday, 1999)
Obituary: Ken MacKenzie (The Daily Telegraph, 6 June 2009)
Bomber Command – Remembrance Day (The Bulletin of the Royal Canadian Legion, Riverside Branch 255, November 2009)
Biography – Williams, Eric Ernest (1911–1983) (Contemporary Authors Online, 2006, via Amazon.com)
Featured Writer – Eric Williams (The Observer, 3 July 1977)
Times Literary Supplement (28 March 1968)
Yale Review (June 1968)
The London Gazette (19 August 1941)
The London Gazette (30 September 1941)
The London Gazette (1 July 1941)
The London Gazette (11 December 1942)
The London Gazette (27 April 1944)
The London Gazette (12 May 1944)
The London Gazette (17 May 1946)
The Daily Chronical, Centralia, Washington State (25 March 1952)
Union Bulletin, Walla Walla, Washington State (26 March 1952)
Lebanon Ohio Daily News (28 June 1952)
Sandusky Register (1 July 1952)
The London Times (1 February 1947)
The London Times (26 March 1952)
The London Times (29 March 1952)
The London Times (20 December 1947)
Marriage Register (by District), UK, 1948 (pages 41, 303, 401 and 539)
Birth Register (by District), UK, 1920 (page 42)
War Hero Tom Wilson Tells of Great Escape in Coleshill (The Coventry Telegraph Online, 29 January 2010)

Tom Wilson Returns to the Site of the Great Escape (Spaghetti Gazette, West Midlands, UK,6 April 2009)
Great Escape Mementos to go Under the Hammer (The Telegraph Online, 9 September 2006)
War Hero to Tell All About Lesser-Known Attempt to Escape (This Is Tamworth Online, 29 April 2011)

Unprovenanced British and/or Canadian newspaper articles:
Helped to Make the Escaper's 'Wooden Horse'
Harrogate Man to Tell His Own Story of the 'Wooden Horse'

National Archives/Imperial War Museum
Paper:
History of Escape Activities Stalag Luft III (AIR40/285)
Official Camp History Stalag Luft III (AIR40/2645)
Recommendation for DSO, Codner, Richard M.C, Captain, RFA w/Escape Report of Flight Lieutenant Williams, Eric E. RAF, and Captain R. M.C. Codner, RFA (WO 373/94)
Private Papers and Escape Paraphernalia of Philpot, O.L.S, Flight Lieutenant MC, DFC (Catalogue Number 13456/ Box Reference 05/65/1A)
Escape Report, O.L.S. Philpot (WO208/3317)
Escape Report, E.E. Williams and R.M.C. Codner w/Addendum to Report By Sybil Williams (WO 208/3317)
Private Papers and Escape Paraphernalia of Williams, E.E. Flight Lieutenant, MC. (Catalogue Number 4077/ Box Reference 03/11/2 & 2A)
Papers of Ward, Ralph Bagshaw, Group Captain, 1911-1992, Liddell Hart Centre for Military Archives, King's College London (Reference No. GB 0099 KCLMA Ward [Former ISAAR ref: GB/NNAF/P46760])
Returned PoW Report/Dallas Laskey (WO 344-180/1)
Returned PoW Report/Thomas Calnan (WO 344-531/1)
Letter From Colonel von Lindeiner to Senior British Officers of East Compound, Dated 1 November 1943 (IWM Catalogue No.13444, Box Ref: Misc 3505A)
Papers of Lamond, H. W, Wing Commander (IWM Catalogue No.6293, Box Ref: 96/41/1)

Sound Recordings:
Imperial War Museum Interview with Oliver Philpot, Full Recording (Reels 1 to 9), Recorded 1987, IWM Catalogue No.09938
Imperial War Museum Interview with Edward Frederick Chapman, Reels 1, 2 and 3, Recorded 12 February 1990, IWM Catalogue No.11194
Imperial War Museum Interview with Edward Frederick Chapman, Reel 2, Recorded 3 DEecember 1996, IWM Catalogue No.17156
Imperial War Museum Interview with Leonard Lawrence Pearman, Reels 2 and 3, recorded 16 January 1989, IWM Catalogue No.11191
Imperial War Museum Interview with Jack Best, Full Recording, Recorded 1999, IWM Catalogue No.21745
Imperial War Museum Interview with Geoffrey Cornish, Full Recording, Recorded 28 May 2003, IWM Catalogue No.23327
Imperial War Museum Interview with Eric Norman Foinette, Full Recording, Recorded 1982, IWM Catalogue No.6095
Imperial War Museum Interview with Leslie James Edward Goldfinch, Full Recording, Recorded September 2005, IWM Catalogue No.28416

The Second World War Experience Centre

Interview with Wing Commander Joseph R. Kayll, by Peter Liddle, September 1996, Tape Nos. 292 and 293

"For you Tommy, the war is over". Not necessarily so; Escape and Evasion in Europe, an article by Peter H. Liddle for the Second World War Experience Centre.

Miscellaneous

Prisoner's Log Book of Flying Officer Philip Marchildon, RCAF (Department of National Defence Collection / Library and Archives Canada Ref.1996-212 NPC)

Papers and Escape Ephemera of R.M.C. Codner, Michael Codner/Codner family

Great Escapes of World War Two A History Channel presentation by Robert Kirk and Scott Paddor, 2001

The Wooden Horse (British Lion Film Corporation, London, 1950)

Multidisciplinary Investigations at Stalag Luft III Allied Prisoner-of-war Camp: The Site of the 1944 'Great Escape,' Zagan, Western Poland, Treatise by J.K. Pringle, P. Doyle, and L.E. Babits

Yellow Sands and Penguins: The Soil of 'The Great Escape' Peter Doyle, Larry Babits and Jamie Pringle Soil and Culture 2009, Part 6, 417-429, DOI: 10.1007/978-90-481-2960-7_25

Live Interviews

Dallas Laskey (telephone) 15 April 2010

Martin Calnan (telephone) 4 January 2011

Thomas and Gabi Wilson (e-mail) continuing 28 December 2010–April 2012

Thomas Wilson/Leslie Sidwell, recorded message to Freddie McKay, 1973 – Courtesy Peter Wilson

Thomas Wilson, BBC interview, August 1990 – Courtesy Peter Wilson

Peter Wilson, (telephone/e-mail) continuing 28 December 2010–December 2011

Leslie Sidwell, BBC interview, undated, probably early 1970's

Michael Codner (e-mail) continuing 27 August 2010–March 2012

Marc Stevens (telephone/e-mail) continuing 6 January 2010–April 2012

Steve Martin (telephone) 12 January 2011, 18 January 2011

Donald 'Pappy' Elliot (telephone) 10 January 2011, 12 January 2011

Ewen McDonald (e-mail) continuing 20 March 11–April 2012

Allan Hunter (e-mail) continuing 1 August 2011–April 2012

Index

Abwehr *See* 'Ferrets'
Anderson, Fg Off. Alex, 131
Ash, Plt Off. William 'Tex', 56, 253, 259
Asselin, Plt Off. Eduard 'Eddie', 56, 65, 67, 100, 257

Bader, Wg Cdr. Douglas, 25, 259
Barber, Flt Lt. Anthony, 27-8, 131, 257
Barrett, Wg Cdr. John, 131
Barthropp, Sqn Ldr. 'Paddy', 131, 259
Beaton, Fg Off. Edward, 244-45, 250
Best, Plt Off. John 'Jack', 26
Black Saturday, 179-87
  Germans attempt photographic check, 180
  Kommandant's admonishment, 184-86
  second photographic check attempt, 183-84
  soccer football incident, 182-83
Breed, Plt Off. Desmond, 129, 131, 145, 256
Bressey, Flt Lt. Phillip, 63
Brickhill, Flt Lt. Paul, 19
Broili, Hauptmann, 177-81
Brownlie, Sqn Ldr. Ian, 63
Buckley, Lt Cdr. James, RN, 22, 29, 58, 63
Bushell, Sqn Ldr. Roger, 29, 69-71, 91, 109, 118, 126, 136
Butterworth, Lt Cdr. Peter, RN, 72, 260

Calnan, Sqn Ldr. Thomas 'Tommy':
  advice sought By Williams and Codner, 65
  as East Compound book censor, 68
  as 'Little S' at Sagan, 64
  asked to join wooden horse effort, 110-11
  at Dulag Luft, 12
  at Oflag IX A/H, 13
  background, 252
  escape from East Compound Vorlager, 81, 111, 255, 256
  first attempted mole tunnel, 27-8
  first escape attempt, 252
  opinion of 'Charlie' Piltz, 85
  philosophy on escapers, 30
  second attempted mole tunnel, 55
  with German cockpit drills, 69
Chapman, Plt Off. Edward, 131
Clark, Lt Col. Albert 'Bub' USAAF, 25-6
Clayton, Flt Lt. John, 63
Codd, Fg Off. David, 90, 179
Codner, Lt. Richard Michael Clinton:
  activities at Dulag, 49-51, 252
  arrival at Dulag Luft, 48-9
  arrival at Schubin *See* Williams
  association/background with 78th Division, 45-6
  background of, 44-5
  capture of, 42-4, 46-8, 252
  escape efforts at Schubin, *See* Williams
  friendship with Williams, 50-1
  late life and legacy, 232-34
  meets Philpot, *See* Philpot
  meets Williams, 49
  post-escape activities to England, *See* Williams: Post-Escape Activities to England
  transfer to Sagan, *See* Williams
  transfer to Schubin, 51
  Wooden Horse idea, *See* Wooden Horse Tunnel: Idea Born and Philpot, Introduced to Wooden Horse Idea
  work on wooden horse project, *See* Wooden Horse Tunnel
Colditz Castle, 111, 187
Collard, Wg Cdr. 179, 182-85, 259, *See also* Tunnels
Cooper, Flt Lt. Douglas, 83
Craig, Flt Lt. Dudley 'Dud', 63, 80, 81, 253
Crawley, Flt Lt. Aiden 'Stafford', 63, 67, 101-102, 105-107, 131, 141, 147, 152, 159, 196, 215, 219, 253

Daix, Sgt. Henri, 220, 222-26, 260
Davies, Sub Lt. Rupert, RN, 72
Dawkins, Plt Off. Jerry, 145
Day, Wg Cdr. Harry 'Wings', 12, 22, 29, 54, 253
Dodge, Maj. John 'Johnny', 52
Dulag Luft/Oberursel:
  history of, 10
  first RAF tunnel from, 11-2
Dunmall, Sgt. Kenneth, 32-3, 252

Edge, Plt Off. Richard 'Dickie', 66
Edwards, Plt Off. Kenneth, 131
Elliot, Plt Off. Donald 'Pappy', 88-9, 131, 255
Eperson, Plt Off. A.G., 131
Escape:
  Delouser Escape, 74
  'Goonskins', description of, 22
  methods of, 22-5
  Operation Olympia, *See* Oflag VIb/Warburg
  problems of, 22
  Toft and Nichols Escape, 23-4
  Wire job, *See* Escape, methods of
Escape Committee:
  at North Compound, Sagan, 69-70, 74

at Schubin, 54-5
forgery: Dean & Dawson, 63, 146, 152, 259
forgery: Thomas Cook's Tours, 63
function and organization, 21-2, 257
organization at East Compound, Sagan, 63
tailoring: Puller's of Perth, 63

Fair, Sgt. Donald, 259
Fancy, Sgt. John, 27
Fessler, Plt Off. Morris, 23
'Ferrets':
blitz searches, 104, 127
'Dopey', 122-23
in tunnels, 256
'Lofty', 88-9, 177, 256
organization and description, 20-1, 255
routines, 21, 24, 28, 72, 91, 102, 106, 125, 129, 255
'Rudy', 91
Floody, Plt Off. 'Wally', 24
Fortune, Maj Gen. Victor, 12
Frith, Flt Lt. Claude, 146

Goldfinch, Fg Off. Leslie 'Bill', 25
Goon in the Block book, 236-38
Gordon, Plt Off. J.A.C. 'Flash', 248
Grain, Elsie S. M. 'Sybil', 236-42

Haller, Lt., 184
Harding, Plt Off. Peter, 131
Harris, Fg Off. John, 106
Harvie, Fg Off. John, 244-45, 250
Hawthorn, Plt Off. Thomas, 101
Hellfachs, Hauptmann, 71, 178, 180-81, 187, 247, 254
Hesse, Cpl. Eberhard 'Nikki', 68, 152
Hester, Plt Off. Roy, 3
Hjelm-Jensen, Sigmund, 222, 224, 226, 260
Hunter, Plt Off. William 'Red', 68, 143, 196, 234

James, Plt Off. Bertram 'Jimmy', 94
'Jo-Jo' the Corsican, 218-22

Kayll, Wg Cdr. Joseph, 63, 80, 81, 86, 99, 107-10, 253, 255-56
Kee, Plt Off. Robert, 99, 113, 172, 256, 259
Kellett, Gp Capt. Richard 'Dickie', 63, 139, 158, 183-84, 245, 249, 257, 259
Kirk, Flt Lt. Ian, 101

Lamond, Fg Off. Henry 'Piglet', 25
Laskey, Plt Off. Dallas:
relief at discovery of tunnel exit, 176
selected for tunnel second try, 141
shoot down and arrival at Sagan, 117-19
takes over vaulting, 131
vaulting participation, 123, 125
Lechten, Dr. 116, 123, 170-71
Lewis, Flt Lt. W.J. 'Mike', 101, 143, 176, 255
Lubbock, Lt. David, RNVR (FAA), 102, 131, 141, 159, 160, 174
Lynch-Blosse, Fg Off. Hugh, 179, 184

MacDonell, Gp Capt. Donald, 63
Macfie, Flt Lt Colin, 131
MacKenzie, Flt Lt. Kenneth, 63
Marsh, Fg Off. Marcus 'Rackets', 50, 68-9, 84, 140, 152, 249
Massey, Gp Capt. Herbert, 69, 254
Maw, Wg Cdr. Roger, 70, 82-4, 145, 156, 181-82, 184-85, 254-55
Maycock, Gp Capt. 208, 229-31
McIntosh, Plt Off. Kenneth 'Digger', 82, 255
McKay, Flt Lt. 'Freddie' RNZAF, 135, 148-49, 160-61, 178, 245-49, 260
Mennill, Plt Off. Joseph, 131
Mercer, Lt. Johnny RN (FAA), 145
Miller, Fg Off. Gordon 'Moose', 118, 131, 256
Millett, Lt. Jack, *See* Tunnels
Miner, Sgt. Alf, 27
Monteuis, Dr. Edward 'Twee', 116, 119

Niner, Plt Off. Aubrey, 131
Nutting, Cpl. Clive, 146, 257

Oflag VIb/Warburg:
escape attempts, 22, 54-5, 68
wooden horse effort, *See* Tunnels
Oflag IX A/H/Spangenburg:
'Arab Quarter', 13
description of, 12
Oflag XXIb/Schubin:
Abort tunnel, 56, 58-9, 253
escape efforts at, 54, 59
escape of Sgt. P.T. Wareing, 55-6
Gestapo control of, 58
history of, 53-4
Oliver, Plt Off. A.E.V., 131
Olson, Capt. E. Ostrup, 225-26, 260

Paget, Flt Lt. John, 63
Parker, Plt Off. Vincent 'Bush', 84
Pearman, Plt Off. Leonard, 131, 257
Pedersen, Olaf, 222-26, 260
Pennock, Sgt. 118
Peschel, Maj. 27
Philpot, Flt Lt. Oliver L.S.:
arrival at Dulag Luft of, 9- 10
arrival at Sagan of, 14
background of, 3-6
birth of 'Jon Jorgenson' and early escape preparations of, 66-9
capture of, 6-8
disposal of tunnel spoil, 100-102, 105-107, 128-29, 142
enters tunnel for the first time, 112-13
escape plan with Sqn Ldr. Woodruff of, 12-3
escape, *See* Wooden Horse Escape
first escape attempt of, 8-9

introduced to wooden horse idea, 77-80
joins wooden horse project as member, 112
late life and legacy, 234-35
leaves first mess at Sagan, 99, 258
life at Sagan the second time around, 71-3
medical care by the Germans of, 8
meets Williams and Codner, 64
philosophy on being a prisoner of war, 11, 28
post-escape activities to England, 228-31
random escape activities at Sagan of, 28
Schubin escape efforts of, 59
second escape attempt of, 13-4
shoot-down of, 1-3
takes idea to committee, 80-1
transfer to Oflag IX A/H/Spangenburg of, 12
transfer/arrival back at Sagan of, 59, 63-5
transfer to/arrival at Schubin of, 52-3
transfer to Stalag Luft III/Sagan of, 13
Piltz, Unteroffizier Karl 'Charlie':
description of, 84-5, 256
examines wooden horse, 85, 88-90
near cookhouse on day of escape, 160
preparing to flush tunnel, 184
searches cookhouse, 102-104
second search of cookhouse, 127-28
upon discovery of tunnel, 177-78
Poulton, Plt Off. 184

Roe, Plt Off. William 'Bill', 131
Rothwell, Flt Lt. Talbot, 72, 260
Ruffel, Plt Off. 184
Runciman, Sgt. 118

Sargeaunt, Sqn Ldr. James 'Jimmie', 83, 157, 245
Searcy, Plt Off. Phillip, RAAF, 26
Shaw, Plt Off. Eric, 146
Shore, Plt Off. E.H.L. 'Bushy', 63
Sidwell, Plt Off. Leslie 'Sid', 96, 99, 111, 113-14, 131, 142, 161, 241, 256, 258, 260
Simoleit, Maj. Gustav, 177, 181, 182, 184
Smallwood, Flt Lt. Neville, 147
Smith, Flt Sgt. Freddie, 3, 8-9
Smith, Plt Off. Martin, 94
Stairs, Mr. 208, 227
Stalag Luft I/Barth, 16, 26, 84, 253
Stalag Luft III/Sagan:
Lt Col. 'Bub' Clark's 'Crap in Comfort' campaign, 252
description of sick quarters, 116
description of, 18-20, 251
evacuation of, 250
German administration of, 20-2
in relation to Sagan district, 62
introduction to, 14-5, 62
occupancy of in 1944, 246
opening of North Compound, 63
post-war use of, 240
reasons for location of, 15-6
tunnelling problems, 16-8
typical East Compound day, 70-1
weather patterns, 74
Stark, Flt Lt. Robert, 102, 161
Stevens, Flt Lt. John, 75, 82-3, 88-9, 91, 94, 111, 254-55
Stevens, Flt Lt. Peter, 68, 143, 253, 255
Stolen Journey book, 235
'Stooge'/'Stooging', 252, *See also* Escape Committee: function and organization
Street, Sgt. William, 27
Strong, Sqn Ldr. Malcolm, 147
Stuhlmeyer, Feldwebel, 71-3, 159-60, 177, 181-82, 246, 248, 254
Sutton-Pratt, Col. 'Reggie', 209, 227, 229, 231

Tettenborn, Phillip, BOAC, 147
The Great Escape, 7, 19, 69-70, 186, 239, 251, 253-55, 258-59
The Wooden Horse film, 239-41
The Wooden Horse (The Sagan Horse) book, 238-39, 242
Tomlinson, Sqn Ldr. Peter, 163, 230
Tunnels:
Hut 68 project, 126-28
'Margaret', 245-50
first crisis, 247-48
operations suspended/recommenced, 249
operations abandoned by evacuation of camp, 250
project commences, 246
second crises, 248
'Mole' tunnel, 25-7
feasibility of wooden horse tunnel, 75, 77-8, 80, 86, 96, 100, 142, 148, 177
results of, 27
Tunnel 'Tom' found, 126
Washhouse tunnel, *See* White, Plt Off. William 'Bill'
Wooden horse effort from Warburg, 79

Voice, Sgt. James, 33-6, 39
Von Lindeiner-Wildau, *Kommandant*, 20, 127
activities following wooden horse escape, 183-84
character of, 186
letter to Gp Capt. Kellett, 139
Williams visits post-war, 239-40
written edict following wooden horse escape, 185-86

Walters, Plt Off. 184
Ward, Sqn Ldr. Ralph Bagshaw, 63, 131, 145, 147, 157, 178-80, 182-83
Wardell, Sqn Ldr. R. N. 'Rusty', 144, 257
Warnings against escape from Germans, 138-40
Webster, Plt Off. Daniel, 65
Weir, Plt Off. John 'Scruffy', 24
White, Plt Off. William 'Bill', 65-6, 72-5, 127
Willetts, Gp Capt. 184

Williams, Flt Lt. Eric Ernest 'Bill':
  arrival at Dulag Luft of, 40-2
  arrival at Sagan, 62
  arrival at Schubin, 56-7
  background of, 34-5
  capture of, 38-40
  collapses from exhaustion and taken to infirmary, 115
  escape efforts at Schubin, 57-8
  evasion of, 35-8
  first escape attempt, 39-40
  late life and legacy, 235-43
    literary career, 241-43
    return to Germany, 237
  meets Codner, 42
  meets Philpot, *See* Philpot
  post-escape activities to England, 228-32
  recapture of, 40
  shoot down of: 32-4
  time in infirmary, 116-17, 119-20
  transfer to Sagan, 59
  transfer to Schubin, *See* Codner
  wooden horse idea, *See* Wooden Horse Tunnel, Idea Born and Philpot, Introduced to Wooden Horse Idea
  work on wooden horse project, *See* Wooden Horse Tunnel and Project
Wilson, Plt Off. Thomas:
  assists with 'Margaret' project, 247-48, 255
  comments on 'Charlie' not discovering wooden horse tunnel, 177
  comments on difficulties faced by vaulters, 89, 92, 97, 255
  comments on golfers, 132
  joins vaulting team, 83
  plays final part in wooden horse effort, 151
  plays part in 'Black Saturday' activities, 181-83
  post-war comments on first knowledge of Williams' book, 239
  post-war reputation as headmaster of school, 260
  provides distraction during tunnel fall incident, 114-15
  returns to team in diversionary roll, 142
  sees movie, 241
  shot down/arrival at Sagan, 83
  suffers injury during vaulting, 132
Wooden Horse: Breakout and Escape:
  day of escape, (am), 156-57
  day of escape, (pm), 157-66
  diversions, 162-63
  escape of Philpot:
    arrives at British Legation in Stockholm, 208
    breakout, 165
    climbs onto ship, 201-202
    first night in hotel, 195-96
    Frankfurt to Küstrin, 188-89
    from camp to train station, 169
    greets Williams and Codner, 209
    harbour trip, finds ship, 196-99
    hidden by crew, 203-207
    Küstrin to Danzig, 189-93
    police check, 192
    slips into dock, 199-200
  Escape of Williams and Codner:
    breakout, 164-65
    finally get ship, 222-23
    first night out, in air-raid shelter, 214
    from camp to train station, 167-69
    from Copenhagen to Stockholm, 224-27
    from Frankfurt to Küstrin, 210-11
    inspect docks, 216-17
    Küstrin to Stettin, 212-13
    meet Philpot at British Legation, 227
    narrowly miss police check, 213
    second night, in hotel/begin making contacts, 205-16
    widen contact field, 217-22
  Last feet of tunnel dug, 161-64
  Last trip of the horse, 160-61
  Purchasing train tickets and waiting at the station, 169-70, 258
  Train to Frankfurt and first night out, 172-75
  Tunnel discovered, 176-77
    'Charlie' crawls the tunnel, 177-78
    Germans attempt roll call, 178-79
Wooden Horse: Final Escape Preparations:
  Breakout prep, 148-49
  final details, 151-53
  forgery, 143-44, 146
  of Philpot, 119-21, 144-45, 147
  of Williams and Codner, 119-22, 145-48
  timing and trains, 149-51
Wooden Horse: Tunnel and Project:
  construction of horse, 83-6
  descriptions of tunnel work, 92-3, 94-6, 123-25, 133-34, 137, 140-42, 256
  descriptions of vaulting and procedure, 91-2, 93-4, 97-8, 108, 123-24, 129-33, 255
    controversy of committee intervention, 108-110
  digging begins, 90
  first day, 88-90
  idea born, 75-7, 254
  idea explained to committee, 86-7
  initial recruitment of vaulters, 82-3
  legacy, 244-45
  material acquired, 81-2
  negative opinion changes, 140-41
  pinpoint of tunnel track/progress, 134-36
  problems with golfers, 99, 132
  question of sound detectors, 136-37
  recruitment of third team member, 110-12
  security concerns, 96-8, 102-104, 106, 128, 131-32, 136, 149
    collapse of tunnel, 113-15
    first search of canteen, 104-05
    second search of canteen, 128
  tunnel progress, 107-108
Woodruff, Sqn Ldr. RAAF, 12-3

'X' Organization, *See* Escape Committee